MICROSOFT WORKS KEYBOARD AND MOUSE SHORTCUTS

Paragraph-Formatting Keyboard Shortcuts

Center	Ctrl-C	D	Ctrl-2
Hanging Indent	Ctrl-H	Left Indent	Ctrl-N
Justified	Ctrl-J	Left-Align	Ctrl-L
Normal Paragraph	Ctrl-X	Right-Align	Ctrl-R
Single-Space	Ctrl-1	Undo Left Indent	Ctrl-M
Undo Hanging Indent	Ctrl-G	1 1/2-Space	Ctrl-5

Spreadsheet Tool

Editing Keys

Absolute Reference	F4	Copy Cell above Highlight	Ctrl-'
Copy Selection	Shift-F3	Display Chart	Shift-F10
Edit Cell	F2	Go to Spreadsheet View	F10
Help	F1	Move Selection	F3
Repeat Copy or Format	Shift-F7	Repeat Search	F7

Keys for Moving the Highlight

Beginning of row	Home	End of row	End
Beginning of file	Ctrl-Home	End of file	Ctrl-End
Next screen	PgDn	Previous screen	PgUp
Screen right	Ctrl-PgDn	Screen left	Ctrl-PgUp
Next block down	Ctrl-↓	Previous block up	Ctrl-↑
Block to the right	Ctrl-→	Block to the left	Ctrl-←
Cell	F5		

Selection Keys

Extend selection	F8	Row	Ctrl-F8
Column	Shift-F8	Spreadsheet	Ctrl-Shift-F8

Selecting with the Mouse

Extend selection	Click-and-drag, or shift-and-click
Row	Click on row number
Column	Click on column letter
Spreadsheet	Click on intersection of row numbers and column letters

(continued on inside back cover)

MASTERING MICROSOFT WORKS ON THE IBM PC

MASTERING MICROSOFT® WORKS ON THE IBM® PC

REBECCA BRIDGES ALTMAN

SAN FRANCISCO • PARIS • DÜSSELDORF • SOEST

Acquisitions Editor: Dianne King
Developmental Editor: Eric Stone
Copy Editor: Richard Mills
Technical Editor: Nick Dargahi
Production Editor: Carolina L. Montilla
Word Processors: Scott Campbell, Deborah Maizels, and Chris Mockel
Series Designer: Eleanor Ramos
Chapter Art and Layout: Ingrid Owen
Technical Art and Screen Graphics: Delia Brown
Typesetters: Winnie Kelly and Len Gilbert
Proofreaders: Vanessa Miller, Rhonda Holmes, and Martha Barrera
Indexer: Ted Laux
Cover Designer: Thomas Ingalls + Associates
Cover Photographer: Michael Lamotte
Screen reproductions produced by XenoFont

Library of Congress Card Number: 90-70331
ISBN: 0-89588-690-1

Manufactured in the United States of America
10 9 8 7

To my best friend
and favorite author...
my husband, Rick Altman

acknowledgments

First of all I would like to thank the person who got me started in the computing business eight years ago: Carole Fleming. Without the support and encouragement she gave me at the beginning of my career, I probably would never have gotten involved with personal computers, and would never have written this book.

The editors at SYBEX were superb, and deserve special recognition. I especially appreciated that they pointed out the things they liked in the manuscript instead of only concentrating on the corrections that needed to be made. Many thanks to Eric Stone, my developmental editor, and Richard Mills, my copy editor. They were a pleasure to work with.

I would also like to thank Microsoft for supplying me with the Works software and for developing an excellent product.

contents at a glance

contents

part five THE COMMUNICATIONS TOOL

introduction

Learning a new software program is always a challenge, especially if you are a new computer user. You open up the box, stare at a stack of disks, and ask, "Now what?" The answer is: "Read this book." *Mastering Microsoft Works* takes you through the major aspects of using the Works program (version 2.0) on an IBM PC or IBM-compatible computer. You will learn how to set up Works on your PC, start the program, and use all the important Works features.

This book was written with the new computer user in mind. If Works is the first software program you have ever used, this is the book for you. I use ordinary, everyday analogies to define each technical term as it is introduced. And though this book is aimed at beginners, it is equally appropriate for more experienced users. If you learned the basic Works features on your own and feel like you need to fill in the gaps, you can pick up many shortcuts and pointers throughout this book.

Mastering Microsoft Works is a tutorial, with easy step-by-step exercises that you can follow at your computer. This book takes a hands-on approach; you will learn by doing. Pictures of the screen are provided at key points so that you can check to make sure you are on the right track. If your screen matches the figure in the book, you can safely assume you followed the instructions correctly.

You can also use this book as a reference guide when you need to review a topic. Use the Index or the Table of Contents to locate the subject, and then read through the text to refresh your memory.

HOW TO USE THIS BOOK

The book is divided into six parts. The first part gives you an overview of Works and what it can do for you. The next four parts concentrate on the Works tools (word processor, spreadsheet, database, and communications). Interspersed throughout the book are many examples of how you can integrate data from the different tools (for example, copying a spreadsheet table into a word processing report). The last part discusses some general topics (windows and macros).

Your use of this book depends on two factors: your level of experience with Works, and which tools you plan on using. If you are new to Works and will be using all the tools, you should read the book in the order the chapters are presented. You can skip over the tools for which you don't have any need, except for the word processor tool. Because the word processor is the first tool that is covered, this part contains important information on the basic operation of Works. Also, be sure not to miss chapters 15 and 16, because these chapters contain information that can be used in any tool. If you are an experienced Works user, you may want to skip the first introductory chapter, and then turn to the parts that focus on the tools you want to learn more about.

At the end of each chapter are exercises that give you additional practice in using the features covered in the chapter. Unlike the exercises that appear throughout each chapter, these final exercises do not tell you every key to press or every command to use. Instead, the exercises are more like story problems. I give you general steps to guide you through the exercise and refer you to the appropriate section in the chapter to turn to if you get stuck. (It's not considered cheating to look back in the chapter; it's considered smart.) If you are able to complete the exercises in a chapter without too much struggle, you can feel confident about proceeding to the next chapter.

HOW THIS BOOK IS ORGANIZED

This book is divided into six parts and five appendices. The chapters in each part are briefly described below.

PART I: INTRODUCTION TO WORKS

Chapter 1 introduces you to Microsoft Works and describes its many capabilities. This introductory chapter discusses how to start Works, how to use the mouse and keyboard, and how to select menu options.

Chapter 2 explores the three useful accessories that are built into Works: the calculator, the alarm clock, and the auto-dialer.

PART II: THE WORD PROCESSOR TOOL

Chapter 3 explains how to type short documents, such as memos and letters. You will learn how to correct typing errors, print documents, move text to a different location in a document, and automatically correct mistakes with the spelling checker.

Chapter 4 explains how to enhance the appearance of your text. You will learn how to boldface words, change fonts, center lines, and double-space a document.

Chapter 5 discusses the features that are specific to longer documents. You will learn how to automatically print page numbers on every page and how to copy text between different documents.

PART III: THE SPREADSHEET TOOL

Chapter 6 introduces you to Works's powerful electronic spreadsheet. In this chapter, you will build a spreadsheet from the ground up. You will enter data, do calculations, and enhance the appearance of the spreadsheet before you print it.

Chapter 7 covers additional spreadsheet topics, such as inserting and deleting data, sorting, and copying a spreadsheet into a document.

In Chapter 8, you create graphs of the numbers in your spreadsheet. Because the spreadsheet and charting features are packaged in one tool, you can quickly and easily create graphs of your spreadsheet data. You will also see how you can include a chart in the middle of a word processor document.

PART IV: THE DATABASE TOOL

Chapter 9 teaches you the fundamentals of database creation. You design and modify a data entry form, enter and edit data, search for a specific record, and print the data in a form. This chapter concentrates on the first way of viewing your database: Form view.

Chapter 10 explores two more views in the database tool: List and Query. With List view, you can display, edit, and print your database in a row-and-column format. With Query view, you can specify which records you want to be displayed.

In Chapter 11, you create, modify, format, and print columnar reports.

In Chapter 12, you learn all the steps involved in doing a mass mailing: creating a database of your mailing list information, typing a form letter, and printing individualized letters. You also learn how to print the address block on mailing labels and envelopes.

PART V: THE COMMUNICATIONS TOOL

Chapter 13 introduces you to the basics of telecommunications. It explains commonly used communications terminology and settings that are important to successful telecommunications. You will learn how to connect to and disconnect from a remote computer, how to transfer files back and forth, and how to save a log of your communications session.

Chapter 14 shows you how to log on to and log off of several remote computer services: CompuServe, MCI Mail, Bank of America's HomeBanking, and an electronic bulletin board.

PART VI: WINDOWS AND MACROS

Chapter 15 demonstrates how to take advantage of one of Works's most powerful features: windows. Works lets you have up to eight windows (files) open at a time.

Chapter 16 shows you how to use Works's Macro feature to automate your commands and typing. In the process of learning how to create macros, you will build a useful collection of macros that you can use in the various Works tools.

APPENDICES

Appendix A takes you through the steps of installing Works on a hard disk or on a floppy disk system. You should turn to this appendix first if you haven't yet created your working copy of Works.

Appendix B contains all the documents referred to in Chapter 5. You can type the documents before you begin the chapter or create them as you follow the exercises.

Appendix C explains all 57 built-in functions that are available in the spreadsheet and database tools. Each function is illustrated with at least one example.

HOW I USE WORKS

I wrote every single word of this book in Works's word processor tool. I typed each chapter in a separate file, used Works's conversion program to convert it to a Microsoft Word file, and then mailed it to the publisher for editing. In the process of writing this book, I relied heavily on Works's windowing feature. I placed the chapter outline in one window and the manuscript in another, and opened a third window for the exercise I was writing. When I needed to look up something in another chapter, I opened yet another window. It was extremely convenient to be able to compose in the program I was writing about.

Although my hard disk is packed with all the heavyweight software programs (WordPerfect, Lotus 1-2-3, Symphony, Excel, dBASE), I prefer using Works for all but the most sophisticated projects. I use the spreadsheet tool for my home budget and monthly financial statements. I type all my memos and letters in the word processor tool. I keep my client information in the database tool. I use the communications tool for HomeBanking, connecting to electronic bulletin boards, and transferring files.

I appreciate the luxury of staying in one program and not having to load and exit several different software programs throughout the day. More important, I find Works to be a very friendly environment to work in. I hope you will too.

part one

INTRODUCTION TO WORKS

AN OVERVIEW OF WORKS

1

Microsoft Works is an all-in-one software package containing four distinct *tools:* word processor, spreadsheet, database, and communications. Let's look at each of these in more detail.

With the word processor tool, you can create and revise letters, memos, and long reports and documents. This tool takes the place of your typewriter.

With the spreadsheet tool, you can do financial planning, analysis, budgets, projections, and forecasts. It takes the place of accounting ledger paper, a pencil, a calculator, and a big eraser. You can also use it to graph data.

With the database tool, you can keep track of information, such as client records or a mailing list. You can search, sort, and create reports. The database tool takes the place of your filing cabinet and Rolodex.

With the communications tool, you can transfer information between two computers over the telephone lines. You can send someone a budget or a report, or you can connect to a service like HomeBanking. You might say that the communications tool takes the place of the post office and other delivery services.

Because all four tools are contained in one package, you can easily transfer information between different types of *files.* (A file is a single word-processed document, a spreadsheet table, a set of communications options, or a database that has a name assigned to it.) Here are several examples of how you can transfer information in Works:

- You can copy a spreadsheet into a word processing document.
- You can create a graph in the spreadsheet tool of stock prices that you received from an online stock information service in the communications tool.
- You can print personalized letters in the word processor tool to everyone who is on your mailing list in the database tool.

Another advantage to an all-in-one package is that you don't have to learn several different *programs.* A program, or *software package* as it is sometimes called, is a set of instructions that performs a specific task. If you weren't using Works, you would have to purchase four different programs to get the same power as Works: a word processing program, a spreadsheet program, a database program, and a communications program. Because these programs are not related to one another, each one of them operates differently. But with Works, the menus and commands are consistent from tool to tool.

MOUSE VS. KEYBOARD

You can use Works with just your keyboard or with a combination of the mouse and the keyboard. A *mouse* is a device that has one or more buttons on top (the mouse's ears, supposedly) and is connected to your computer with a thin cable (the mouse's tail). By moving the mouse on your desktop, you move a pointer on the screen. You use the buttons (primarily the left one) to perform such tasks as selecting text, scrolling the screen, and choosing menu commands.

You don't have to have a mouse to use Works. However, some commands are faster or more convenient with the mouse. If you haven't used a keyboard much or are competing for World's Worst Typist, you will enjoy using this little critter. But don't overuse the mouse—sometimes it makes more sense to perform a task using the keyboard. After using Works for a while, you will discover which tasks work better with the mouse and which work better with the keyboard. I will also make recommendations throughout this book.

Even if you use a mouse, you still have to type letters, numbers, and other characters with your keyboard. The keyboard layout you have depends on what type of computer you have. Figure 1.1 displays the three most common layouts. The center part of the keyboard (containing the letters, numbers, and symbols) is similar to a typewriter; however, the Caps Lock key is a little different from a typewriter's Shift Lock key. All it does is capitalize letters; it does not lock in the Shift key for special symbols. So if you want to type a dollar sign, you must hold down the Shift key, regardless of whether Caps Lock is on or off. To return to lowercase letters, press Caps Lock again. Some keyboards have a separate Caps Lock indicator light. Works lets you know when Caps Lock is on by displaying *CL* at the bottom of the screen.

The *function keys* are labeled F1 through F10 (or F1 through F12 on some keyboards) and appear on the left side or top row of the keyboard. These keys are shortcuts to commonly used commands. For example, instead of using the Works menu to get help (at least three keystrokes), you can simply press the F1 function key. Or, instead of using the menu to move a paragraph, you can press F3. You will learn the specific functions throughout this book.

A function key provides additional commands when you use the Shift or Ctrl (Control) key in tandem with the function key. For example, Ctrl-F6

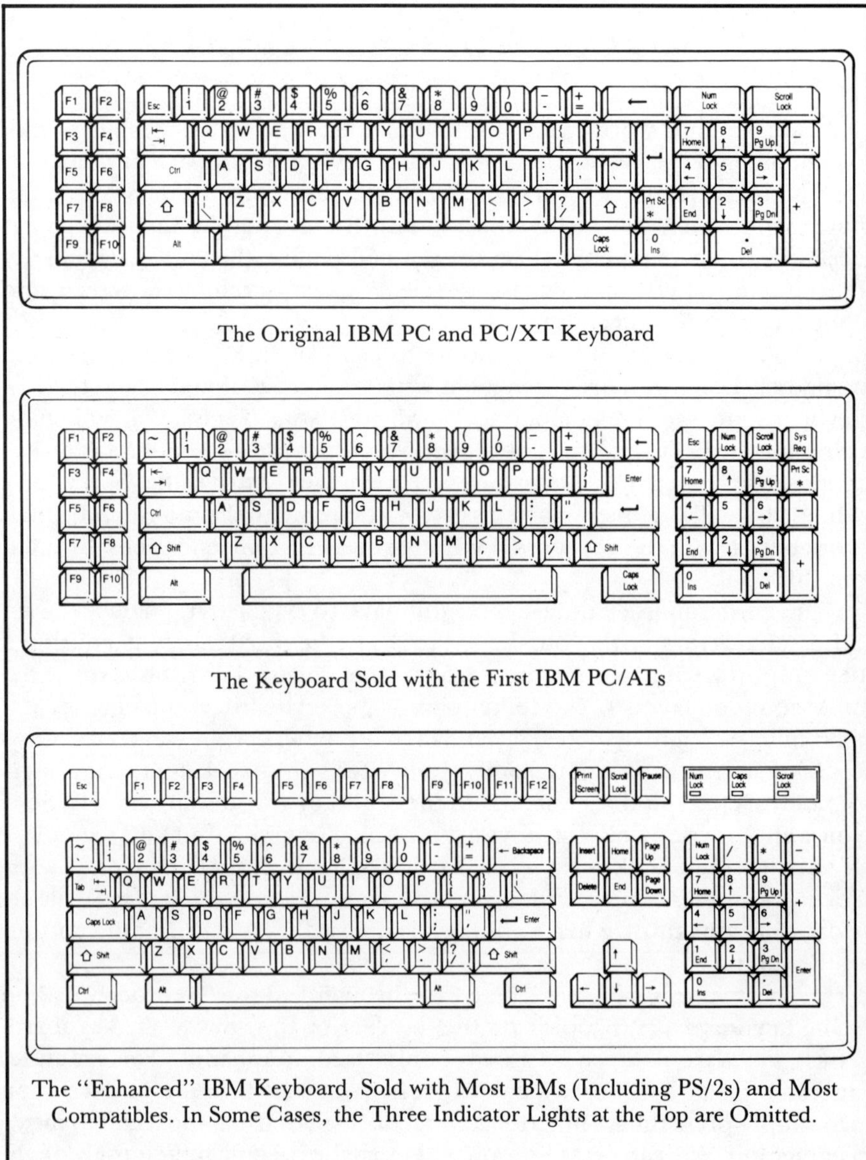

The Original IBM PC and PC/XT Keyboard

The Keyboard Sold with the First IBM PC/ATs

The "Enhanced" IBM Keyboard, Sold with Most IBMs (Including PS/2s) and Most Compatibles. In Some Cases, the Three Indicator Lights at the Top are Omitted.

Figure 1.1: The IBM PC, PC/AT, and enhanced keyboards

is the Next Window command—you press the Ctrl key and continue holding it down while pressing and releasing the F6 function key. This technique is like changing gears in a manual transmission car: You must hold down the clutch (press the Ctrl key) before and during the time you change gears (press the function key).

On the far-right side of the keyboard is a cluster of keys labeled with both numbers and arrows. (For example, there is a key that has the number 6 and a right arrow on it.) This keypad allows you to perform two functions: entering numbers and moving the *cursor.* The cursor is a short, flashing line on the screen that indicates where the characters you type will appear. You can move the cursor around with the arrows on the keypad, and with the Home, End, PgUp (Page Up), and PgDn (Page Down) keys.

The Num Lock key lets you switch between typing numbers and moving the cursor. When Num Lock is on, the keypad produces numbers and *NL* appears at the bottom of the screen. When Num Lock is off, the keypad moves the cursor and no indicator appears on the screen. Your keyboard may also have an indicator light to let you know when Num Lock is on.

Some keyboards, such as the enhanced IBM keyboard, have a second keypad dedicated to cursor movement so that you can keep Num Lock on at all times. This keypad is usually to the left of the numeric keypad. The advantage of keyboards that have this keypad is that you can move the cursor and use the keypad to enter numbers, without having to press Num Lock.

If your keyboard has only the numeric keypad, you may prefer to leave Num Lock off so that the cursor movement keys are readily available. You then have to use the numbers on the top row of the keyboard.

Another important key is Esc (Escape). It does just what it sounds like it might do: It allows you to escape from an action (usually something you don't want to do). You use it to cancel commands.

STARTING WORKS

Complete instructions for setting up Works to run on your computer appear in Appendix A. If you haven't yet copied Works to your hard disk or haven't made working copies to run on floppy disks, you should turn to Appendix A now and return here when you are finished.

The procedure for starting Works depends on whether you have a hard disk drive. To start the Works program from a hard disk, follow these steps:

1. Turn on your computer. After the computer warms up and does a few self-tests, you will see the DOS prompt: *C:\>*.
2. Change to the subdirectory where you copied Works. For example, if you named the subdirectory MSWORKS, type **CD\MSWORKS** and press Enter. Or, if you named the subdirectory WORKS, type **CD\WORKS** and press Enter.
3. To start the program, type **works** and press Enter.

If you have only floppy disk drives, follow these steps:

1. Place the DOS disk in drive A.
2. Turn on your computer. After the computer warms up and does a few self-tests, you will see the DOS prompt: *A>*.
3. Remove the DOS disk from drive A, and insert your working copy of the Works program disk in drive A.
4. Insert a blank, formatted disk in drive B. (This disk will store the documents you create.)
5. To start the program, type **works** and press Enter.

HOW TO USE MENUS IN WORKS

When you first start the Works program, you see the screen shown in Figure 1.2. The *menu bar* across the top of the screen displays three options: File, Options, and Help. The File *pull-down menu* is automatically displayed for you as well. A pull-down menu displays command options on a vertical list.

The screen display is similar to a restaurant menu. The main options on the Works menu bar (File, Options, Help) correspond to the food categories on a restaurant menu (Appetizers, Salads, Entrees, Desserts). The choices on the pull-down menu (Create New File, Open Existing File, Save, etc.) correspond to the specific dishes (Cherries Jubilee, Baked Alaska, Mud Pie, etc.) listed within a food category.

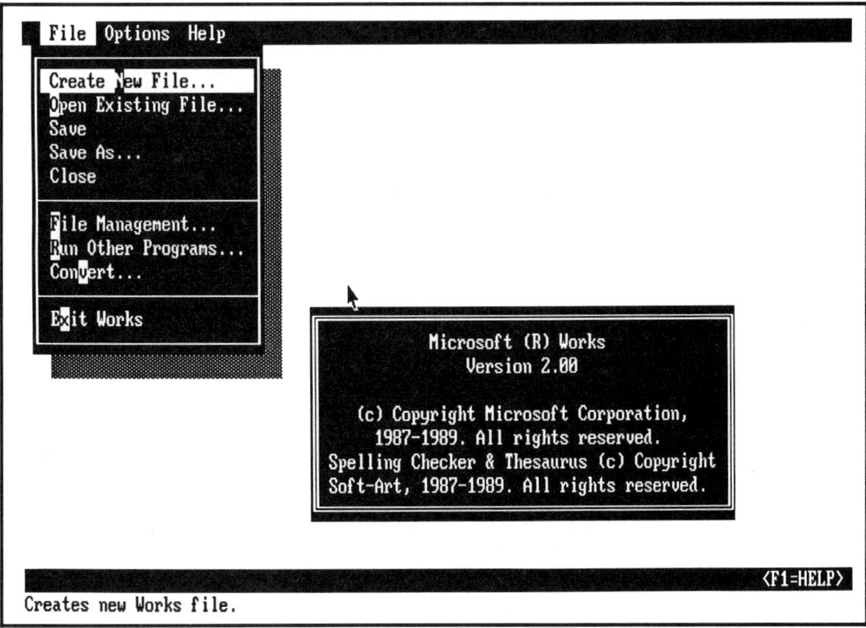

Figure 1.2: The Works opening screen

The Works menu is different from a restaurant menu in that you can't see all the dishes at once. On a restaurant menu, you can see all the appetizers, salads, and entrees, usually on a two-page spread. In Works, you can only see one "food category" (pull-down menu) at a time. For example, when you start Works, you can only see the "dishes" in the File menu. If you press →, you can see the choices in the Options menu. Press → again and you can see what's cooking in the Help menu. Press → one more time and you are back to the File menu.

Notice that the first option in the File menu, Create New File, looks different from the other options—it has a black background, and the other options all have a light background. The black background indicates that the option is *highlighted.* A brief description of the highlighted option appears in the bottom-left corner of the screen. When you start Works, this description reads *Creates new Works file.* Press ↓ and notice that the next option, Open Existing File, is highlighted and the description now reads *Opens existing Works file.* In the next section, you will learn how to select menu options.

Press the Esc (Escape) key to move out of the File pull-down menu. The menu bar is still visible, but none of the pull-down menus are available right now.

ACTIVATING MENUS WITH THE KEYBOARD

How you use and activate menus differs depending on whether you are using the mouse or the keyboard. To activate the menu bar from the keyboard, press the Alt key. (Do this now.) You then see one letter in each option highlighted differently. Usually it is the first letter, but if two menu options begin with the same letter, a different letter is highlighted. To choose a menu option, you either type the highlighted letter in the command name or use the arrow keys to highlight the command and press Enter.

Let's display the File pull-down menu now: Press F for File. At this point, a pull-down menu displays the commands available for that menu option. Notice that some of the commands have a highlighted letter and some don't. The options without a highlighted letter (Save, Save As, and Close) are not available now. You can select a command either by typing the highlighted letter or by highlighting the command with ↓ and pressing Enter. Just for practice, choose the File Management command, using either of these two techniques: Press ↓ to highlight File Management and then press Enter, or press F (the highlighted letter in File Management).

A box of choices appears after you select the command. Since you don't want to use this command right now, press Esc to cancel it. The box disappears, and the menu is deactivated. To give another command, you have to press Alt again to reactivate the menu. If you press Alt accidentally, or if you no longer want to work with the menu, press Esc to deactivate the menu.

ACTIVATING MENUS WITH THE MOUSE

If Works is installed to work with a mouse, you see either an arrow or a square block in the middle of your screen when you start Works. This symbol is called the *mouse pointer*—it moves as you roll the mouse on your desktop.

To use the mouse in the menu bar, you move the mouse pointer to the desired option, and click the left mouse button once. You then see a pull-down menu. Place the pointer on the option you want in this menu, and click the left button. For practice, select the File Management option in the

File pull-down menu:

1. Place the mouse pointer on File in the menu bar.
2. Click the left mouse button.
3. Place the mouse pointer on File Management in the pull-down menu.
4. Click the left mouse button.
5. Press Esc to cancel this command and deactivate the menu.

CONVERSING WITH DIALOG BOXES

If a menu option has three dots after it (for example, *Open Existing File...*), a ***dialog box*** appears when you select the option. A dialog box is a fill-in-the-blank form that prompts you to supply further information. In our restaurant-menu analogy, a dialog box is the equivalent of a waitress asking you questions after you have given her your order: "Do you want soup or salad?"; "Thousand Island, Ranch, or Italian salad dressing?"; "How would you like your steak prepared?"; "Would you prefer rice or baked potato?"

Dialog boxes ask you similar questions—not about food but about the particular command you have selected. For example, if you choose the Open Existing File command, a dialog box asks you for the name of a file to open. Some options in dialog boxes require you to type in numbers or text, and others have you choose from a list.

To select an option in a dialog box, press the Tab key until the cursor moves to the section of the dialog box where you want to carry out an action. If the option contains a list, use the arrow keys to make your selection. As an alternative to using the Tab and arrow keys to get around the dialog box, you can press the Alt key in combination with the highlighted letter in an option's name.

To see how a typical dialog box operates, follow these steps:

1. Press Alt to activate the menu bar.
2. Press F for File.
3. Press O for Open Existing File. A dialog box appears, like the one in Figure 1.3.

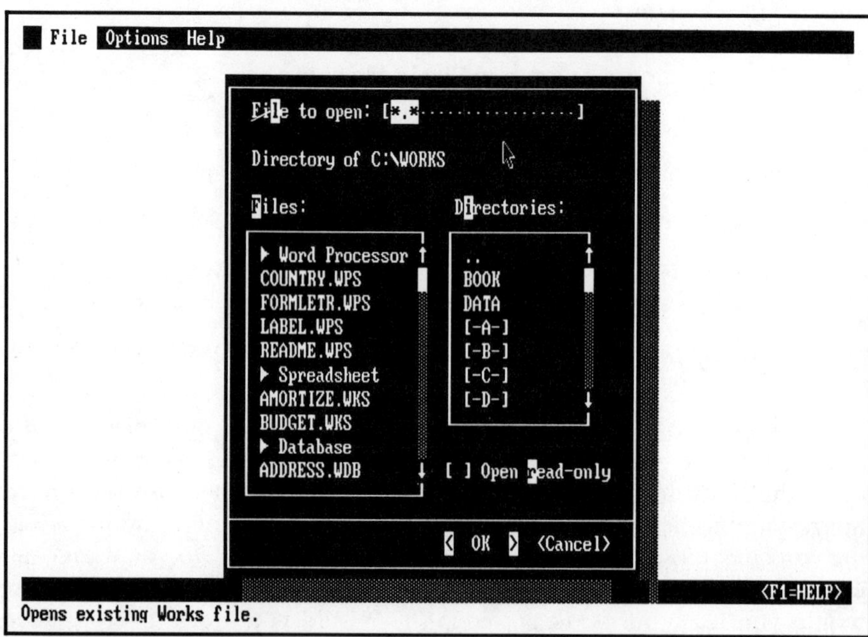

Figure 1.3: The Open Existing File dialog box

4. The dialog box has several different areas: ***File to open***, ***Files***, ***Directories***, and ***Open read-only***. The cursor is next to ***File to open***. To go to the next area (*Files*), press Tab or Alt-F. The cursor now blinks in the Files list.
5. Press ↓ to highlight different file names in the list. If you wanted to open one of these files, you would highlight the name and press Enter—*do not* do this now.
6. To move the cursor to the next area (*Directories*), press Tab or Alt-I. You can press ↓ to highlight different disk-drive letters and subdirectory names, but *do not* press Enter.
7. To remove the dialog box without making any selections, press Esc.

If you are using the mouse, moving around in a dialog box is easy: just position the mouse pointer in the area of the dialog box where you want to carry out an action, and click the left button once. For practice, follow these steps:

1. Move the pointer to File in the menu bar. Click the left button.
2. Move the pointer to Open Existing File in the pull-down menu. Click the left button. The dialog box is displayed.
3. The cursor is next to the option *File to open.* To highlight a file in the list of names, position the pointer on a file name in the Files list and click the left button once. The file name you click on is highlighted.
4. Position the pointer on an option in the Directories list and click once.
5. To remove the dialog box without making any selections, place the pointer on Cancel, and click the left button.

The bottom of every dialog box displays a way to execute the command and a way to cancel it. Usually, you see *OK* and *Cancel*, as you saw in the Open Existing File dialog box. If you are using the keyboard, you can simply press the Enter key to choose OK or press the Esc key to cancel the command. If you are using a mouse, you have an alternative to clicking on OK: Click twice quickly on the last option you want to select in the dialog box. This is called *double-clicking.* If your hands are already on the keyboard typing something, it may be easier to simply press the Enter key.

WORKING WITH FILES AND USING WINDOWS

The File menu (see Figure 1.4) lists all the actions you can perform on your files: creating, opening, saving, and closing them. (Don't select any of these options just yet.) If you choose the option Create a New File, you are asked to choose the type of file: Word Processor, Spreadsheet, Database, or Communications. Notice that these file types correspond to the four Works tools. You then see a blank screen on which you can create the type of file you specified. You don't name the file until you choose the Save or Save As option.

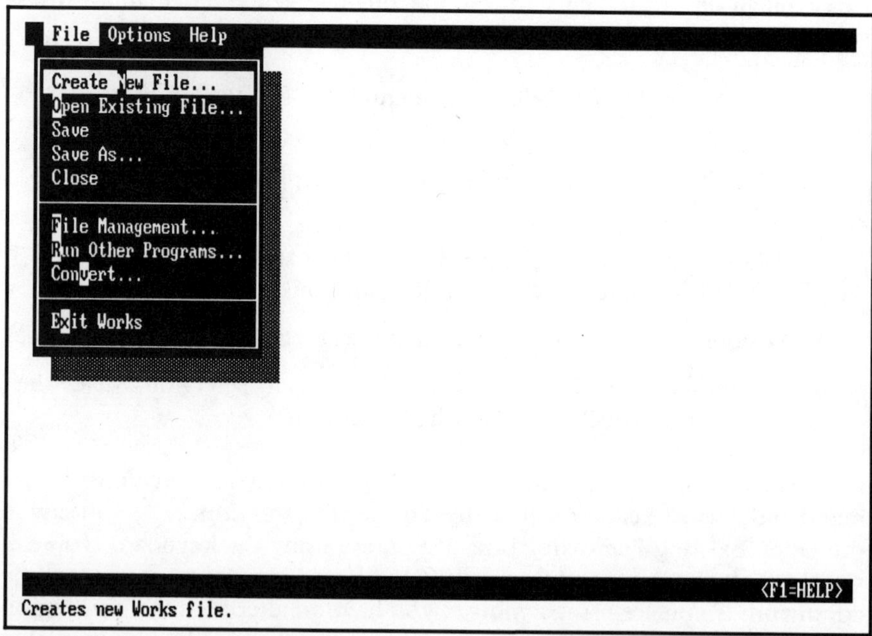

Figure 1.4: The File menu

Saving your files is an extremely important part of using a computer. The letters, reports, graphs, and tables you create in Works are stored in the computer's temporary memory (RAM). Until you execute the Save command, the file is not permanently recorded on your hard disk or floppy disk. If the power goes off before you save, you lose your work.

A friend of mine related the following sad story to me. Someone (not me!) showed him how to create a document in a word processing program, and he spent an entire evening merrily typing away. After typing and editing 20 pages, he turned off the computer and went to bed, tired, but pleased with all the work he had accomplished. The next morning, he turned on his computer and alas, he couldn't find his document. Whoever showed him how to use the computer forgot one important step: saving the file to disk.

You use the Save As command to assign a new name to your file and the Save command when you have already named a file and want to save it with the same name.

To recall a file you have already saved, use the Open Existing File command. When you have finished working with a file, use the Close command.

If you have made any changes since you last saved, Works asks you if you want to save your changes—you needn't worry about accidentally closing a file that you haven't saved.

One of the more powerful features of Works enables you to have more than one file open at a time. Each file is stored and displayed in its own *window*. A window is simply a bordered container for a file. You don't need to go through any special steps to open multiple files. If there is a file already open on your screen when you open another file or when you create a new one, the first file is placed in a window behind the second one. You can have up to eight files open at a time. If you no longer want to work on a file, be sure to close it before opening another one. Open files take up space in memory and on the screen, so it's best to close a file when you're finished with it.

Figure 1.5 shows a file named DEPTS.WKS that was opened after the file named JOHNSON.WPS. Notice that you can still see the name of the first file and the window's left border. For more information on windows, see Chapter 15.

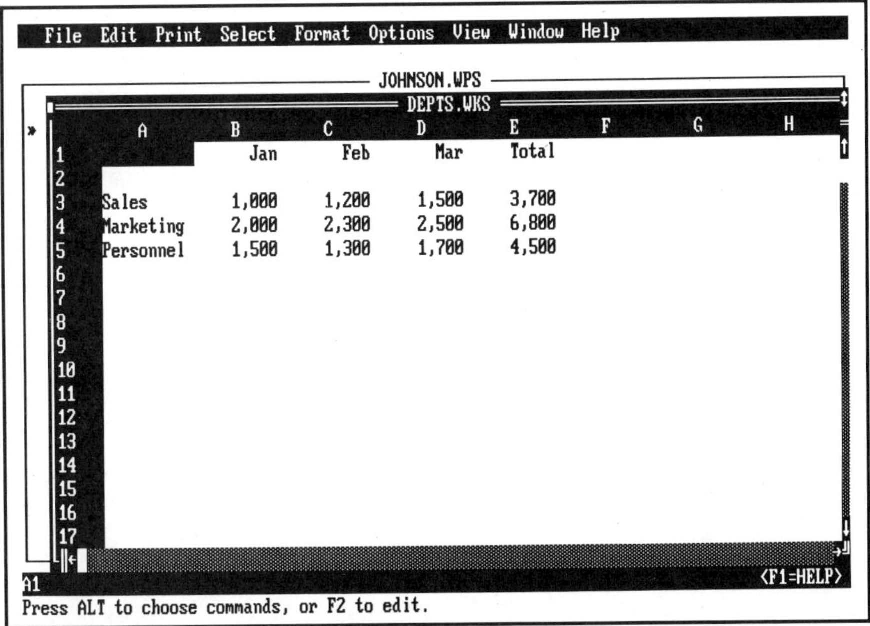

Figure 1.5: Two open files, each in its own window

SUMMARY

In this chapter, you were introduced to working with the basic Works features: using the mouse and the keyboard, selecting menu options, filling in dialog boxes, and saving files. The next chapter discusses several accessories that come with Microsoft Works: the calculator, the alarm clock, and the auto-dialer.

EXERCISES

In the following exercises, you have an opportunity to practice what you learned in Chapter 1. You will start up the Works program, choose options on the menu bar and pull-down menus, and fill in dialog boxes. You can use the keyboard or the mouse, whichever you prefer. If you get stuck, hints and references to the appropriate sections in the chapter are indicated inside parentheses.

1. Exit Microsoft Works by choosing Exit Works on the File menu.
2. Start the Works program (see "Starting Works," page 7).
3. Check the computer's current date and time. (If you aren't sure how to choose the menu options, see "How to Use Menus in Works," page 8.)
   - Choose File Management on the File menu.
   - Choose Set Date & Time.
   - If the date and/or time are not accurate, enter the correct values.
   - Choose OK.
4. Cancel the File Management menu.
5. Open the FORMLETR.WPS file (see "Conversing with Dialog Boxes," page 11). FORMLETR.WPS is a word processor file that comes with Works; if you can't find this file, choose another one. (If you don't see any file names on the Files list, skip this exercise.) Follow these steps to open a file:
   - Choose Open Existing File on the File menu.
   - Highlight the name on the Files list (for example, FORMLETR.WPS).
   - Press Enter (or double-click the left mouse button).
6. Close the open file by choosing Close on the File menu.

USING THE ACCESSORIES

2

Works offers several useful accessories that let you display a calculator, set an alarm, and dial a phone number, regardless of which tool you are using. These accessories allow you to use your computer for tasks you normally carry out with other devices. By working through this chapter at your computer, you will not only learn how to use these accessories in any Works tool, you will also get practice in working with menus and dialog boxes.

In this chapter you will also learn how to use the Help facility to look up general information on using Works and how to receive specific instructions on using a particular command.

USING THE CALCULATOR

You no longer need to keep a calculator next to your computer—Works comes with its own on-screen version of one. Any time you need to make a quick calculation, you can use the Works calculator. You can even insert a result in your document, spreadsheet, or database.

Follow these steps to display the calculator using the keyboard:

1. Press the Alt key.
2. Press O to choose Options.
3. Press ↓ to highlight Calculator.
4. Press Enter. You then see the on-screen calculator displayed in Figure 2.1.

Follow these steps to display the calculator using the mouse:

1. Move the pointer to Options.
2. Click the left mouse button. A pull-down menu is displayed.
3. Move the pointer to Calculator.
4. Click the left mouse button.

To enter numbers in the calculator, you can use the numbers on the top row of the keyboard or on the numeric keypad. Since the numbers on the

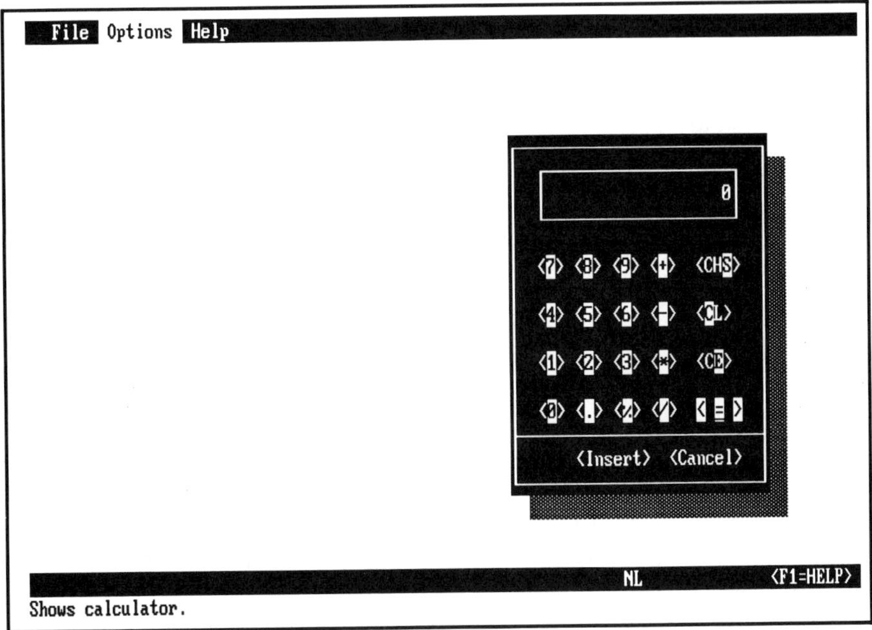

Figure 2.1: The on-screen calculator

numeric keypad are in the same positions as they are on the on-screen calculator, you will probably prefer to use the numeric keypad. Remember, though, that this keypad controls both cursor movement and numbers; it only types numbers when Num Lock is turned on. (Works displays *NL* at the bottom of the screen to indicate that Num Lock is on.)

To do a calculation, you type a number, then the mathematical symbol for the operation you want to perform (for example, + to add), type another number, and then press Enter or = (equals sign) to see the result. The box at the top of the calculator is the equivalent of the display window on a hand-held calculator; it displays the numbers you type and the results of your calculations. Table 2.1 describes the keys you can use with the calculator.

For practice, multiply 175.25 by 7%. Follow these steps:

1. Type **175.25**.
2. Press *. (There are two asterisks on the keyboard—you can use either one.)

Table 2.1: Calculator Key Functions

KEY	FUNCTION
+	Add
−	Subtract
*	Multiply
/	Divide
C	CL (Clears all)
E	CE (Clears entry)
S	CHS (Changes sign from positive to negative or negative to positive)
I	Insert

3. Type 7%.
4. Press Enter or press the equals sign (=) to calculate the answer.

If you did this exercise correctly, the answer *12.2675* is displayed. Press Esc to leave the calculator, or you can enter another calculation, if you like.

If you are working on a document, spreadsheet, or database, you can paste the result *12.2675* into the file by choosing the Insert command at the bottom of the calculator (click on the Insert command or press I). Since you are not in a file right now, however, you cannot insert the result. Press the Esc key to close the calculator, or select Cancel with the mouse and click the left button.

USING THE ALARM CLOCK

You can set an alarm in the alarm clock to remind yourself to do an important task, such as making a phone call, going to a meeting, or getting the laundry out of the dryer (some of us work out of our homes...). The reminder can be for the current day or a day in the future. You can also set the frequency of an alarm so that it goes off on a regular basis. Figure 2.2 shows the alarm-clock dialog box. The section in the upper-right side of the box shows the frequency intervals you can set for each alarm. You may want to enter the birthdays of friends and relatives as yearly alarms.

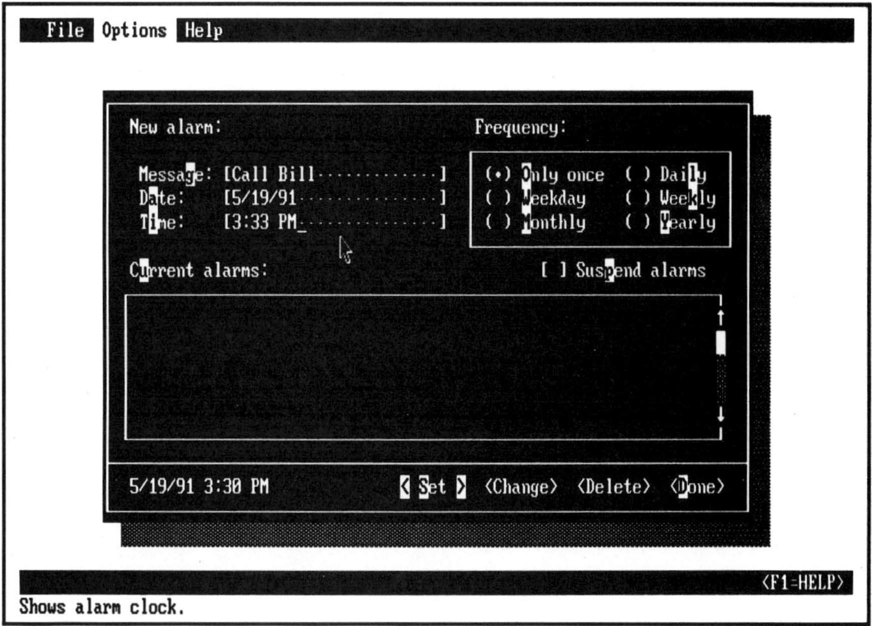

Figure 2.2: The alarm-clock dialog box

To see how the alarm clock works, let's set an alarm to go off in several minutes.

1. Choose Alarm Clock on the Options menu. (Look at the current date and time at the bottom of the dialog box. If this information is not correct, refer to your computer manual to reset the clock.)
2. Type **Call Bill** after Message. (Your message can be up to 60 characters long.)
3. Press Tab or ↓ to move the cursor to the next option, Date.
4. Type today's date in the same format that is shown in Figure 2.2.
5. Press the Tab key or ↓ to move the cursor next to Time.
6. Type in a time 3 minutes from the time shown at the bottom of the dialog box. The time can be entered in the 24-hour time format (for example, *15:00* for 3:00 in the afternoon) or in the standard 12-hour time format (for example, *3:00 PM*). Be sure to specify AM or PM if you are using the 12-hour format.

7. To set the alarm, press Enter, or move the mouse pointer to Set and click the left button. The alarm is now listed in the *Current alarms* section of the screen.

8. To close the alarm-clock dialog box, press Esc or Alt-D (for Done) or click on Done.

When the alarm beeps, a message box pops up on the screen, giving you three options: Snooze, Reset, or OK. If you press Enter, this chooses OK. This command cancels the alarm and clears the message from the screen. *Snooze* works just like the snooze button on your real alarm clock—if you choose it, the alarm will sound again in 10 minutes. *Reset* lets you reset the alarm for a future date or time. Choosing this option takes you directly into the alarm-clock dialog box.

What happens if your computer is not turned on or you are not in Works when the alarm is supposed to go off? The alarm hibernates until the next time you load the Works program. As soon as you enter Works, the alarm will beep and the message will be displayed. Better late than never!

AUTO-DIALING

To use the auto-dialer, you need to have a *modem* connected to your PC. A modem is a device that connects your computer to the telephone line. (For more information, see Chapter 13.)

Using Works's dialing feature, you can automatically dial any phone number listed in a document, spreadsheet, or database. For example, you might want to type your phone list into a file and open the file whenever you want to make a call. The auto-dialing feature saves you the time you would spend looking up a phone number in your Rolodex or phone book and then manually dialing the number. You simply select the phone number and choose Dial This Number from the Options menu. As long as you have a modem connected to your PC and the modem is plugged in and turned on, Works dials the number for you and instructs you to "Pick up phone and press OK to answer." While the phone is ringing, you pick up the telephone receiver and press Enter to choose OK.

GETTING HELP

Works has a comprehensive *online help* facility. You may have noticed that the lower-right corner of the screen displays *F1 = HELP* and that one of the main menu options is Help.

1. Select the Help option on the menu bar and look at the various options on the pull-down menu (see Figure 2.3).
2. Choose the first option, Using Help, which tells you how to operate the Help feature. Notice the triangle pointing downward at the bottom right-hand side of the screen. This symbol lets you know that more information is available.
3. Press the PgDn key to look at the next Help screen, or if you have a mouse, click on Page Down. When you reach the last Help screen on the topic, you see two squares where the triangle was.

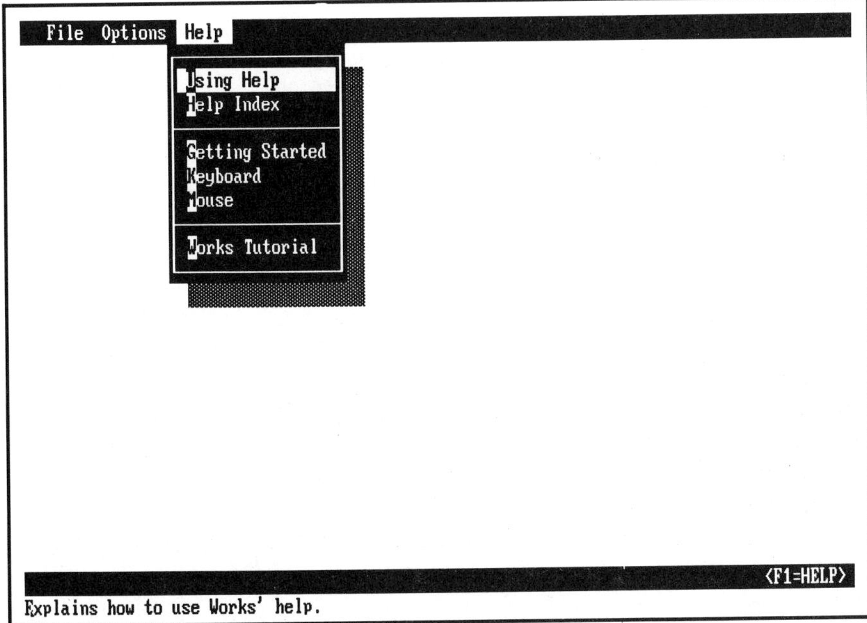

Figure 2.3: The Help menu

A *help index* is also available. Help Index is an option on the Help pull-down menu, and it is always an option listed at the bottom of any Help screen (except if you are already in the index). The cursor automatically highlights this option so you can press Enter to go into the index. Your screen should look similar to Figure 2.4.

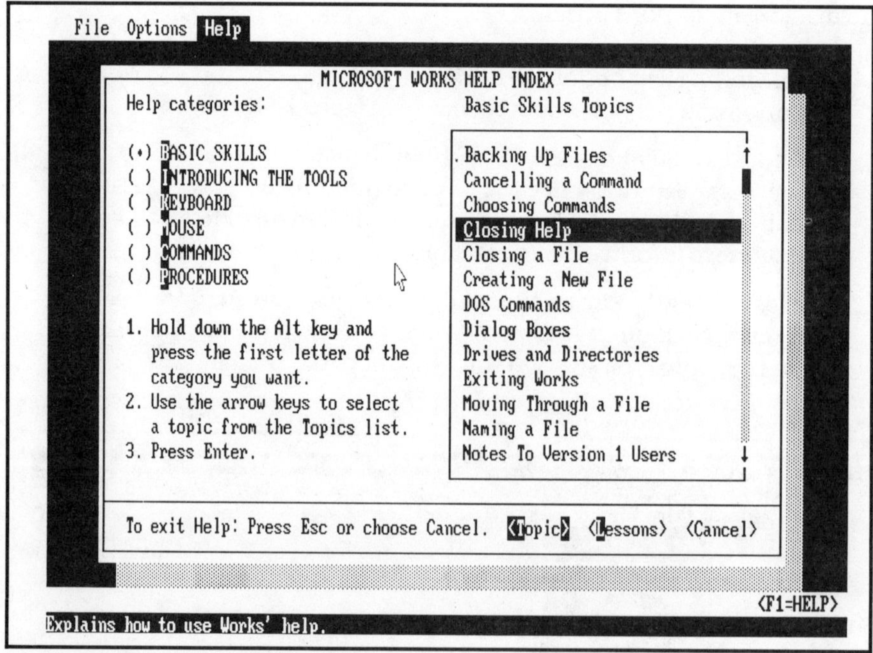

Figure 2.4: The Help Index

The left side of the index screen lists general Help categories, and the box on the right side lists specific topics for the chosen category. To choose a different Help category, press Alt in combination with the highlighted letter of the category name or click inside the parentheses next to the name. For example, press Alt-I to choose Introducing the Tools. The box on the right now contains tools-related topics. Use the arrow keys or the mouse to highlight a topic.

Because you will learn the word processor tool in the next chapter, highlight Getting Started in the WP and press Enter (or double-click on the topic). Read each Help screen and press PgDn (or click on Page Down) until you see the double squares. If you keep pressing PgDn at the end of a topic, the next topic is automatically displayed.

Another way to use Help is to press F1 while you are in the middle of a command. Works automatically displays the Help screen for the command you are using. This feature is called *context-sensitive help.* For example, if you are in the middle of a command and you need help, press F1 and instructions appear for using that command. When you find the information you need, press Esc to clear the Help screen, and you are returned to the command you were in when you requested help. To see how context-sensitive help operates, follow these steps:

1. Press Esc to clear the Help screen.
2. Choose Alarm Clock on the Options menu.
3. Press F1.
4. Read the Help screen, and press PgDn (or click on Page Down) to view the other Help screens.
5. Press Esc to cancel Help. You are brought right back to where you were when you requested help.
6. Press Esc to cancel the Alarm Clock command.

You might want to browse through the Help Index and read about various features. Press F1 when you need instant help on a specific command.

Another option on the Help pull-down menu is Works Tutorial. The tutorial, called Learning Works, gives you an instructional tour of Works's tools and features. All instructions for using the tutorial are on the screen. The tutorial may be a useful supplement to the exercises in this book.

SUMMARY

In this chapter, you learned how to use the three accessories that are included in Works: the calculator, the alarm clock, and the auto-dialer. You can use these accessories in any Works tool. You also got acquainted with Works's online help facility.

The next chapter introduces you to the word processor. Even if you don't plan on doing a lot of word processing, you should still read through the chapter. It acquaints you with many skills that are helpful in using any Works tool, such as using the scroll bars, and saving and opening files.

EXERCISES

In the following exercises you will practice using the Works accessories. You will set alarms in the alarm clock, perform calculations with the calculator, and use the Help feature. If you get stuck, refer to the sections indicated inside parentheses.

1. Set an alarm to remind you of a friend's birthday. The alarm-clock dialog box should look similar to the one shown in Figure 2.5. Notice that the frequency is set to Yearly. (See "Using the Alarm Clock," page 22.)

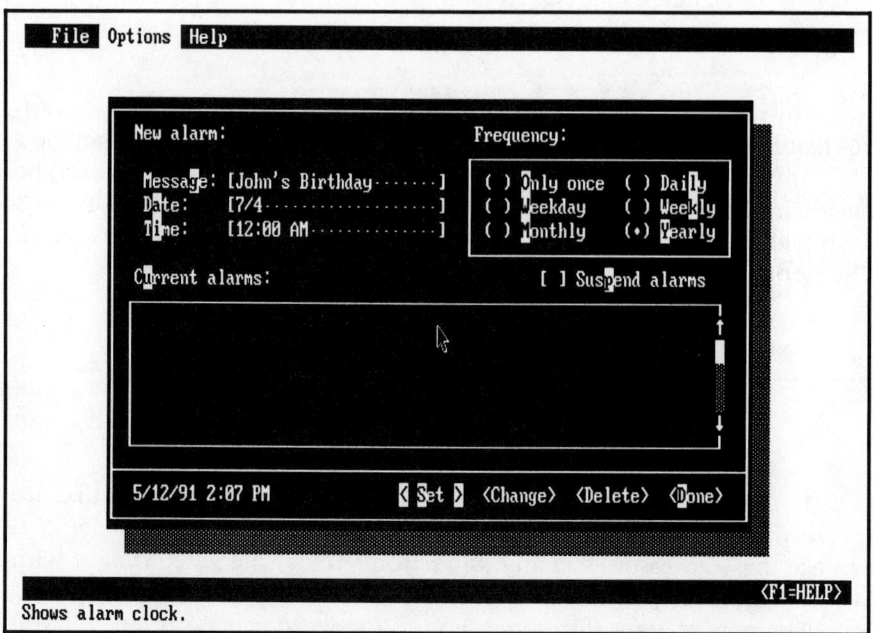

Figure 2.5: Setting an alarm to remind you of a friend's birthday

2. Set an alarm that will go off in 5 minutes to remind you to get up and stretch. Clear the alarm-clock dialog box from the screen (choose Done or press Esc).

3. Use the calculator to make the following calculations (see "Using the Calculator," page 20):

   - 255 divided by 5 (answer: *51*)
   - 999 multiplied by 8 (answer: *7992*)
   - The sum of 356, 120, and 265 (answer: *741*)
   - The difference between 4020 and 2040 (answer: *1980*)

4. Get help while you are in the calculator (see "Getting Help," page 25). The Help screens are specific to using the calculator since you are in the calculator. When you are finished reading the Help screens, clear them and the calculator.

5. Display the Help Index, and choose Dialog Boxes from the Basic Skills Topics list on the right side of the screen. Read all the Help screens on this topic. Cancel the Help screens. (See "Getting Help," page 25.)

part two

THE WORD PROCESSOR TOOL

CREATING, EDITING, AND PRINTING A DOCUMENT

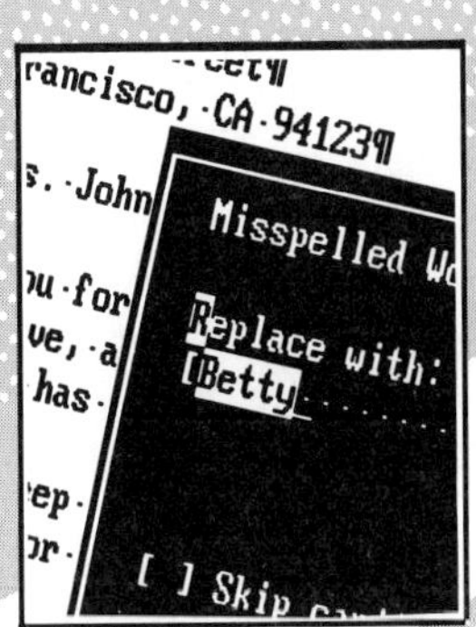

I have taught word processing classes for years, and I have yet to meet anyone who wanted to go back to using a typewriter after learning a word processing program. I ask my students what they like so much about word processing, and they invariably come up with the following responses:

- It's easy to correct typos.
- You can move sections of text around without having to physically cut-and-paste.
- You can automatically center and underline text.
- You can change margins and line spacing without having to retype.
- The word processor can check your document for spelling errors.

Another advantage of word processors is that they have ***automatic word wrap.*** Unlike when you use a typewriter, you don't have to wait for the bell to ring at the end of each line. When you reach the right margin, the word you're typing automatically "wraps" or moves down to the beginning of the next line. The only time you need to press Enter in Works's word processor tool is

- to end a paragraph,
- to end a short line (such as *Dear Mr. Jones:*), or
- to create a blank line.

CREATING A WORD PROCESSOR FILE

To begin typing a word processor document, you need to create a file. Follow these steps:

1. Choose the File command on the menu bar. As discussed in Chapter 1, you can access the menu bar with the mouse or with the keyboard. With the mouse, click on the option—File, in this case. With

the keyboard, press Alt and then press the underlined or shaded letter in the menu option—the letter *F,* in this case.

2. Press Enter to select Create New File, the first option displayed on the pull-down menu, or click on it with the mouse. A list of the four file types (tools) appears.
3. Press Enter to select New Word Processor, which is already highlighted on the screen.

An empty *word processor window* now appears, with the menu bar at the top of the screen. The Works screen gives you a lot of information once you know how to interpret it. Figure 3.1 points out the important parts of the word processor screen.

EXPLORING THE WORD PROCESSOR WINDOW

Inside the window, you see several symbols:

Underline	Your cursor.
Diamond	Indicates the end of the document. You cannot move the cursor beyond this symbol.
Double right-pointing arrows	Indicate the beginning of a page. This symbol appears at the top of each page.
Arrow or square block	The mouse pointer.

Notice that Figure 3.1 has a paragraph mark (¶) displayed as well. If you do not see a paragraph mark on your screen, choose Show All Characters on the Options menu (using the techniques described in Chapter 1). With this option turned on, you see special symbols, such as paragraph marks, tabs, and dots for blank spaces. All the figures in this chapter have this option turned on so that you can see exactly what to type when you follow the examples at your computer.

The window's top border, called the *title bar,* displays the file name. Since you haven't saved the file yet, a generic name, WORD1.WPS, is displayed. Directly underneath the title bar is a numbered *ruler.* The square

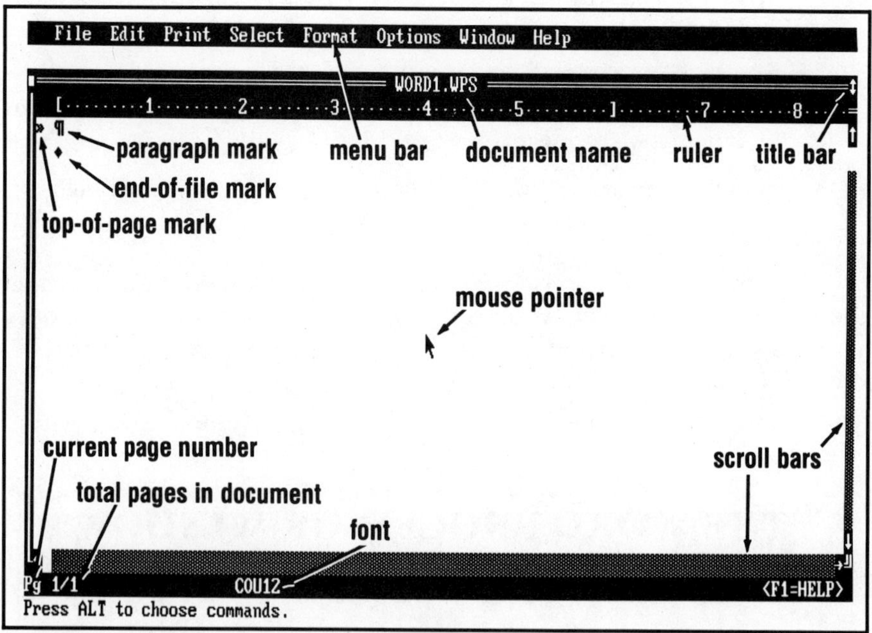

Figure 3.1: The word processor window

brackets in the ruler indicate where your lines of text begin and end. The numbers are in inches. By default your lines of text are 6 inches long.

The bottom border of the window displays information about the pages in your document. Right now it displays *Pg 1/1*. The first number indicates the page number of the cursor location. The second number indicates the total number of pages in the document. (*Pg 4/12* would indicate that your cursor is on page 4 of a 12-page document.)

The bottom border also displays the current *font,* such as *COU10,* which is an abbreviation for Courier 10-point. Fonts are discussed in Chapter 4. If Caps Lock or Num Lock is turned on, *CL* or *NL* appears in the bottom border. You also see a reminder that the F1 function key displays Help screens.

The right border of the window contains a vertical *scroll bar.* Notice another scroll bar at the bottom of the window that you use to scroll the screen horizontally. Use the scroll bars to display different parts of a long document that doesn't fit on the screen all at once. You learn how to use the vertical scroll bars in the section "Getting Around a Document."

Other symbols in the corners of the windows are used to change the size of the window and are discussed in Chapter 15.

TYPING A DOCUMENT

Now that you understand the different parts of the word processor screen, you are ready to begin typing your first document. Type the document in Figure 3.2 at your computer now, keeping the following points in mind:

- Let the text automatically "wrap" to the next line when you are typing paragraphs—press Enter only to end paragraphs, create blank lines, or end short lines (where you see the ¶ symbol in the figure).
- Don't worry about mistakes! As you will soon see, changing your typing errors is quick and easy. If you want to correct a mistake as you are typing, use the Backspace key (marked ⟵ on the top row of the keyboard) to back up and erase what you have just typed.

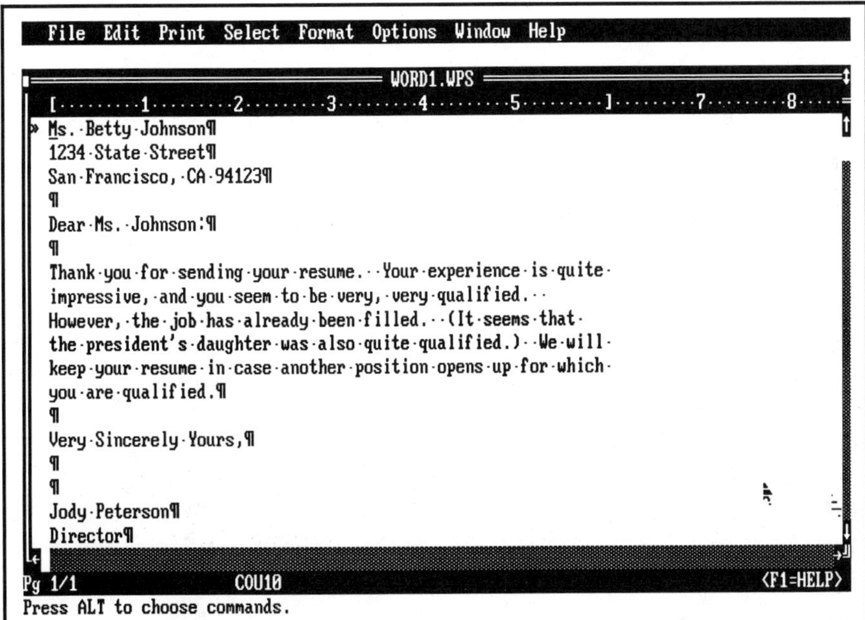

Figure 3.2: A sample letter for you to type

SAVING YOUR WORK

Save your work to disk about every 15 minutes. It doesn't take very long to save, but it could take a long time to recreate something you have typed, especially if you compose as you type. Always save before you leave your computer unattended.

The File menu offers two ways to save: Save and Save As. The first time you save a file, you can choose either of these options. Works first prompts you for a file name and then saves the file to the disk. If you continue working on the document and you add more text or revise the existing text, you should resave the document. The Save option saves the file with the same name you gave it previously, the Save As option lets you assign a new name to the file. Thus, if you want to replace the previously saved version with the new version, choose Save. If you want to keep the original file, and create a different file from the new version, choose Save As.

All the usual DOS file-naming rules apply to Works file names, as follows:

- A file name can be up to 8 characters long. Try to make the name descriptive of what is contained in the file.
- A file name can contain letters and numbers.
- Many of the special symbols (such as the * and ?) are not allowed. If you type an invalid character, Works displays an error message.
- Do not use spaces or periods.
- Do not type an extension. Works automatically assigns the appropriate extension for each tool (.WPS for word processing files, .WKS for spreadsheet files, .WDB for database files, and .WCM for communications files).

Follow these steps to save the document you just typed:

1. Pull down the File menu.
2. Choose Save As. The default file name, WORD1.WPS, appears next to *Save file as*.
3. Type **JOHNSON**. As soon as you start typing, the default name disappears.
4. Press Enter.

The title bar at the top of the window now displays the name JOHNSON.WPS. Works automatically assigned the extension .WPS.

Where exactly was this file saved? Go back into the Save As command and look directly underneath the file name. The default directory is displayed—for example, *C:\WORKS.* This means that the file will be saved on the C drive in the WORKS subdirectory. Your screen may show a different drive or subdirectory, depending on how your system is set up. Later on you will learn how to save and retrieve files from other drives and subdirectories. Press Esc to cancel the Save As command.

CLOSING A FILE

A file remains on the screen in its own window until you close it. To see how this works, choose Close on the File menu. The screen should now be clear except for the menu. If you hadn't just saved your latest changes, Works would have asked you if you wanted to save; unless you had made a mistake that you didn't want saved, you would choose Yes to save the current document and close the file.

CORRECTING MISTAKES

In this section, you open an existing file, move the cursor around the document using the keyboard, and scroll the screen using the mouse. You also learn how to *edit* the document. When you edit, you make corrections to your work.

OPENING AN EXISTING FILE

To display a document you have already saved and closed, use the Open Existing File command on the File menu. Choose this command now and you should see the screen displayed in Figure 3.3. This screen has several different areas: the Files box and the Directories box. The Files box on the left contains a list of files in the current directory, C:\WORKS. If you don't know the exact name of the document you want to open (or you don't feel like typing the name), you can use the mouse or arrow keys to point to the name.

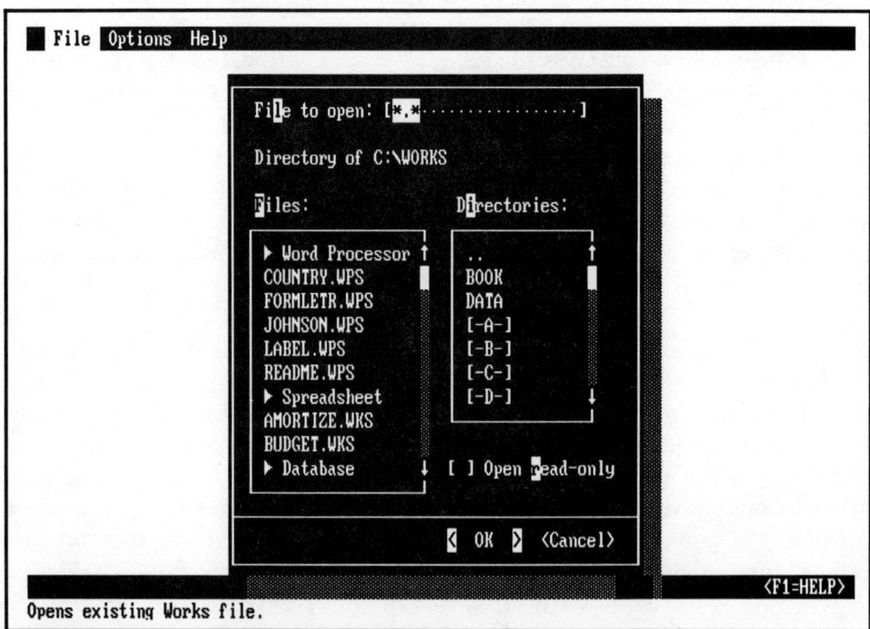

Figure 3.3: The Open Existing File dialog box

The Files list is in alphabetical order within each file type to make the process of finding a file easier. All the word processor files are grouped together, all the spreadsheet files are grouped together, etc. Files without the standard Works extensions are dumped into the Other Files category, at the bottom of the Files list. Except for JOHNSON.WPS, the files listed in Figure 3.3 are ones that come with the Works program. The Directories list on the right displays other drives and subdirectory names. The double dot (..) at the top of the list refers to the directory at the previous level. To open a file in another drive or subdirectory, you choose it from the Directories list.

To redisplay the JOHNSON document you just created, you can either type *JOHNSON* next to *File to open* or point to the name in the Files list. If you have a mouse, point to the name JOHNSON.WPS, and double-click the left mouse button. Otherwise, press ↓ until JOHNSON.WPS is highlighted, and press Enter.

What if you don't see the file name listed in the Files box? It's possible that the name is not shown because it is farther down in the list. You can use any of the following techniques to display additional file names:

- Press ↓ to scroll a file at a time.
- Press PgDn to scroll a whole box at a time.
- Press Ctrl-End to go to the end of the list.
- Press Ctrl-Home to go to the top of the list.
- Type the first letter of the file name. The cursor jumps to the first file starting with that letter.

If you have a mouse, you can use the scroll bar on the right side of the Files box. Here's how to use the scroll bar:

- Click on a scroll arrow to scroll the list a file at a time.
- Click anywhere in the middle of the scroll bar to scroll a whole box at a time.
- Click on the scroll box, hold the button down, and drag the scroll box to the bottom of the scroll bar. This action displays the files at the end of the list. Drag the box to the top of the bar to move to the beginning of the list.

GETTING AROUND A DOCUMENT

You should now have the JOHNSON document displayed on your screen. To correct mistakes, you need to move the cursor to them. To move the cursor to a location currently on the screen, use your arrow keys (up, down, left, right) or the mouse. Moving the cursor with the mouse requires two steps:

- Place the pointer on the character you want to move the cursor to.
- Click the left button.

Besides the arrow keys, Works offers many other ways—faster ways—to move the cursor. Table 3.1 lists these keyboard shortcuts.

If the text you want to move the cursor to is not currently displayed on your screen, you can use the mouse to access the vertical scroll bar to scroll to different parts of the document. Table 3.2 lists ways of scrolling the

Table 3.1: Keyboard Shortcuts for Moving the Cursor

MOVEMENT OF CURSOR	KEYSTROKE
Right one word	Ctrl-→
Left one word	Ctrl-←
Beginning of line	Home
End of line	End
Next paragraph	Ctrl-↓
Previous paragraph	Ctrl-↑
Next screen	PgDn
Previous screen	PgUp
Top of window	Ctrl-PgUp
Bottom of window	Ctrl-PgDn
Beginning of file	Ctrl-Home
End of file	Ctrl-End

Table 3.2: Mouse Scrolling Commands

DIRECTION OF SCROLLING	ACTION
Down one line	Click on down arrow in scroll bar
Down continuously	Click on down arrow in scroll bar, and hold the left button down
Up one line	Click on up arrow in scroll bar
Up continuously	Click on up arrow in scroll bar, and hold the left button down
Down one screen	Click on scroll bar underneath the scroll box
Up one screen	Click on scroll bar above the scroll box
Beginning of file	Click and drag scroll box to top of scroll bar
End of file	Click and drag scroll box to bottom of scroll bar

screen with the mouse. The scroll box in the scroll bar indicates where you are in relation to the length of the entire document. For example, if the scroll box is in the middle of the scroll bar, you are currently working in the middle of the document.

However, scrolling with the scroll bar does not actually move the cursor. If you use the scroll bar, you must click the mouse in the text to actually move the cursor to the screen you scrolled to. If you use the arrow keys before clicking in the text, the cursor moves back to where it was before you began scrolling.

Practice the shortcuts in Tables 3.1 and 3.2 until you feel comfortable moving the cursor and scrolling. Because the JOHNSON document is only one screen long, some of the commands will not apply (such as PgDn and PgUp).

INSERTING AND DELETING TEXT

The three most common typing mistakes are to leave out characters, to type the wrong characters, or to type extra characters. If you discover that you have left out text, you need to *insert* new text, and if you have typed the wrong or extra characters, you need to *delete* them.

Inserting Text

Works is always in Insert mode—whatever you type, wherever you type it, the text is added to whatever is already there. Text is inserted to the left of the cursor, while text to the right of the cursor is pushed forward as you type.

In the JOHNSON document, let's insert the word *us* in the first paragraph. This word is underlined in Figure 3.4 to help you locate it—the text on your screen should not be underlined. Follow these steps:

1. Place the cursor on the word *your,* type **us**, and press the spacebar.
2. Insert the other underlined words shown in Figure 3.4 and any other words or characters you omitted in the letter.
3. To insert an extra blank line after *Very Sincerely Yours,* place the cursor at the end of this line (or on one of the blank lines below it) and press Enter.

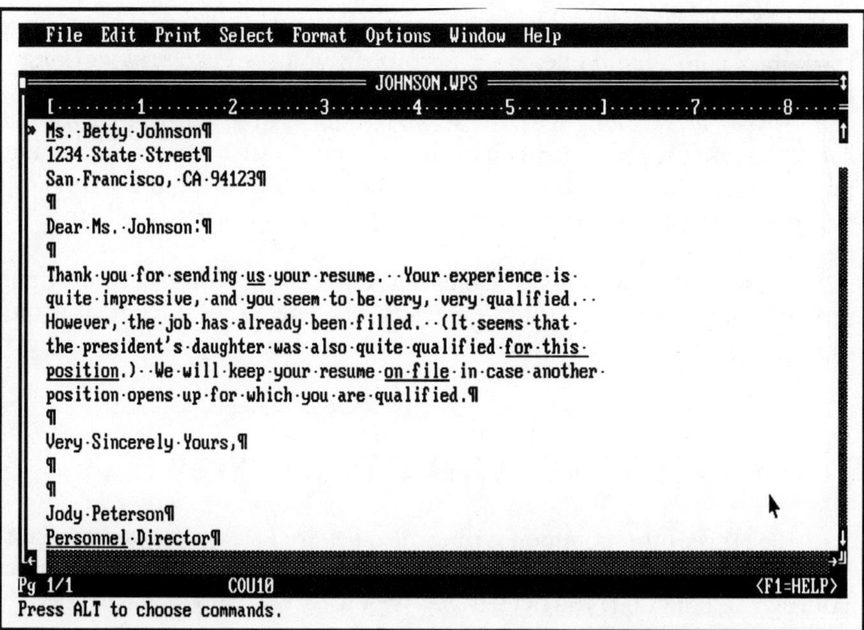

Figure 3.4: The document, with words to insert (underlined)

4. To divide a paragraph into two, you place the cursor on what you want to be the beginning of the second paragraph, and press Enter. Divide the paragraph in the JOHNSON document into two, as shown in Figure 3.5. To do this, place the cursor at the beginning of the sentence *We will keep...*, and press Enter twice.

Deleting Text

In general, to delete an incorrect or extra character, place the cursor directly on the character, and press the key marked Del (or Delete). The character is removed and characters to the right shift over to take its place. Take a look at Figure 3.6. Each of the words that are crossed out in the figure should be deleted. For example, delete the word *quite* by placing the cursor on the *q* and pressing Del six times. Make all the deletions indicated in Figure 3.6.

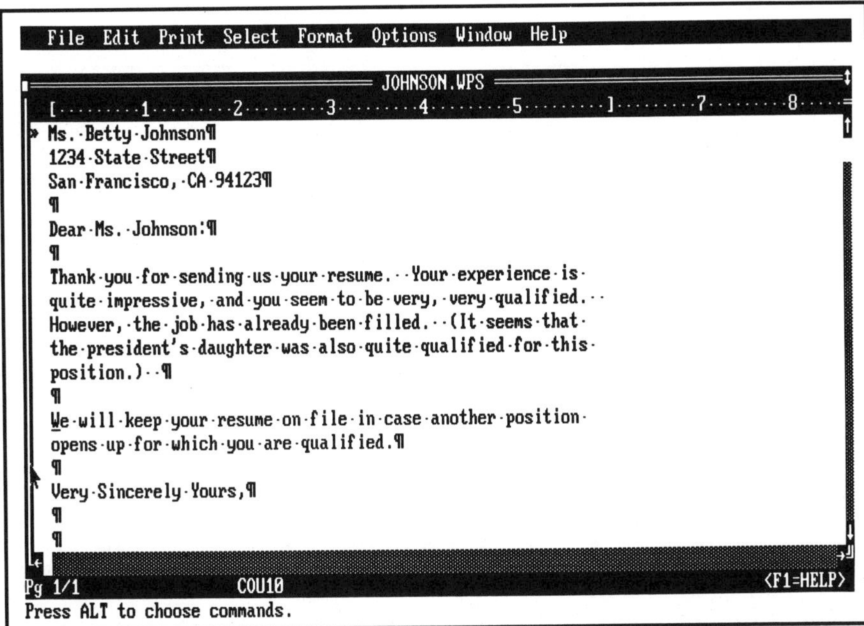

Figure 3.5: A single paragraph divided into two paragraphs

Backspace is another way to delete characters. While Del removes the character directly on the cursor, Backspace deletes the character to the *left* of the cursor. Thus, to delete characters with Backspace, make sure you place the cursor to the right of what you want to delete. For example, to delete the word *quite*, you would place the cursor in the space after the word and press Backspace six times.

The Del and Backspace keys, as you have been using them so far, only delete one character at a time. As you'll see in the upcoming section, Works offers shortcuts for deleting larger chunks of text.

SELECTING TEXT TO DELETE, MOVE, OR COPY

Works provides several commands for performing electronic cut-and-pastes. You can delete an entire page, move a paragraph from one location in

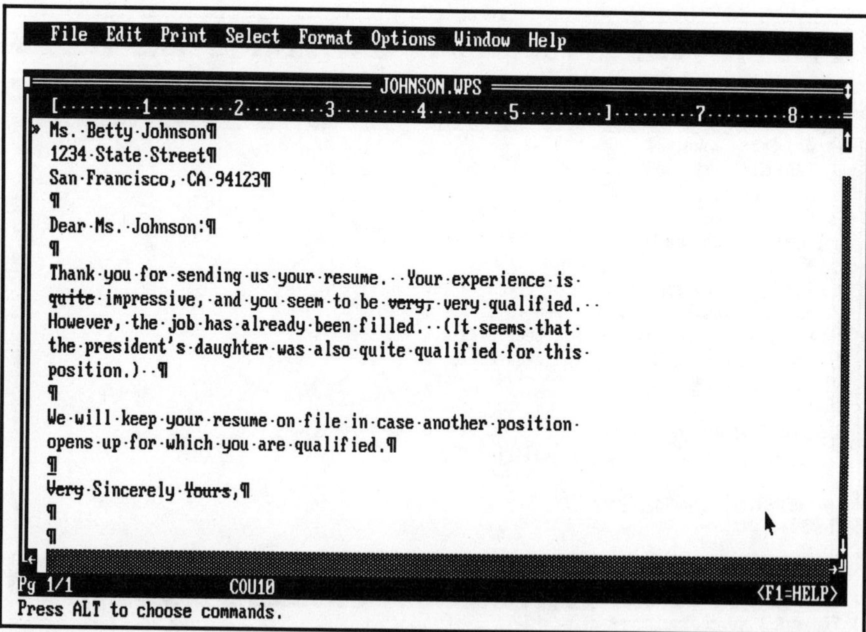

Figure 3.6: The document, with words to delete

a document to another, or make copies of similar text passages so that you don't have to retype anything. These actions require you to select the text before you issue the command to delete, move, or copy it. *Selecting* is the process of highlighting or shading text on the screen. Table 3.3 lists selection methods you can use with the keyboard. The cursor can be anywhere in the

Table 3.3: Selecting Text with the Keyboard

SELECTED TEXT	ACTION
Word	Press F8 twice
Sentence	Press F8 three times
Paragraph	Press F8 four times
Entire document	Press F8 five times, or choose All on the Select menu
Extend selection	Press F8 once, or choose Text on the Select menu, or hold Shift down with arrow key

word, sentence, or paragraph you want to select. For example, to select a paragraph, you can place the cursor at the paragraph's beginning, end, or anywhere in the middle.

If you need to select an "odd" amount of text, such as three words or two paragraphs, press the Extend Selection key, F8, just once (or choose Text on the Select menu). *EXT* appears at the bottom of the screen, indicating that you are in Extend mode. When you are in this mode, text is selected as you move the cursor with any of the usual cursor movement keys (such as →, ↓, Ctrl-→, End, PgDn, Ctrl-PgDn).

If you get into Extend mode accidentally, press the Esc key. Esc does not clear the highlighting; it cancels Extend mode. But as soon as you next move your cursor, the highlighting disappears. If you accidentally select too much text, you can use your cursor movement keys (such as ↑, ←, and PgUp) to unselect text. You can also press Esc to cancel the Extend mode and start over.

Another way to select text is to hold down the Shift key while you press the arrow keys. Be sure to keep the Shift key down the whole time, though, or you will lose the highlighting.

The F8 key has a few idiosyncrasies that you should watch out for. First, F8 includes the paragraph mark in the sentence selection when you select the last sentence of a paragraph. Most of the time, you will want to press ← to exclude the paragraph mark from the selection. Let's try this.

1. Place the cursor anywhere in the last sentence of the first paragraph (*It seems that the president's daughter...*).
2. Press F8 once. *EXT* appears in the bottom window border.
3. Press F8 a second time. The word is selected.
4. Press F8 a third time. The sentence *and* the paragraph mark are selected. (If you were selecting any other sentence in the paragraph, the mark would not be selected—this idiosyncrasy occurs only when you select the last sentence.)
5. Press ← to exclude the paragraph mark.
6. Cancel the selection by pressing Esc, followed by any arrow key.

Another idiosyncrasy is that sometimes the fourth press of the F8 key (instead of the fifth) selects the entire document. This happens if the cursor is on the paragraph mark when you start pressing F8 or if the paragraph is only one sentence long. If you aren't paying attention, you could accidentally select the entire document and then delete it when all you wanted to do was delete a paragraph! As you press F8, watch your screen to make sure you have selected what you intended to select. If you accidentally select too much text, press Esc and start over.

Table 3.4 lists ways to select text with the mouse. To choose an odd amount of text with the mouse, you have two methods available. The first is to use the *click and drag* method, as follows:

- Click the left mouse button on the first character you want to select.
- Hold the button down.
- Drag the cursor to the last character.
- Let go of the button.

Table 3.4: Selecting Text with the Mouse

SELECTED TEXT	ACTION
Word	Click right button on the word
Sentence	Click left and right buttons on the sentence
Line	Click left button in the left margin
Paragraph	Click right button in the left margin
Document	Click left and right buttons simultaneously in left margin
Extend selection	Click and drag, or shift and click

The second method requires you to use the keyboard and the mouse, as follows:

- Click on the first character.
- Move the mouse pointer after the last character.
- Hold down the Shift key while clicking the left mouse button.

Experiment with both methods to find your preference. Once you've selected the text, you can delete, move, or copy it.

Deleting Selected Text

To delete selected text, simply press the Del key (never Backspace), or choose Delete on the Edit menu. Let's use the selection techniques discussed above to delete the word *quite* in the first paragraph.

1. Place the cursor anywhere in the word (it doesn't have to be on the *q*), and give the word-selection command: Click the right mouse button or press F8 twice. Notice that the space after the word is automatically included.
2. Press Del to delete the word.

Try deleting an entire sentence—the last sentence in the first paragraph (see Figure 3.7).

1. Place the cursor anywhere in the sentence.
2. Give the sentence-selection command: Click the right and left mouse buttons or press F8 three times.

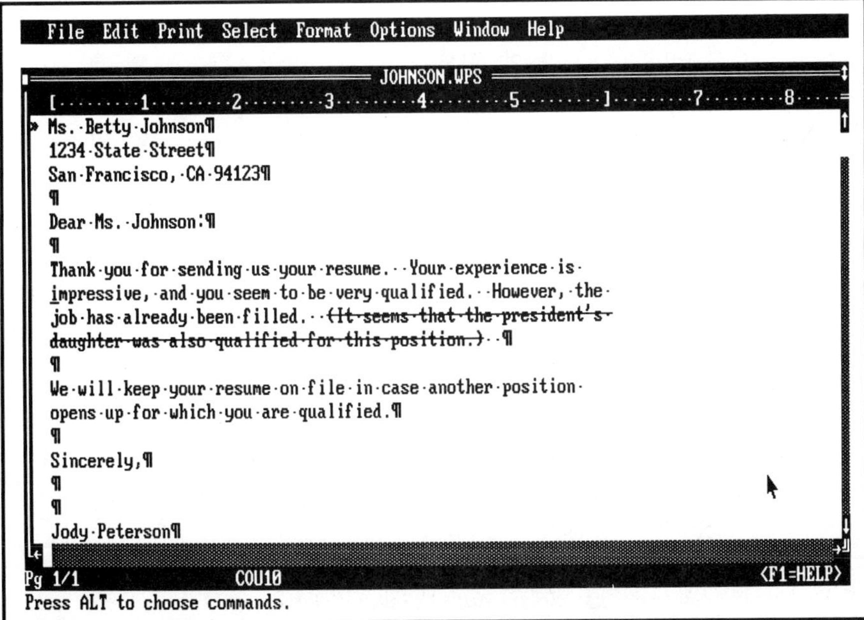

Figure 3.7: The document, with a sentence to delete

3. Because the sentence is at the end of the paragraph, the selection includes the paragraph mark. You do not want to delete this, so press ← once before you press Del to remove the sentence. If you selected the sentence with the mouse, you have to hold down the Shift key and click on the paragraph mark to remove the selection from the symbol.
4. Press Del to remove the selected sentence.

Moving Text

To move text from one location to another within a document, follow these general steps:

- Select the text to be moved, using any of the selection commands listed in Tables 3.3 and 3.4.
- Select Move on the Edit menu, or press F3. Works lets you know exactly what to do next:

  Select new location and press ENTER. Press ESC to Cancel.

  The bottom border of the window also displays *MOVE*, indicating the command you selected.
- Place the cursor at the point where you want to move the selection. You can use any of your cursor movement keys or mouse scrolling techniques to position the cursor. As soon as you start moving the cursor, the highlighting of your selection disappears. Don't worry, this is supposed to happen.
- Press Enter to complete the move.

Moving Tips

Here are a few tips for moving entire paragraphs:

- Make sure your selection includes the paragraph mark at the end of the paragraph. If it doesn't, the text will be joined with the next paragraph in the new location because it doesn't have its own paragraph mark.
- If you have double spacing between paragraphs, be sure to select the blank line after the paragraph. If you forget to include this line,

you will end up with an extra blank line in the original location and no blank line in the new location. The paragraph selection commands (pressing F8 four times or clicking the right mouse button in the left margin) do *not* include the blank line after the paragraph. To include the extra line, press ↓ once. (If you have a mouse, you must hold down Shift while clicking on the paragraph mark.)

- The new location for the paragraph is at the beginning of the paragraph that will immediately follow the moved paragraph.

If you select the paragraph incorrectly or specify the wrong new location, your paragraph spacing will be off. However, you can easily rectify these types of mistakes. To remove an extra blank line, press Del on the line's paragraph mark. To add a blank line, press Enter (lines are inserted *above* the cursor).

Moving Practice

Just for practice, move the first paragraph in the JOHNSON document after the second. If you don't have a mouse, or you prefer using the keyboard, follow these steps:

1. Place the cursor at the beginning of the first paragraph (*Thank you for sending...*).
2. Press F8 to turn on the extend-selection command.
3. Press ↓ until the entire paragraph and the blank line are selected.
4. Press F3 to move the paragraph. Notice the message at the bottom of the screen.
5. Place the cursor at the new location, on *Sincerely*, and press Enter. The paragraph moves, as shown in Figure 3.8.

Follow these steps if you have a mouse:

1. Click and drag from the beginning of the paragraph (*Thank you for sending...*) to the blank line after the paragraph.
2. Choose Move on the Edit menu. Notice the message at the bottom of the screen.
3. Place the mouse pointer cursor at the new location, on *Sincerely*, click the left button, and press Enter.

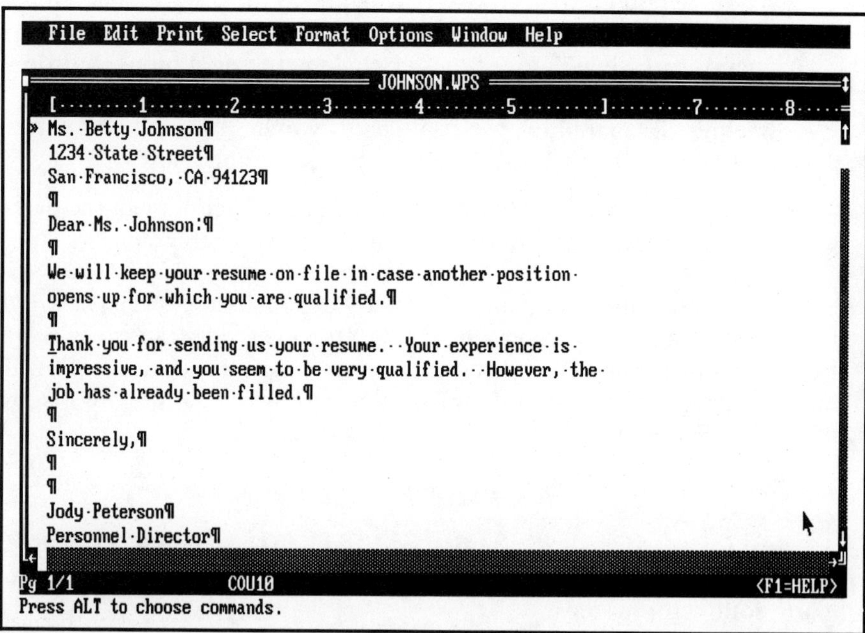
File Edit Print Select Format Options Window Help

JOHNSON.WPS

Ms. Betty Johnson¶
1234 State Street¶
San Francisco, CA 94123¶
¶
Dear Ms. Johnson:¶
¶
We will keep your resume on file in case another position opens up for which you are qualified.¶
¶
Thank you for sending us your resume. Your experience is impressive, and you seem to be very qualified. However, the job has already been filled.¶
¶
Sincerely,¶
¶
¶
Jody Peterson¶
Personnel Director¶

Pg 1/1 COU10 <F1=HELP>
Press ALT to choose commands.

Figure 3.8: A paragraph that has been moved

It doesn't really make sense to move the paragraph where you did, so now move the paragraph back to its original location, using the techniques you just learned.

If you forget to make a selection before choosing the Move command, Works displays the error message "Make selection first." Press Enter to OK the message and start over.

Copying Text

Copying is similar to moving, except it leaves the text in its original location and places a copy in the new location. Use the Copy command to copy sections of text that are similar or identical. For example, if you need to type a procedure that has steps similar to a section you have already typed, use the Copy command and then modify the copy as necessary.

To copy text from one location to another within a document, follow these general steps:

- Select the text to be copied, using any of the selection commands listed in Tables 3.3 and 3.4.
- Select Copy on the Edit menu, or press Shift-F3. Works lets you know exactly what to do next:

  Select new location and press ENTER. Press ESC to Cancel.

  The bottom border of the window displays *COPY,* indicating the command you selected.
- Place the cursor at the point where you want to copy the selection. You can use any of the cursor movement keys or mouse scrolling techniques to position the cursor. As soon as you start moving the cursor, the highlighting of your selection disappears.
- Press Enter to complete the copying.

To make multiple copies of the same section of text, follow the above steps to make the first copy. Then, place the cursor at each new location and press Shift-F7 for Repeat Copy. You can use other commands or do other operations (such as typing new text or deleting text) while you are in the process of repeating a copy. Works "remembers" the selected text you want to copy until you copy or move another selection.

Replacing Selected Text

Unlike some word processors, Works does not have a way to go into an "overtype mode" in which your typing replaces the existing text at the cursor position, character for character; Works is always in "insert mode." However, Works does offer an option similar to overtype mode—it's called *Typing Replaces Selection* and is on the Options menu. If you turn on this feature, you do not need to delete existing selected text before inserting something in its place. Just select the text you want replaced, and start typing. The selected text immediately disappears as soon as you begin typing.

Once you turn on the Typing Replaces Selection feature, a mark appears next to the option in the menu. The feature remains on even when you open another document or exit Works. The only way to cancel it is to choose Typing

Replaces Selection again to turn off the mark. This option is a *toggle*—the same command turns the feature on and off.

Follow these steps to try replacing selected text in the JOHNSON document:

1. Make sure your Typing Replaces Selection feature is on.
2. Place the cursor on the word *job* in the first paragraph.
3. Select *job* by pressing F8 twice or clicking the right mouse button. (The word should be selected as shown in Figure 3.9.)
4. Type **position**, and press the spacebar. (As soon as you start typing, the word *job* disappears.)

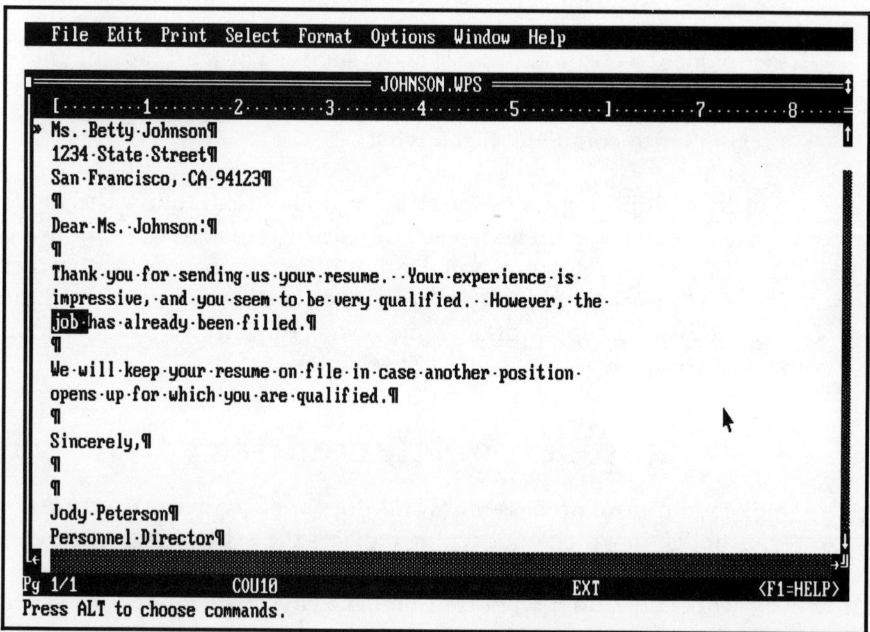

Figure 3.9: The selected word *job,* before being replaced with *position*

If you accidentally type something when text is selected and Typing Replaces Selection is on, you lose the selected text. Fortunately, Works offers a way to undo mistakes.

UNDOING MISTAKES

One of the biggest fears new computer users have is making mistakes. To a great extent, this fear can be alleviated in Works, thanks to its Undo feature. The Undo option on the Edit menu reverses the last command you issued or operation you performed. (You can also press Alt-Backspace to undo the last command you gave.) Undo is a lifesaver if you delete text accidentally. It is not limited to deleting, however. You can undo the following:

- Commands on the Edit menu.
- Commands on the Format menu.
- Text you have typed or deleted since the cursor was last moved.
- Text you have replaced with the Typing Replaces Selection feature. (Undo undeletes the selected text and deletes the text you inserted.)
- Spelling-checker changes (see next section).

You can only undo the *most recent* change to your document. You can't, for example, undo the deletion you made before you moved something. Nor can you undo an undo.

To see how the Undo feature works, follow these steps:

1. Press F8 twice to select the word *very* in the first paragraph.
2. Press Del. The word is deleted.
3. Choose Undo on the Edit menu or press Alt-Backspace. The word "magically" reappears.

CHECKING YOUR SPELLING

Another way to edit your document is to let Works do it for you. The spelling checker scans your document and stops at words that are potentially misspelled, allowing you to correct them. Even if you won all your school spelling bees, you still may want to use the spelling checker because it locates typing mistakes (unless you were also the school typing champ).

Options for Correcting Misspelled Words

When Works spell-checks, it checks the spelling of each word in your document against its 100,000-word dictionary. If a word is not in the dictionary, it stops at the word and presents a dialog box to let you correct it. Figure 3.10 displays the spelling-checker dialog box with all its options at the bottom. The options are described in Table 3.5.

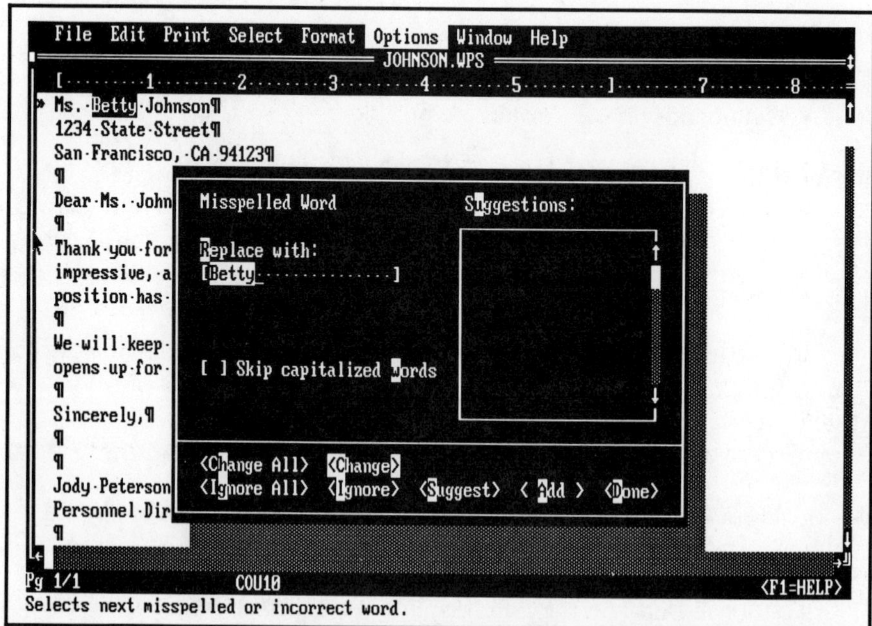

Figure 3.10: The spelling-checker dialog box

The spelling checker sometimes stops at words that are correctly spelled. Proper names, abbreviations, acronyms, and technical terms may not be in the dictionary. Thus, the spelling checker would think the following words are misspelled: *Ferdinand, DMV, Microsoft,* and *sulfathiazole.* The spelling checker would stop at these words even though they are not misspelled.

The options you can use to deal with these types of words are Ignore, Ignore All, and Add. If you are not likely to use a particular word in other documents, choose Ignore or Ignore All. For a word you will use frequently,

Table 3.5: Spelling-Checker Options

OPTION	KEYBOARD SHORTCUT	FUNCTION
Change	Alt-C	Replaces the word with the corrected spelling
Change All	Alt-H	Replaces the word, and all other words misspelled the same way, with the corrected spelling
Ignore	Alt-I	Leaves the word as it is
Ignore All	Alt-G	Bypasses all occurrences of the word throughout the document
Suggest	Alt-S	Gives a list of possible correct spellings
Add	Alt-A	Inserts the word in your personal dictionary so that Works will recognize it as correctly spelled the next time you use the spelling checker
Done	Alt-D	Exits the spelling checker

add it to your personal dictionary by choosing Add. By customizing your dictionary, you streamline the spell-checking process.

If the word is not spelled correctly, follow these basic steps to correct its spelling:

- The misspelled word is displayed after *Replace with* so that you can edit it as needed; use → and ↓ (or click with the mouse) to position the cursor.
- Delete and insert characters to correct the word.
- Press Enter to choose the Change option. If you consistently misspelled the word throughout the document, choose Change All instead, so the spelling checker won't stop at each occurrence.

If you are not sure how the word is spelled, follow these steps to have the spelling checker list possible correct spellings:

- Choose the Suggest option. The list of words appears in the Suggestion box.
- Use the arrow keys to select the correct word. If you are using the mouse, click on the correct spelling.
- Press Enter, and the word is corrected in the document.

Spell-Checking Your Document

The JOHNSON document you have been working with in this chapter probably doesn't have any spelling or typing mistakes because you corrected them already. So that you can have some typos to correct with the spelling checker, insert the following mistakes:

- Delete the *i* from *experience.*
- Insert an extra *s* in *impressive.*
- Delete the second *e* from *Sincerely.*

The spelling checker starts correcting at the cursor location and checks all words after that point in the document. If your cursor is not at the beginning of the document when you start the spelling checker, Works checks the words from the cursor to the end of the document and then asks if you want to spell-check the beginning of the document.

If you want to check text in the middle of the document or check the spelling of a single word, select the text before spell-checking. Works then checks only the selected text.

For practice, try the following exercise:

1. Press Ctrl-Home to move to the beginning of the document.
2. Choose Check Spelling from the Options menu. The first word highlighted is *Betty* because it is a proper name and is not in the dictionary. It is spelled correctly, so you can either add it to your personal dictionary or ignore it.
3. Since Betty is not a word you use frequently, choose Ignore.

4. The next highlighted word is *Johnson*. Because Johnson appears twice in the document, choose Ignore All so that the spelling checker won't stop at other occurrences. Ignore *Francisco* as well.
5. When the spelling checker stops at the first actual mistake, *experence,* choose Suggest. The Suggestion box shown in Figure 3.11 displays a list of possible correct spellings. The correct spelling is the first one.
6. Press Enter (or double-click) to select the correct spelling. The word is corrected in the document, and the next misspelled word that Works finds is *impresssive.*
7. Use the arrow keys to position the cursor on the extra *s* and press Del.
8. Press Enter to select the Change command.
9. Finish correcting the document using the skills you've just learned.

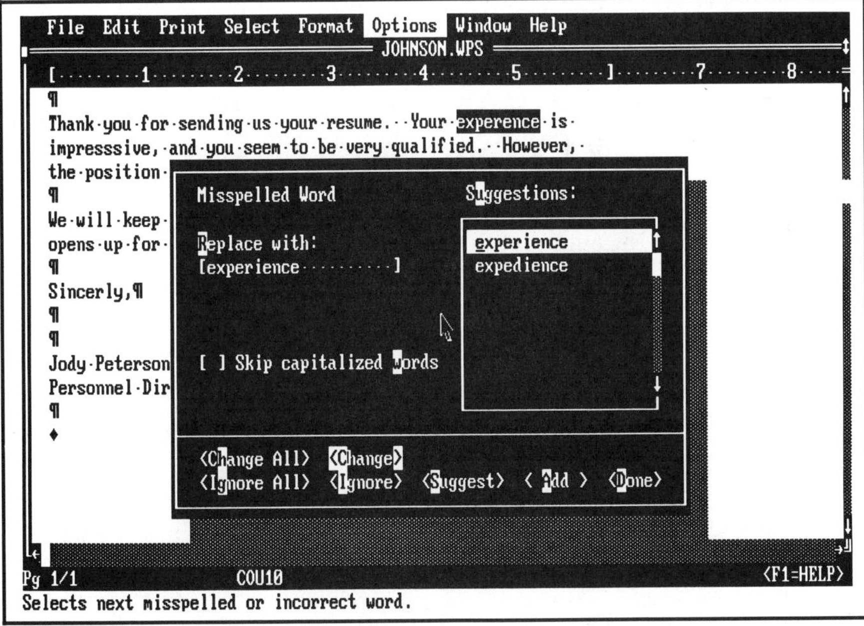

Figure 3.11: A list of suggested correct spellings

Other Spell-Check Features

The spelling checker does more than just check for misspelled words; it also checks for double words, for example, "He went across *the the* street." When the spelling checker encounters this type of mistake, the message "Repeated word" appears in the upper-left corner of the spelling-checker dialog box. (Normally, the message "Misspelled word" appears here.) A single word already appears in the *Replace with* line. Since Change is the default response, press Enter to correct this mistake.

To speed up spell-checking of a document containing many acronyms, you can turn on the *Skip capitalized words* option on the spell-check screen. With this option turned on, the spelling checker does not stop at words in which all letters are capitalized. However, since it won't stop at these words, you cannot add them to your personal dictionary, so think twice about whether you want to activate this option.

Though the spelling checker is great for finding your typing and spelling mistakes, it does not replace your own proofreading. It only checks words, not context. So if you type *I red the book,* the spelling checker will not find anything wrong because *red* is a word.

SETTING MARGINS

Margins are the amount of white space, in inches, between the printed text and the edge of the paper. By default, Works assigns the following margins to your document:

Top:	1″
Bottom:	1″
Left:	1.3″
Right:	1.2″

To change the margins in your JOHNSON document, follow these steps:

1. Choose Page Setup & Margins on the Print menu. A dialog box displays the current margins and page dimensions.

2. Use the mouse, the Tab key, or the arrow keys to move the cursor next to *Left margin.*
3. Type **1**.
4. Move the cursor next to ***Right margin.***
5. Type **1**.
6. Choose OK. (When entering margins, you must convert fractions to decimals; for example, 1½ must be entered as *1.5.*)

The ruler line displays the length of each typed line, according to the margins and page dimensions you indicate on the Page Setup & Margins screen. Thus, with standard page size (8.5″ × 11″) and left and right margins reset to 1 inch, the left bracket in the ruler line is at 0 and the right bracket is at 6.5. This 6.5-inch line-length is calculated by subtracting the left and right margins (2 inches total) from the page width (8.5 inches). Fortunately, Works calculates the line length for you—all you have to do is enter the page size and margins.

PRINTING

Before you print for the first time, follow the steps below to make sure Works is set up for your printer:

1. Choose Printer Setup on the Print menu.
2. Look at the printer name highlighted in the Printers list. If this name is not correct, and you see your printer listed, highlight it.
3. If your printer name is not listed, run the Setup program (see Appendix A). You can choose TTY, a generic printer name, but you may not be able to print out special text effects, such as boldface, certain fonts, and underlining.
4. Look at the printer model highlighted in the Model list. If this is not correct, press Alt-D to move to the list, and highlight (or click on) the correct model.
5. Press Enter or click on OK when you are done.

PRINTING A DOCUMENT

As long as Works is installed for the right printer, printing is a breeze. Follow these general steps:

- Make sure your printer is turned on and has paper.
- Open the file that you want to print.
- Choose the Print command on the Print menu. The Print dialog box is displayed.
- Click on Print or press Enter. The document soon begins printing. The message "Press ESC to cancel printing" is displayed at the bottom of the screen. You cannot work on this document, or any other document, until this message disappears. As soon as it does—even though your printer may still be printing—you can work on any document.

STOP THE PRESSES!

If you need to stop printing for one reason or another (for example, you put the wrong paper in the printer, or you discover a mistake in the printout), press Esc. The printing may not stop immediately, however, if your printer has a large *buffer.* A buffer is an area of memory storage inside the printer where the document is placed temporarily until the printer is ready to print it out. A buffer is necessary because the computer can send information to the printer much faster than the printer can print it. If your printer has a one-line buffer, printing stops almost immediately when you press Esc. But if your printer has a four-page buffer, four pages print after you cancel printing.

PREVIEWING ON THE SCREEN

To get an idea of what your printed page will look like without having to waste a piece of paper, use the Preview command on the Print menu. Though you cannot see the text in detail when you are previewing, you can see what the whole page looks like with the current margins. For example, the preview lets you see if you need to specify different margins to center the text on the page. Follow these steps to try it:

1. Select Preview on the Print menu.
2. Press Enter or click on Preview. Your previewed page should look similar to Figure 3.12.

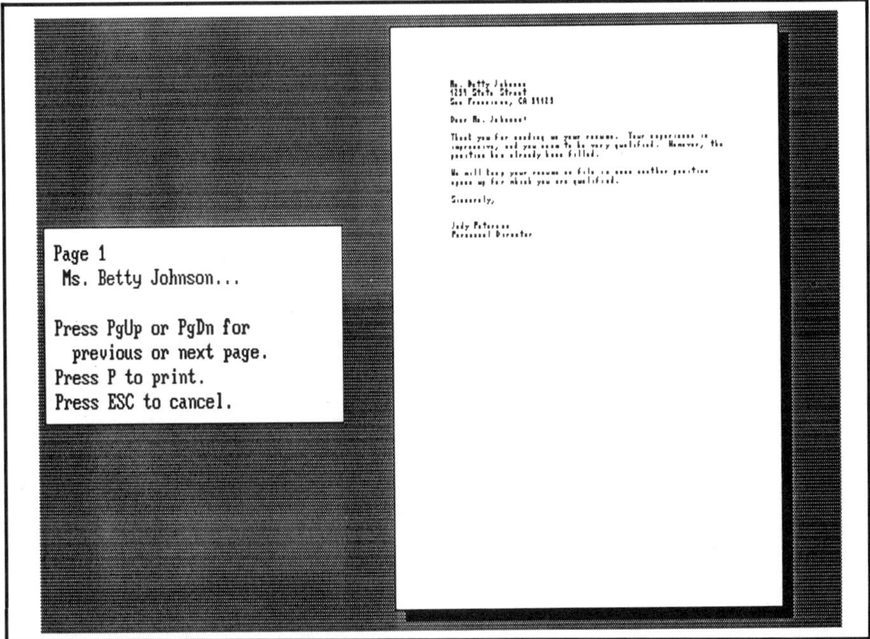

Figure 3.12: A preview of the printed page

Notice that the letter is top-heavy. You have two alternatives for pushing it down the page. You could press Enter a number of times at the top of the document. Use this technique if the letter is more than one page long. Or you could set a larger top margin using the Page Setup & Margins command. Let's try the second technique; follow these steps:

1. Press Esc to cancel Preview.
2. Choose Page Setup & Margins on the Print menu.
3. Type **3.5** (inches) for Top Margin and press Enter.
4. Select Preview on the Print menu.

5. Press Enter or click on Preview. The letter is now centered on the page. If it wasn't quite centered yet, you could repeat the above steps with a different top margin.
6. When you are pleased with what you see in the preview, press P for Print, as instructed on the Preview screen.

You are now finished editing the JOHNSON document. Follow these steps to save and close the document:

1. Choose Save on the File menu.
2. Choose Close on the File menu.

SUMMARY

This chapter showed you how to create, edit, and print a document in the word processor tool. You learned how to correct mistakes by inserting, deleting, and moving text. You also learned how to use Works's built-in spelling checker to let Works do some of the editing for you.

In the next chapter you will learn how to improve the layout and appearance of your documents. This process is called *formatting*.

EXERCISES

```
Mr. Peter Anderson
P.O. Box 987
Palo Alto, CA  94302

Dear Mr. Anderson:

As a member of the Board of Directors of the Palo Alto
Chamber of Commerce, I want to congratulate you on your
decision to become a member of our organization.  It goes
without saying that all of us associated with the Chamber
are dedicated to promoting the interest of business.

Once again, congratulations on making what I feel will be a
wise investment decision.  I look forward to seeing you at
future Chamber functions.

The key to success for any organization is a vibrant and
involved membership, and I hope that you will take an active
role. If you would like to participate, please let us know.

Sincerely,


Hamilton Burger
```

Figure 3.13: A practice document

In the following exercises you get to practice creating and editing a word processor document. You will create a word processor file, type and revise the document shown in Figure 3.13, run the spelling checker, set the margins, and print the document. As you edit the document, refer to Figure 3.14, the final printed letter. If you get stuck, refer to the sections indicated inside parentheses.

1. Create a word processor file (see "Creating a Word Processor File," page 34).
2. Type the document shown in Figure 3.13 (see "Typing a Document," page 37).
3. In the first paragraph, delete the following phrases (see "Deleting Text," page 44):
   - *It goes without saying that* (capitalize the *A* in *all*)
   - *the interest of*

4. At the end of the first paragraph, insert *in our community* (see "Inserting Text," page 43).
5. Move the second paragraph after the third paragraph (see "Moving Text," page 50).
6. Insert the following sentence between the two sentences in the second paragraph: *Volunteers are always needed to assist on our committees.*
7. Spell-check the document to correct any typing mistakes (see "Checking Your Spelling," page 55).
8. Change the top margin to 3 inches and the left and right margins to 1 inch each (see "Setting Margins," page 60).
9. Save the document under the name ANDERSON (see "Saving Your Work," page 38).
10. Print the document (see "Printing a Document," page 62).
11. Close the file (see "Closing a File," page 39).

```
Mr. Peter Anderson
P.O. Box 987
Palo Alto, CA  94302

Dear Mr. Anderson:

As a member of the Board of Directors of the Palo Alto Chamber of
Commerce, I want to congratulate you on your decision to become a
member of our organization.  All of us associated with the
Chamber are dedicated to promoting business in our community.

The key to success for any organization is a vibrant and involved
membership, and I hope that you will take an active role.
Volunteers are always needed to assist on our committees.  If you
would like to participate, please let us know.

Once again, congratulations on making what I feel will be a wise
investment decision.  I look forward to seeing you at future
Chamber functions.

Sincerely,


Hamilton Burger
```

Figure 3.14: The final document

FORMATTING YOUR DOCUMENTS

4

The Format menu in the word processor tool offers an abundance of ways to improve the appearance of your documents. First, you can add style to your text: Words can be boldfaced, underlined, and italicized. Second, you can change the alignment, line spacing, tab stops, and indents of certain paragraphs or the entire document. You can also create lines and boxes around sections of your document.

FORMATTING YOUR TEXT

Works offers many ways to make words stand out in your document. By boldfacing, underlining, italicizing, or changing the font of words, you can emphasize important text.

You can format documents using the Format menu or with commands that you invoke directly from the keyboard. You will probably find the keyboard shortcuts faster (see Table 4.1).

Table 4.1: Keyboard Shortcuts for Character Styles

STYLE	KEYSTROKE
Bold	Ctrl-B
Underline	Ctrl-U
Italic	Ctrl-I
Strikethrough	Ctrl-S
Subscript	Ctrl- =
Superscript	Ctrl- +
Plain Text	Ctrl-spacebar

ADDING STYLE TO YOUR CHARACTERS

Bold, underline, and italic are called *character styles.* The process of assigning each of the character styles to text is similar.

Changing the Style of Existing Text

To change the style of text you have already typed, follow these general steps:

- Select the text to be changed.
- Choose the appropriate style on the Format menu (Bold, Underline, or Italic), or use the keyboard shortcut (Ctrl-B for Bold, Ctrl-U for Underline, Ctrl-I for Italic).

Let's add some character styles to the JOHNSON document that you created in Chapter 3. First, open the document.

1. Choose Open Existing File on the File menu.
2. Highlight JOHNSON.WPS in the Files list and press Enter. The document is displayed on your screen.

Refer to Figure 4.1 to add the following styles:

1. Select the words *very qualified* and underline them by pressing Ctrl-U.
2. Select the name *Jody Peterson* and make it bold with Ctrl-B.
3. Select *Personnel Director* and italicize it with Ctrl-I.

You are done with the JOHNSON document for now, so save it and close the file.

1. Choose Save on the File menu.
2. Choose Close on the File menu.

Changing the Style as You Type

To assign a style to text as you type, turn on the style before you start typing and then return to plain text afterward. Follow these general steps:

- Turn on the style using the appropriate option on the Format menu (Bold, Underline, or Italic), or use the keyboard shortcut (Ctrl-B, Ctrl-U, or Ctrl-I). You may turn on more than one style.

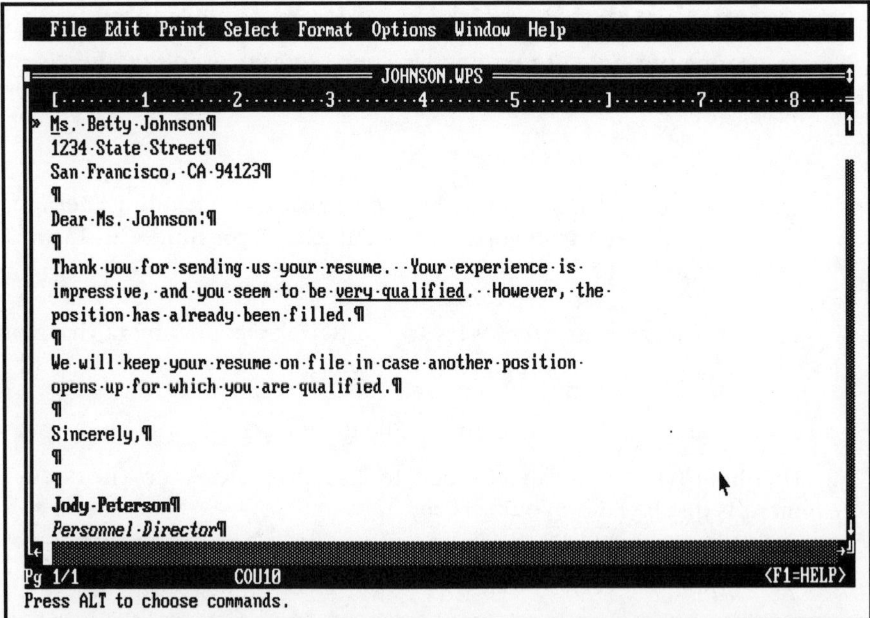

Figure 4.1: Character styles (bold, underline, italic) shown on-screen

- Type the text. It should appear on the screen in the appropriate style and a letter (*B, U,* or *I*) should appear in the bottom window border. (If you don't see the style on your screen, read the section "Viewing Text Styles.")
- Turn off the style by choosing Plain Text on the Format menu or by pressing Ctrl-spacebar. Check the bottom window border to make sure that the letter disappeared. If you chose multiple styles (for example, bold and underline), they are all cleared when you choose the Plain Text command.

Let's practice some of these formatting commands in a new document. Choose Create New File on the File menu and choose New Word Processor. Type the text shown in Figure 4.2, specifying the styles as you type.

1. Boldface *JOB OPENINGS.*
2. Underline *Project Manager* and *Networking Engineers.*
3. Italicize the last sentence in each paragraph.

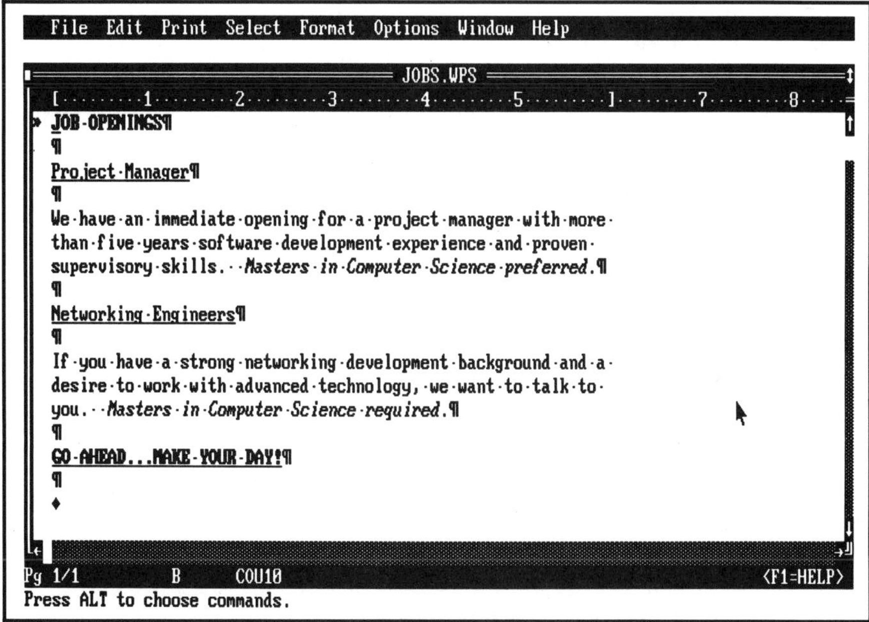

Figure 4.2: A document with different character styles

4. Boldface and underline *GO AHEAD...MAKE YOUR DAY!*
5. Save the file with the name JOBS.

Removing Text Styles

To remove styles you have already assigned, select the text and choose the Plain Text command on the Format menu or press Ctrl-spacebar.

Viewing Text Styles

Works offers two screen modes for viewing your formatting styles. *Text mode* shows styles in different colors on a color monitor, but does not indicate styles on a monochrome display. To see what style is being used on a monochrome display in Text mode, you must look in the bottom window border. Whenever the cursor is on stylized text, you see a letter (*B* for Bold, *U* for Underline, or *I* for Italic) in the bottom window border. *Graphics mode* displays styles exactly how they will print. If the text does not appear different from plain text, you are probably in Text mode rather than Graphics mode, or your monitor does not have graphics capabilities.

To change the screen mode, use the Works Settings command on the Options menu. The dialog box displays two options for Screen Mode: Text and Graphics. The mode with the mark next to it is the current mode. Try choosing a different mode to see which you prefer.

CHANGING FONTS

A *font* is the set of all characters in a given typeface (for example, Courier, Helvetica, or Times Roman) and size (for example, 10- or 14-point). The *point* is a measure of type size used in the publishing world that refers to the character's height and width. The larger the point size, the larger the character. To give you an idea of how large a point is, there are 72 points to an inch. You will probably use 10- or 12-point for most of your text. Ten-point type is roughly the size of elite type on your typewriter, and 12-point is the equivalent of pica type.

The fonts you can use are a function of your printer's capabilities. If you have a simple dot-matrix printer (such as the Epson) or a letter-quality printer (such as the Diablo), your font selections are limited to pica and elite. If you have a laser printer (such as the Hewlett-Packard LaserJet), you can use its built-in fonts, Courier 12-point and Line Printer 8-point. If you have purchased any font cartridges, you can use the fonts they contain as well. For example, if you have Hewlett-Packard's B cartridge, you can use Helvetica 14-point and Times Roman 8- or 10-point.

Selecting a Typeface

Let's change the title *JOB OPENINGS* to a different font.

1. Select the title and then choose Font & Style on the Format menu. A dialog box similar to Figure 4.3 appears. (Your Fonts list will probably be different.)
2. If you have a mouse, click on the font name (your choice), or if you don't see the name, use the Font box's scroll bar to display additional fonts.

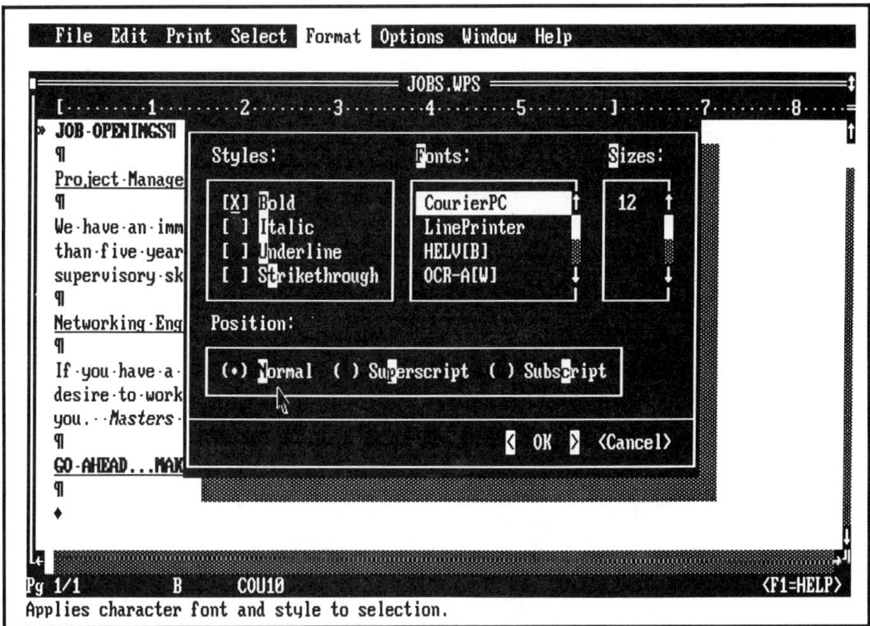

Figure 4.3: The Font & Style dialog box for a Hewlett-Packard LaserJet printer

3. If you want to use the keyboard, press Alt-F to go to the Fonts list, and then use ↓ or PgDn to scroll the list. (You can also press the first letter of the typeface name to move to the first font beginning with this letter.)

Before you press Enter to select a typeface, you need to consider the font size.

Choosing a Font Size

As you highlight different typefaces, different sizes appear on the Sizes list. The sizes displayed are the only point sizes you can choose for that typeface. Even though you may want a larger or smaller size, you cannot choose it unless it is displayed on the list. Click on the size you want with your mouse, or if you are using the keyboard, press Alt-S to go to the Sizes list and then use ↓ to highlight the size. Before you press Enter, look at the Styles list in the dialog box.

Adding Style to a Font

You can select character styles using the methods described in the section "Adding Style to Your Characters," or you can assign them when you are changing a font. The styles are included in the Font & Style dialog box for your convenience so that you don't have to assign fonts and styles in separate steps.

An additional style available to you in the Font & Style dialog box is *Strikethrough*. This style is most frequently used in legal documents where text to be deleted is indicated by striking through each letter with a dash or slash. This style was chosen in Figure 3.6 to show you what text to delete.

You can select any combination of styles in the Styles box. Click inside the square brackets to select (or unselect) a style. A mark appears inside the brackets when the style is chosen. If you're using the keyboard, you should press Alt in tandem with the shaded letter of the style (for example, Alt-B to choose Bold). To unselect a style using the keyboard, press Alt with the shaded letter again; the mark disappears.

Once you have selected the font, size, and style, you can press Enter or click on OK to complete the command. You do not actually see the font or size on the screen, though you do see the style if you are in Graphics mode. The bottom window border displays an abbreviation of the font and size (for example, COU12 for Courier 12-point and TMS10 for Times 10-point).

Follow these steps to choose another font for the subtitle *Project Manager:*

1. Select *Project Manager.*
2. Choose Font & Style on the Format menu.
3. Highlight one of the fonts in the Fonts box (your choice).
4. Highlight a point size in the Sizes box.
5. Choose OK.

Repeat the above steps to change the font of *Networking Engineer.*

Assigning Fonts as You Type

In the above examples, you changed the font of text that had already been typed in. Follow these general steps to change the font of text before typing it:

- Select the Font & Style command on the Format menu.
- Choose the font, size, and style.
- Press Enter or click on OK. Check the bottom window border to make sure you selected the font correctly.
- Type in the text.
- Repeat the first three steps to return to the original font.

Fitting Text on the Screen

By default, Works shows the exact amount of text that can fit on a line, given the margins and fonts you have set. However, if you have chosen a small font size, so many characters can fit on a line that you cannot see the end of a line without scrolling the screen or moving the cursor there.

You may want to change the default setting so that you can see all the text on the screen while you are typing and editing. Choose the Wrap For Screen command on the Options menu. This command only changes text-wrap on the screen, not on the printed document.

Like other options you have seen, the Wrap For Screen command is a toggle. You can turn it on and off by choosing the same command. To check your current setting, look to the left of the option. If a mark is there, the option is turned on.

FORMATTING PARAGRAPHS

In the previous section, you learned different ways to format characters. In this section, you learn how to format entire paragraphs. You'll see how to center lines of text, justify a document, set line spacing, and indent paragraphs.

The following general rules apply to paragraph formatting commands—keep these in mind as you read through this section:

- To format a single paragraph, just place the cursor anywhere in that paragraph and give the command; you don't need to select the paragraph first.
- To format several consecutive paragraphs, select them first.
- To change the paragraph format of the entire document, select the entire document first.
- If you set a paragraph format while you are typing new text, the format automatically carries forward to the next paragraph when you press Enter.
- Paragraph formatting instructions are actually stored in the paragraph mark. If you delete the paragraph mark, you delete the formatting. Use the Undo command if you delete the mark accidentally.

CHANGING PARAGRAPH ALIGNMENT

Four types of paragraph alignment are available: Left, Center, Right, and Justified. You can assign paragraph alignment in three different ways:

- Use the appropriate command listed on the Format menu.
- Use keyboard shortcuts (see Table 4.2 for a list of all the paragraph-formatting keyboard shortcuts).
- Use the Indents & Spacing command on the Format menu. This command allows you to enter any combination of paragraph formats (alignment, spacing, and indents) using a single command.

The default paragraph alignment is Left—that is, text is lined up at the left margin. An alternative to left alignment is Justified. In justified text, spaces are inserted between words so that you have smooth left and right margins.

The other types of paragraph alignment, Center and Right, are usually applied to single-line paragraphs, rather than word-wrapped paragraphs. Use center alignment to center a title, or right alignment to line up a date with the right margin.

Table 4.2: Keyboard Shortcuts for Paragraph Formats

FORMAT	KEYSTROKE
Centered	Ctrl-C
Left-aligned	Ctrl-L
Justified	Ctrl-J
Right-aligned	Ctrl-R
Left Indent	Ctrl-N
Undo Left Indent	Ctrl-M
Hanging Indent	Ctrl-H
Undo Hanging Indent	Ctrl-G
Single Spacing	Ctrl-1
Double Spacing	Ctrl-2
1½ Spacing	Ctrl-5
Normal Paragraph	Ctrl-X

Centering a Line

Automatic centering is one of the most convenient features of a word processor. When you have it, you no longer need to go to the center of the page and back up one space for every two characters, as you did with your typewriter. You simply type the line at the left margin and give the Center command.

To center a single-line paragraph in your JOBS document, follow these simple steps:

1. Place the cursor on the *JOB OPENINGS* line. It doesn't matter whether the cursor is at the beginning, end, or anywhere in the middle of the line.
2. Choose Center on the Format menu, or press Ctrl-C.
3. Repeat the above steps to center the line *GO AHEAD...MAKE YOUR DAY!*

If there are several consecutive lines you want to center, select them before choosing the Center command. If you only need one line centered, you do not need to select it.

When you go back to center a line that you already typed, that's all there is to it. However, if you centered the line while you were typing, you need to cancel the centering on the next line. To bring the cursor back to the left margin, choose Left on the Format menu, or press Ctrl-L.

Justifying Text

You will probably not want to justify letters or memos, because you want these types of documents to look personalized, not computerized. With other types of documents, such as reports and proposals, you may find justification looks more professional.

Normally, when you use justification, you want it for the entire document. If you are thinking about using it before you start typing, choose Justified on the Format menu (or press Ctrl-J). Then all your text is justified as you type. You can see the difference on the screen between spaces you type in and justification spaces inserted by the word processor if you have the Show All Characters option turned on. Spaces you insert with the spacebar appear as dots, whereas justification spaces show as blank space.

If you forget to turn on justification before you start typing, you can change it later by selecting the text and issuing the Justified command. As you have already learned (see tables 3.4 and 3.5), the following techniques are available for selecting the entire document:

- Choose All on the Select menu.
- Press F8 five times.
- Click the right and left mouse buttons at the same time in the left margin.

If you center lines of text before you justify the entire document, you lose all centering. This is because a paragraph can have only one alignment associated with it.

Justify the two long paragraphs in your JOBS document by following these steps:

1. Place the cursor in the first paragraph.
2. Choose Justified on the Format menu (or press Ctrl-J).

3. Repeat the procedure for the second paragraph. (You could have selected the entire document and pressed Ctrl-J but you would have uncentered the two lines.)

Your document should look similar to Figure 4.4.

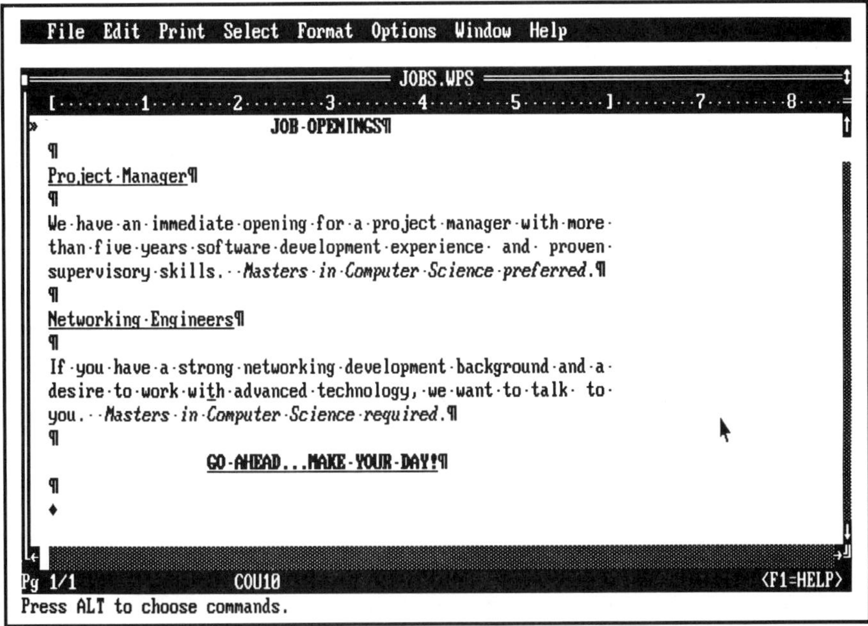

Figure 4.4: A document with centered lines and justified paragraphs

CHANGING LINE SPACING

Line spacing can be changed for the entire document or for any paragraph or section. When you want to switch to different line spacing in the middle of your typing, use one of the following methods:

- Choose Double Space or Single Space on the Format menu.
- Press Ctrl-2 (you have to use the numbers on the top row of the keyboard) to double-space, Ctrl-1 to single-space, or Ctrl-5 to 1½-space the text.

- Choose Indents & Spacing on the Format menu, and enter the desired number next to *Line spacing.* Spacing must be entered using decimals (for example, 2.5 for 2½ spacing).

Text you have already typed must be selected before you indicate the spacing change, unless you are formatting a single paragraph. For example, to double-space an entire document, choose All on the Select menu and then press Ctrl-2. However, because double spacing shows half as many lines on the screen as single spacing, you might want to type the document single-spaced so you can see more lines, and then format it for double spacing before you print it.

Let's try different line spacings for the first paragraph in the JOBS document.

1. Place the cursor in the first paragraph and press Ctrl-2. The paragraph is displayed as double-spaced on your screen.
2. Press Ctrl-1 to go back to single spacing.
3. Press Ctrl-5 to choose 1½ spacing. The document looks double-spaced, but it will print 1½ spaced.
4. Since 1½ and double spacing look the same on the screen, double-check the setting by choosing Indents & Spacing on the Format menu. The line spacing for the current paragraph is displayed next to *Line spacing.*
5. Return the paragraph to single spacing by pressing Ctrl-S to move the cursor next to *Line spacing* (or by clicking next to it with the mouse) and typing **1**. Press Enter.

INDENTING PARAGRAPHS

As you saw in Chapter 3, the Page Setup & Margins command changes the margins for the entire page. But what if you want to change the margins for part of the page—for example, for a single paragraph. The Indent command lets you move text in from the margins.

For practice, indent the paragraph as shown in Figure 4.5. The paragraph is indented 1 inch from the left margin and 1 inch from the right.

1. Put the cursor anywhere in the paragraph.
2. Choose Indents & Spacing on the Format menu.

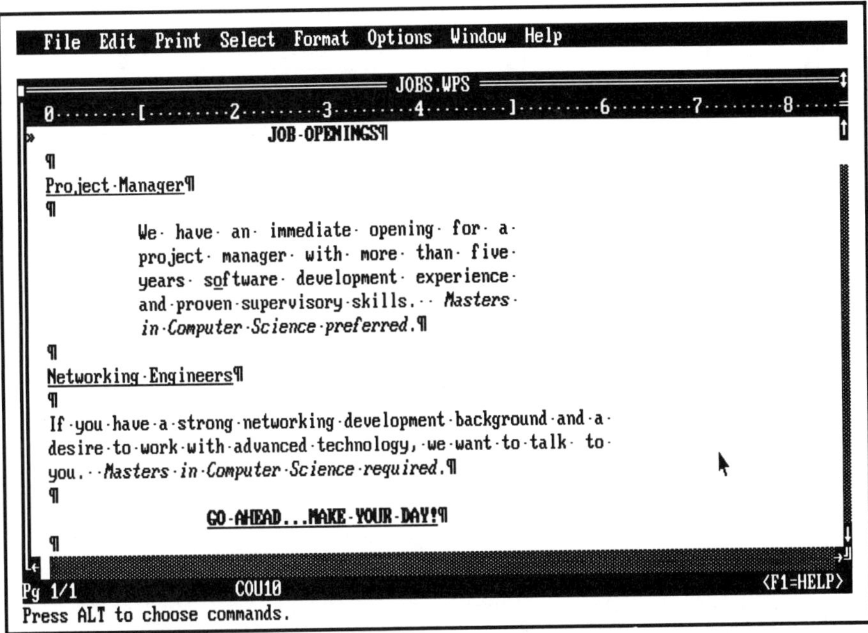

Figure 4.5: A paragraph indented from the left and right margins

3. Next to Left Indent, type **1**.
4. Move the cursor next to Right Indent and type **1**.
5. Press Enter.

Repeating the Last Formatting Command

The other paragraph should be indented the same way. Rather than going back to the Indents & Spacing command, you can instruct Works to repeat the last formatting command you gave. The Repeat Format command is actually the same key combination as the Repeat Copy command, Shift-F7.

1. Place the cursor in the second paragraph.
2. Press Shift-F7.

If you have several consecutive paragraphs you want to indent, select them all before you use the Indents & Spacing command.

You are now finished with your JOBS document. Save and close the file.

1. Choose Save on the File menu.
2. Choose Close on the File menu.

Indenting as You Type

If you specify the indent as you are typing, paragraphs continue to be indented until you cancel the indent. Follow these general steps to indent as you type:

- Choose Indents & Spacing from the Format menu.
- Enter the desired left and right indents.
- Type the text to be indented.
- For the first paragraph that you do not want indented, choose Indents & Spacing on the Format menu, and enter **0** for the left and right indents.

Works offers a keyboard shortcut for indenting on the left: Ctrl-N. This command indents a half-inch every time you press it. To reduce the indent a half-inch at a time, press Ctrl-M. There are no shortcuts for indenting on the right or for indenting on both the right and left.

Hanging Indents

Another type of indent is a ***hanging indent.*** In a hanging indent, text (such as a bullet or a number) ''hangs'' to the left of the indented paragraph. Figure 4.6 gives an example of hanging indents. The easiest way to create one is to use the keyboard shortcut Ctrl-H.

Typing Paragraphs with Hanging Indents

To type the hanging indents shown in Figure 4.6, follow these steps:

1. Create a new word processor file.
2. Press Ctrl-H to begin a hanging indent.

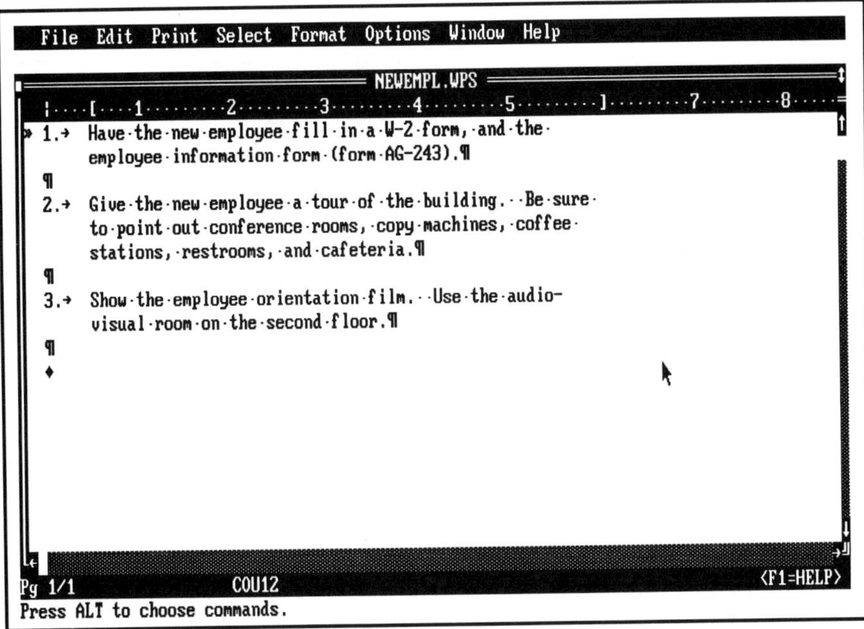

File Edit Print Select Format Options Window Help
NEWEMPL.WPS
1.→ Have·the·new·employee·fill·in·a·W-2·form,·and·the·employee·information·form·(form·AG-243).¶
¶
2.→ Give·the·new·employee·a·tour·of·the·building.··Be·sure·to·point·out·conference·rooms,·copy·machines,·coffee·stations,·restrooms,·and·cafeteria.¶
¶
3.→ Show·the·employee·orientation·film.··Use·the·audio-visual·room·on·the·second·floor.¶
¶
Pg 1/1
COU12
<F1=HELP>
Press ALT to choose commands.

Figure 4.6: A document with hanging indents

3. Type **1.** and press Tab. The Tab symbol appears on the screen, and the cursor moves to the left indent position. (Note: The Tab symbol does not print; it is on the screen to let you know what you have typed.)
4. Type the text. The text automatically wraps to the left indent, not the left margin. Press Enter to complete the paragraph.
5. Repeat steps 3 and 4 for the other two paragraphs.
6. When you want to go back to wrapping to the left margin, instead of the left indent, press Ctrl-G in the *next* paragraph. (If your cursor is still in the indented paragraph, the Ctrl-G command cancels the hanging indent in that paragraph.)

Each time you give the hanging indent command, you increase the indent of the first line of the paragraph and the left indent by a half-inch each. For example, the first time you press Ctrl-H, the first-line indent is at zero (that is, the left margin) and the left indent is at a half-inch. The second time you press Ctrl-H, the first-line indent is at a half-inch and the left indent is at 1 inch.

Customizing Hanging Indents

If you don't want hanging indents in half-inch increments, you need to use the Indents & Spacing command to enter the Left Indent and 1st Line Indent manually. Think of the Left Indent as where you want the text to word-wrap. The 1st Line Indent is how much you want the hanging characters to go back from the Left Indent. Usually the 1st Line Indent is the negative value of the Left Indent. For example, if your Left Indent is 0.2, then the 1st Line Indent should be −0.2.

You are now finished with this document. You can save and close the file as follows:

1. Choose Save As on the File Menu.
2. Type **NEWEMPL** for the file name.
3. Press Enter.
4. Choose Close on the File menu.

TYPING TABLES

If you have a table with columns or a list you want to include in a document, you can either type it in the spreadsheet tool and then copy it into your document, or type it directly into the document. In this section, you learn various techniques for typing tables in the word processor tool: setting tabs, entering end-of-line marks, and creating borders.

SETTING TABS

By default, Works has tab stops at half-inch intervals. If you need tab stops that are not at equal intervals, you must set each tab individually. In the Tabs dialog box (see Figure 4.7), you specify the position of each tab stop, and then select the Insert command. If you have a mouse, skip to the section ''Setting Tabs with the Mouse.''

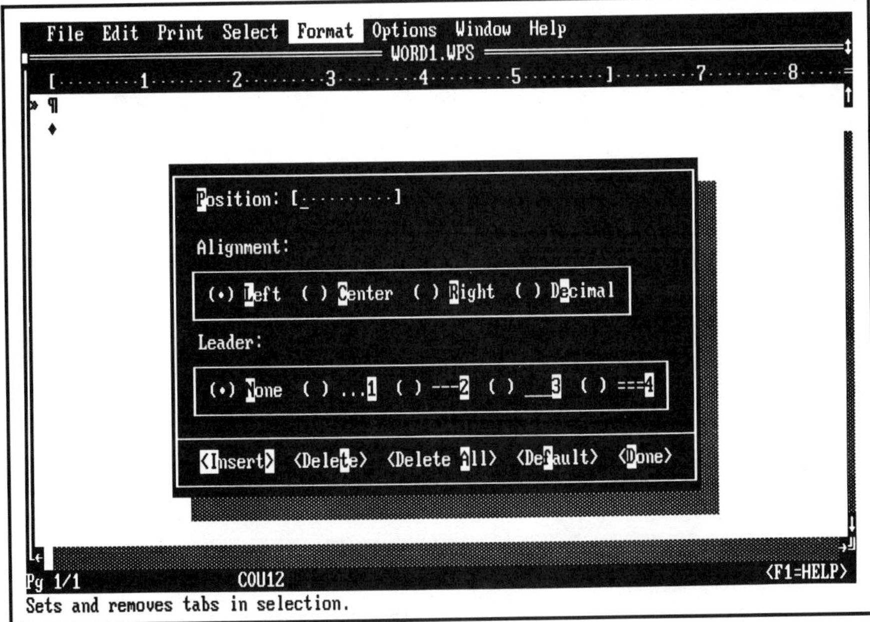

Figure 4.7: The Tabs dialog box

Setting Tabs with the Keyboard

To type the table in Figure 4.8, you need to set tab stops at 2.50″ and 5.50″. There are two ways to set tabs with the keyboard:

- Type the character position.
- Move the cursor in the ruler.

If you know you want to set a tab at a certain character position, the easiest thing to do is to type it in after Position in the Tabs dialog box.

1. Create a new word processor file.
2. Choose Tabs on the Format menu.
3. Type **2.5** to set a tab at the 2.5″ position.
4. Press Enter to select the Insert command; the letter *L* (for left-aligned tab) will appear in the ruler at 2.5″.

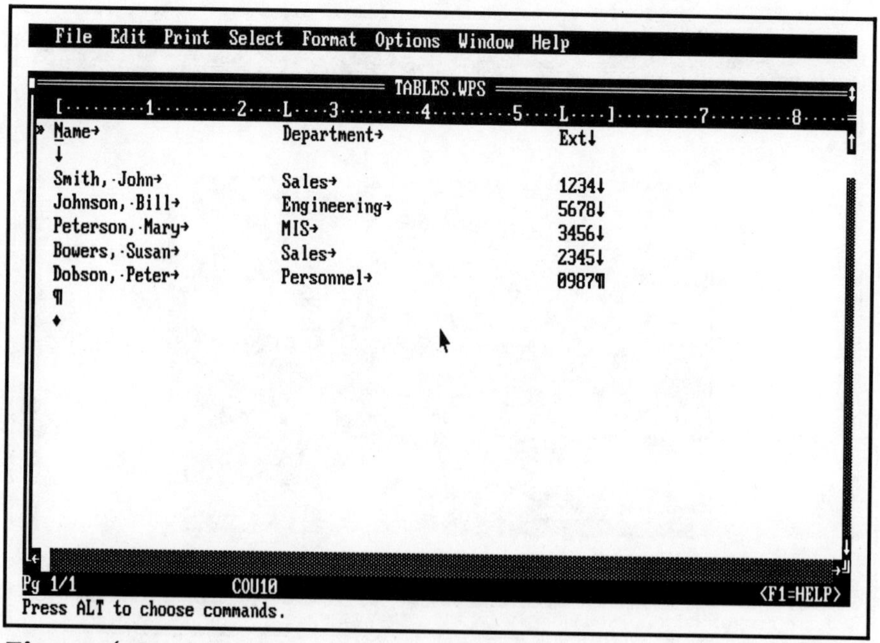

```
 File  Edit  Print  Select  Format  Options  Window  Help
═══════════════════════════ TABLES.WPS ═══════════════════════════
 [·········1·········2···L···3·········4·········5···L···]·········7·········8·····
» Name→                      Department→                 Ext↓
 ↓
 Smith,·John→               Sales→                      1234↓
 Johnson,·Bill→             Engineering→                5678↓
 Peterson,·Mary→            MIS→                        3456↓
 Bowers,·Susan→             Sales→                      2345↓
 Dobson,·Peter→             Personnel→                  0987¶
 ¶
 ♦

Pg 1/1              COU10                                          <F1=HELP>
Press ALT to choose commands.
```

Figure 4.8: A table with tabs set at 2.50″ and 5.50″

Alternatively, you can set tabs directly in the ruler. To move the cursor in the ruler, you press Ctrl-→ and Ctrl-←.

1. The Tabs dialog box should still be open on your screen. To set the second tab stop, press Ctrl-→ until the cursor is at 5.5″.
2. Press Enter to insert the tab. Your ruler should show an *L* at 2.5″ and at 5.5″.
3. Choose Done to leave the Tabs dialog box.

You might think that setting tabs in the ruler takes more effort than typing the tab position in inches. The ruler method, however, allows you to think of setting tabs in relation to each other rather than thinking of each tab stop in terms of inches. Also, if you don't know the exact position of a tab stop that you want to delete, it's easier to go to it in the ruler than to guess its position.

If you don't have a mouse, skip to the section "Typing a Table."

Setting Tabs with the Mouse

Another way to set tabs is to click the mouse pointer in the ruler. If you have a mouse, use it; it offers the fastest and easiest way to set tab stops.

1. Create a new word processor file.
2. Choose Tabs on the Format menu to bring up the Tabs dialog box.
3. Click the mouse in the ruler at the position you want to set the first tab stop: 2.5.
4. Click on Insert (this sets the tab). The letter *L* (for left-aligned tab) appears in the ruler at 2.5″.
5. Click at 5.5 in the ruler.
6. Click on Insert to set the tab.
7. Click on Done when all tabs are set. The Tabs dialog box closes.

TYPING A TABLE

The best way to type a table is to press Shift-Enter, rather than Enter, at the end of each line. The Enter key begins a new paragraph, while the Shift-Enter key combination just starts a new line. Because of the way Works treats paragraph formatting, it is better to type a table as a single paragraph. That way, it is easy to change the format of the table (for example, its spacing or indents) or to change the tab stops. All you have to do is place the cursor anywhere in the table and give the format command. If you enter each line as a separate paragraph, you have to select each line in the table before you format it. The new-line command, Shift-Enter, makes table formatting easier.

When you press Shift-Enter at the end of the line, you see the new-line symbol (an arrow pointing downward) instead of the paragraph mark. If you accidentally press Enter (which is easy enough to do since it's probably your natural instinct), move to the paragraph mark, press Shift-Enter, and then delete the paragraph mark.

1. Type the table shown in Figure 4.8, pressing Tab to move between columns and Shift-Enter to move to a new line.
2. Press Enter twice after typing the last line of the table.
3. Save the file with the name TABLES.

ADJUSTING TAB STOPS

More times than not, your tab stops will not be perfect the first time you set them. Setting tabs is sometimes a trial-and-error process, so you may have to adjust your tabs several times before you get them just right. Fortunately, you can adjust tab stops without having to retype anything in the table—the columns in the table reposition themselves automatically.

The last tab stop in your table is a little too far to the right. Adjusting this tab stop is a two-step process: Delete the existing tab, and insert the new tab. Before you do anything, though, place the cursor in the table. This is very important! If your cursor is below the table, you can not change the tab stops of the table. Like line spacing, alignment, and indents, tabs are associated with paragraphs, and the cursor has to be in the paragraph whose format you want to change. If you have a mouse, skip to the section "Changing Tabs with the Mouse."

Changing Tabs with the Keyboard

Let's reset the tab from 5.5″ to 5″.

1. Make sure the cursor is in the table.
2. Bring up the Tabs dialog box by choosing Tabs on the Format menu.
3. Type **5.5**.
4. Press Alt-T for Delete. (You can also press Ctrl-→ to move to the tab stop—the *L* at 5.5″—and then press Alt-T.) The *L* disappears from the ruler.
5. Type **5**.
6. Press Alt-I for Insert. The *L* appears at the 5″ mark in the ruler.
7. Press Alt-D for Done.

The third column automatically adjusts to the new tab setting. If you don't have a mouse, skip to the section "Adding Borders."

Changing Tabs with the Mouse

Make sure the cursor is in the table (on any line) before you bring up the Tabs dialog box. To adjust tab stops with the mouse, you go into the ruler and click where you want to insert and delete tabs. Follow these steps:

1. Click anywhere in the table.
2. Choose Tabs on the Format menu to display the Tabs dialog box.
3. Click on the L at 5.5″ in the ruler.
4. Click on Delete.
5. Click on the 5″ mark in the ruler.
6. Click on Insert to set the new tab.
7. Click on Done when you are finished. The table now reflects the new tab setting.

If your next paragraph has tab stops completely different from the ones you previously set, the easiest thing to do is to use the Delete All command in the Tabs dialog box. Before you choose this option, check your cursor location: The command deletes the tab stops in the current paragraph. Therefore, if the cursor is in an existing table, you will delete all the tab stops you so carefully entered!

ADDING BORDERS

You can place lines around your tables (or any paragraph) to separate them from other tables or text on the page. Works calls these lines *borders.* Figure 4.9 shows the phone list, with borders above and below it.

Follow these steps to put top and bottom borders on the phone list:

1. Place the cursor anywhere in the table.
2. Choose Borders on the Format menu. Figure 4.10 displays the Borders dialog box that appears. The Outline border places lines around all four sides of the paragraph; you can select any combination of Top, Bottom, Left, and Right. The line style can be Normal (single line—the default), Bold (dark single line), or Double.
3. Click next to Top and Bottom (or press Alt-T and Alt-M).
4. Select OK. The table should look similar to Figure 4.9.

Save and close the file.

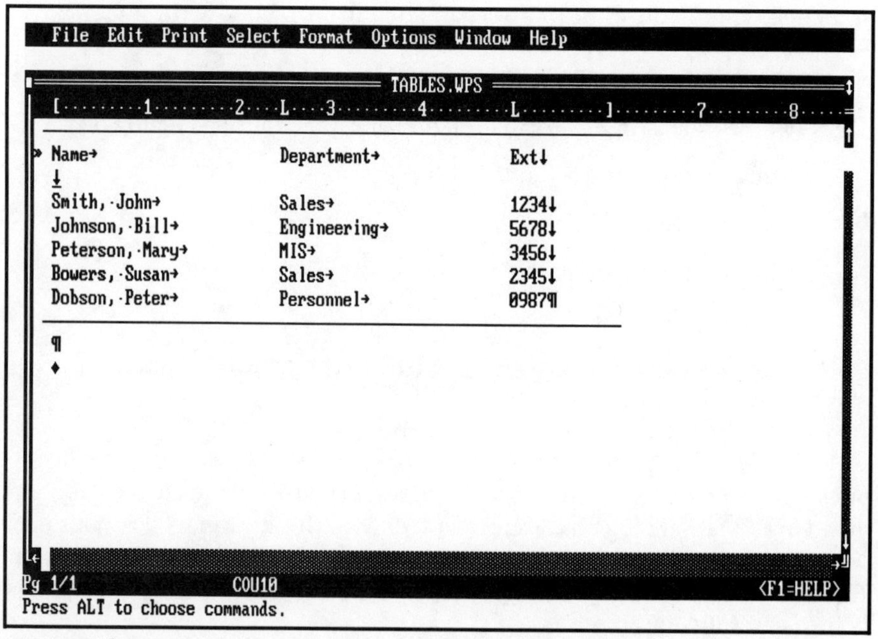

```
 File  Edit  Print  Select  Format  Options  Window  Help
                              TABLES.WPS
 [·········1·········2···L····3·········4·········L·········]·········7·········8·····
 Name→                      Department→                 Ext↓
 ↓
 Smith,·John→               Sales→                      1234↓
 Johnson,·Bill→             Engineering→                5678↓
 Peterson,·Mary→            MIS→                        3456↓
 Bowers,·Susan→             Sales→                      2345↓
 Dobson,·Peter→             Personnel→                  0987¶
 ¶
 ♦
Pg 1/1              COU10                                                  <F1=HELP>
Press ALT to choose commands.
```

Figure 4.9: The phone list with top and bottom borders

SUMMARY

This chapter showed you how to format documents so that the final product looks attractive and emphasizes key points on the page. You learned how to specify character styles (bold, underline, italic) and select different fonts. You also learned how to center lines, justify text, change line spacing, create indents, and draw border lines. Furthermore, you learned how to set tab stops and type a table.

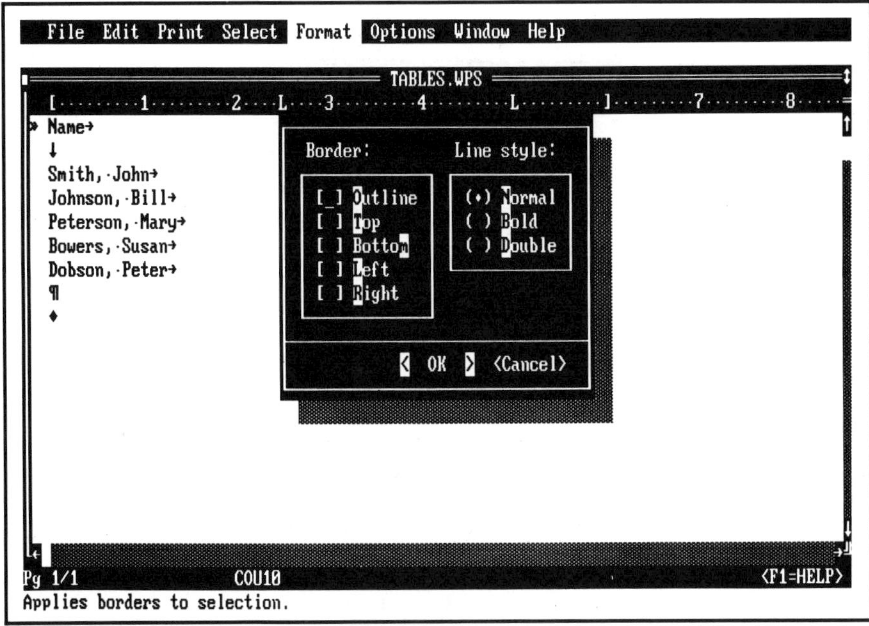

Figure 4.10: The Borders dialog box

All the features you learned in this and the previous chapter will help you create attractive letters, memos, and tables. However, if you work with longer documents, read the next chapter to learn the specific skills that you need for multipage documents.

If you are eager to learn another Works tool right away, skip to Chapter 6 to explore the spreadsheet. You can return to Chapter 5 later if you need to learn more advanced word processor features.

EXERCISES

In the following exercises you will practice formatting a document. You will center lines, bold and underline words, create hanging indents, justify and double-space paragraphs, and draw border lines. As you format the document, refer to Figure 4.12, the final printed letter. If you get stuck, refer to the sections indicated inside parentheses.

1. Create a word processor file.
2. Keep the following in mind as you create the document shown in Figure 4.11:
   - Bold and underline the indicated words *as you type* (see "Changing the Style as You Type," page 69).
   - Center the top two lines as you type (see "Centering a Line," page 77).
   - Create hanging indents in the bulleted paragraphs (see "Typing Paragraphs with Hanging Indents," page 82), and cancel the hanging indent in the last paragraph.

Additional Information
About Your Benefits

Your medical plan pays benefits for these services and supplies:

o Hospital room and board charges, the average semi-private room rate for the hospital of your choice, and any other hospital-furnished inpatient medical services and supplies.

o Approved confinement in a nursing care facility for the first 30 days each calendar year.

o X-rays, laboratory examinations, anesthetic and its administration.

o Services of a physician.

Other covered supplies include: blood and blood plasma; rental or purchase of a wheelchair or hospital-type bed; and oxygen and rental of equipment for its administration.

Figure 4.11: A sample document

3. Double-space the first and last paragraphs as shown in Figure 4.12 (see "Changing Line Spacing," page 79).
4. Justify the bulleted paragraphs (see "Justifying Text," page 78).
5. Create a top border for the first centered line as shown in Figure 4.12 (see "Adding Borders," page 89).
6. Create a bottom border for the second centered line as shown in Figure 4.12.
7. Save the file with the name BENEFITS.
8. Print the document.
9. Close the file.

Additional Information
About Your Benefits

Your medical plan pays benefits for these services and supplies:

o Hospital room and board charges, the average semi-private room rate for the hospital of your choice, and <u>any other hospital-furnished inpatient medical services and supplies</u>.

o Approved confinement in a nursing care facility for the first 30 days each calendar year.

o X-rays, laboratory examinations, anesthetic and its administration.

o Services of a physician.

Other covered supplies include: blood and blood plasma; rental or purchase of a wheelchair or hospital-type bed; and oxygen and rental of equipment for its administration.

Figure 4.12: The final document

5

WORKING WITH MULTIPLE PAGE DOCUMENTS

In Chapters 3 and 4, you learned how to create, edit, and format documents in the word processor tool. This chapter continues with word processing but concentrates on the features specific to longer documents. You will learn how to control page breaks, how to number pages, how to get around a long document, and how to copy text between separate documents.

Appendix B contains all the documents used in this chapter's exercises. To follow along with the exercises, you should create these documents on your own. The two-page document CLASS is used in most of the examples, so you may want to create it before reading the rest of this chapter.

PAGINATION

Pagination is the process of dividing a document into pages. As pointed out in Chapter 3, Works displays a symbol (double right-pointing arrows) to show where each new page begins. The bottom window border also indicates on which page your cursor is and the total number of pages in the document (for example, *Pg 4/7*).

How does Works determine where to put the page break? The process involves a little math, but fortunately Works performs all the calculations. It calculates the number of printed inches on the page by subtracting the top and bottom margins from the page length. (These measurements are specified in the Page Setup & Margins dialog box on the Print menu.) It then factors in your line spacing and font size to determine the number of lines that will fit on the page.

Thus, if you want to fit more or fewer lines on a page, you have several alternatives:

- Change the margins.
- Change the line spacing (for example, try 1½ spacing instead of double spacing).
- Use a different font size.

Do not change the Page Length to try to get more or less on a page! The Page Length is the physical size of the paper, and if you change it needlessly, pages will not print properly.

INSERTING YOUR OWN PAGE BREAKS

Works inserts page breaks automatically according to the formula described in the previous section. But what if you want a page break before Works inserts one? For example, you may want a new chapter or report section to start on its own page. To insert a *manual page break,* place the cursor at the beginning of the line where you want the new page to begin. Then choose Insert Page Break from the Print menu, or simply press Ctrl-Enter. A dotted line appears, running across the page, representing a manual page break. Figure 5.1 displays a manual page break.

If you change your mind about the manual page break, or if you inserted it in the wrong place, you can delete it. Put the cursor on the dotted line, and press Del once.

PAGINATE NOW!

Works automatically paginates your document as you type. Occasionally, however, the pagination lags behind when you issue commands that

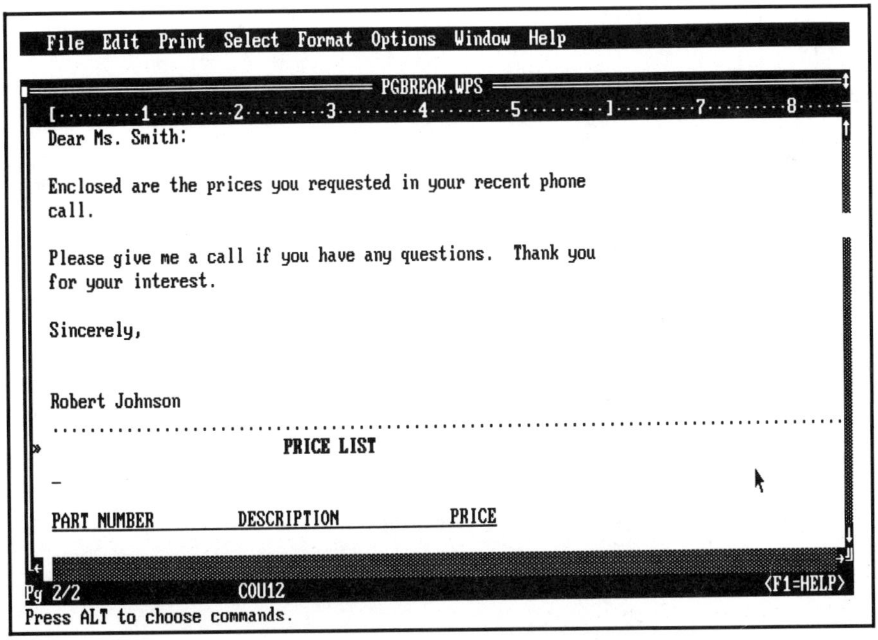

```
File  Edit  Print  Select  Format  Options  Window  Help
                         PGBREAK.WPS
[·········1·········2·········3·········4·········5·········]·········7·········8·····
Dear Ms. Smith:

Enclosed are the prices you requested in your recent phone
call.

Please give me a call if you have any questions.  Thank you
for your interest.

Sincerely,


Robert Johnson
...............................................................................
»                        PRICE LIST

-

PART NUMBER          DESCRIPTION          PRICE

Pg 2/2               COU12                                              <F1=HELP>
Press ALT to choose commands.
```

Figure 5.1: A manual page break inserted with Ctrl-Enter

affect pagination (such as Insert Page Break), or when you do substantial editing (such as moving text between pages) or formatting (such as changing line spacing). You know that Works has fallen behind in pagination when you don't see a page number in the bottom window border.

If this happens, you can either wait for Works to catch up with you, or if you are impatient and must see your current page breaks right now, you can choose Paginate Now on the Options menu (or press F9). The message "Press ESC to cancel pagination" appears at the bottom of the screen. You must wait until this message disappears before you can continue working on the document. For short documents (under 10 pages), the message may flash so quickly that you don't even see it. When the message disappears, your current page breaks appear.

NUMBERING PAGES AUTOMATICALLY

By issuing a single command, you can have page numbers automatically printed on every page; you do not have to manually enter the number on each page. The correct page numbers always print on each page, even after you edit the document. You specify page numbering using the Headers & Footers command on the Print menu. A *header* is text that is printed at the top of a page. A *footer* is text that is printed at the bottom. You do not actually see the headers and footers in your document—only when you print or preview the pages.

Let's say you want the page number centered at the bottom of the page of your CLASS document.

1. Create or open the CLASS document (see Appendix B).
2. Choose Headers & Footers on the Print menu.
3. Move next to *Footer* and type **&C&P**. &C is the code for centering and &P is the code for page numbering. Table 5.1 lists the codes you can use in your headers and footers. We'll explore some of the other codes shortly.
4. Press Enter to complete the command.

Table 5.1: Header and Footer Codes

CODE	FUNCTION
&L	Align with left margin
&R	Align with right margin
&C	Center between left and right margins
&P	Insert page number
&F	Insert file name
&D	Insert current date
&T	Insert current time

Follow these steps to preview and print the current page so that you can see the page number:

1. Choose Preview on the Print menu.
2. Press Enter.
3. To see the next page, press PgDn.
4. If the footer looks OK, press P to print. Otherwise, press Esc to exit Preview and return to the document.

Often you do not want to print the page number on the first page of the document—if you don't, choose *No footer on 1st page* (Alt-O) or *No header on 1st page* (Alt-N) in the Headers & Footers dialog box.

PRINTING TEXT ON EVERY PAGE

As shown in Table 5.1, headers and footers can also contain the file name, date, and time. If you don't specify the alignment (&L, &C, or &R) in a header or footer, the text is automatically centered. You can also type text, such as a title, a revision number, or a person's name. Let's look at a few examples.

If you want dashes around the page number (for example, -2-), you create this footer: *&C-&P-*. Or if you want parentheses around the page number, you type *&C(&P)*.

The header *&LMr. Jones&R&D* prints *Mr. Jones* at the left margin and the current date (for example, *12/4/90*) at the right margin, as shown below:

Mr. Jones 12/4/90

The footer, *&L&F&C&P&RRev. No. 12,* prints the file name at the left margin, the page number in the center, and *Rev. No. 12* at the right margin, as shown below:

REPORT1.WPS 3 Rev. No. 12

CREATING MULTILINE HEADERS AND FOOTERS

Only single-line headers and footers can be entered in the Headers & Footers dialog box. If your header or footer is two lines long or more, you have to create it at the top of the document in what are called ***header and footer paragraphs.*** Follow these general steps:

- Display the Headers & Footers dialog box.
- Select *Use header and footer paragraphs* (Alt-U).
- Choose OK.

This command inserts codes at the beginning of the document as shown in Figure 5.2. The line beginning with *H* is where you type your header. To get multiple lines, use the new-line command, Shift-Enter. The line beginning with *F* is the footer line. As Figure 5.2 illustrates, a default footer is set up for you automatically. This footer prints *Page* - followed by the page number, centered at the bottom of the page. Notice that multiline footers don't use the same code as single-line footers—the code **page** (instead of *&P*) prints the page number. If you don't want the default footer, you can delete the text.

Look at the ruler in Figure 5.2 and notice the *C* and *R*—these are center- and right-aligned tab stops. (In Chapter 4 you set left-aligned tabs, indicated by an *L* in the ruler.) These tabs were set up for you so that you can easily use the Tab key to align the different parts of your header and footer. You do not use the &L, &C, and &R codes that you used in single-line headers and footers.

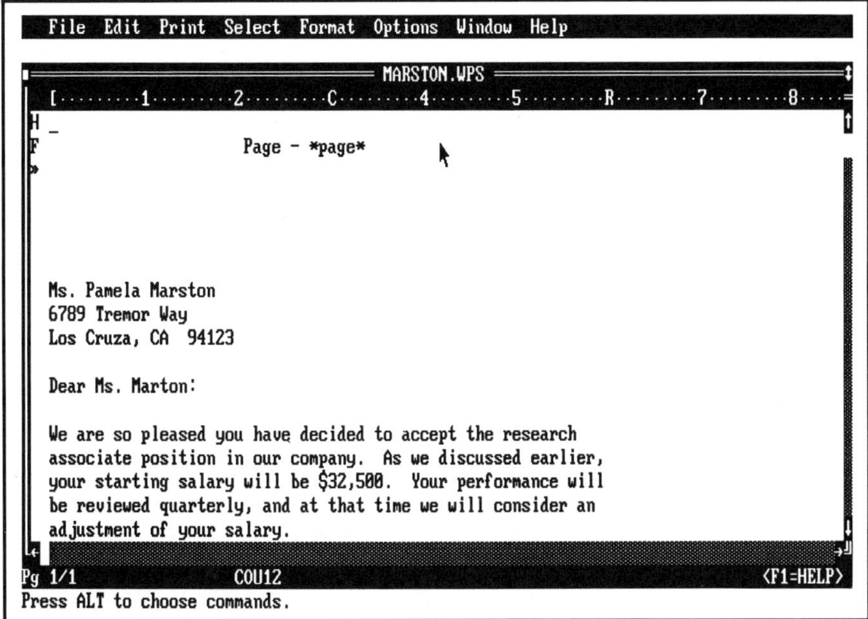

Figure 5.2: The default header and footer paragraphs

You can insert the page number, date, time, and file name in any line of the header or footer. Place the cursor where you want to insert the code and use the following:

COMMAND	DESCRIPTION	SCREEN CODE
Ctrl-P	Page number	*page*
Ctrl-F	File name	*filename*
Ctrl-D	Date	*date*
Ctrl-T	Time	*time*

If you can't remember the Ctrl-key commands to insert these header/footer codes, an alternative method is available:

- Choose the Insert Special command on the Edit menu.

- Select one of the following commands from the displayed list:

  Print page

  Print file

  Print date

  Print time

- Choose OK.

When you issue one of these commands, the code listed above appears in the header or footer. When you print the document, the code is replaced with the actual text.

Figure 5.3 displays an example of a multiline header. The first line of the header has the name *Ms. Pamela Marston,* the second line has the date, and the third line has the word *Page*, followed by the page number. This header is one you might use on multipage letters. Since you don't want footers in a letter, the default footer text is deleted.

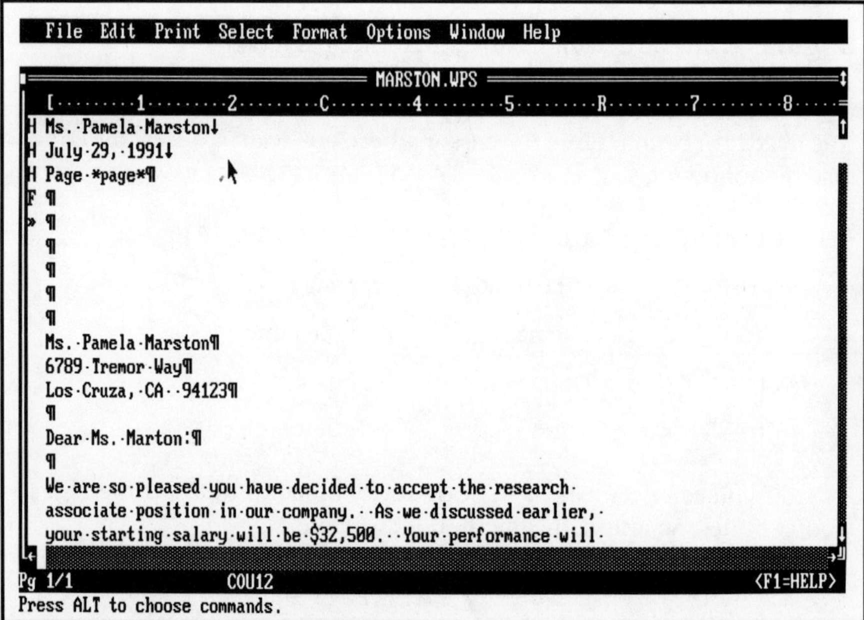

Figure 5.3: A multiline header

With the default margins, you can fit a one- or two-line header on the page. If you try to print the three-line header in Figure 5.3, Works displays the error message "Header too tall: reduce header margin or increase top margin." As the message indicates, you can create room for the header by reducing the space between the top edge of the paper and the start of the header (the header margin) or by increasing the space between the top edge of the paper and the first line of the document (the top margin). The default top margin is 1″; the default header margin is 0.5″. To get the three-line header to print, you have to increase the top margin to 1.25″ or reduce the header margin to 0.25″.

Figure 5.4 illustrates the locations of the different margins on the page, along with their default settings.

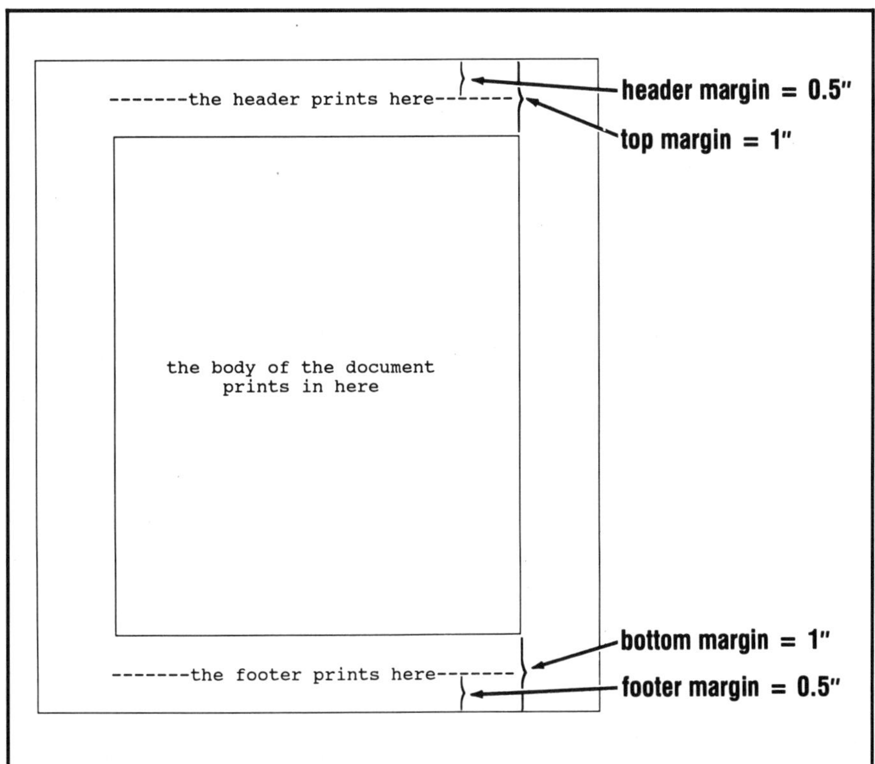

Figure 5.4: The default margins on the page

The same rules apply for multiline footers. If you get an error message that the footer is too tall, reduce the footer margin (the space between the bottom edge of the paper and the top of the footer) or increase the bottom margin (the space between the bottom edge of the paper and the last line of the document). Please note that the footer margin includes the space below the footer *and* the footer text itself. It is *not* the distance between the last line of the footer and the bottom edge of the page.

If you no longer want to use multiline headers and footers in your document, turn off *Use header & footer paragraphs* in the Headers & Footers dialog box. You no longer see the headers and footers at the beginning of the document. However, just by turning on the option again, you can make the header/footer symbols and text reappear.

PRINTING SPECIFIC PAGES

Sometimes you may want to print only certain pages of a long document. By default, when you select Print, Works prints the entire file, but you can specify whichever pages you want. The dialog box in Figure 5.5 will print pages 3–5 and page 8. To print specific pages, you need to choose two options while in the Print dialog box.

1. Turn on the ***Print specific pages*** option (Alt-S). You should see an *X* next to the option.
2. Choose *Pages* (Alt-G), and enter the page numbers.
3. To specify a range of pages, separate the numbers with either a colon or a dash (for example, 3:5 or 3–5).
4. To specify noncontiguous pages or ranges, type a comma between each page number as shown in Figure 5.5.

Works remembers the specified page range the next time you print, so be sure to check the Print dialog box. If you want to go back to printing the entire document, choose *Print specified pages* to turn off the option. (The *X* should disappear.) You do not need to delete the numbers next to *Pages.*

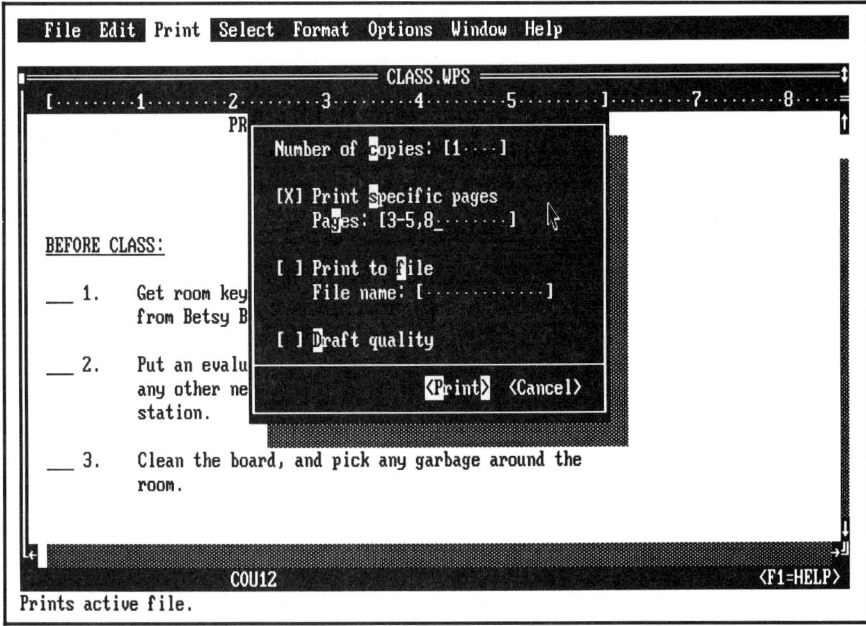

Figure 5.5: Printing specified pages in a document

GETTING AROUND A LONG DOCUMENT

Chapter 3 discussed many ways to move the cursor around and to scroll the screen in a document. If you need to refresh your memory of the keyboard shortcuts for moving the cursor, refer back to Table 3.2. Table 3.3 lists the ways you can scroll with the mouse. The keyboard commands that are especially useful for long documents are PgDn and PgUp (to scroll a screen at a time) and Ctrl-Home and Ctrl-End (to move to the top or bottom of a document). If you have a mouse, you can position the box in the scroll bar to accomplish the same tasks. The Goto key, F5 (or Go To on the Select menu), moves you to a specific page.

In this section, you learn even faster ways to get around a multipage document.

SEARCHING FOR TEXT

Using the Search command is probably the fastest way to move your cursor in a long document. You can use this feature to go directly to a word or phrase you need to correct or to move the cursor quickly to the heading of a section you want to work on. I used the Search command frequently when writing this book. After printing a chapter and marking it up with corrections, I used the Search command to locate each mistake. This saved me a lot of time and effort scrolling through the document, scanning for the passage I needed to correct.

Using the Search Command

The Search feature searches from the cursor location forward through the document. To begin a search from the top of a document, press Ctrl-Home before starting the search.

To search for the word *pick* in the CLASS document so that you can correct a mistake there (see Figure 5.6), follow these steps:

1. Open the CLASS document. (If you haven't already typed in this document, refer to Appendix B where it is typed in its entirety.)
2. Place the cursor at the beginning of the document.
3. Choose Search on the Select menu.
4. Type **pick** as the text to search for and press Enter. The cursor moves to and selects the word.
5. Change *pick* to *pick up.* Once you find a word or phrase you're searching for, you can do whatever it is you want to do there—you don't need to cancel the command.

In this example, there was only one occurrence of *pick,* so the cursor moved right where you wanted to go. If a document contains multiple occurrences of the word you are searching for, continue the search by pressing F7. Keep pressing F7 until you find the right occurrence. If you want to see how Repeat Search works, search for the word *class;* press F7 to go to each occurrence.

If you aren't sure how a word is spelled in a document, you can use a *wildcard.* In poker a wildcard can be any card you want it to be. In Works a wildcard in a search string can be used in place of individual characters. It

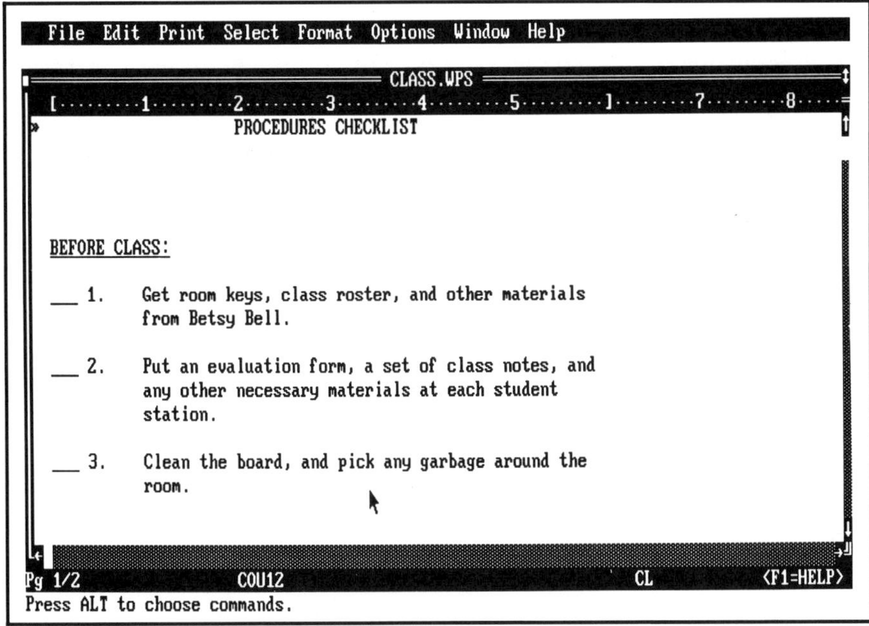

Figure 5.6: Searching for the word *pick*

is represented by a question mark. For example, if you search for *Thomps?n,* Works locates *Thompson* or *Thompsen.* You can use more than one wildcard in a search string.

Narrowing the Search

To save yourself the effort of pressing the F7 key many times, you need to make the search string as unique as possible. One way of narrowing the search is to search for a *phrase* rather than a word. By typing a phrase, you will most likely go directly to the occurrence you want. A phrase is more likely to be unique than a single word, so you will not need to stop at as many occurrences. To go to *class* in item 2 in Figure 5.6, you could search for *class notes* instead of just *class.*

Another way to reduce the number of occurrences that you land on during a search is to use the options in the Search dialog box. The *Match whole word* option only finds your search text if it appears as a complete word in the document. Without this option, Works locates the word even if it's in the middle of another word. For example, if you search for *other* using this option, Works does not find *another, smother,* or *others.* When you turn on the *Match whole word* option, Works only finds *other* when it is a complete word.

The *Match upper/lower case* option only finds text in the document that matches the exact case you enter. So, if you search for *Class,* Works does not locate *CLASS* or *class.*

You can choose both of these options at the same time to narrow your search even further. The options remain selected for subsequent searches unless you turn them off or exit Works.

REPLACING TEXT

The Replace feature takes the Search command one step farther: It searches for a word or phrase and replaces it with another. If you find that you have consistently misspelled someone's name throughout a document, you can search for the incorrectly spelled name and replace it with the correctly spelled one.

Another way you can use the Replace feature is to customize a generic form. In a legal contract, for example, the word *NAME* may appear throughout the document. You can customize the contract for a specific person by searching for *NAME* and replacing it with someone's actual name, for example, *Joe Smiley.* You get to practice this procedure a little later.

My favorite way to use Replace is to have it replace shorthand codes I've typed throughout the document. If there is a cumbersome word or phrase (like a company name or a technical term) that appears frequently in a document, I type an abbreviation in its place. For example, as I wrote this book, instead of typing *Microsoft Works,* I typed *msw.* Then I had Works replace *msw* with *Microsoft Works* in one easy procedure.

To use the Replace feature, follow these general steps:

- Place the cursor at the beginning of the document.
- Select Replace on the Select menu.
- After *Search for,* type the text to be searched for. Do not press Enter yet! (If you press Enter without specifying text to replace with, the search text is replaced with nothing. In other words, the search text is deleted.)

- Move down to the *Replace with* option. Click the mouse next to it or press ↓ or press Alt-W.
- Type the text that will replace the text you're searching for.
- Select the *Match whole word* and/or the *Match upper/lower* case option, if desired.
- Choose Replace, the default, to replace each occurrence one by one. Choose Replace All to replace all occurrences without having to individually confirm each one.

Replacing Words Automatically

Be very careful when you use the Replace All option. If you are not 100 percent certain that you want every occurrence automatically replaced, choose Replace, not Replace All. Let's say you want to replace all occurrences of *her* with *him* in a document. If you forget to choose the *Match whole words* option *and* you choose Replace All, Works replaces the letters *her* in *here,* forming the word *hime.* The word *other* becomes *othim* and *there* becomes *thime.*

As you see, you can end up with some pretty funny-looking words. Fortunately, you can use the Undo feature to correct your mistake—press Alt-Backspace or choose Undo on the Edit menu. (Because Undo cancels your last command only, if you don't notice the mistake right away, you have to use the Replace command again and search for *him* and replace it with *her*—but this time you choose Replace, not Replace All.)

Replacing Words One by One: Playing It Safe

As mentioned in the previous section, you should only choose Replace All when you are certain you want every single occurrence of a word or phrase replaced. If you are not sure, play it safe and choose Replace. Works then stops at each occurrence and asks, "Replace this occurrence?" If you choose Yes, Works replaces the word and moves on to the next. If you select No, Works just goes to the next occurrence. Choose Cancel to stop the Replace command.

Using Replace to Customize a Form

The contract in Figure 5.7 is a standard form that contains the word *NAME* instead of a specific name. You can use the Replace command to customize the contract.

1. Type the document shown in Figure 5.7.
2. Save the file with the name CONTRACT.
3. Press Ctrl-Home to move the cursor to the beginning of the document.
4. Replace all occurrences of the word *NAME* with *Joe Smiley.*
5. Replace *agreement* with *contract,* except in the last paragraph. (Hint: use Replace, not Replace All.)

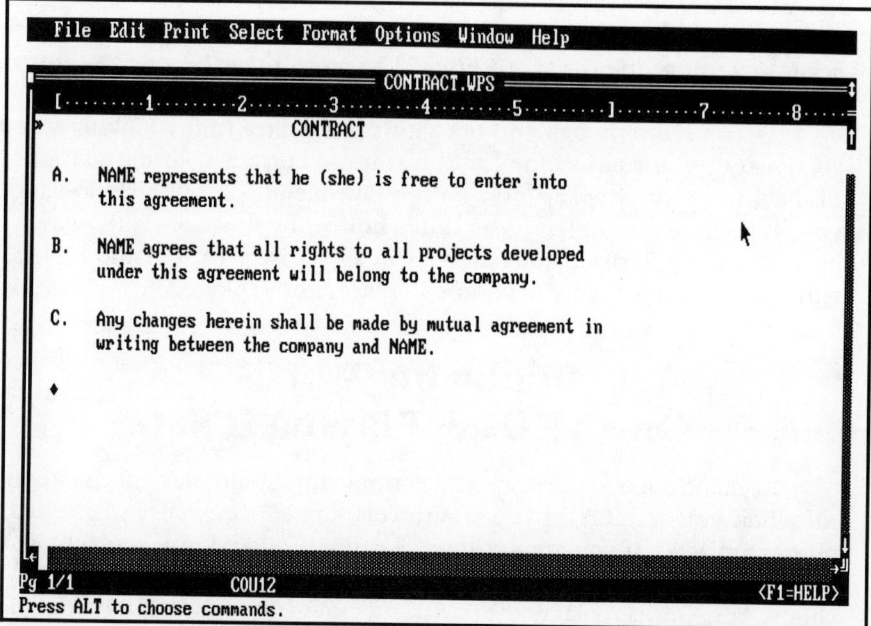

Figure 5.7: A standard contract that can be customized with the Replace command

Whenever you customize a form with the Replace command, you will want to save the document under a new name by using the Save As command. This way your original form remains generic. You should save the customized document shown in Figure 5.7 under the name JSMILEY and then close the file.

COPYING TEXT BETWEEN DOCUMENTS

Because Works allows you to have more than one file open at a time, you can easily exchange information between documents. The general steps are as follows:

- Open both documents.
- Press Ctrl-F6 to switch between windows.
- Select the text to be copied.
- Press Shift-F3 to Copy, or choose the Copy command on the Edit menu.
- Press Ctrl-F6 to switch to the other window.
- Position the cursor at the point where you want to copy the selected text and press Enter.

You cannot *move* text between documents. You have to *copy* the text, and then delete it from the original document.

For practice, open a couple of your existing files. When you have multiple files on-screen, the last file you opened takes center stage. However, you can still see the left edge of the window behind it; the title bar with the file name of the background window appears at the top. Figure 5.8 shows the document REQUEST behind the document PRICES. (These documents are in Appendix B if you want to create them.)

To move between windows, use Ctrl-F6, the Next Window command. If you have only two files open, Ctrl-F6 switches you back and forth between the two windows. For more information on working with windows, see Chapter 15.

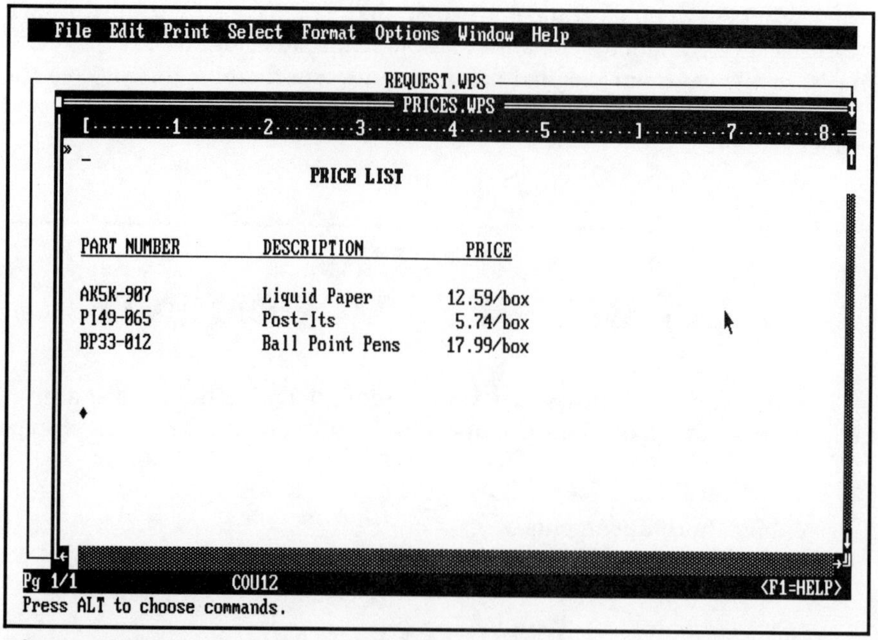

```
File  Edit  Print  Select  Format  Options  Window  Help
REQUEST.WPS
PRICES.WPS

                    PRICE LIST

PART NUMBER        DESCRIPTION          PRICE

AK5K-907           Liquid Paper        12.59/box
PI49-065           Post-Its             5.74/box
BP33-012           Ball Point Pens     17.99/box

Pg 1/1            COU12                                   <F1=HELP>
Press ALT to choose commands.
```

Figure 5.8: Two document files open at once

Following the steps listed above, practice copying a section of one document into another. When you are finished with the file you are copying from, go to that window (press Ctrl-F6), and choose the Close command on the File menu. If you have made any changes to the file, Works asks you if you want to save them.

To include an entire document inside another, you follow the same basic steps, except you select the entire document before you initiate the copying procedure. You can select the entire document by choosing All on the Select menu or by pressing F8 five times or by clicking both mouse buttons simultaneously in the left margin.

SUMMARY

In this chapter you learned the commands and features that are exclusive to, or are especially useful for, multipage documents. You made pages break exactly where you wanted them to, set up headers and footers, moved around a long document, and exchanged information between documents.

In the next chapter, you will learn how to create spreadsheets using another Works tool.

EXERCISES

In the following exercises you will practice working with a multipage document. Specifically, you will create the document shown in Figure 5.9, insert page breaks, copy text between two documents, use the Replace feature, add a header, and print a document. As you do the exercises, refer to Figure 5.10, the final printed document. If you get stuck, refer to the sections indicated inside parentheses.

1. Create the document shown in Figure 5.9.
2. Insert a page break at the bottom of the document (see "Inserting Your Own Page Breaks," page 97).
3. Open the BENEFITS file that you created in the Chapter 4 exercises, and copy all the text in this file onto page 2 of the new document (see "Copying Text between Documents," page 111).
4. Go to the top of the document and use the Replace command to replace all occurrences of *medical plan* with *major medical plan* (see "Replacing Text," page 108). You should make four replacements.

Important Facts About Your Coverage

GRACE PERIOD: Your medical plan provides a 31-day grace period for the payment of your quarterly premiums.

BENEFITS AFTER AGE 65: Coverage will terminate on the Medicare Eligibility Date, or age 65, whichever comes first.

OUT-OF-POCKET EXPENSES: The out-of-pocket expense amount of your medical plan must be satisfied during each calendar year before 100% of eligible expenses can be paid.

CARRY-OVER PROVISION: Eligible expenses used to satisfy the deductible amount of your medical plan in the last 3 months of a calendar year may be used to satisfy the deductible amount for the next calendar year.

Figure 5.9: A practice document

Major Medical Plan Page 1

Important Facts About Your Coverage

GRACE PERIOD: Your major medical plan provides a 31-day grace period for the payment of your quarterly premiums.

BENEFITS AFTER AGE 65: Coverage will terminate on the Medicare Eligibility Date, or age 65, whichever comes first.

OUT-OF-POCKET EXPENSES: The out-of-pocket expense amount of your major medical plan must be satisfied during each calendar year before 100% of eligible expenses can be paid.

CARRY-OVER PROVISION: Eligible expenses used to satisfy the deductible amount of your major medical plan in the last 3 months of a calendar year may be used to satisfy the deductible amount for the next calendar year.

Major Medical Plan Page 2

Additional Information About Your Benefits

Your major medical plan pays benefits for these services and supplies:

o Hospital room and board charges, the average semi-private room rate for the hospital of your choice, and any other hospital-furnished inpatient medical services and supplies.

o Approved confinement in a nursing care facility for the first 30 days each calendar year.

o X-rays, laboratory examinations, anesthetic and its administration.

o Services of a physician.

Other covered supplies include: blood and blood plasma; rental or purchase of a wheelchair or hospital-type bed; and oxygen and rental of equipment for its administration.

Figure 5.10: The final document

5. Create a header that contains the title *Major Medical Plan* and the page number (see "Printing Text on Every Page," page 99).
6. Save the document under the name MAJORMED.
7. Print the document.
8. Print page 1 only (see "Printing Specific Pages," page 104).
9. Close both files.

part three

THE SPREADSHEET TOOL

BUILDING A SPREADSHEET

6

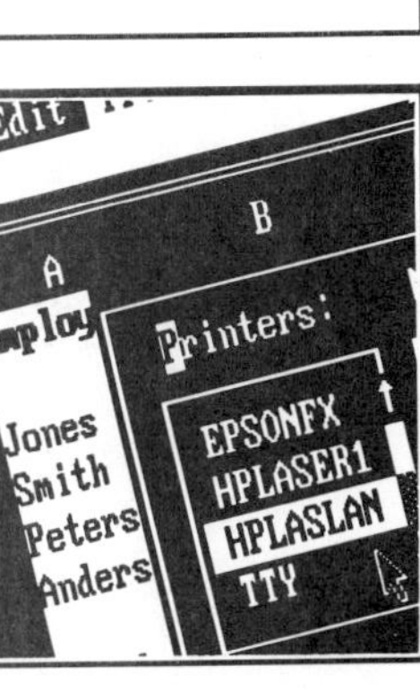

The spreadsheet is the tool to use for all your number crunching. It's ideal for doing budgets, forecasts, projections, and financial analysis. Though this tool is primarily designed for working with numbers, you can also use it to create columnar tables; the columns are already set up so that you don't have to set tab stops.

An electronic spreadsheet is the computerized version of ledger paper—you know, the yellow paper with the green and brown lines. Using the old ledger paper has its problems. If you forget a line, you either have to redo the spreadsheet, write really small between the lines, or cut-and-paste. In Works's spreadsheet tool, you can simply issue the command to insert a row.

If you enter an incorrect number on ledger paper, you have to white it out or erase it, enter the new number, and then get out your calculator and reenter all the calculations that use that number. In Works, you type the new number (you don't even have to erase the old one), and all the calculations are updated automatically.

One of the biggest advantages of an electronic spreadsheet is its ability to play "what if" games with the assumptions underlying a projection or forecast. I know people who, before the advent of electronic spreadsheets, stayed up all night recreating forecasts, a different one for each set of assumptions. First, for example, they might develop a spreadsheet with the assumption that sales of a given product would increase by 10 percent a year. Then they got out another piece of paper, rewrote the spreadsheet, and recalculated the results for a 15 percent increase. They repeated this process for each scenario. It doesn't sound like a pleasant way to spend an evening.

With the electronic spreadsheet you can spend your evenings at the movies or at ballgames instead of recreating spreadsheets. To revise a forecast in Works, all you have to do is type the new percentage and you instantly have your new spreadsheet. It takes only seconds to play "what if" games in an electronic spreadsheet—call me a nerd, but I even think it's fun.

CREATING A SPREADSHEET FILE

To create a spreadsheet, choose Create New File from the File menu and select New Spreadsheet from the list of file types. The spreadsheet window, shown in Figure 6.1, appears.

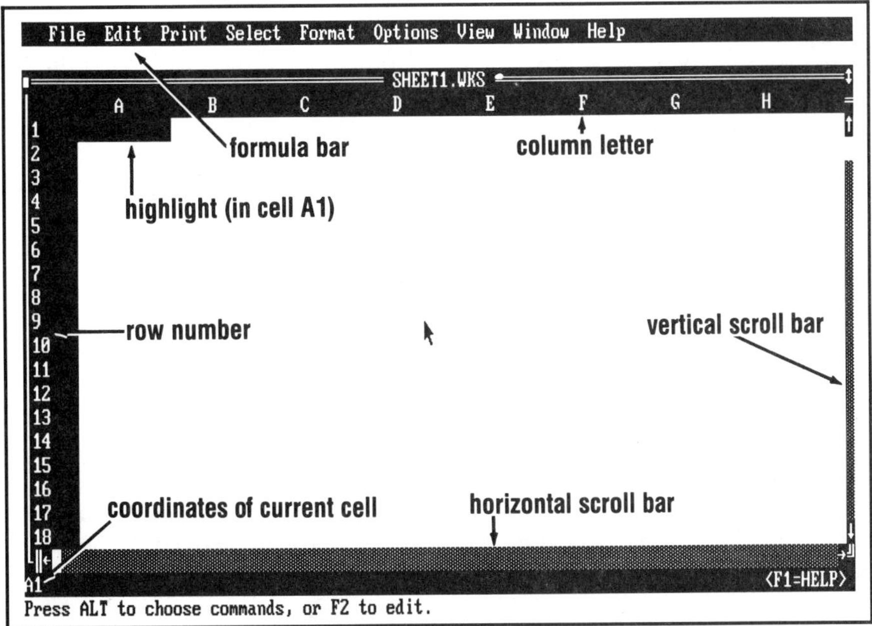

Figure 6.1: The spreadsheet window

Like the word processor file, the spreadsheet file is contained in a bordered window with mouse scroll bars on the right and at the bottom. Figure 6.1 points out the different parts of the spreadsheet window. The title bar contains the name of the file (*SHEET1.WKS* is displayed until you give the file a name).

Notice that the columns are labeled with letters (A, B, C, D, etc.) across the top window border and that the rows are labeled with numbers (1, 2, 3, 4, etc.) down the left side of the window. The intersection of a row and a column is called a *cell.* A cell is a box in which you type text or numbers. You refer to a cell by its coordinates, designated by the column letter and row number where it is located. Right now the ***highlight*** (the rectangular bar) is in cell A1. Always refer to a cell by its column letter first and then its row number.

For practice, use your arrow keys to move around to different cells in the spreadsheet window. When you are in the middle of the screen, it's sometimes difficult to tell what the current cell coordinates are. However, you don't need to guess—just look at the bottom-left corner of the screen. The information in this corner always tells you your current cell location.

How large is the spreadsheet grid? To find out, press → to see what happens when you move past the last column on your screen (either G or H, depending on your monitor). Is the world flat? Do you fall off the edge? No, you get more columns. Column A scrolls off the screen to the left and you see another column (on the right). What happens when you get to column Z? The alphabet starts doubling up (AA, AB, AC, ...; BA, BB, BC, ...; CA, CB, CC, etc.) and continues through column IV (the letters I and V)—that's 256 columns.

How many rows are there? Even if you use the PgDn key to go 18 rows at a time, it would take you quite some time to find the bottom of the spreadsheet. There are 4096 rows.

This spreadsheet grid, containing 1,048,576 cells, should be large enough for most of your computing needs. You would probably run out of computer memory before you ran out of available spreadsheet space.

To bring your highlight back to cell A1, the beginning of the spreadsheet, press Ctrl-Home. (Recognize this command from the word processor tool?) We'll be learning more ways to move the highlight in Chapter 7.

ENTERING DATA

Entering numbers and text in the spreadsheet is easy. Follow these general steps:

- Place the highlight where you want to type the data. You can use the arrow keys or simply click the mouse pointer on the cell.
- Type the data in the cell. As you type, the characters appear both in the cell and in the *formula bar.* The formula bar is the single line between the menu bar and the spreadsheet window. Figure 6.2 shows the word *SALES* in cell A1. (Notice that the text appears in the formula bar and in the cell.)
- If you make a mistake while you are typing, press the Backspace key to back up and correct it.

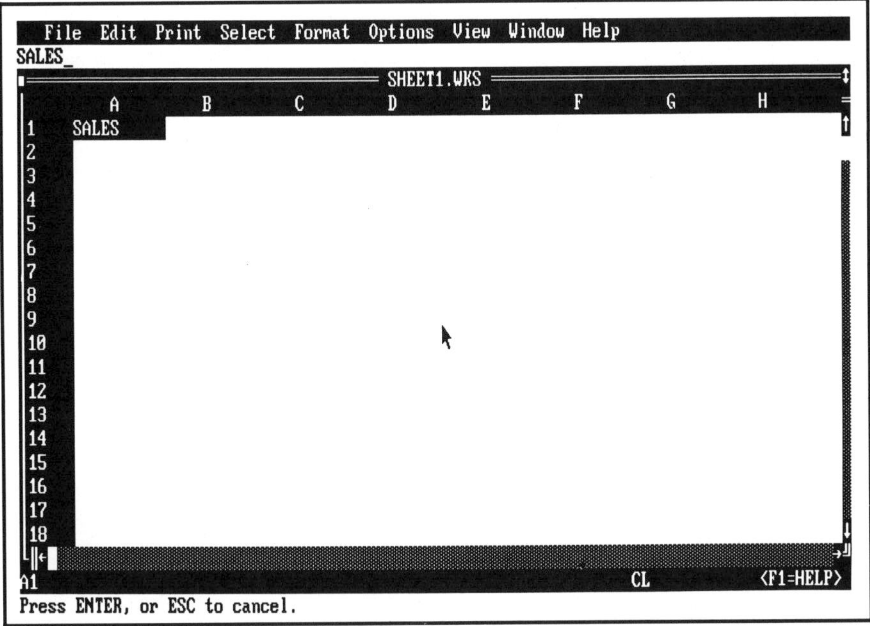

Figure 6.2: Text typed in cell A1

- When you are finished typing the data, you can press any of the following keys to complete the entry:

Enter	Leaves the highlight on current cell
Tab	Moves the highlight to the right
Arrow keys	Moves the highlight in the direction of the arrow

The arrow keys actually perform double-duty. They enter data in a cell *and* move the highlight to the location where you want to type next. For example, when entering a column of data, press ↓ instead of pressing Enter and then ↓. This technique saves you one keystroke per cell. When entering a row of information, use Tab or →.

If you have a mouse, you can click the pointer in the next cell where you want to enter data. However, if you are entering data in consecutive cells, you'll probably want to stick with the arrow keys, since your hands are already on the keyboard. It just doesn't make much sense to take your hand off the keyboard to use the mouse, unless the cell you want to go to is farther away on the screen. Do the following exercise:

1. Type the word **SALES** in cell A1.
2. Press Enter, then look in the formula bar. The formula bar contains the contents of the cell in which the highlight is positioned. Notice that the word is preceded by a quotation mark (*"SALES*). Works automatically places a quotation mark in front of *text* as a way of distinguishing text from numbers. Works does not insert a symbol in front of numbers.
3. To confirm this rule, put the highlight in A2 and type **4000**.
4. Press Enter and study the formula bar.

Notice that the label *SALES* is aligned on the left side of the cell and the number *4000* is aligned on the right. These alignments are the defaults for text and numbers. Later in this chapter you will learn how to change cell alignment.

If you enter something in the wrong cell, you can use the Del or Backspace key to clear it out. (The spreadsheet tool does not have an Undo feature, so be very careful when erasing cells.) To try it, do the following:

1. Put the highlight on the cell to delete, A1.
2. Press Del. The cell contents are cleared, and the bottom of the screen displays "Press ENTER, or ESC to cancel." By pressing Esc, you can cancel the command and redisplay the cell contents (in case you cleared the cell accidentally). By pressing Enter, you can erase the cell. (Tab and the arrow keys work also.)
3. Press Enter.
4. Repeat steps 1–3 to erase cell A2.

For the rest of this chapter and part of Chapter 7, you will be working with an employee-raise spreadsheet model. It calculates the amount of employee raises and new salaries for a company's personnel department. The spreadsheet also totals and averages the salaries and raises.

Type the spreadsheet in Figure 6.3, keeping the following in mind:

- Type the information in the exact cells shown in Figure 6.3. All examples throughout this and the next chapter refer to these cells.

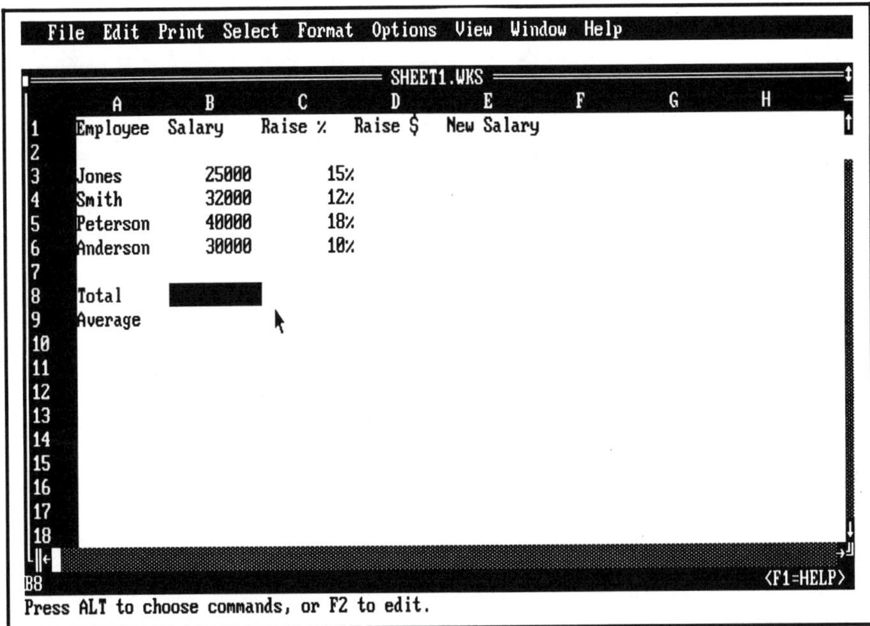

Figure 6.3: The data for the employee-raise spreadsheet

- If you make a mistake after you press Enter, clear it with the Del key or retype the data correctly.
- Do not type commas in the numbers. (Commas are added with a formatting command.)
- Be sure to type the percent signs for the raise percentages.
- Because Works automatically aligns text and numbers, the column headings may not line up with the numbers. You will fix the alignment later.

BUILDING FORMULAS

Formulas perform calculations with the numbers in your spreadsheet. In the employee-raise spreadsheet, you will type formulas to calculate the dollar amount of the raise, the new salary, and the total and average salaries for all employees. You type formulas in the cell where you want the answer to appear. A formula contains references to the cells containing the numbers rather than the actual numbers. For example, if you wanted to do a calculation with Jones's salary in Figure 6.3, the formula would refer to cell B3, not the number 25000. That way, no matter what numbers are in the cells, the calculation is accurate. Formulas always begin with the equal sign (=).

CREATING SIMPLE FORMULAS

Simple formulas are formulas that refer to individual cells. You can create simple formulas to add, subtract, multiply, or divide numbers in two or more cells. The *Raise $* and *New Salary* columns are simple formulas. The total and average rows use built-in functions and are covered in a later section.

You can use the following mathematical operations:

+	Addition
–	Subtraction
/	Division
*	Multiplication

Typing a Simple Formula

To calculate the dollar amount of the raise, you multiply the salary by the raise percentage. Remember, you refer to cells, not numbers, in your formulas. Thus, the formula to calculate Jones's raise is *=B3*C3*.

1. Put the highlight in cell D3, where you want the answer to appear.
2. Type the formula **=B3*C3**
3. Press Enter.

The answer, *3750,* appears in the cell; the formula appears in the formula bar. As you can see, the formula is permanently recorded in the cell.

To see how Works automatically recalculates its formulas when you enter new values, do the following:

1. Put the highlight in cell B3.

2. Type **52000**.
3. Press Enter. The new answer, *7800,* is automatically displayed, without your having to do a thing. How's that for powerful!
4. Return B3 to its original value, *25000.*

You are probably wondering how to calculate the raises for the other three employees. You do not need to retype the formula for each row. Because the formula is the same for each employee (the salary multiplied by the raise percentage), you can copy the formula. We will do this a little later in the chapter. For now, let's enter the other formulas.

Entering a Formula by Selecting Cells

Works offers another way to enter formulas. The technique you just used to enter the raise formula is called the *typing* method. The alternative technique is called the *selecting* method. In the typing method, you type everything: the mathematical operators (+ , − , *, /) and the cell references. In the selecting method, you still type the operators, but instead of typing the cell references, you move the highlight to them.

To try this method, follow these steps to calculate the dollar amount for New Salary (the salary plus raise amount):

1. Place the highlight in cell E3.
2. Begin the formula by typing = .
3. Move the highlight to B3 either by clicking on it with the mouse or by pressing ←. The formula bar displays *=B3.*
4. Type + . The highlight jumps back to where you are building the formula.
5. Move the highlight to D3. The formula bar now displays *=B3+D3.*
6. Press Enter to complete the formula. Your spreadsheet should now look similar to Figure 6.4.

The selecting method has several advantages over the typing method. First, you don't have to figure out what cells the numbers are in; you simply put the highlight on the cell and Works fills in the cell reference. Second, it is more accurate. It's easy to make a typing mistake when typing a cell reference. For example, you might accidentally type *B33* instead of *B3.* You

```
 File  Edit  Print  Select  Format  Options  View  Window  Help
=B3+D3
                              SHEET1.WKS
        A         B          C          D          E          F          G          H
1   Employee  Salary     Raise %    Raise $   New Salary
2
3   Jones         25000       15%      3750      28750
4   Smith         32000       12%
5   Peterson      40000       18%
6   Anderson      30000       10%
7
8   Total
9   Average
10
11
12
13
14
15
16
17
18
E3                                                                        <F1=HELP>
Press ALT to choose commands, or F2 to edit.
```

Figure 6.4: The spreadsheet after formulas for Raise and New Salary have been entered

don't have to worry about this kind of mistake if you select cells with the highlight.

When you create spreadsheets on your own, experiment with the two methods to see which one you prefer. When writing formulas that refer to cells all over a large spreadsheet, you might find it tedious to select each cell. In this case, it would be easier to write down the cell coordinates you want to use in the formula and then use the typing method to enter the formula.

USING BUILT-IN FUNCTIONS

Works comes with more than 50 built-in functions that you can use in your formulas. These functions are categorized as *mathematical, statistical, logical, date,* and *special.* Appendix C contains a list with complete descriptions of each function. Probably the most commonly used function is SUM, which totals columns and rows.

Totaling a Column

The SUM function requires you to indicate the *range* of cells containing the numbers to be totaled. A range is a rectangular group of cells. For example, =*SUM(B3:B6)* totals the range of cells from B3 to B6. One way of indicating a range is to type it; you use a colon (:) to separate the beginning cell and the ending cell. The other way to specify a range is to select it, using either the keyboard or the mouse.

With the mouse, you use the *click and drag* technique to select the range: Click on the first cell in the range, hold down the left mouse button, and move the pointer to the last cell. You can also use the *shift and click* technique: Click on the first cell, hold down the Shift key, and click on the last cell.

To select a range with the keyboard, use the arrow keys. Place the highlight on the first cell in the range, and then choose one of the following methods to extend the selection:

- Hold down the Shift key and press the arrow keys.
- Press F8 (Extend) and press the arrow keys.
- Choose Cells on the Select menu and press the arrow keys.

The range will be selected (highlighted) as you press the arrow keys. If you are using the Shift key to select, you must keep the Shift key down the entire time. If you let go, you have to start over.

In the employee-raise spreadsheet, you need to total the salary column. Use the selection technique to indicate the range.

1. Place the highlight in cell B8.
2. Type **=SUM(** to begin the formula. (Both simple formulas and functions must begin with an equal sign.)
3. If you want to use the keyboard, select from B3 to B6. (Move the highlight to B3, press F8 or hold down the Shift key, and then move the highlight down to B6.) If you want to use the mouse, click and drag from B3 to B6. (Click on B3, hold down the mouse button, and move down to B6.)
4. Type **)** and press Enter. As shown in Figure 6.5, the answer appears in the cell, and the formula appears in the formula bar.

Finding an Average

Usually, to find an average you have to total the numbers, count how many entries there are, and then divide the total by this number. In Works, all these steps are built into the AVG function. All you have to do is indicate the range of numbers to average.

To average the salaries in the employee-raise model, follow these steps:

1. Place the highlight in cell B9.
2. Type **=AVG(** to begin the formula.
3. To use the keyboard, select from B3 to B6. To use the mouse, click and drag from B3 to B6.
4. Type **)** and press Enter. The answer, *31750,* appears in the cell, and the formula, *=AVG(B3:B6),* appears in the formula bar.

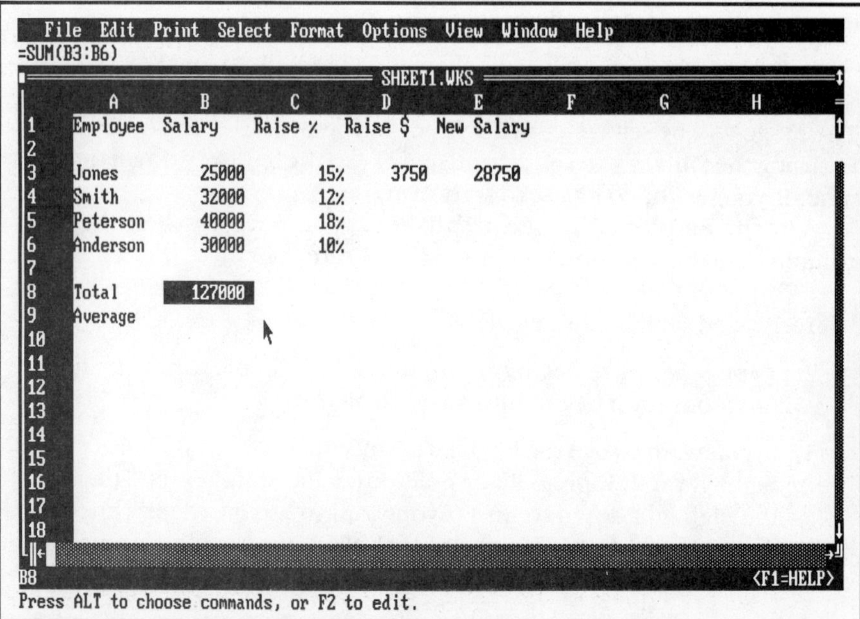

Figure 6.5: Using the SUM function to add up a column

SAVING A SPREADSHEET FILE

You have done quite a bit of work on your spreadsheet, so it's time to save it to disk. As you have already seen, the File menu offers two ways to save: Save and Save As. Remember, use the Save As command to assign a new name to a file, and use Save to save the file with the same name you gave it previously. Actually, the first time you save the file, you can choose Save or Save As; either option prompts you for a file name. The default file name, SHEET1.WKS, will be displayed. However, you will want to assign a more descriptive name, such as RAISE.

Save the spreadsheet with the name RAISE, using the techniques you learned in Chapter 3. You will then see the file name, RAISE.WKS, in the title bar at the top of the window. Works automatically assigns the extension .WKS to the files you create in the spreadsheet tool. Your screen should now look similar to Figure 6.6.

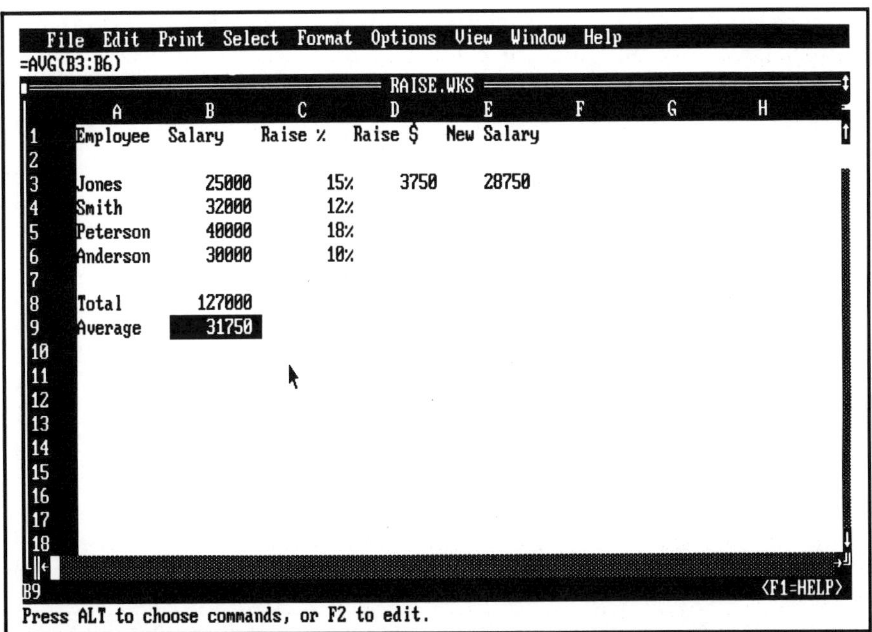

Figure 6.6: The spreadsheet saved with the name RAISE

COPYING DATA IN THE SPREADSHEET

You can copy anything in the spreadsheet, including text, numbers, and formulas. Works is smart when it comes to copying formulas—it assumes that you want to copy the formula, not the answer, so when it copies, it changes the cell references relative to where you are copying the formula. For example, when you copy the raise formula from row 3 to row 4, Works adjusts the formula so that the copied formula multiplies the salary and raise percentage in row 4.

FILLING ACROSS OR DOWN

When copying down a column or across a row, use the Fill Down or Fill Right command on the Edit menu. Before you choose the command, though, you must select the range. The range includes the cell or cells you want to copy from (for example, the cell(s) containing the formula) ***and*** the cells you want to copy into (the blank cells to the right or below).

Table 6.1 lists the different ways to select a range, some of which you have already learned.

Follow these steps to copy the raise formula:

1. Select the range D3:D6.
2. Choose Fill Down on the Edit menu. The formulas copy down the column, as shown in Figure 6.7.
3. Place the highlight in D4 and look at the formula bar. Notice that the formula automatically adjusts to the row it copies into.

Repeat the steps just listed to copy the formula for New Salary. (You could have copied both formulas, Raise $ and New Salary, at the same time by selecting the range D3:E6.)

You can copy the Total and Average formulas in a similar fashion, except this time you use the Fill Right command. Let's copy both formulas at the same time.

1. Select B8:E9.
2. Choose Fill Right on the Edit menu.

Table 6.1: Selecting Cells

WITH THE KEYBOARD	
Row	Ctrl-F8, or choose Row on Select menu
Column	Shift-F8, or choose Column on Select menu
Spreadsheet	Ctrl-Shift-F8, or choose All on Select menu
Extend selection	F8 once, or choose Cells on Select menu, or hold down Shift and select with arrow keys
WITH THE MOUSE	
Row	Click on row number
Column	Click on column letter
Spreadsheet	Click on intersection of row numbers and column letters
Extend selection	Click and drag, or shift and click

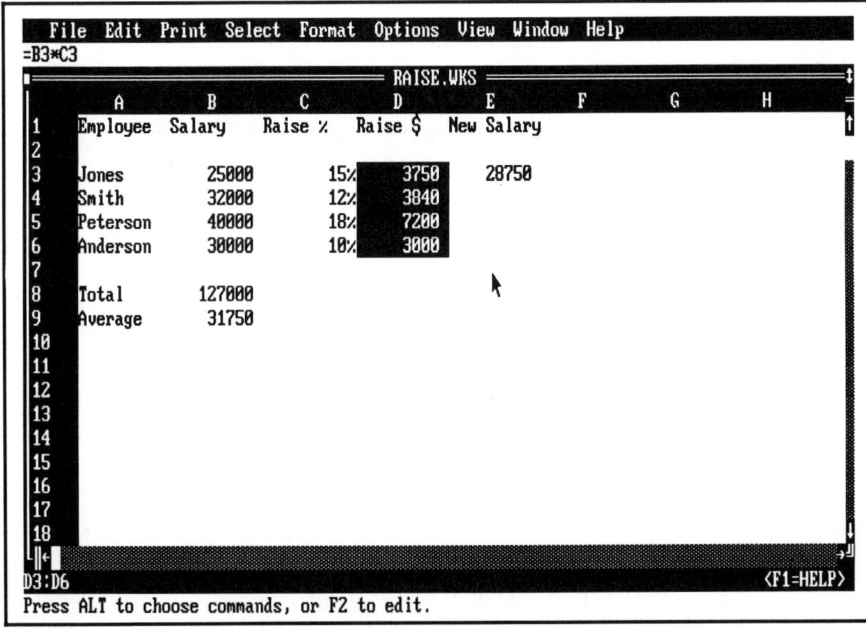

Figure 6.7: Copying the raise formula down a column

Your screen should look similar to Figure 6.8. Notice that some of the numbers have decimal places and some don't, and that the raise percentages are displayed without percent signs. Although these numbers are screaming ''Format me!'' you will ignore their cries until the ''Enhancing the Spreadsheet'' section (coming up very soon, I promise).

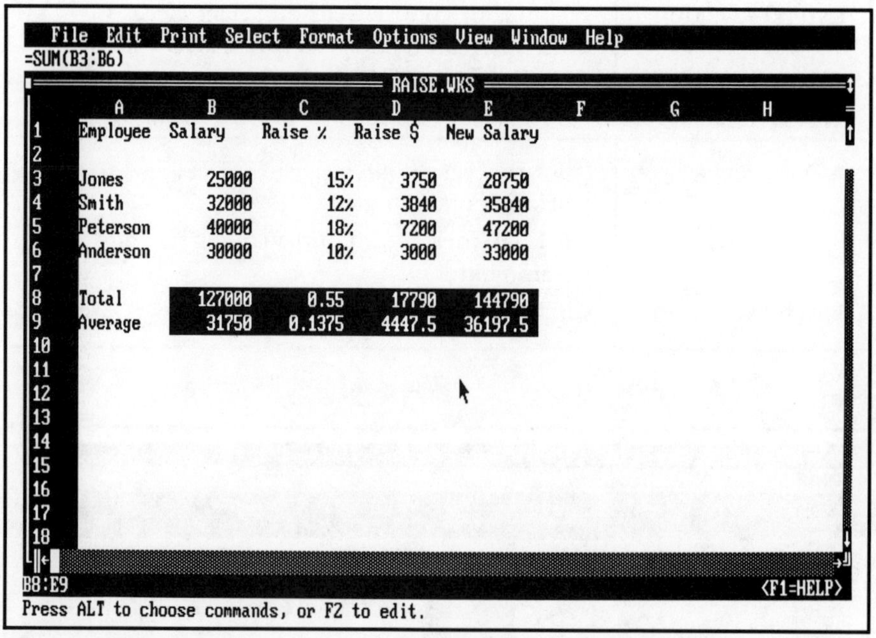

```
 File  Edit  Print  Select  Format  Options  View  Window  Help
=SUM(B3:B6)
                         RAISE.WKS
       A          B          C          D          E          F          G          H
1  Employee   Salary     Raise %    Raise $    New Salary
2
3  Jones          25000        15%       3750      28750
4  Smith          32000        12%       3840      35840
5  Peterson       40000        18%       7200      47200
6  Anderson       30000        10%       3000      33000
7
8  Total         127000       0.55      17790     144790
9  Average       31750      0.1375     4447.5    36197.5
10
11
12
13
14
15
16
17
18
B8:E9                                                                   <F1=HELP>
Press ALT to choose commands, or F2 to edit.
```

Figure 6.8: The Total and Average formulas copied to the right

Because it doesn't make sense to sum the raise percentages, clear the contents of cell C8. Move the highlight to the cell, and press Del, then Enter.

COPYING TO ANOTHER LOCATION

The Edit menu contains two other commands for copying: Copy and Copy Special. Copy Special is for consolidating data from different spreadsheets—it does not copy formulas. You will use this command in

Chapter 7. The Copy command (Shift-F3) copies a range to another location. For example, this little spreadsheet you set up is just for the Personnel Department. To create spreadsheets for other departments, you could copy this spreadsheet with the Copy command. This command lets you copy to another location in the same file or to a different spreadsheet file. You can even copy to a document in the word processor tool (as explained in Chapter 7).

To see how the Copy command works, follow these steps to copy your spreadsheet to another location in the file:

1. Select the range A1:E9.
2. Choose Copy on the Edit menu, or press Shift-F3. The message "Select new location and press ENTER. Press ESC to cancel" appears at the bottom of the screen.
3. Move the highlight to cell A11. (The selection highlighting disappears as soon as you start moving the highlight—this is supposed to happen.)
4. Press Enter.

The entire spreadsheet is copied—text, numbers, and formulas. The formulas automatically adjust to their new location.

Now let's make a third copy of the spreadsheet. Rather than going through the Copy command again, you can tell Works to make another copy.

1. Move the highlight down to cell A22.
2. Press Shift-F7, the Repeat command.

You can continue this process until you have as many copies as you need.

Actually, you don't want this spreadsheet copied just yet because it's not quite finished. To erase the copied ranges, do the following:

1. Select the range A11:E30.
2. Choose Clear on the Edit menu. (The Del and Backspace keys clear only one cell, not a selected range.) The copied ranges are erased.
3. Press Ctrl-Home to go back to the beginning of the spreadsheet.

COPYING THE CELL ABOVE THE HIGHLIGHT

As you have seen, Works has quite a few ways to copy cells. But wait, there's one more: You can copy the contents of the cell above the highlight. This command is useful if you are entering a column of data, and you have two identical entries in a row—just press Ctrl-' (single quotation mark). This command is for text and numbers only; it does not copy formulas. If the cell above is a formula, it copies the result.

When you press Ctrl-', Works displays the contents in the formula bar, and the message "Press ENTER, or ESC to cancel" is displayed at the bottom of the screen. If you want an exact copy, press Enter or an arrow key. If you need to revise the entry, you can use the Backspace key before pressing Enter.

ENHANCING THE SPREADSHEET

Although your employee-raise spreadsheet has all the correct results, it doesn't look very pretty. Works offers a plethora of formatting options to enhance the spreadsheet. You can add symbols and punctuation to the numbers (like dollar signs, commas, and decimal places), align the headings with the numbers, change column widths, set styles (bold, underline, and italic), and change the font.

FORMATTING THE NUMBERS

Works offers the following format options for numbers:

General The default format

Fixed No punctuation, definable decimal places

Currency Dollar signs, commas, and definable decimal places

Comma Commas, definable decimal places

Percent	Percent signs, definable decimal places
Exponential	Scientific notation

The default format, *General,* displays numbers with the greatest possible precision. If the number doesn't have any decimal places, no decimals are displayed. If the number has decimal places, it displays as many decimals as can fit in the column width. If the number is larger than can fit in the column width, the General format displays exponential notation (for example, the number *1234567890* is displayed as *1.235E + 09*).

After you select a numeric format on the Format menu, you are usually asked to enter a number of decimal places. The number you enter controls the digits to the right of the decimal point. For example, the number *1.368* formatted with two decimal places is displayed as *1.37*. Notice that the formatted number is rounded. This rounding applies only to the display of the number; Works uses the actual number (*1.368*) in its calculations.

This screen rounding can get you into trouble, though. Look at the example below:

BEFORE FORMATTING	**FORMATTED WITH NO DECIMALS**
1.4	1
1.4	1
----	--
2.8 (total)	3 (total)

The apparent mistake in the answer formatted with no decimals happens because Works adds the actual numbers (1.4 and 1.4) in its calculation of the total, not the rounded numbers. Keep your eye out for these kinds of rounding problems. You may have to display more decimal places so that your results are accurate.

Whenever possible, select an entire row or column when formatting. This method offers several advantages over selecting a range in a row or a column. First, you can use keyboard and mouse shortcuts to select entire columns or rows (see Table 6.1). Second, if you later insert rows or columns (as you will do in Chapter 7), the new cells will already be formatted. If you are going to have multiple spreadsheets within a file, though, you probably do not want to format entire rows and columns, because the other tables might have different kinds of data requiring different kinds of formatting.

If you want the entire spreadsheet formatted in a certain way, select the entire spreadsheet before choosing the format. (See Table 6.1 for the selection methods.)

Figure 6.9 displays the formatting for numbers in the employee-raise spreadsheet. The Salary, Raise $, and New Salary columns have the Comma format, the Raise % column has the Percent format with one decimal place, and the Total and Average rows have the Currency format. To add commas in the Salary, Raise $, and New Salary columns, do the following:

1. Select the Salary column by pressing Shift-F8 with the highlight in column B (or click on the column letter *B* with the mouse).
2. Choose Comma on the Format menu. You are asked to enter the number of decimal places; *2* is the default.
3. You don't want any decimal places, so type **0** and press Enter.

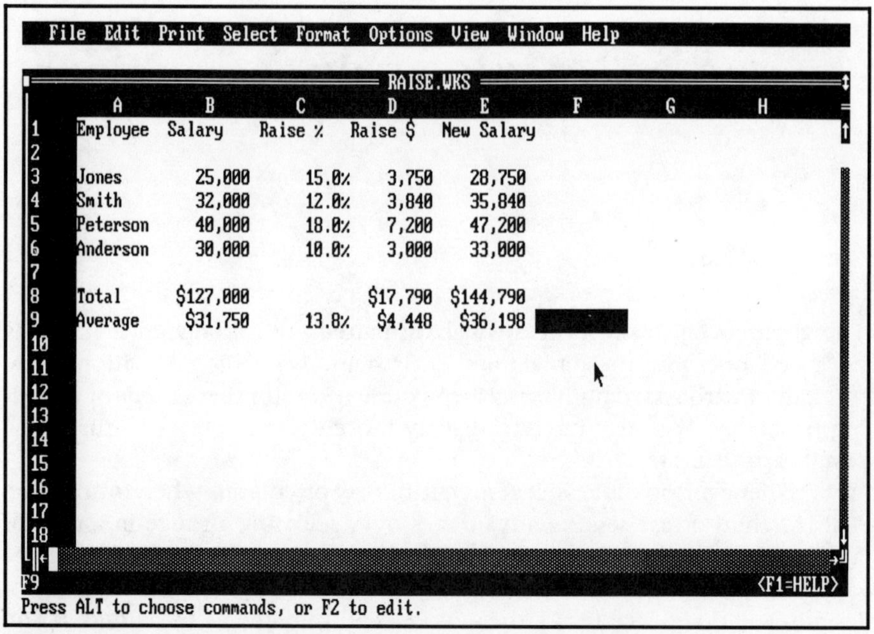

File Edit Print Select Format Options View Window Help

RAISE.WKS

	A	B	C	D	E	F	G	H
1	Employee	Salary	Raise %	Raise $	New Salary			
2								
3	Jones	25,000	15.0%	3,750	28,750			
4	Smith	32,000	12.0%	3,840	35,840			
5	Peterson	40,000	18.0%	7,200	47,200			
6	Anderson	30,000	10.0%	3,000	33,000			
7								
8	Total	$127,000		$17,790	$144,790			
9	Average	$31,750	13.8%	$4,448	$36,198			
10								
11								
12								
13								
14								
15								
16								
17								
18								

F9 <F1=HELP>

Press ALT to choose commands, or F2 to edit.

Figure 6.9: The spreadsheet with formatted numbers

This same format should be applied to the last two columns. If you are using the keyboard, you can select two adjacent columns by following these steps:

1. Place the highlight in column D.
2. Press Shift-F8 to select the column.
3. Press F8 for Extend Selection (or hold down the Shift key).
4. Press → to select column E.

If you have a mouse, click and drag on the column letters D and E.

Both columns (D and E) should now be selected. Specify Comma format with no decimal places.

The Total and Average rows should have the Currency format. To select rows 8 and 9, follow these steps:

1. Place the highlight in row 8.
2. Press Ctrl-F8 to select the row.
3. Press F8 for Extend Selection (or hold down the Shift key).
4. Press ↓ to select row 9.

If you have a mouse, click and drag on the row numbers 8 and 9.

When you have selected rows 8 and 9, choose the Currency format with no decimal places. Notice that the raise percentage, which was in the middle of the range, is now displayed as *$0* since 0.1375 rounds to 0 when no decimal places are displayed. Don't worry, you haven't lost the number. Put the highlight on cell C9 and look in the formula bar; the formula, =AVG(C3:C6), is still there.

Format the Raise % column to Percent with one decimal place. Make sure you select the entire column first. Your formatted spreadsheet should now look like Figure 6.9.

ALIGNING COLUMN HEADINGS

In the default alignment, text lines up on the left side of the cell and numbers line up on the right side. However, if you have alphanumeric column headings (with letters or a combination of letters and numbers), they will not line up with the numbers below.

This problem has a simple solution—Works allows you to change the alignment of text and numbers. You can find the alignment options hiding in the Style dialog box; they are not on the main Format menu like they are in the word processor tool. The Style command lets you choose alignments (General, Left, Right, or Center) and styles (Bold, Underline, and Italic). The General alignment is the default—text on the left, numbers on the right. You can select one alignment and any combination of styles.

All the headings over columns of numbers in the employee-raise example need to be right-aligned.

1. Select the range B1:E1.
2. Choose Style on the Format menu; the dialog box is displayed.
3. Choose Right (use the mouse or ↓, or press R).
4. Choose OK.

The headings look much better when they are aligned with the numbers, don't they?

Next, center the percentages in column C.

1. Select all of column C by pressing Shift-F8 or by clicking on the column letter *C* with the mouse.
2. Choose Center alignment in the Style dialog box.

Your spreadsheet, with its aligned column headings and percentages, should look similar to Figure 6.10.

BOLDFACING AND ITALICIZING CELLS

The Style dialog box also contains options for Bold, Underline, and Italic. You will use the Underline option in the next section. Let's boldface all the column headings in the spreadsheet.

1. Select row 1.
2. Choose Style on the Format menu.
3. Select Bold (click next to it or press B).

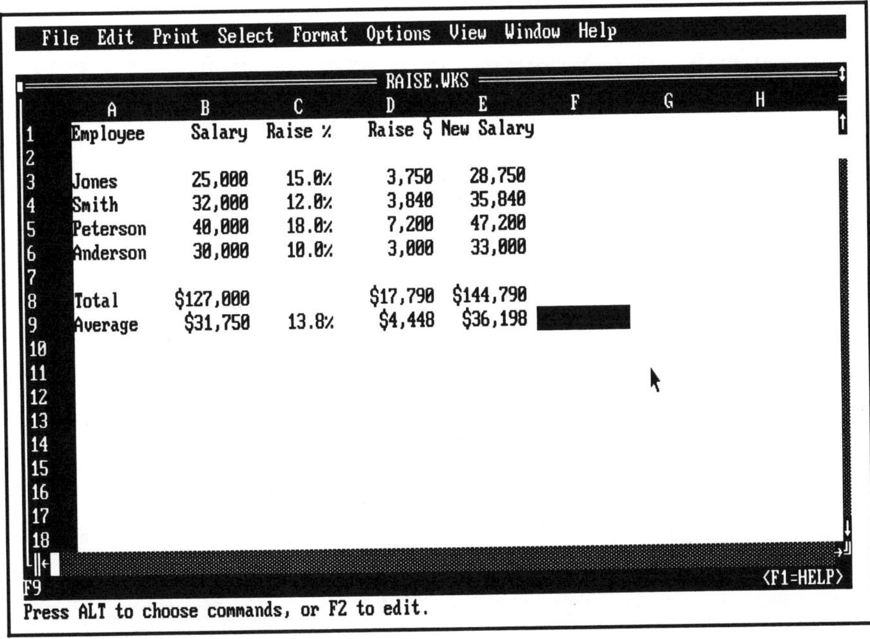

Figure 6.10: Right-aligned column headings and centered percentages

4. Choose OK. Move the highlight so that you can see the style more clearly.

Specify the Italic style for the text in column A.

1. Select the range A3:A9.
2. Choose Style on the Format menu.
3. Select Italic (click next to it, use the arrows, or press I).
4. Choose OK. Move the highlight so that you can see the style more clearly.

CREATING LINES

Lines (dashed or solid) make a spreadsheet easier to read because they separate and organize the different parts of the spreadsheet. You will use lines in your spreadsheets above the column totals and/or under the column headings. The Underline option in the Style dialog box provides one way of creating lines. You can also type dashes for single-dashed lines or equal signs for double-dashed lines. Let's look at both of these techniques.

1. Select the last row of numbers above the total: B6:E6.
2. Choose Style on the Format menu.
3. Select Underline.
4. Choose OK.
5. Move the highlight so that you can see the underlining as shown in Figure 6.11.

The underline extends from one edge of the cell to the other when the cells contain numbers. (With text, though, the underline covers only the characters.)

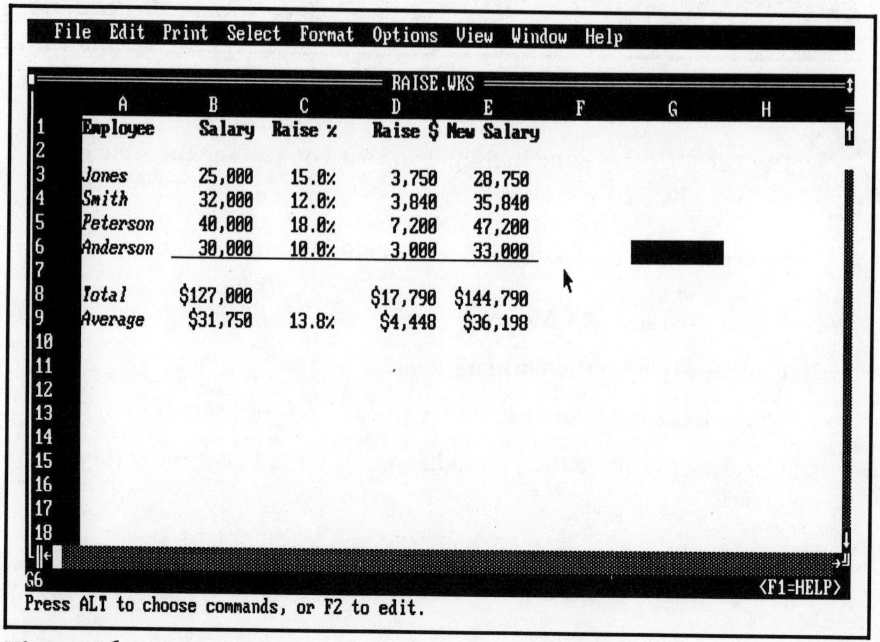

File Edit Print Select Format Options View Window Help

RAISE.WKS

	A	B	C	D	E	F	G	H
1	Employee	Salary	Raise %	Raise $	New Salary			
2								
3	Jones	25,000	15.0%	3,750	28,750			
4	Smith	32,000	12.0%	3,840	35,840			
5	Peterson	40,000	18.0%	7,200	47,200			
6	Anderson	30,000	10.0%	3,000	33,000			
7								
8	Total	$127,000		$17,790	$144,790			
9	Average	$31,750	13.8%	$4,448	$36,198			
10								
11								
12								
13								
14								
15								
16								
17								
18								

G6 <F1=HELP>
Press ALT to choose commands, or F2 to edit.

Figure 6.11: A solid line created with the Underline style

The bottom line of a spreadsheet often has double underlines. The only way you can create a double-dashed line is to type equal signs in one cell and then copy the cell across the width of the spreadsheet. Because the equal sign is what you use to start a formula, you have to precede the equal sign with a quotation mark, the text identifying symbol. As mentioned earlier, Works identifies your text entries by placing a quotation mark at the beginning of the cell contents. You do not see the quote mark in the cell—it appears in the formula bar when you place the highlight on the cell.

You type " = = = = = = = = = = = = under the first cell you wanted to be double-underlined. When you press Enter, you see the lines in the cell, but not the quotation mark. The quote mark only shows in the formula bar. You can then use the Fill Right command to copy the double lines across. If you forget to type the quotation mark, Works displays the following error message when you press Enter: "Missing operand." Choose OK to clear the message and then type the quotation mark.

One problem with the Underline style is that it doesn't span the complete column width when you underline text; it only underlines the characters in the cell. If you want a line that completely fills the cell, you need to enter dashes in the cell below. This technique is similar to the one described for creating double-dashed lines. Again, you need to precede the dashes with a quotation mark, and then use Fill Right to copy the line across.

This manual method for creating lines has one drawback: If you later expand the column width, the line does not completely fill the cell anymore; it falls short. You then have to add extra dashes or equal signs and recopy across. You can avoid this pitfall by entering more dashes than you currently need. In other words, plan ahead for future column-width expansion.

CANCELING STYLES AND ALIGNMENTS

To cancel a style or alignment you have previously assigned to a cell, place the highlight on the cell, and display the Style dialog box. The current alignment setting is marked, and the style has an X next to it. To turn off a format, simply select it again; the *X* will disappear.

To turn off a setting for a range of cells, the procedure is slightly different. As an example, let's turn off the Italic style for column A.

1. Select the range A3:A9.
2. Display the Style dialog box. This time no marks appear next to the alignment or style options because each cell in the selected range

could have a different setting. To turn off a setting, you must mark it and then unmark it.

3. To cancel the Italic style, choose Italic twice.
4. Choose OK and move the highlight so you can see that the style has been canceled.

SETTING COLUMN WIDTHS

The default column width is 10 characters, but you can change column widths for any particular column, a range of columns, or all columns. You need to widen column widths when the number or text doesn't fit in the cell. If a number is too large for the current column width, number signs (######) are displayed instead of the number. (Look at Figure 6.12 for an example of column widths that are too narrow.) As soon as you widen the columns, though, the actual numbers reappear. If text is longer than the column width, the text is automatically displayed in the next cell unless the next cell has something in it. If the next cell is not blank, the text is truncated (both on the screen and on the printout). Look at column A in Figure 6.12 for an example of truncated text.

Sometimes you may want to adjust column widths for purely aesthetic reasons. You may think the columns will look better if they have a little more white space between them. Or you may want to narrow a column that contains only a few characters per cell. Also, by setting the column width to 0, you can hide a column. The hidden column won't appear on the screen or on your printouts.

In the employee-raise spreadsheet, let's change all column widths at the same time.

1. Select the entire spreadsheet by doing one of the following:
    - Choose All on the Select menu.
    - Press Ctrl-Shift-F8.
    - Click on the row and column intersection.
2. Select Column Width on the Format menu.
3. Type 7.
4. Press Enter.

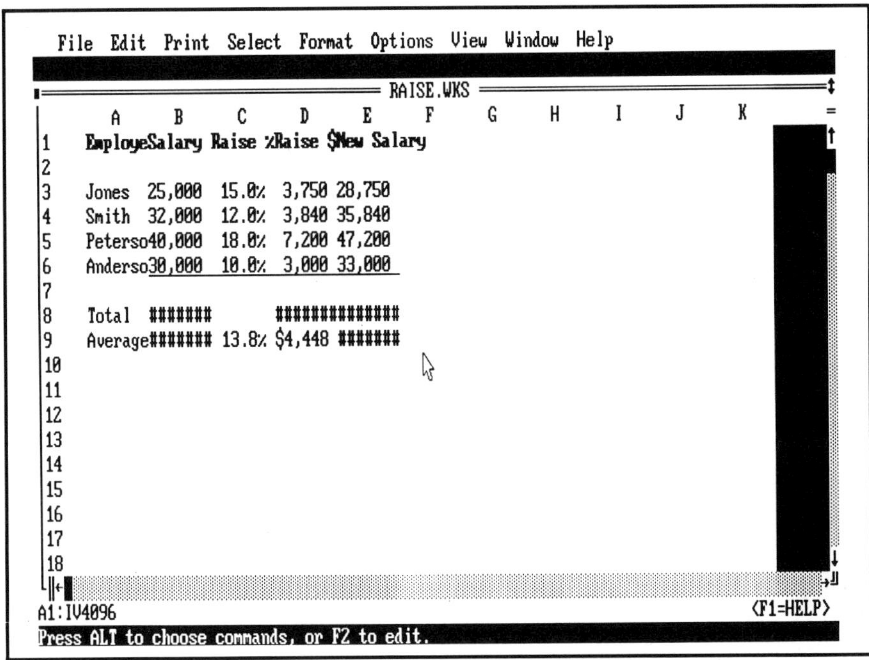

Figure 6.12: Columns that are not wide enough

Because the columns aren't wide enough to display the totals and averages in the Currency format, number signs are displayed in rows 8 and 9. Furthermore, some of the text in column A is truncated. Your spreadsheet is somewhat of a mess, as shown in Figure 6.12.

To correct these problems, all you need to do is widen the columns. Make sure all the columns are still selected, and using the techniques you just learned, change the column width to 12. This time, all the numbers and text are displayed, and you have extra space between columns.

The Employee and Raise % columns do not really need to be so wide, but because the columns are not adjacent, you must set each one separately.

1. Place the highlight anywhere in column A (you don't have to select the entire column).
2. Specify a column width of 10.
3. Place the highlight in column C.

4. Press Shift-F7, the Repeat command. This column adjusts to 10 as well.

Your spreadsheet is now complete and should look like Figure 6.13.

File Edit Print Select Format Options View Window Help

RAISE.WKS

	A	B	C	D	E	F	G
1	Employee	Salary	Raise %	Raise $	New Salary		
2							
3	Jones	25,000	15.0%	3,750	28,750		
4	Smith	32,000	12.0%	3,840	35,840		
5	Peterson	40,000	18.0%	7,200	47,200		
6	Anderson	30,000	10.0%	3,000	33,000		
7							
8	Total	$127,000		$17,790	$144,790		
9	Average	$31,750	13.8%	$4,448	$36,198		
10							
11							
12							
13							
14							
15							
16							
17							
18							

G7 <F1=HELP>

Press ALT to choose commands, or F2 to edit.

Figure 6.13: The final, formatted employee-raise spreadsheet

CHANGING THE DEFAULT FONT

As explained in Chapter 4, a *font* consists of a typeface (such as Courier, Helvetica, or Times Roman) and a type size (like 10- or 14-point). The larger the point size, the larger the character. But unlike the word processor tool, which allows you to choose different fonts for different parts of the document, the spreadsheet tool allows you only one font for the entire file. Because of this, you don't have to select a cell or a range before choosing the Font command on the Format menu.

The most common reason for changing the font in a spreadsheet is because you need a smaller point size so that you can print more on a page. If you have a Hewlett-Packard LaserJet printer, you can choose the Line

Printer font, which prints in 8-point. On a dot-matrix printer, such as the Epson FX-80, you can choose Pica 8-point.

Choose Font on the Format menu. A dialog box, similar to the one in Figure 6.14, is displayed. Your Fonts list may have different choices depending on the kind of printer you have. The Fonts list has its own scroll bar for use with the mouse. If you want to use the keyboard, you can use ↓ or PgDn to scroll the font list. (You can also press the first letter of the typeface name to move to the first font beginning with the letter.)

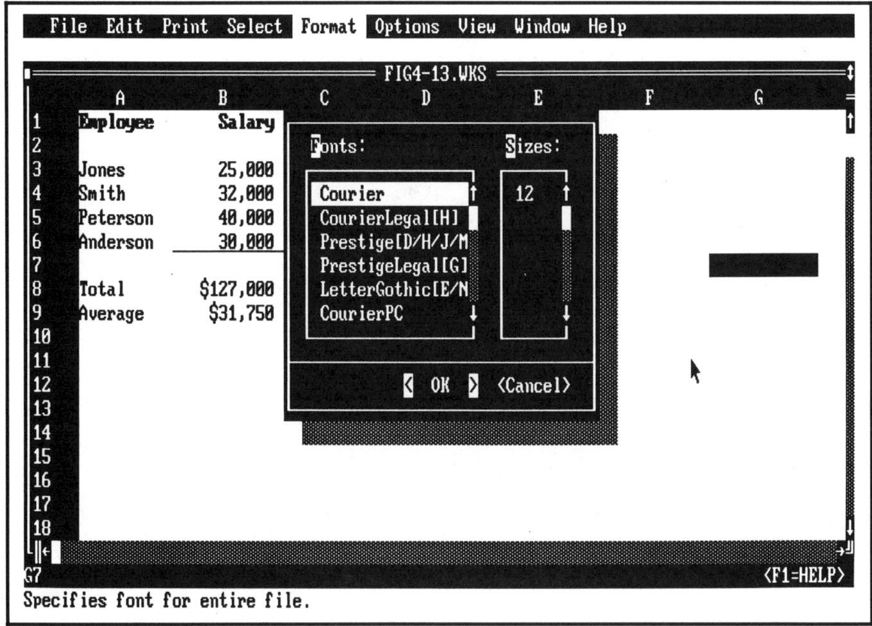

Figure 6.14: The Font dialog box for a Hewlett-Packard LaserJet printer

As you highlight different typefaces, different sizes appear on the Sizes list. Remember from Chapter 4 that the displayed sizes are the only point sizes you can choose for that typeface. Click on the desired size with the mouse, or if you are using the keyboard, press Alt-S to go to the Sizes list and then use ↓ to highlight the size.

You can experiment with different fonts and sizes for the employee-raise spreadsheet, but be sure to return it to a 12-point font before you continue. (Do not choose a proportionally spaced font for your spreadsheet. If you do, the columns will not line up when you print.)

PRINTING THE SPREADSHEET

Printing a spreadsheet is similar to printing a document: You use the Print command on the Print menu. The Print dialog box in the spreadsheet has an additional option: *Print row and column labels.* You would turn on this option to print column letters and row numbers. This option is helpful for rough drafts of your spreadsheet. By default the letters and numbers are not printed.

PREVIEWING ON THE SCREEN

It's useful to preview your spreadsheet on the screen to see if all the columns will fit on the printed page. If you see that they won't fit, you can make adjustments without wasting time printing.

1. Choose Preview on the Print menu.
2. Select the *Print row and column labels* option.
3. Choose Preview. Only four of the five columns are displayed on page 1 (see Figure 6.15).
4. Press PgDn to see that page 2 contains the last column.
5. Press Esc to go back to the spreadsheet.

What can you do to make all the columns fit on a page? You can try any of the following:

- Narrow some, or all, of the column widths.
- Select a different font with a smaller size.
- Reduce the right and left margins.
- Print in a landscape (horizontal) orientation.

You already know how to change the column widths and the default font. Let's look at the other two methods.

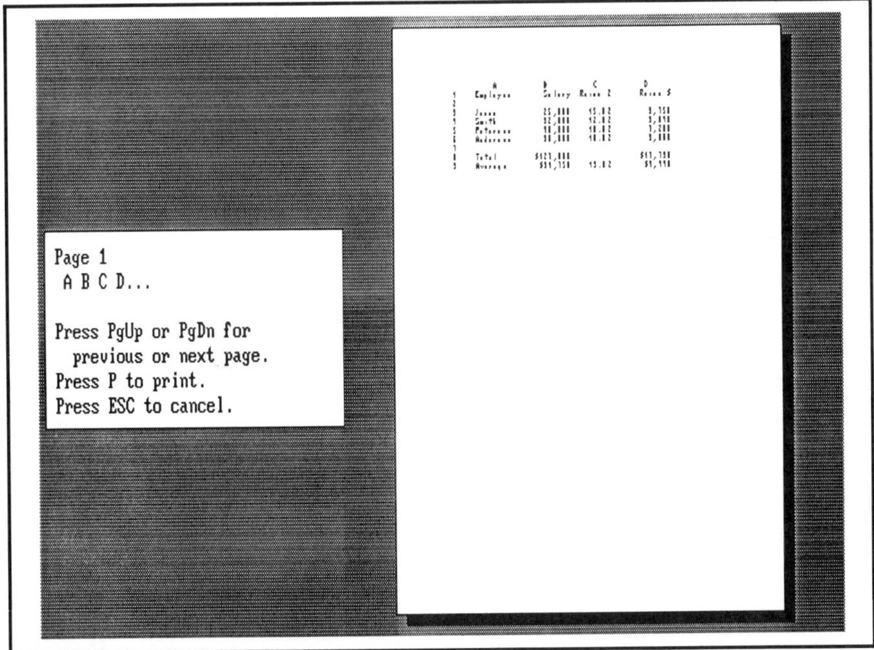

Figure 6.15: Print preview showing that the entire spreadsheet will not fit on one page

CHANGING THE MARGINS

To change the spreadsheet's margins, use the same command as you did in the word processor: *Page Setup & Margins* on the Print menu. The default margins are quite generous. The left margin is set at 1.3″ and the right margin at 1.2″. With a spreadsheet, you are usually trying to cram as many columns on the page as possible, so you want to reduce the left and right margins. To permanently change the default spreadsheet margins, see your documentation.

Let's see if we can fit all the columns on the page by reducing the margins.

1. Display the Page Setup & Margins dialog box.
2. Move the cursor next to Left margin and type **0.5″**. (You don't need to type the inch mark.)
3. Move the cursor next to Right margin and type **0.5″**.
4. Choose OK.

It's best to preview on the screen before actually printing.

1. Use the Preview command to preview the spreadsheet. This time all the columns fit on one page (see Figure 6.16).
2. If your printer is ready, press P to print. Otherwise, press Esc to return to the spreadsheet.

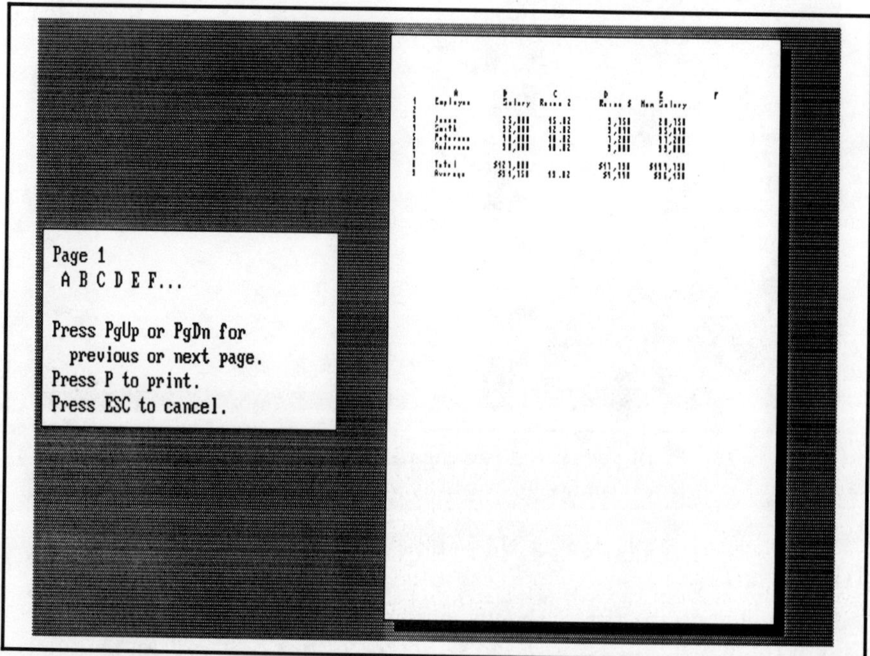

Figure 6.16: The previewed page with smaller margins

Use the Save command on the File menu to save your recent changes to disk. The file is saved with the same name, RAISE.

PRINTING THE PAGE HORIZONTALLY

In *landscape* orientation, the spreadsheet prints horizontally so you can fit more columns across the page. All laser printers can print in landscape mode, but most other types of printers cannot.

To print in landscape mode, you need to change two settings.

1. Select a landscape printer in the Printer Setup dialog box.
2. Change the page length and width in the Page Setup & Margins dialog box.

You *must* do both steps.

To see if you have a choice for a landscape printer, choose the Printer Setup command on the Print menu. Look at the list of printers on the left side of the dialog box. Figure 6.17 displays a printer list for three types of printers: Epson, Hewlett-Packard LaserJet, and TTY (Teletype—a generic printer name). Notice that there are two choices for HP: HPLASER1 and HPLASLAN. HPLASER1 is the printer for *portrait* (vertical) printing. HPLASLAN is the printer for *landscape* (horizontal) printing. If you do not have a choice for landscape printing and you know your printer can do it,

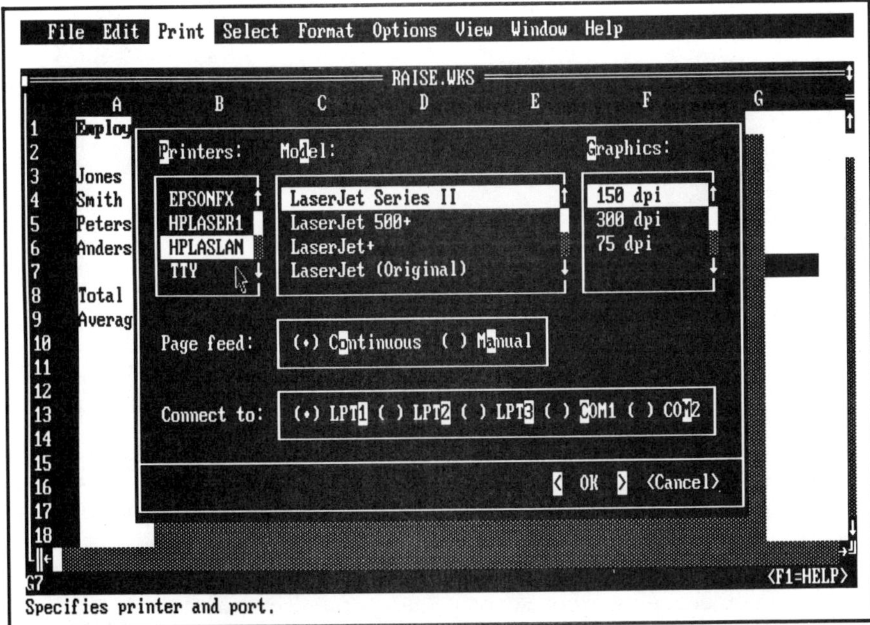

Figure 6.17: The Printer Setup dialog box

you have to run the Setup program to install Works for another printer. (See Appendix A for details.)

1. If you have a choice for a landscape printer, select it and choose OK.
2. Go into the Page Setup & Margins dialog box.
3. Reverse the *Page length* and *Page width* settings. Change the page length to 8.5 and the page width to 11.
4. Choose OK.
5. Preview the spreadsheet on the screen. It should look similar to Figure 6.18.

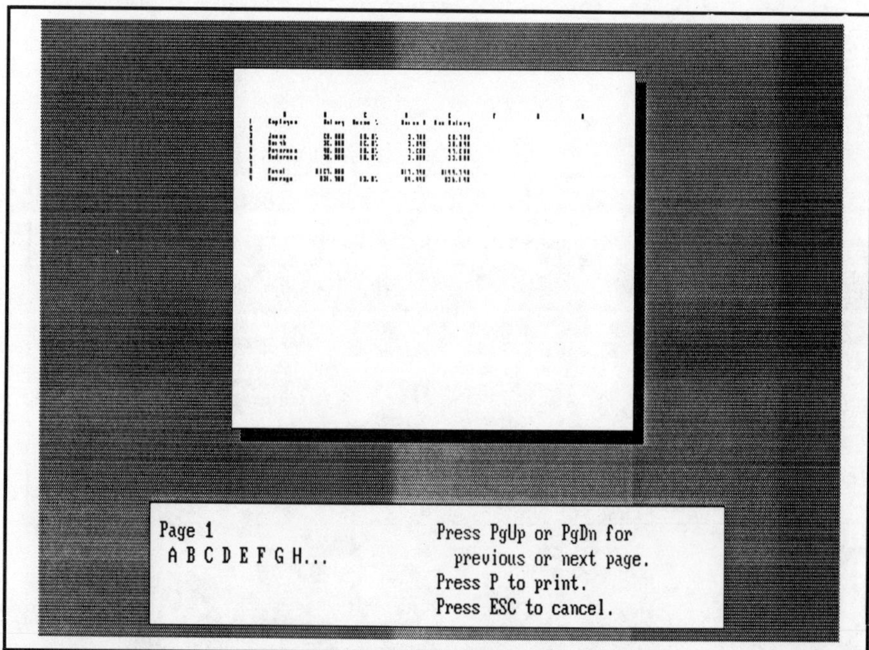

Figure 6.18: A preview of the spreadsheet printed in landscape mode

The printer you specify in Printer Setup is permanently saved with the program. If you change to a landscape printer for a spreadsheet, the next file you print—even a word processor document—prints in landscape mode. Remember to check Printer Setup before you print, or you could end up with surprising results. If you preview on the screen, you can identify the problem before accidentally printing a long word processor document in landscape mode.

If you are going to read Chapter 7 now, you can leave the RAISE spreadsheet on your screen. Otherwise, you can save and close the file. Do not delete it, though, because you will need it for Chapter 7.

SUMMARY

In this chapter you learned all the basics for building a spreadsheet: entering data, creating formulas, copying, formatting, and printing. At this point you should be able to create and format simple spreadsheets. Once you start building larger and more involved spreadsheets, you'll need to read the next chapter. In Chapter 7, you will discover how to modify an existing spreadsheet, how to sort data alphabetically and numerically, and how to work with large spreadsheets, and you will learn many more tips and shortcuts.

EXERCISES

In the following exercises you will build a practice spreadsheet (Figure 6.19) to compare 1989 and 1990 sales of a product. In the process of building it you will enter text and numbers, change column widths, create and copy formulas, and format the spreadsheet before you print it. While you are doing the exercises, refer to Figure 6.20, the final spreadsheet. If you get stuck, refer to the sections indicated inside parentheses.

1. Create a spreadsheet file and enter the data shown in Figure 6.19 (see "Entering Data," page 122). You will need to widen column A to 17 characters (see "Setting Column Widths," page 144).
2. Enter the following simple formulas (see "Creating Simple Formulas," page 126):
   - In cell D6, calculate the CHANGE between 1989 and 1990 (you will format the numbers later).

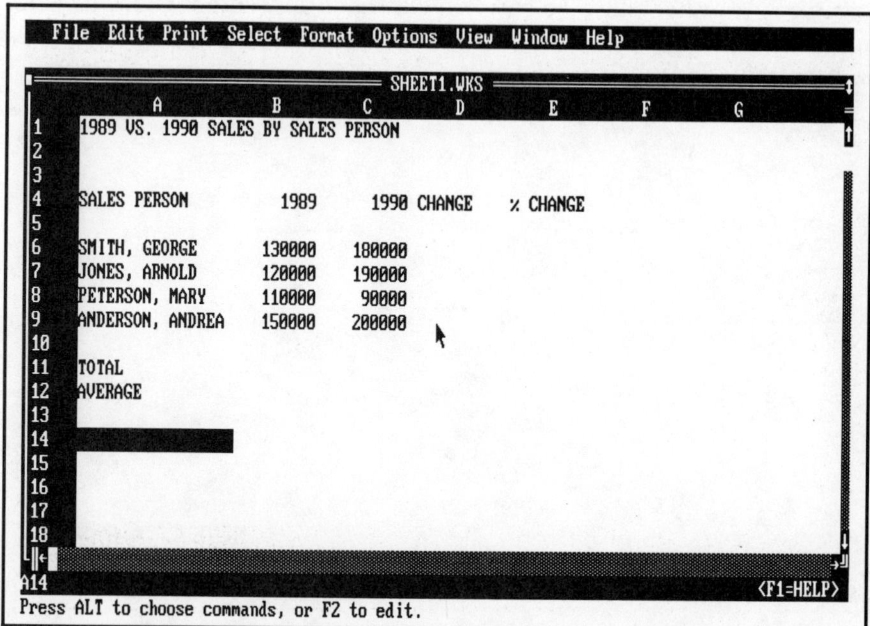

Figure 6.19: A practice spreadsheet

- In cell E6, calculate the % CHANGE (CHANGE divided by 1989 Sales).

3. Use the Fill Down command on the Edit menu to copy the formulas (see "Filling Across or Down," page 132).
4. Enter the following formulas (see "Using Built-in Functions," page 128):
    - In cell B11, sum the 1989 column.
    - In cell B12, average the 1989 column.
5. Use the Fill Right command to copy the formulas across (see "Filling Across or Down," page 132).
6. Change the alignment of the column headings (see "Aligning Column Headings," page 139).
    - Center the headings in cells B4 and C4.
    - Right-align the headings in cells D4 and E4.

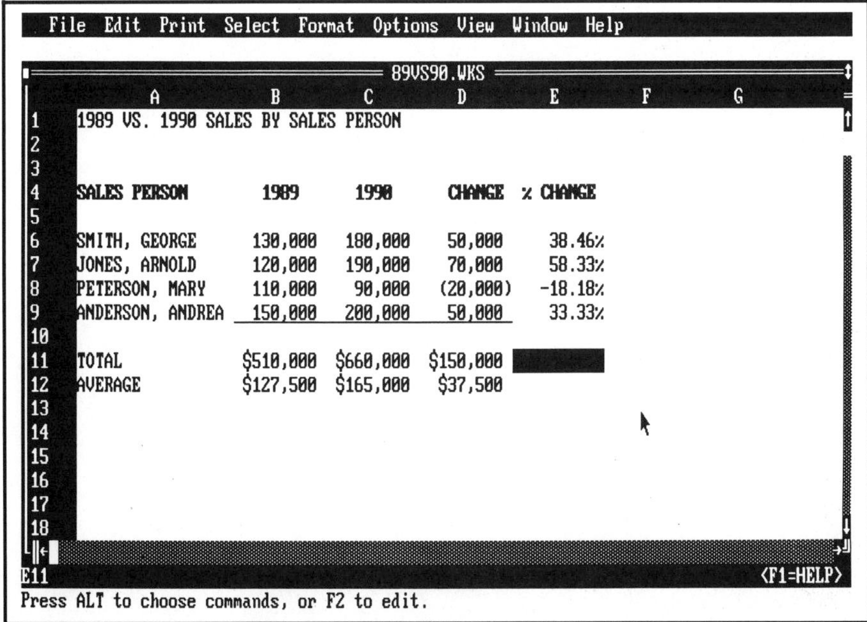

Figure 6.20: The final spreadsheet

7. Format the numbers (see "Formatting the Numbers," page 136).
   - The % CHANGE column should be Percent format with 2 decimal places.
   - The 1989, 1990, and CHANGE columns should be Comma format with no decimal places.
   - The TOTAL and AVERAGE rows should be Currency format with no decimal places.
8. Boldface the column headings (see "Boldfacing and Italicizing Cells," page 140) and underline the row of numbers above the totals (see "Creating Lines," page 141).
9. Save the spreadsheet under the name *89VS90* (see "Saving a Spreadsheet File," page 131).
10. Print the spreadsheet (see "Printing the Spreadsheet," page 148).
11. Close the file.

MODIFYING SPREADSHEETS

7

The spreadsheet tool has much more to offer than just what you saw in Chapter 6. As you will see in this chapter, you can modify an existing spreadsheet by editing, inserting, deleting, erasing, and moving. You will also learn the many features Works provides that are especially useful in a large spreadsheet: shortcuts for getting around quickly and printing selected pages or a range of a spreadsheet. In addition, you will learn how to sort data and how to copy a spreadsheet into a document.

MODIFYING A SPREADSHEET

One of the major advantages of using an electronic spreadsheet is that you can easily make changes to it. You can edit the contents of a cell, insert rows and columns, delete rows and columns, clear a cell or a range, and move cells from one location to another.

In this section, you will use the employee-raise spreadsheet created in Chapter 6. If necessary, use the Open Existing File command on the File menu to retrieve the spreadsheet called RAISE.WKS. Your screen should look similar to Figure 7.1.

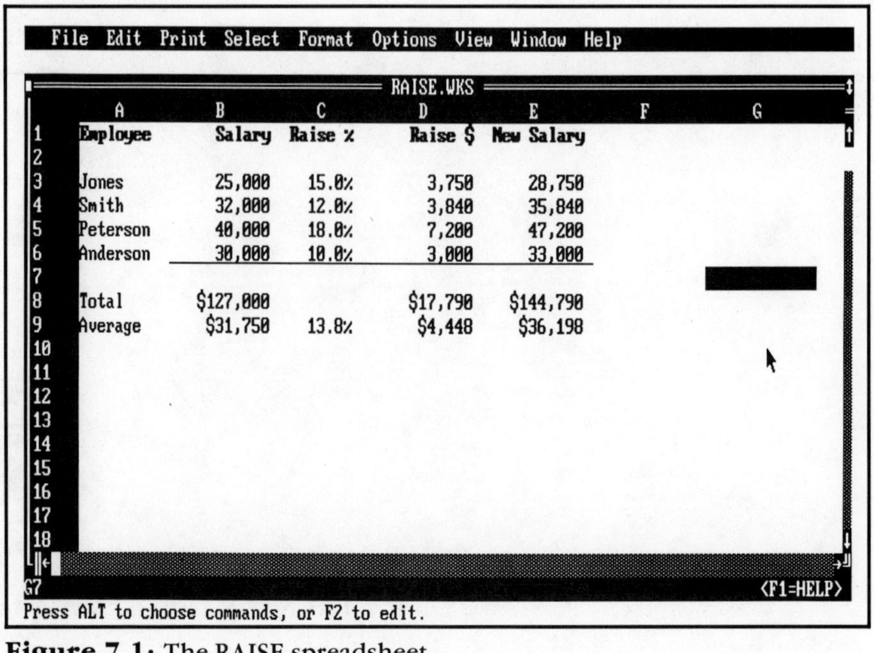

File Edit Print Select Format Options View Window Help

RAISE.WKS

	A	B	C	D	E	F	G
1	Employee	Salary	Raise %	Raise $	New Salary		
2							
3	Jones	25,000	15.0%	3,750	28,750		
4	Smith	32,000	12.0%	3,840	35,840		
5	Peterson	40,000	18.0%	7,200	47,200		
6	Anderson	30,000	10.0%	3,000	33,000		
7							
8	Total	$127,000		$17,790	$144,790		
9	Average	$31,750	13.8%	$4,448	$36,198		
10							
11							
12							
13							
14							
15							
16							
17							
18							

G7 <F1=HELP>

Press ALT to choose commands, or F2 to edit.

Figure 7.1: The RAISE spreadsheet

EDITING CELLS

You already know one way to change the contents of a cell: If you want something completely different in the cell, you can type right over what's there and, as soon as you press Enter, the cell's contents are replaced. However, if you want to make a slight modification to a cell, you can use the Edit function key, F2.

When you press F2, the contents of the cell are displayed in the formula bar, and the cursor appears at the end of the entry. (You will also see the word EDIT on the status line.) You can edit with any of the keys described in Table 7.1. Inserting text in the formula bar is similar to inserting text in the word processor: Position the cursor and start typing. The characters are automatically inserted to the left of the cursor.

Table 7.1: Cell-Editing Keys

EDITING ACTION	KEYSTROKE
Move left one character	←
Move right one character	→
Move to beginning of entry	Home
Move to end of entry	End
Select characters	Shift with arrow key
Delete to left	Backspace
Delete selection	Del

In the RAISE spreadsheet, edit cell C1 to read *% Raise* instead of *Raise %*.

1. Place the highlight on C1.
2. Press F2 for Edit.
3. Press the Backspace key to delete the % sign.
4. Press ← to move to the *R* in *Raise.*
5. Type % and press the spacebar.
6. Press Enter.

Repeat the above steps to change cell D1 to *$ Raise* instead of *Raise $*.

If you have a mouse, you have an alternative way to edit a cell. Instead of pressing F2, click the mouse pointer in the formula bar at the position where you want to start editing. Text is inserted automatically unless you make a selection before you start typing. For example, if the cell contained *Percent Raise,* you could click and drag across *Percent* and then type %. The word *Percent* would be replaced with %.

ERASING A RANGE

Chapter 6 already discussed how to clear a cell and a range. To refresh your memory, here are the general steps again.

To clear a cell:

- Place the highlight on the cell.
- Press Del or Backspace.
- Press Enter or move the highlight.

To clear a range:

- Select the range of cells.
- Choose Clear on the Edit menu.

Since the spreadsheet tool doesn't have an Undo command, be very careful when clearing cells.

Use the Clear command to erase the averages in row 9.

INSERTING ROWS AND COLUMNS

If you discover that you left out a row or column in your spreadsheet, you can insert one very easily using the Insert Row/Column command on the Edit menu. Works offers two ways to insert rows and columns:

- Select an entire row or column, and choose the Insert Row/Column command. A row is inserted *above* the selected row, or a column is inserted to the *left* of the selected column.
- Place the highlight anywhere in the row or column. (Don't select the entire row/column.) Choose the Insert Row/Column command, and then select whether you want to insert a row or a column.

Formulas automatically adjust when you insert rows and columns. If cell locations move after an insertion, Works changes the cell references in the formulas. For example, if you insert a row in the middle of a range that is summed, the sum range automatically expands.

To see how this works, insert a row between rows 4 and 5.

1. Place the highlight in row 5.
2. Select the row. (Press Ctrl-F8 or click on the row number in the window border.)
3. Choose Insert Row/Column on the Edit menu. Everything below the highlight is pushed down one row.
4. To make sure your formulas are still accurate, place the highlight on B9, the Total formula. Before you inserted the row, the formula was *=SUM(B3:B6).* But after the insertion, Works automatically changed the range to *B3:B7.*
5. Type the data shown in row 5 of Figure 7.2. Remember, when you type in the % Raise in cell C5, you must enter *0.14,* not *14.0,* because of the way the cell is formatted (otherwise, you'll get 1400%).

Notice that the numbers are formatted properly. This automatic formatting happens because you selected entire columns when you formatted the spreadsheet in Chapter 6. If you had selected individual ranges, you would have had to format new cells after you inserted rows. The formulas, though, do not automatically copy into the new row; you have to copy them yourself using the Fill Down command.

More often than not, though, you will want to insert a new row at the bottom of the range, not in the middle. Be careful when inserting rows at the bottom—these rows are outside the summed range and therefore are not included in the total. You have to edit the formula to include the new row or rows. If you forget to change the formula, your totals will not be accurate and it will look like you can't add!

Works does offer a way for you to get around this common problem. In your SUM range, include the blank cell underneath the last number in the column you want to add, for example, *=SUM(B3:B8).* Because cell B8 is blank, the total won't be affected. But if you insert rows at the bottom of the range, the formula range expands to include these new rows.

Now let's insert six rows at the top of the spreadsheet so that you can enter a spreadsheet title. To insert more than one row, you select the

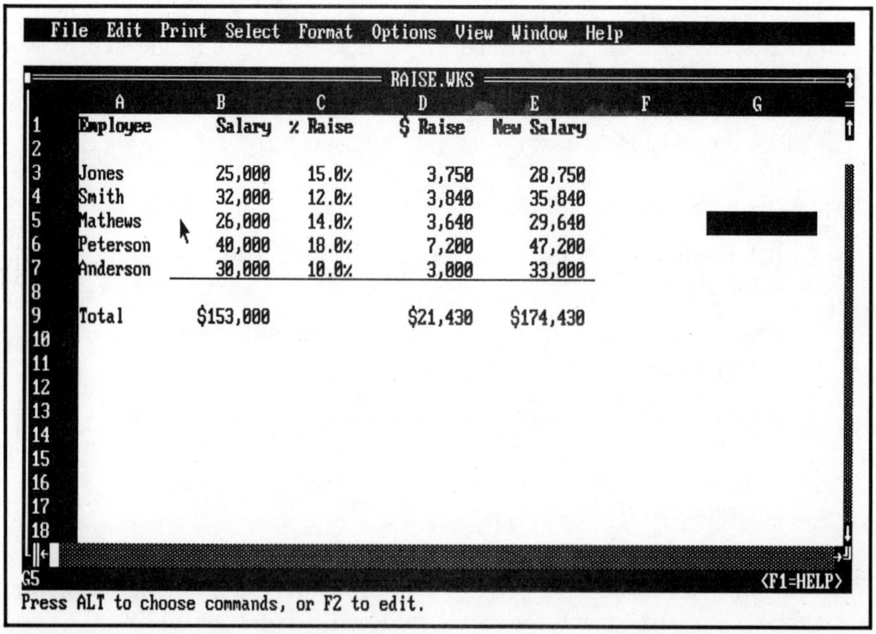

```
 File  Edit  Print  Select  Format  Options  View  Window  Help
                          RAISE.WKS
      A            B        C          D          E          F          G
1   Employee     Salary  % Raise    $ Raise   New Salary
2
3   Jones        25,000   15.0%      3,750     28,750
4   Smith        32,000   12.0%      3,840     35,840
5   Mathews      26,000   14.0%      3,640     29,640
6   Peterson     40,000   18.0%      7,200     47,200
7   Anderson     30,000   10.0%      3,000     33,000
8
9   Total      $153,000             $21,430   $174,430
10
11
12
13
14
15
16
17
18
G5                                                              <F1=HELP>
Press ALT to choose commands, or F2 to edit.
```

Figure 7.2: The spreadsheet with a row for a new employee, Mathews

number of rows you want to insert (one cell in each row is sufficient). Follow these steps:

1. Press Ctrl-Home to move to the beginning of the spreadsheet.
2. Select the range A1:A6.
3. Choose Insert Row/Column on the Edit menu.
4. Press R to choose Row and OK the box. The six blank rows are inserted.
5. Type the spreadsheet titles shown in Figure 7.3.

DELETING ROWS AND COLUMNS

Many of the rules you learned for inserting rows and columns apply to deleting them:

- You don't need to select the entire row/column (one cell is adequate). If you do select an entire row/column, Works automatically

File Edit Print Select Format Options View Window Help

RAISE.WKS

	A	B	C	D	E	F	G
1	Employee Raises						
2	Personnel Department						
3							
4							
5							
6							
7	**Employee**	**Salary**	**% Raise**	**$ Raise**	**New Salary**		
8							
9	Jones	25,000	15.0%	3,750	28,750		
10	Smith	32,000	12.0%	3,840	35,840		
11	Mathews	26,000	14.0%	3,640	29,640		
12	Peterson	40,000	18.0%	7,200	47,200		
13	Anderson	30,000	10.0%	3,000	33,000		
14							
15	Total	$153,000		$21,430	$174,430		
16							
17							
18							

G2 <F1=HELP>

Press ALT to choose commands, or F2 to edit.

Figure 7.3: The spreadsheet with titles at the top

knows what you want to delete and won't ask you whether you want to delete a row or a column.

- To delete more than one row or column, select a range that includes one cell in each row or column you want to delete.
- Formulas automatically adjust when you delete rows or columns.
- It's OK to delete a row or column in the *middle* of a summed range, but you will run into problems if you delete the beginning or end of a range.

This last rule merits further discussion. If you delete rows 10, 11, or 12 in your current version of the RAISE spreadsheet, the range in the SUM formula will contract without a problem. But if you delete row 9 or row 13, you are eliminating the beginning or end of the range. Works gets confused when this happens, and you will get ERR (error) messages; you then have to reenter your cell references. However, if you include the blank cells at the bottom and top of the column in your SUM range, you will not be faced with those dreaded ERR messages when you delete the first or last row of data.

Before you delete anything in the RAISE spreadsheet, save the file.

1. Place the highlight anywhere in Peterson's row.
2. Select the entire row. (Press Ctrl-F8 or click on the row number in the window border.)
3. Choose Delete Row/Column on the Edit menu. The entire row is deleted.
4. Delete two rows at once. Select the range A5:A6 and choose Delete Row/Column. Be sure to choose Row before you OK the box. Two of the blank rows you inserted earlier are now deleted.

MOVING CELLS

Just as you can move text in the word processor tool, you can move cells in the spreadsheet. Unlike the word processor's Move command, though, the spreadsheet's Move command will not work properly unless there is open space in the cell you are moving text to. If there is not open space, you can use the Insert Row/Column command to open up space before moving the cells. There is one exception to this rule: If you select an entire row or column, the cells automatically are inserted in the new location.

To position the spreadsheet titles in the center of the page, use the Move command, as explained below:

1. Select the range A1:A2.
2. Choose Move on the Edit menu (or press F3). The bottom of the screen displays the message "Select new location and press ENTER. Press ESC to cancel."
3. Move the highlight to C1, the middle column of the spreadsheet.
4. Press Enter.

Both cells move. Notice that you don't have to select C1:C2 as the new location; you only need to specify the first cell to move into.

Because *Employee Raises* is shorter than *Personnel Department,* the two titles are not centered with respect to each other. The only way to center them is to insert a couple of spaces before *Employee Raises.*

1. Place the highlight on C1.
2. Press F2 for Edit.
3. Move the cursor to the *E* in *Employee.*
4. Press the spacebar twice.
5. Press Enter to complete the entry.

The titles are now centered over the table as shown in Figure 7.4. Save and close this file.

File Edit Print Select Format Options View Window Help

RAISE.WKS

Employee Raises
Personnel Department

Employee	Salary	% Raise	$ Raise	New Salary
Jones	25,000	15.0%	3,750	28,750
Smith	32,000	12.0%	3,840	35,840
Mathews	26,000	14.0%	3,640	29,640
Anderson	30,000	10.0%	3,000	33,000
Total	$113,000		$14,230	$127,230

G1 <F1=HELP>
Press ALT to choose commands, or F2 to edit.

Figure 7.4: Centered titles in the RAISE spreadsheet

WORKING WITH LARGE SPREADSHEETS

When your spreadsheets start to grow, you are likely to encounter one or all of these problems:

- It takes a long time for you to get to the different parts of your spreadsheet.
- You can't find the section you want to go to.
- You must print the whole spreadsheet when you need only part of it.

Judged from this list, working with large spreadsheets doesn't sound like much fun. Works, however, provides solutions to each of these problems.

GETTING AROUND THE SPREADSHEET

A large spreadsheet can be cumbersome to work with unless you know a few tricks and techniques. This section lets you in on all the shortcuts for getting around a spreadsheet.

Moving the Highlight

Up to this point, you haven't used many shortcuts for moving the highlight. You've used the arrow keys to move the highlight a cell at a time and Ctrl-Home to go to the beginning of the file. Actually, you probably haven't felt a need for shortcuts because your spreadsheets have been quite small so far. Table 7.2 lists the keyboard shortcuts for moving the highlight.

A *block* is a range of cells that is bordered by blank cells. The block commands jump the cursor from one block to another, in the direction of the arrow you press. For example, if the highlight is on cell A5 (look at Figure 7.4) and you press Ctrl-↓, the highlight moves to the beginning of the next block, cell A7. Press Ctrl-↓ again and the highlight moves to the end of the block, cell A10. The third time you press Ctrl-↓ the highlight moves to the next block, cell A12. The block commands use blank cells as their "stop signs."

Table 7.2: Moving the Highlight in the Spreadsheet

MOVEMENT OF HIGHLIGHT	KEYSTROKE
Beginning of row	Home
End of row	End
Beginning of file	Ctrl-Home
End of file	Ctrl-End
Next screen	PgDn
Previous screen	PgUp
Screen right	Ctrl-PgDn
Screen left	Ctrl-PgUp
Next block down	Ctrl-↓
Previous block up	Ctrl-↑
Block to the right	Ctrl-→
Block to the left	Ctrl-←
Cell	F5

You can use any of the shortcuts for moving the highlight when you select cells. To select from the highlight to the end of the row, press F8 (Extend) and End. To select from the highlight to the bottom of the block, press F8 and Ctrl-↓. These keyboard shortcuts are big time-savers.

The Goto function key, F5 (or the Go To command on the Select menu), takes you to a specific cell. For example, if you know you want to move the highlight to cell AA1, you can press F5, type *AA1,* and press Enter to go there directly. But do not overuse the Goto key! If you are in B5 and want to go to B7, just use your arrow keys. Restrict your use of the Goto key to moving the highlight to a cell off the screen.

Scrolling with the Mouse

If you have a mouse, you can move quickly around a spreadsheet by taking advantage of the scroll bars. The vertical scroll bar on the right side of the window scrolls the screen up and down; the horizontal scroll bar at the bottom of the window scrolls the screen to the right and to the left. You are already acquainted with the vertical scroll bar in the word processor tool.

To practice scrolling, open the file BUDGET.WKS. This spreadsheet is included with Works and should be in your Works program directory

(C:\WORKS). The BUDGET spreadsheet should look like Figure 7.5. If you can't find this file, choose another file, preferably one that is large. As you can see in Table 7.3, the scroll arrow functions in the spreadsheet are similar to those in the word processor. You click on them to scroll a row or column at a time. Click below the scroll box to scroll forward through the spreadsheet.

The major difference in scrolling in the two tools is the position of the scroll box. In the word processor tool, the scroll box's location in the scroll bar indicates where you are in relation to the length of the current document (for example, if the scroll box is halfway down the scroll bar, you are in the middle of the document). In the spreadsheet tool, though, the vertical scroll bar indicates where you are in relation to the entire spreadsheet grid (256 columns by 4096 rows). For example, if the scroll box is in the middle of the scroll bar, you are currently working in the middle of the grid (at around row 2000).

To go to the first row of the spreadsheet when the scroll box is still at the top of the scroll bar, just click once on the scroll box. If the scroll box is not at the top of the scroll bar, slide the box upward by using the click-and-drag technique. You do the same thing to scroll to the first column of the spreadsheet, except you use the horizontal scroll bar.

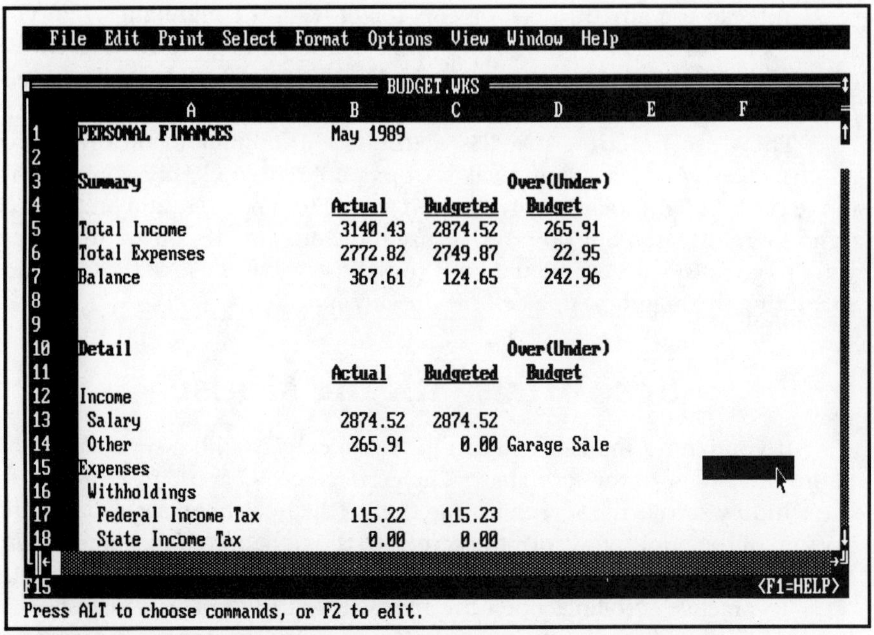

```
 File  Edit  Print  Select  Format  Options  View  Window  Help

                              BUDGET.WKS
            A                    B         C          D          E        F
1  PERSONAL FINANCES          May 1989
2
3  Summary                                         Over(Under)
4                              Actual   Budgeted   Budget
5  Total Income               3140.43   2874.52     265.91
6  Total Expenses             2772.82   2749.87      22.95
7  Balance                     367.61    124.65     242.96
8
9
10 Detail                                          Over(Under)
11                             Actual   Budgeted   Budget
12 Income
13  Salary                    2874.52   2874.52
14  Other                      265.91      0.00 Garage Sale
15 Expenses
16  Withholdings
17   Federal Income Tax        115.22    115.23
18   State Income Tax            0.00      0.00
F15                                                               <F1=HELP>
Press ALT to choose commands, or F2 to edit.
```

Figure 7.5: The BUDGET spreadsheet included with Works

Table 7.3: Mouse Scrolling Commands

Scroll down one row	Click on ↓ in vertical scroll bar
Scroll down continuously	Click on ↓ in vertical scroll bar, and hold the button down
Scroll up one row	Click on ↑ in vertical scroll bar
Scroll up continuously	Click on ↑ in vertical scroll bar, and hold the button down
Scroll right one column	Click on → in horizontal scroll bar
Scroll right continuously	Click on → in horizontal scroll bar, and hold the button down
Scroll left one column	Click on ← in horizontal scroll bar
Scroll left continuously	Click on ← in horizontal scroll bar, and hold the button down
Scroll down one screen	Click on vertical scroll bar, underneath the scroll box
Scroll right one screen	Click on horizontal scroll bar, to the right of the scroll box
Row 1	Click and drag scroll box to top of vertical scroll bar
Column A	Click and drag scroll box to left of horizontal scroll bar

Scrolling with the scroll bar does not actually move the highlight. If you use the scroll bar, you must still click with the mouse on a cell to move the highlight to the screen you scrolled to. If you use the arrow keys before clicking on a cell, the highlight moves back to where it was before you began scrolling.

Freezing Titles

When you move the highlight off the screen, either with the keyboard or the mouse, your row and column headings scroll off the screen. If you can't see your headings, it may be difficult to understand the data on your screen. The Freeze Titles command on the Options menu lets you lock your titles on the screen.

Before you select this option, your highlight should be positioned below and to the right of your headings. If you are using the BUDGET spreadsheet, for example, place the highlight on cell B5. The cells above and to the left are frozen on the screen after you choose Freeze Titles. Now when you move the highlight down or scroll with the mouse, the column headings do not scroll off the top of the screen. Figure 7.6 shows how rows 1–4 remain on the screen while you move to the bottom of the spreadsheet. If your spreadsheet were wide, the row headings in column A would remain on the screen when you scrolled to the right.

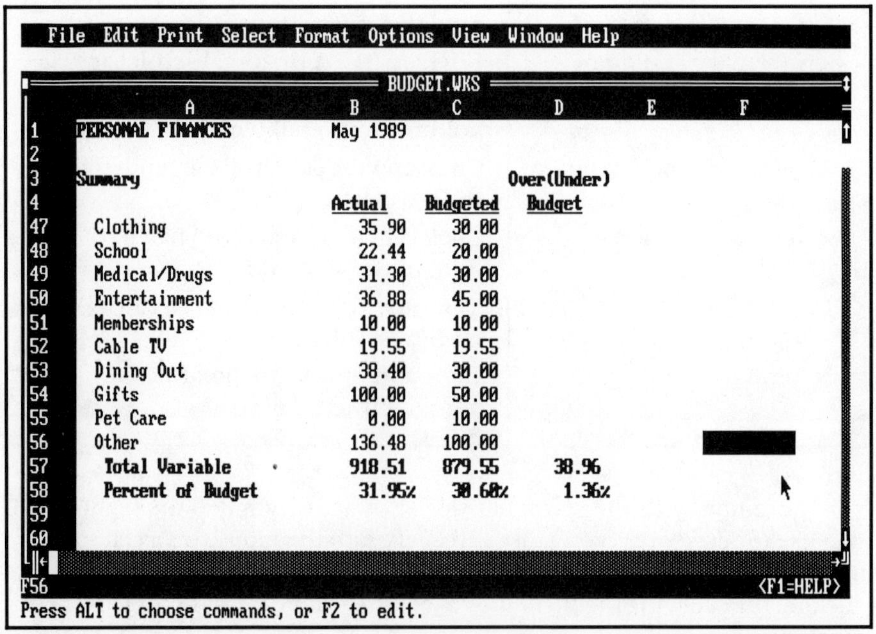

File Edit Print Select Format Options View Window Help

BUDGET.WKS

	A	B	C	D	E	F
1	PERSONAL FINANCES	May 1989				
2						
3	Summary			Over(Under)		
4		Actual	Budgeted	Budget		
47	Clothing	35.90	30.00			
48	School	22.44	20.00			
49	Medical/Drugs	31.30	30.00			
50	Entertainment	36.88	45.00			
51	Memberships	10.00	10.00			
52	Cable TV	19.55	19.55			
53	Dining Out	38.40	30.00			
54	Gifts	100.00	50.00			
55	Pet Care	0.00	10.00			
56	Other	136.48	100.00			
57	Total Variable	918.51	879.55	38.96		
58	Percent of Budget	31.95%	30.60%	1.36%		
59						
60						

F56 <F1=HELP>

Press ALT to choose commands, or F2 to edit.

Figure 7.6: The spreadsheet with frozen titles

When you freeze your titles, you cannot use your keyboard controls (such as the arrow keys) to move the highlight into the frozen area. If you need to edit in this area, you have several alternatives:

- Unfreeze your titles.
- Click in the frozen area.
- Use the Goto key, F5, to move to the cell.

The last two methods temporarily make a duplicate copy of the frozen rows and columns. Make your desired change, and then move the highlight off the screen and back again to remove the duplicate rows and columns. You must use your keyboard controls to move the highlight; scrolling with the mouse does not remove the duplicate ranges.

To unfreeze your headings, choose Unfreeze Titles on the Options menu.

Searching in the Spreadsheet

Locating a particular area or cell in a large spreadsheet can be tedious and frustrating. When you need to look up a number, correct a mistake, or update data, you have to scroll screen by screen, scanning for the item you want. An easier method is to use the Search feature to have Works do the scanning for you. The Search feature is similar to the one offered in the word processor.

In the BUDGET spreadsheet, update the amount budgeted for Cable TV. Use the Search command to take you right there:

1. Choose Search on the Select menu. (The highlight can be anywhere and you don't need to select any cells.)
2. Next to *Search for,* type **cable.** It doesn't matter whether you type uppercase or lowercase letters.
3. To speed up the search, you can tell Works to search by rows or by columns. In our example, the text is in the first spreadsheet column, so it is faster to search by columns. Choose Columns (Alt-C).
4. Choose OK in the dialog box. The highlight is brought directly to Cable TV. If your titles are still frozen, you temporarily see a duplicate copy of column A; if this bothers you, unfreeze the titles.
5. Now that you have located Cable TV, change the Actual and Budgeted amounts to *22.20.*

In the previous example, Works took you directly to the phrase you wanted to find. Sometimes, though, the spreadsheet contains multiple occurrences of the text you want to locate. In a case like this, you can press F7 to search for the next occurrence of the text. To see how this works, search for *auto* in the BUDGET spreadsheet and press F7 to see each occurrence.

The Search command searches for the series of characters you specify. Works doesn't care if you enter only part of the word; it locates each occurrence in which those characters appear. So if you search for *auto,* Works also finds *automobile* and *automatic.* By typing the complete word or phrase you are looking for, you can narrow the search so that Works doesn't stop at as many occurrences.

If you aren't sure how a word is entered in the spreadsheet, you can use *wildcards* to take the place of the characters you aren't sure of. Two wildcards are available: the asterisk and the question mark. The asterisk matches any group of characters; the question mark matches only a single character. For example, if you search for *ti?ing,* Works locates all words that have any single character between *ti* and *ing* (for example, *timing* or *tiling*). If you search for *ti***ing,* Works locates all words that start with *ti* and end with *ing* (for example, *timing, tilling, ticking,* and *tinkering*).

Assigning Range Names

Another way to get around a large spreadsheet is to assign names to its different sections, and then use the Goto key to go to them. Besides letting you quickly move to a section of your spreadsheet, range names can be used in formulas and to select ranges.

Going to a Range Name

The Goto key lets you go to a specific cell, assuming you know the exact cell coordinates of where you want to go. But how often does that happen? For example, it's unlikely you will be able to remember that the Withholdings section begins in A16 and that Finance Payments starts in A25. That's where range naming comes in handy. You don't even have to remember the exact name—you can choose it from a list.

In the BUDGET spreadsheet, assign the name *Withholdings* to the range of withholding expenses:

1. Select the range A16:E24.
2. Choose Range Name on the Edit menu. The dialog box shown in Figure 7.7 is displayed. Notice that *Withholdings* is automatically filled in next to *Name.* No, Works is not a mind reader; it picked up the name from the first cell in the range. (Also notice that this file already has some range names in the Names list. These names were created by whoever built the BUDGET spreadsheet. You will use

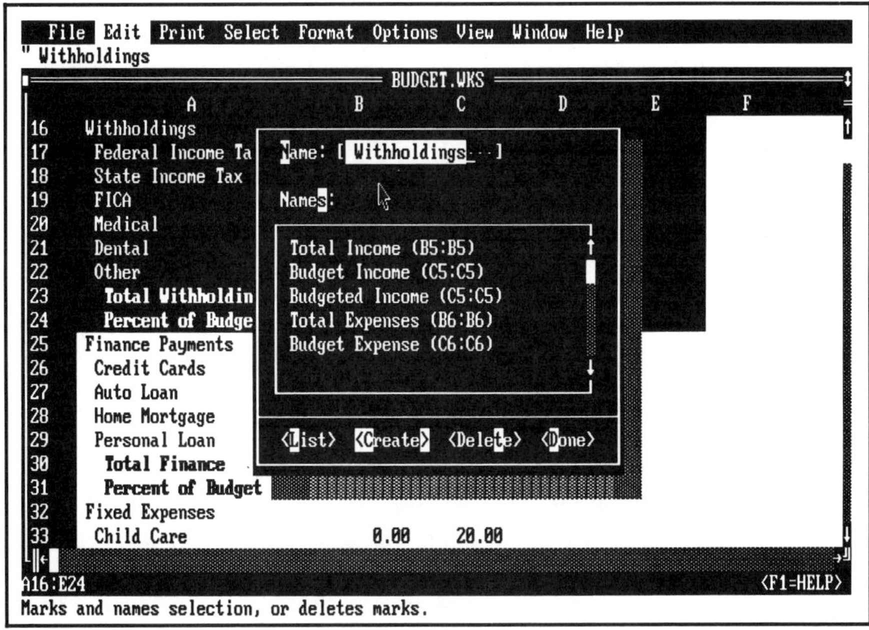

Figure 7.7: The Range Name dialog box

these names in the following section, "Using Range Names in Formulas.")

3. Press Enter to choose Create.

Repeat the above steps to assign names to each of the following expense sections:

Finance Payments	A25:D31
Fixed Expenses	A32:D41
Variable Expenses	A42:D58

If the range name exceeds 15 characters, Works truncates the name after the 15th character. In the range names you just created, only the first 15 characters of Finance Payments and Variable Expenses are used.

Let's go to one of your new range names.

1. Press the Goto key (F5) or select Go To on the Select menu.
2. Select *Withholdings* from the Names list. The entire Withholdings section is selected.
3. To remove the selection and position the highlight in the upper-left corner of the range, press Esc. Alternatively, you can leave the range selected and do something to the range (clear, move, copy, format, or print it).

Using Range Names in Formulas

As you may have noticed in the previous section, the BUDGET spreadsheet already has several range names in it. Figure 7.7 lists the spreadsheet's existing range names. Whoever created the BUDGET spreadsheet created these range names so that they could be used in formulas. Move the highlight over to cell D5 and look in the formula bar: *=Total Income–Budget Income.* Cell D6 also contains a formula with range names. As you can see, formulas are much easier to understand when you name the cells referenced in the formula.

Before you can use a range name in a formula, you have to assign the name using the Range Name command on the Edit menu.

PRINTING A LARGE SPREADSHEET

When your spreadsheet is longer than a single page, you should consider several additional print options. You need to control what prints on each page, and you may want to print page numbers or titles on every page.

Inserting Page Breaks

Works calculates how much of your spreadsheet can fit on a page according to your current margins, font, and column widths. When your spreadsheet is too large to fit on one page, Works inserts page breaks for you. If your spreadsheet is wide, Works determines how many columns can fit on the first page and prints the remaining columns on subsequent pages. You can then tape the pages together. If your spreadsheet is longer than one page, Works calculates how many rows can fit (54 rows using the default margins in portrait orientation; 39 rows in landscape) and prints the remaining rows on the next page(s). If you turn on the ***Print row and column labels*** option, one less line can fit on each page.

Unlike in the word processor tool, automatic page breaks are not displayed on the screen. You have to either print or preview the spreadsheet to see the page breaks.

These automatic page breaks sometimes end up where you don't want them to be, such as in the middle of a section that should not be split over two pages. Just like in the word processor tool, you can insert your own page breaks. However, in the spreadsheet tool, you can control page breaks both horizontally and vertically. Thus, you can determine which rows and which columns print on each page. If your spreadsheet is wide, you can set a vertical page break to control the number of columns on each page. For example, you might want to print the data for January–June on one page and insert a column page break so that the July–December data print on the next page. If your spreadsheet is long, you can insert a horizontal page break where you want the next page to begin.

To insert a vertical page break, follow these general steps:

- Place the highlight on what you want to be the first column on the next page (Column H in Figure 7.8).
- Choose Insert Page Break on the Print menu.
- Select Column. A page break mark appears next to the column letter as shown in column H of Figure 7.8.

To insert a horizontal page break, follow these general steps:

- Place the highlight on the row you want to be at the top of the next page.
- Choose Insert Page Break on the Print menu.
- Select Row. A page break symbol, similar to the one in the word processor tool, is displayed to the right of the row number.

If you place the page break in the wrong place or later need to change the page break location after revising the spreadsheet, you can remove the existing page break and insert a new one. To remove a page break, place the highlight in the row or column you want to remove the break from, and choose Delete Page Break on the Print menu. Use the Preview command to double-check your page breaks before printing.

File Edit Print Select Format Options View Window Help

COLBREAK.WKS

	A	B	C	D	E	F	G	» H
1	Part #	Jan	Feb	Mar	Apr	May	Jun	Jul
2								
3	G-345	2,012	2,213	2,435	2,678	2,946	3,240	3,564
4	A-450	2,269	2,496	2,745	3,020	3,322	3,654	4,020
5	B-123	2,526	2,779	3,056	3,362	3,698	4,068	4,475
6	B-098	2,783	3,061	3,367	3,704	4,075	4,482	4,930
7	C-199	3,040	3,344	3,678	4,046	4,451	4,896	5,386
8	D-564	3,297	3,627	3,989	4,388	4,827	5,310	5,841
9								
10								
11								
12								
13								
14								
15								
16								
17								
18								

H10 <F1=HELP>

Press ALT to choose commands, or F2 to edit.

Figure 7.8: A page break inserted at column H

Setting the Print Area

As you saw in Chapter 6, Works automatically prints the entire spreadsheet. But what if you want to print only part of the spreadsheet? One way is to specify which pages you want to print. Printing selected pages of a spreadsheet is identical to printing selected pages of a document.

To print specific pages, you need to choose two options in the Print dialog box. To display the Print dialog box, choose Print on the Print menu. Turn on the *Print specific pages* option (Alt-S). You should see an *X* next to the option. Then choose *Pages* (Alt-G) and enter the page numbers.

To specify a range of pages, you can separate the numbers with either a colon or a hyphen (for example, *1-3* or *1:3*). You can specify multiple pages or ranges by typing a comma between each one (for example, *1-3,6*).

Works remembers the specified page range the next time you print, so be sure to check the Print dialog box. If you want to go back to printing the entire spreadsheet, choose *Print specific pages* to turn off the option (the X will disappear). You do not need to delete the numbers next to *Pages*.

Another way to print part of a spreadsheet is to select the range of cells you want to print, and then choose the Set Print Area command on the Print menu. Then when you print, only the selected range prints. To go back to printing the whole file, select the entire spreadsheet (for example, choose All on the Select menu), and choose Set Print Area again.

Don't forget about your shortcuts for selecting entire rows and columns (see Table 6.1 in Chapter 6). With the mouse, you can click and drag through row numbers or column letters. With the keyboard, you can select one row or column, press F8 to extend the selection, and then use the arrow keys to select other consecutive rows or columns.

Headers and Footers

Headers and footers—text that prints at the top or bottom of a page—are available in every Works tool, including the spreadsheet. You do not actually see the headers and footers on your screen; you only see them when you print or preview the pages.

Headers and footers can contain page numbers, the file name, the date, and the time. They can also hold text, such as a title or a revision number. I suggest printing the file name and the date at the top or bottom of all your spreadsheets. That way, if you find a printed spreadsheet lying around your office, you'll know what file it came from and how recently it was printed. You won't have to play any guessing games.

The header and footer codes you learned in the word processor tool apply to every tool. Table 7.4 summarizes these codes for you again. To print the file name in the left margin and the date in the right margin, create this header: *&L&F&R&D.* To print a page number centered at the bottom of the page, create this footer: *&C&P.*

Table 7.4: Header and Footer Codes

&L	Align with left margin
&R	Align with right margin
&C	Center between left and right margins
&P	Insert page number
&F	Insert file name
&D	Insert current date
&T	Insert current time

SORTING THE SPREADSHEET

The Sort Rows command on the Select menu arranges your spreadsheet table in alphabetical, numerical, or chronological order. You can sort any column in the table, in either ascending or descending order. Choosing ascending order is more common: It sorts text from A to Z, numbers from lowest to highest, and dates from earliest to latest. Occasionally you might want the highest number or the most recent date at the top of the list. If you do, you want to sort in descending order.

Before you issue the Sort Rows command, you must select the sort range. The sort range consists of all the rows to be sorted. Make sure you do not have any data to the right of the spreadsheet range you are sorting; *everything* on the rows in the sort range is sorted.

Do not include blank rows or column headings. Blank rows are moved to the bottom of the list, and the column headings are sorted within the list. It doesn't matter how many columns you select since the entire row is sorted. It's a good idea, though, to select only the column you want to sort because Works automatically identifies it as your sort column.

Create the spreadsheet shown in Figure 7.9, and save the file with the name SALESJAN. Follow these steps to sort the last-name column:

1. Select the range A5:A11.
2. Choose Sort Rows on the Select menu. The dialog box displays an *A* next to *1st Column.* Works knew you wanted to sort by column A because your sort range was in column A. Also notice that ascending order is the default.
3. Choose OK to accept the dialog box settings. The last names are now sorted alphabetically.

Notice that two people have the last name Smith. When you have duplicate entries in your first sort column, you should specify additional sort columns. As the dialog box indicates, you can sort up to three columns at once. In this example, you need to indicate First Name as the second sort column.

1. With the same sort range selected, display the Sort Rows dialog box. Column A should still be indicated next to *1st column.*
2. Next to *2nd Column,* type **B**.

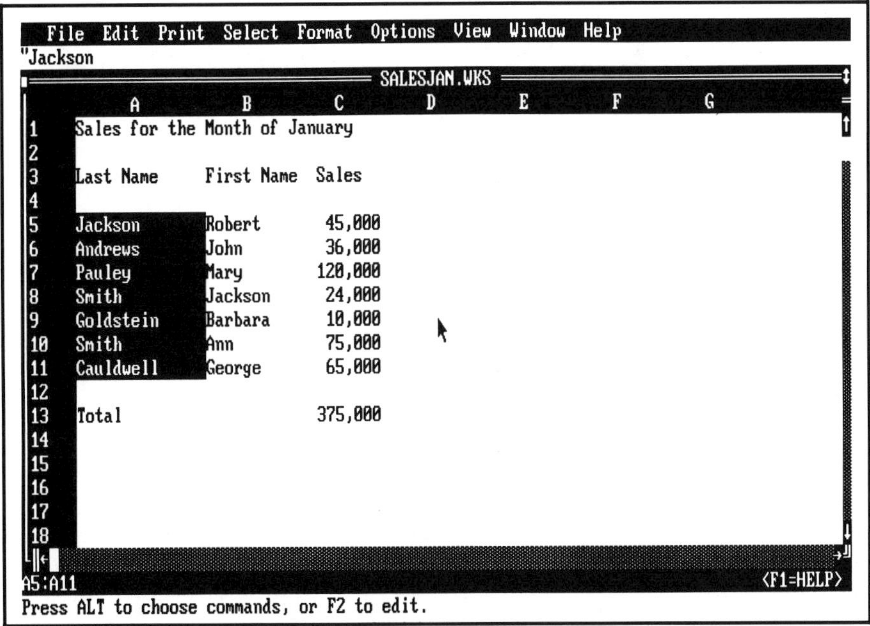

Figure 7.9: The sort range for sorting by last name

3. Press Enter. The last names are sorted, and when two people have the same last name, the first names are sorted.

USING COPY COMMANDS

In Chapter 6, you learned several copying commands: Fill Right to copy across a row, Fill Down to copy down a column, Copy to duplicate a range in another location in the document, and Ctrl-' to copy the cell above the highlight. In this section, you take a look at different ways to use the copy commands. In particular, you learn how to copy a formula without changing a cell reference, how to copy a spreadsheet into a document, and how to consolidate data from different spreadsheet files.

USING ABSOLUTE REFERENCES IN FORMULAS

As you saw in the last chapter, Works automatically adjusts the cell references relative to the location at which you are copying the formula. For instance, when you copied the formula *=SUM(B3:B6)* to column C, the formula became *=SUM(C3:C6)*. Sometimes, though, you don't want a cell reference to change when you copy; you want it to remain constant. To prevent a cell reference from changing when you copy, you need to turn it into an ***absolute reference.***

Figure 7.10 displays an example of a situation where you would want to use an absolute reference. The *% of Total* formula in column D divides each person's sales by the total sales. The total sales in cell C13 should be made absolute because you want the formula to always be divided by C13—you do not want C13 to change. Look in the formula bar of Figure 7.10. The formula in D5 is *=C5/$C$13*. The dollar signs do not have anything to do with currency; they are the symbols that make the cell absolute. Essentially,

File Edit Print Select Format Options View Window Help

=C5/$C$13

SALESJAN.WKS

	A	B	C	D	E	F	G
1	Sales for the Month of January						
2							
3	Last Name	First Name	Sales	% of Total			
4							
5	Andrews	John	36,000	10%			
6	Cauldwell	George	65,000	17%			
7	Goldstein	Barbara	10,000	3%			
8	Jackson	Robert	45,000	12%			
9	Pauley	Mary	120,000	32%			
10	Smith	Ann	75,000	20%			
11	Smith	Jackson	24,000	6%			
12							
13	Total		375,000				
14							
15							
16							
17							
18							

D5 <F1=HELP>

Press ALT to choose commands, or F2 to edit.

Figure 7.10: Using an absolute reference

the first dollar sign says, "Don't change the column," and the second dollar sign says, "Don't change the row" when the formula is copied.

The procedure for making a reference absolute differs depending on whether you enter the formula with the typing or selecting method. If you type the formula, you must type in the dollar signs yourself. If you select the cell references by highlighting them as you build the formula, you can press the Absolute key, F4. For example, to enter the formula = *C5/$C$13* in cell D5, you follow these steps:

1. Type = to begin the formula.
2. Select cell C5.
3. Type / to divide.
4. Select cell C13 and press F4. The dollar signs are automatically inserted in front of the column letter and the row number.
5. Press Enter.
6. Format to Percent with no decimal places.
7. Select the range D5:D11.
8. Choose Fill Down on the Edit menu. Each individual's sales is divided by the total sales in cell C13.

In some cases, you may want partial absolute references. For example, you may want the row number to change but the column letter to remain constant when the formula is copied. In this case, you only need one dollar sign: in front of the column letter (like *$B2*). To keep only the row constant, the dollar sign should be in front of the row number (like *B$2*). The first time you press F4 the reference changes from relative to absolute. The second time you press F4 the reference changes to row-only absolute, the third time to column-only absolute, and finally it switches back to relative.

Creating an absolute reference requires you to think ahead. While you are building the formula, you need to think about whether you need any absolute references when you copy the formula. Frequently, though, you do not think this way. You enter the formula, copy it, and then discover something is awry. If you copy the formula in Figure 7.10 without using an absolute reference, you get error messages because the formula tries to divide by blank cells (that is, by zero). Sometimes you don't get error messages but your results are inaccurate. If you discover that you need an absolute reference *after* you have entered and copied the formula, you must edit the formula, type in the dollar signs in front of the column letter and row number, and recopy the formula.

COPYING A SPREADSHEET INTO A DOCUMENT

One of the major advantages of using an integrated program like Works is being able to share data between the different tools. For example, you may want to include a spreadsheet table in a report you typed in the word processor. Exchanging data between tools couldn't be easier. You just open the two files and use the Copy command. Here are the general steps:

- Open the word processor document.
- Open the spreadsheet file.
- Select the cells to be copied.
- Choose Copy on the Edit menu (or press Shift-F3).
- Press Ctrl-F6 to move to the other window. (Or, if you haven't yet opened the target file after you've begun copying, you can open the file or even create a new file in the middle of the Copy command.)
- Place the cursor where the table should be copied.
- Press Enter.

Let's copy your SALESJAN spreadsheet into the memo shown in Figure 7.11. You can leave the spreadsheet open because you are going to be copying it into another file. Create a new word processor file and type the memo in Figure 7.11. Follow these steps to copy the spreadsheet:

1. Press Ctrl-F6 to move to the SALESJAN window.
2. Select the range A3:D13.
3. Choose Copy on the Edit menu or press Shift-F3.
4. Press Ctrl-F6 to move to the memo window.

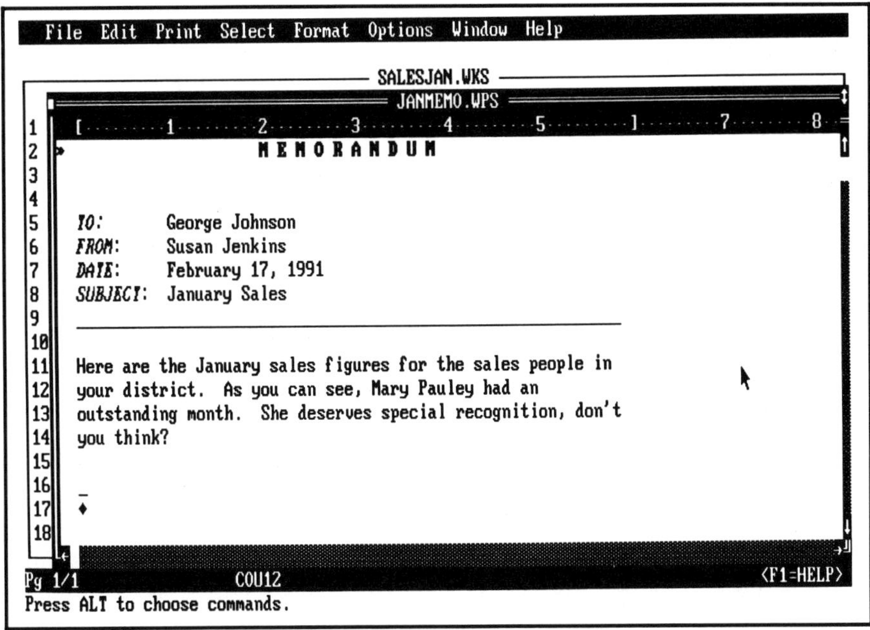

Figure 7.11: A memo

5. Place the cursor at the end of the memo.
6. Press Enter and the table is copied into the memo (see Figure 7.12).

Works even sets tab stops for each column. If you look at the ruler in Figure 7.12, you can see the tabs (*L* for Left and *D* for Decimal tabs). These tabs allow you to easily type additional lines in the table using the word processor tool.

After you have successfully copied the table, you can go to the spreadsheet window by pressing the Next Window command, Ctrl-F6, and then close the file.

Turn on the option Show All Characters (if it's not already on), and notice that there are paragraph marks at the end of each line in the table. As you learned in Chapter 4, a table should have new-line marks (a down-arrow symbol) at the line endings. With new-line marks, the entire table can be formatted as a single paragraph without your having to select each line. This

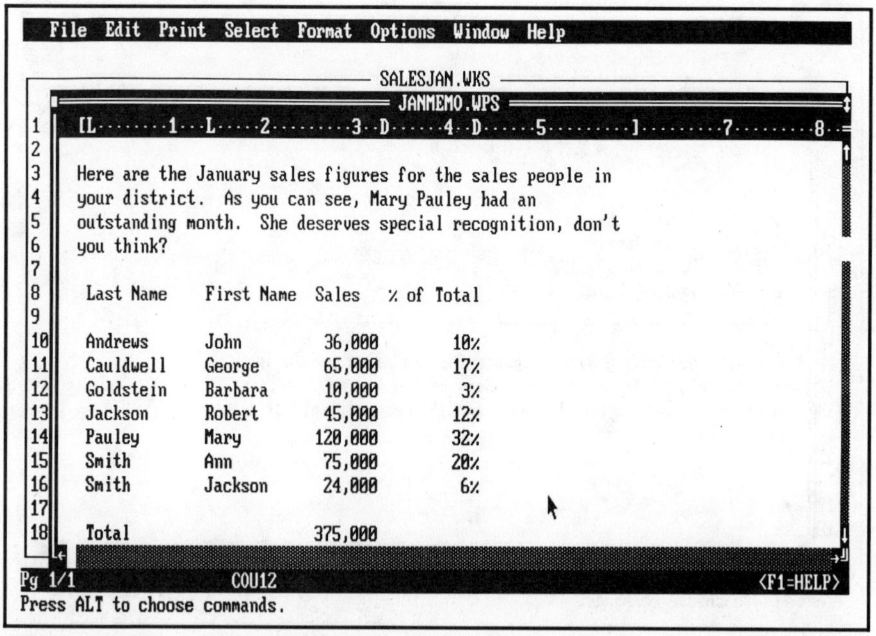

```
 File  Edit  Print  Select  Format  Options  Window  Help
                          SALESJAN.WKS
                          JANMEMO.WPS
1   [L·······1···L·····2·········3··D······4··D······5·········]·········7·········8··
2
3   Here are the January sales figures for the sales people in
4   your district.  As you can see, Mary Pauley had an
5   outstanding month.  She deserves special recognition, don't
6   you think?
7
8    Last Name     First Name  Sales    % of Total
9
10   Andrews       John          36,000        10%
11   Cauldwell     George        65,000        17%
12   Goldstein     Barbara       10,000         3%
13   Jackson       Robert        45,000        12%
14   Pauley        Mary         120,000        32%
15   Smith         Ann           75,000        20%
16   Smith         Jackson       24,000         6%
17
18   Total                      375,000
Pg 1/1              COU12                                          <F1=HELP>
Press ALT to choose commands.
```

Figure 7.12: A spreadsheet copied into a document

saves time when you want to format the table (change tab stops, add a border, create an indent, etc.). Therefore, after copying a spreadsheet into a document, substitute new-line marks (press Shift-Enter) for the paragraph marks. Doing this saves you time in the long run.

You can now save the memo with the name JANMEMO and close the file.

You can also go the other way and copy word-processed tables into a spreadsheet. After typing a table in a document, you may realize later it should be a spreadsheet file. You can follow the same steps listed above, except you copy from the document into the spreadsheet. After copying the table, you usually have to adjust the column widths.

A word-processed table correctly copies into a spreadsheet as long as you used tab stops to align the columns. Works uses the tabs to figure out what to put in each spreadsheet column. If you entered spaces instead of tabs, the data are copied into a single spreadsheet column, not into separate columns.

CONSOLIDATING SPREADSHEET FILES

Using the Copy Special command is a powerful way to copy because it performs three operations at once: it copies values to another location or file (just like Copy), it converts formulas to values, and it adds or subtracts the copied values to the values already in the target location. The Copy Special command is ideal for combining data from different spreadsheet files.

For example, let's say you enter each month's sales data in separate spreadsheet files and you want a report that summarizes the quarterly sales for each salesperson. You could use the Copy command to copy the values side by side and then create formulas to give you your quarterly totals. (Figure 7.13 displays an example of this method.) But you don't really want the monthly sales in the summary—you just need the quarterly totals. With the Copy Special command, you can achieve this result directly; you can copy and add at the same time.

File Edit Print Select Format Options View Window Help

SALESQ1.WKS

1st Quarter Sales

Last Name	First Name	Jan	Feb	Mar	Total
Andrews	John	36,000	39,000	45,000	120,000
Cauldwell	George	65,000	45,000	52,000	162,000
Goldstein	Barbara	10,000	15,000	20,000	45,000
Jackson	Robert	45,000	52,000	56,000	153,000
Pauley	Mary	120,000	140,000	130,000	390,000
Smith	Ann	75,000	65,000	67,000	207,000
Smith	Jackson	24,000	23,000	29,000	76,000
Total		375,000	379,000	399,000	1,153,000

G14 <F1=HELP>

Press ALT to choose commands, or F2 to edit.

Figure 7.13: Consolidating data with the Copy command

In this example, you use three spreadsheet files:

SALESJAN
SALESFEB
SALESMAR

SALESJAN is the file you have been working with in this chapter. Since the other two files are identical to SALESJAN except for the data in column C, you don't need to create each file from scratch. You can enter the data in SALESJAN and save the file with a new name. Follow these steps:

1. With SALESJAN on your screen, enter the February data in column C. (Refer to Figure 7.13 for the February data.)
2. Change cell A1 to *Sales for the Month of February.*
3. Use Save As to save the file with the name SALESFEB.
4. Repeat steps 1–3 for March, and create a file called SALESMAR.

Now do the following:

1. Open all three files, and display SALESJAN on the screen; if necessary, press Ctrl-F6, the Next Window command. SALESJAN is the file into which you will copy the other two months. You can choose any file as the one in which you consolidate data, but it's easier to keep it straight if you consolidate in chronological order.
2. Change the title in cell A1 to *First Quarter Sales* and save as *SALESQ1*.
3. Press Ctrl-F6 to move into the SALESFEB file.
4. Select the range C5:C11.
5. Choose Copy Special on the Edit menu. The bottom of the screen displays the message "Select new location and press ENTER."
6. Press Ctrl-F6 until you are in the SALESQ1 file.
7. Place the highlight on C5, the cell you want to copy to.

8. Press Enter. A box listing the following choices is displayed:

Values only	Replaces existing values with copied values; converts formulas to values.
Add values	Adds copied values to existing values.
Subtract values	Subtracts copied values from existing values.

9. To consolidate data, choose *Add values* and OK the dialog box. The Sales column now contains the total of January and February sales, as shown in Figure 7.14.
10. Press Ctrl-F6 until the SALESMAR file is displayed.
11. Use Copy Special to consolidate the March data. As shown in Figure 7.15, your SALESQ1 file now summarizes the first-quarter sales.
12. Save the file and close all open files.

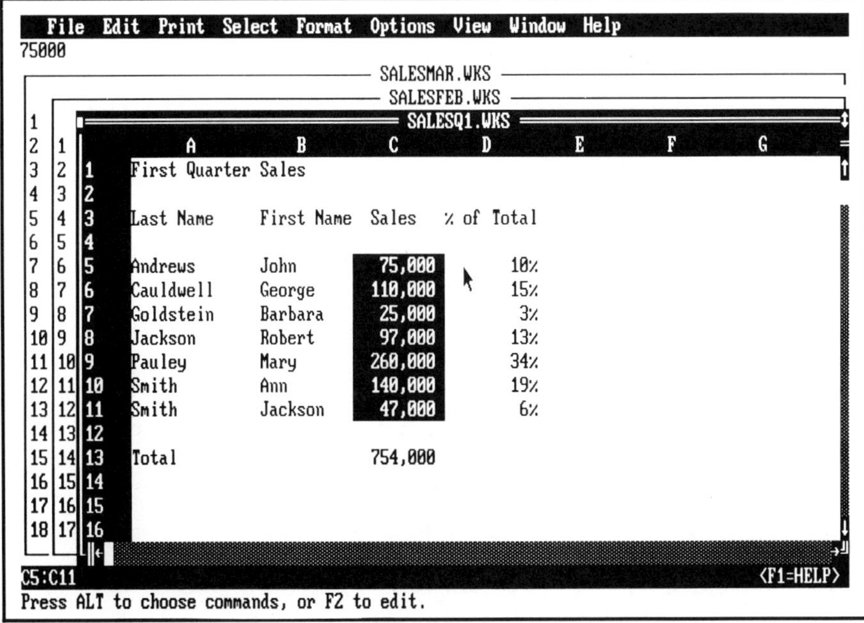

File Edit Print Select Format Options View Window Help
75000
SALESMAR.WKS
SALESFEB.WKS
SALESQ1.WKS
A B C D E F G
First Quarter Sales
Last Name First Name Sales % of Total
Andrews John 75,000 10%
Cauldwell George 110,000 15%
Goldstein Barbara 25,000 3%
Jackson Robert 97,000 13%
Pauley Mary 260,000 34%
Smith Ann 140,000 19%
Smith Jackson 47,000 6%
Total 754,000
C5:C11
<F1=HELP>
Press ALT to choose commands, or F2 to edit.

Figure 7.14: Consolidating January and February sales

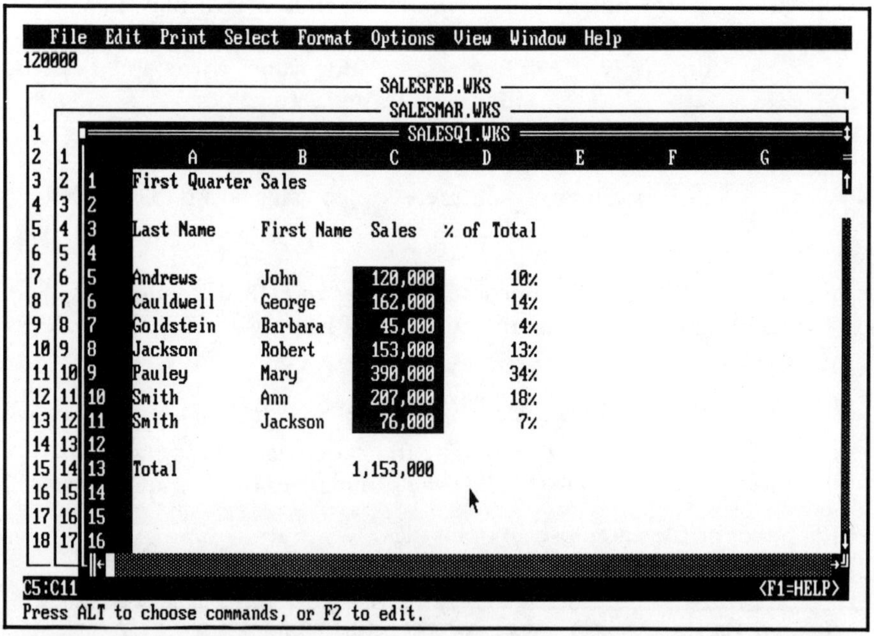

```
 File  Edit  Print  Select  Format  Options  View  Window  Help
120000
                              SALESFEB.WKS
                              SALESMAR.WKS
                              SALESQ1.WKS
        A             B          C          D        E        F        G
 1  First Quarter Sales
 2
 3  Last Name     First Name  Sales    % of Total
 4
 5  Andrews       John        120,000        10%
 6  Cauldwell     George      162,000        14%
 7  Goldstein     Barbara      45,000         4%
 8  Jackson       Robert      153,000        13%
 9  Pauley        Mary        390,000        34%
10  Smith         Ann         207,000        18%
11  Smith         Jackson      76,000         7%
12
13  Total                   1,153,000
14
15
16
C5:C11                                                          <F1=HELP>
Press ALT to choose commands, or F2 to edit.
```

Figure 7.15: Consolidating first-quarter sales

SUMMARY

In this chapter, you built upon the basic skills you learned in Chapter 6. You learned how to modify an existing spreadsheet, get around quickly in a large spreadsheet, and control the printing of a large spreadsheet. You also learned more about copying and how to sort a spreadsheet.

Another aspect of the spreadsheet tool is charting. As you will learn in the next chapter, you can quickly create graphs of your spreadsheet data.

EXERCISES

In the following exercises you modify the spreadsheet you created in the Chapter 6 Exercises, shown again in Figure 7.16. You will delete

File Edit Print Select Format Options View Window Help

89VS90.WKS

	A	B	C	D	E
1	1989 VS. 1990 SALES BY SALES PERSON				
2					
3					
4	SALES PERSON	1989	1990	CHANGE	% CHANGE
5					
6	SMITH, GEORGE	130,000	180,000	50,000	38.46%
7	JONES, ARNOLD	120,000	190,000	70,000	58.33%
8	PETERSON, MARY	110,000	90,000	(20,000)	-18.18%
9	ANDERSON, ANDREA	150,000	200,000	50,000	33.33%
10					
11	TOTAL	$510,000	$660,000	$150,000	
12	AVERAGE	$127,500	$165,000	$37,500	

E11 <F1=HELP>

Press ALT to choose commands, or F2 to edit.

Figure 7.16: The spreadsheet created in Chapter 6

columns, erase ranges, edit a cell, use an absolute reference, and sort. While you are doing the exercises, refer to Figure 7.17 for the final spreadsheet. If you get stuck, refer to the sections indicated inside parentheses.

1. Open the 89VS90 spreadsheet you created in the Chapter 6 Exercises. The spreadsheet should look similar to the one in Figure 7.16.
2. Erase the AVERAGE row (see ''Erasing a Range,'' page 160).

3. Delete the following columns (see ''Deleting Rows and Columns,'' page 162):
    - 1989
    - CHANGE
    - % CHANGE
4. Edit the title in cell A1 so that it reads *1990 SALES BY SALES PERSON* (see ''Editing Cells,'' page 159).
5. Enter and boldface the column heading in cell C4 (see Figure 7.17).
6. In cell C6, enter the formula to calculate Smith's percentage of the total (see ''Using Absolute References in Formulas,'' page 180).
7. Copy the formula down the column.
8. Format column C to Percent with two decimal places.

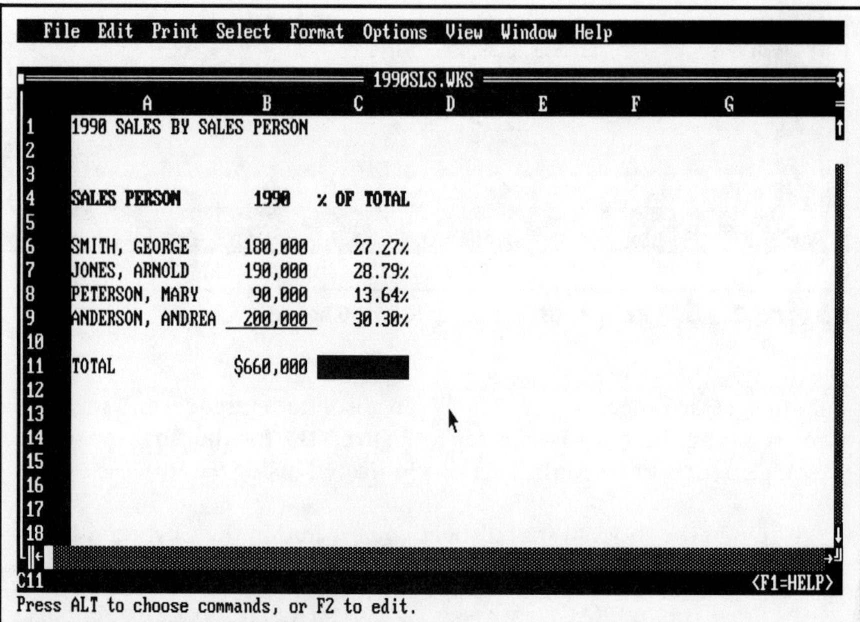

Figure 7.17: The revised spreadsheet

9. Alphabetize the records by last name (see "Sorting the Spreadsheet," page 178).
10. When you sort, the underline moves to the top of the list. Remove the underlining from cell B6 (see Chapter 6, "Canceling Styles and Enhancements," page 143) and then underline cell B9 (see Chapter 6, "Creating Lines," page 141).
11. Save the file with a new name, *1990SLS.*
12. Close the file.

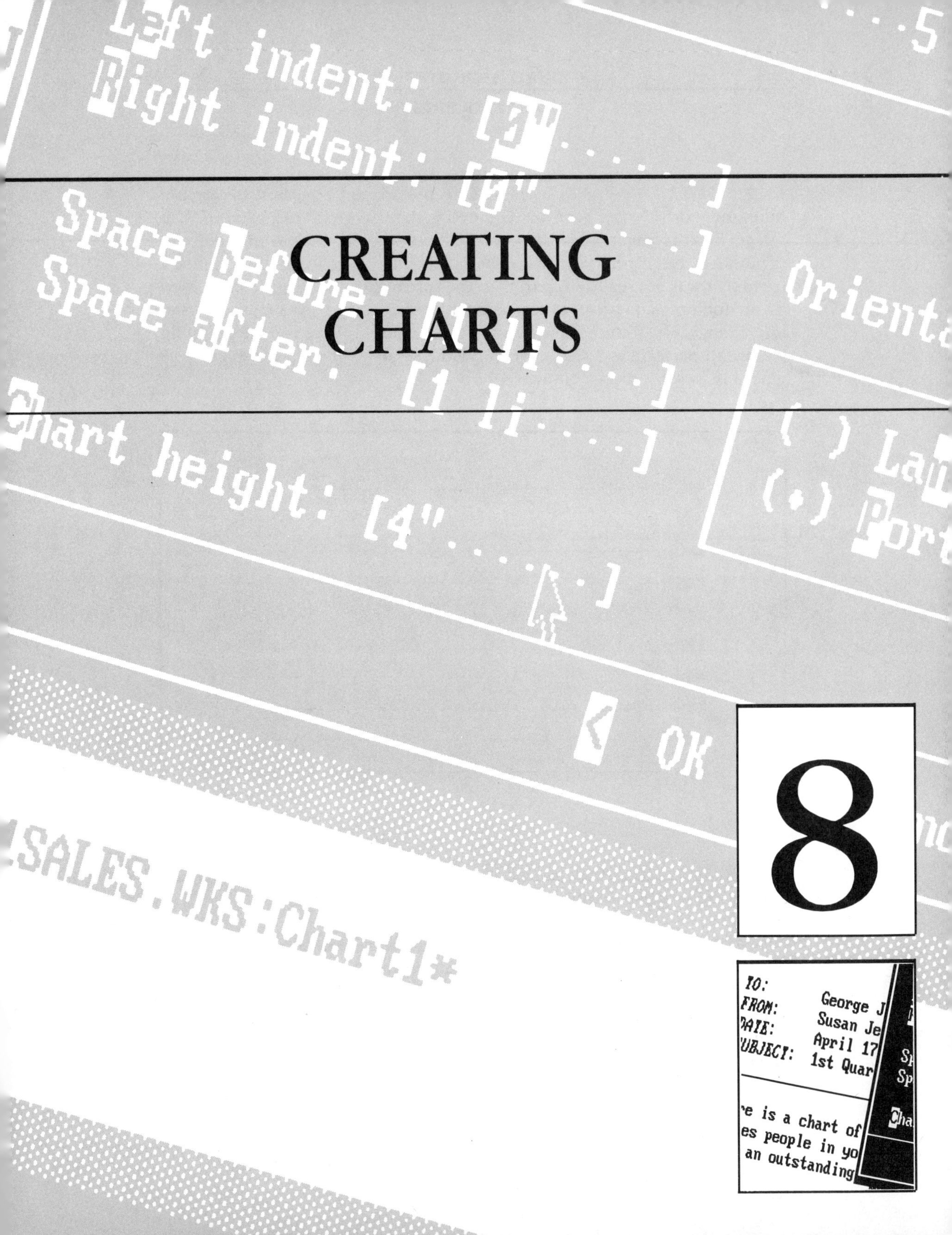

CREATING CHARTS

8

The old adage "a picture is worth a thousand words" must have been coined with business graphs in mind. You can get dizzy trying to interpret a spreadsheet that has column after column of numbers. But if you create a graph of that data, you may instantly notice a trend that was not readily apparent in the spreadsheet (see Figure 8.1). Even if you don't plan on printing any charts (the terms *chart* and *graph* are used interchangeably) for presentations or reports, you still can use the graphing feature to perform a quick on-screen analysis of your data. How quick is quick? Is 10 seconds fast enough for you?

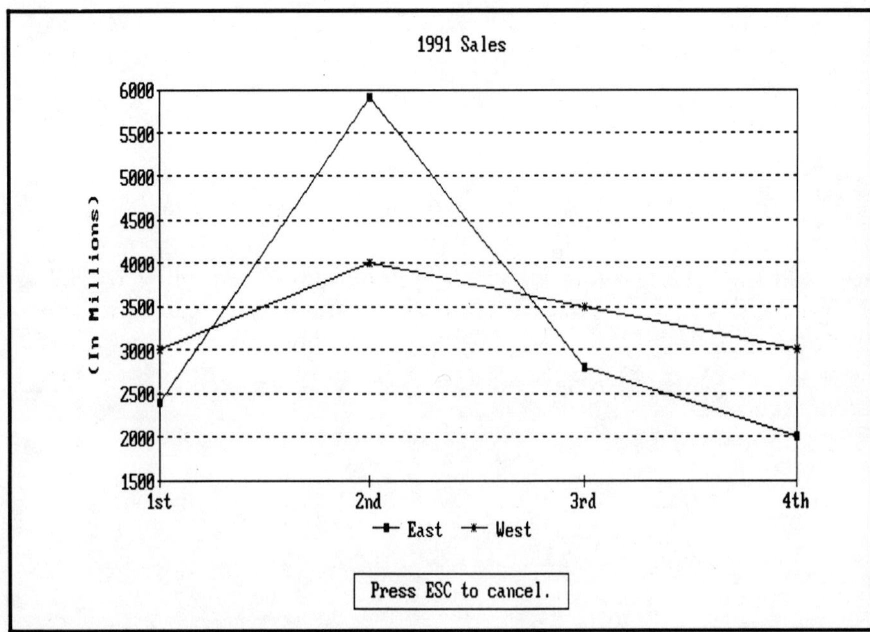

Figure 8.1: A line graph

If you have ever created a graph by hand you know that it's time-consuming, and if incorrect data are used, the graph must be redrawn. However, Works's charting features make creating graphs fast, easy, and even fun. You do not need to be a graphic artist to create a beautiful chart in Works. All you have to do is tell Works what numbers you want to graph and the charting feature takes care of the rest. Throw out your ruler, compass, and colored pens. Needless to say, the graphs you print in Works look much more professional than anything the average person could draw. And you can be assured that all the data points are accurate.

USING CHART VIEW

The spreadsheet tool offers two ways to look at your data: as a columnar table (called the *spreadsheet view*) and as a graph (called the *chart view*). So far you have been using the spreadsheet view to create, edit, and format data. In the chart view, you can build a graph of your spreadsheet data. Charting is built directly into the spreadsheet tool and is accessed from the View menu.

One of the advantages of having an integrated spreadsheet and graphing tool is that you can change any of the numbers in the spreadsheet and the chart automatically includes the revised data. If you create a graph by hand and someone revises a number, you have to redraw the entire chart.

To create a chart, you must first have spreadsheet data. For the first example in this chapter, you will create a graph of the data in Figure 8.2. This spreadsheet keeps track of the quarterly sales for the East Coast and West Coast divisions of a company. Create a new spreadsheet by typing the data exactly as they appear in the figure. Be sure not to leave any blank rows or columns—I'll explain why later.

DEFINING A CHART RANGE

The quickest way to create a graph is to select the spreadsheet range and then switch to chart view. Let's try it:

1. Select the range A1:E3.
2. Choose New Chart on the View menu.

Voilà, the graph is instantly displayed, as shown in Figure 8.3.

When you told Works to create a new chart, Works did the following:

- It created a bar graph (the default graph type).
- It placed the column headings (1st, 2nd, 3rd, 4th) on the x-axis. This range is called the *X-Series*.

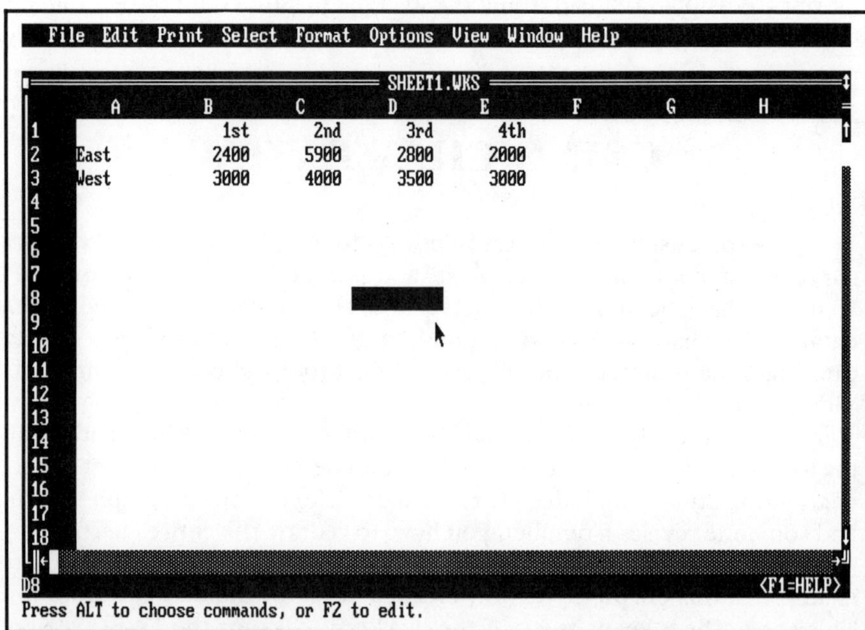

Figure 8.2: The spreadsheet data

- It determined the y-axis scale (0–6000 with even increments of 1000) from the range of numbers in the spreadsheet (2400–5900).
- It placed legends (East and West) below the graph to define the two ranges of data. The legends let you know what each bar pattern or color represents.

Each row of data is called a *series.* The first row, B1:E1, is the X-Series. The second row, B2:E2, is the 1st Y-Series, and the third row, B3:E3, is the 2nd Y-Series. Works allows up to six Y-Series of data, so in this example, you could graph up to six divisions. This six-series limitation is not as severe as it may sound because each series can have an infinite number of values. Works defined these series for you automatically. Later in this section you learn how to define the series yourself.

The automatic graph Works created for you is not perfect, however, and you will soon learn ways to spruce it up. Press Esc to remove the graph from the screen. The Esc key displays your spreadsheet in chart view.

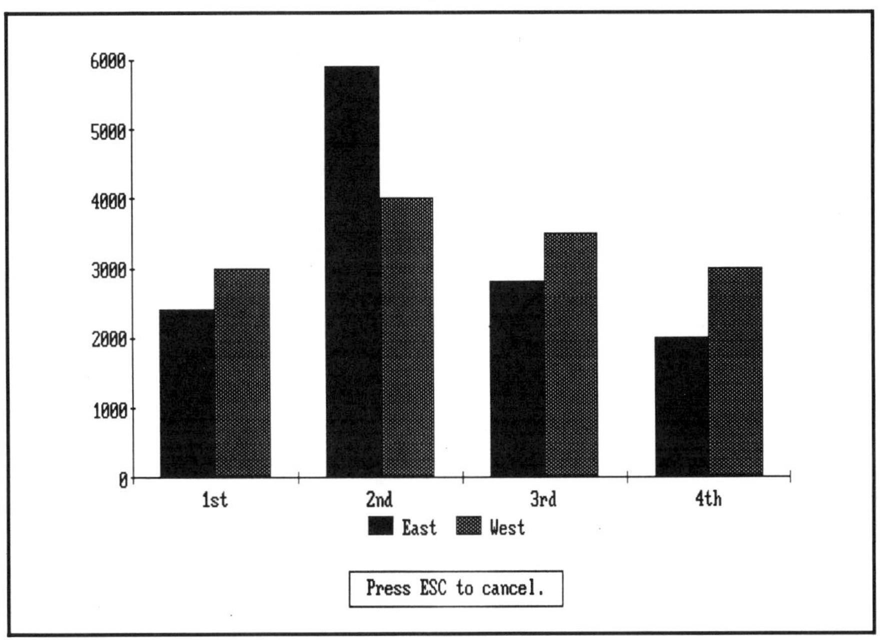

Figure 8.3: A graph created automatically

EXPLORING THE SCREEN

Unless a chart is currently displayed, the chart view is remarkably similar to the spreadsheet view (see Figure 8.4). You still see the spreadsheet grid and all your data. The only visible difference is that the menu bar has different options and the word CHART appears in the bottom window border.

In chart view you can move the highlight, enter and edit data, clear single cells, and select ranges with the keyboard or with the mouse. However, since the menu bar does not offer an Edit option, you cannot make major modifications to the spreadsheet. You cannot insert, delete, move, or copy ranges; you must return to the spreadsheet view to make significant changes.

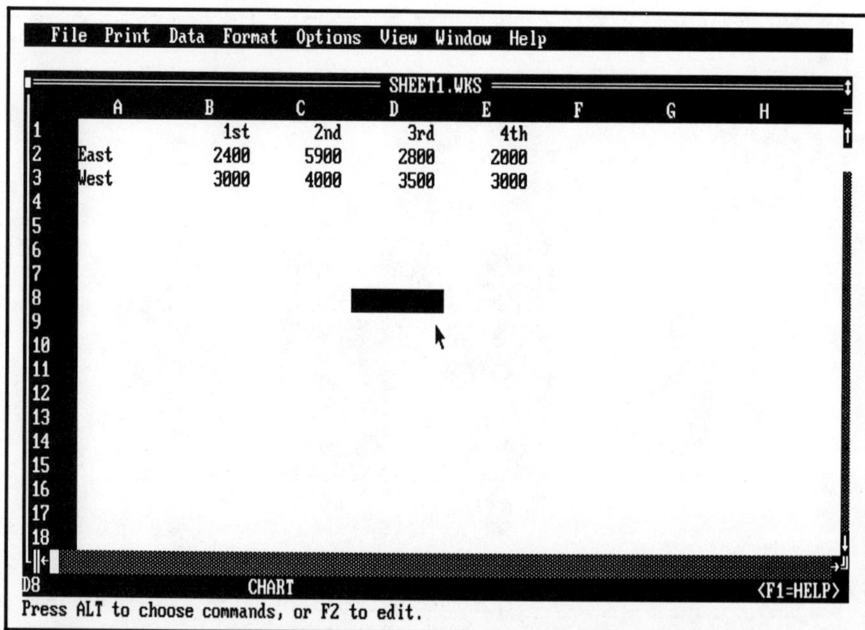

Figure 8.4: The chart window

MODIFYING THE DEFAULT GRAPH

The default graph that Works generates when you select New Chart is not a finished product. This section shows you how to choose a different graph type and how to add supplementary data to the graph to make it more descriptive. At the end of this section, you learn how to create a chart when the spreadsheet is not laid out in the format that chart view expects.

CHANGING THE GRAPH TYPE

The Format menu offers several different graph types to choose from. Table 8.1 and Figure 8.5 describe each of these types. Not all these graph types make sense for the chart you just created, but let's look at a few of them.

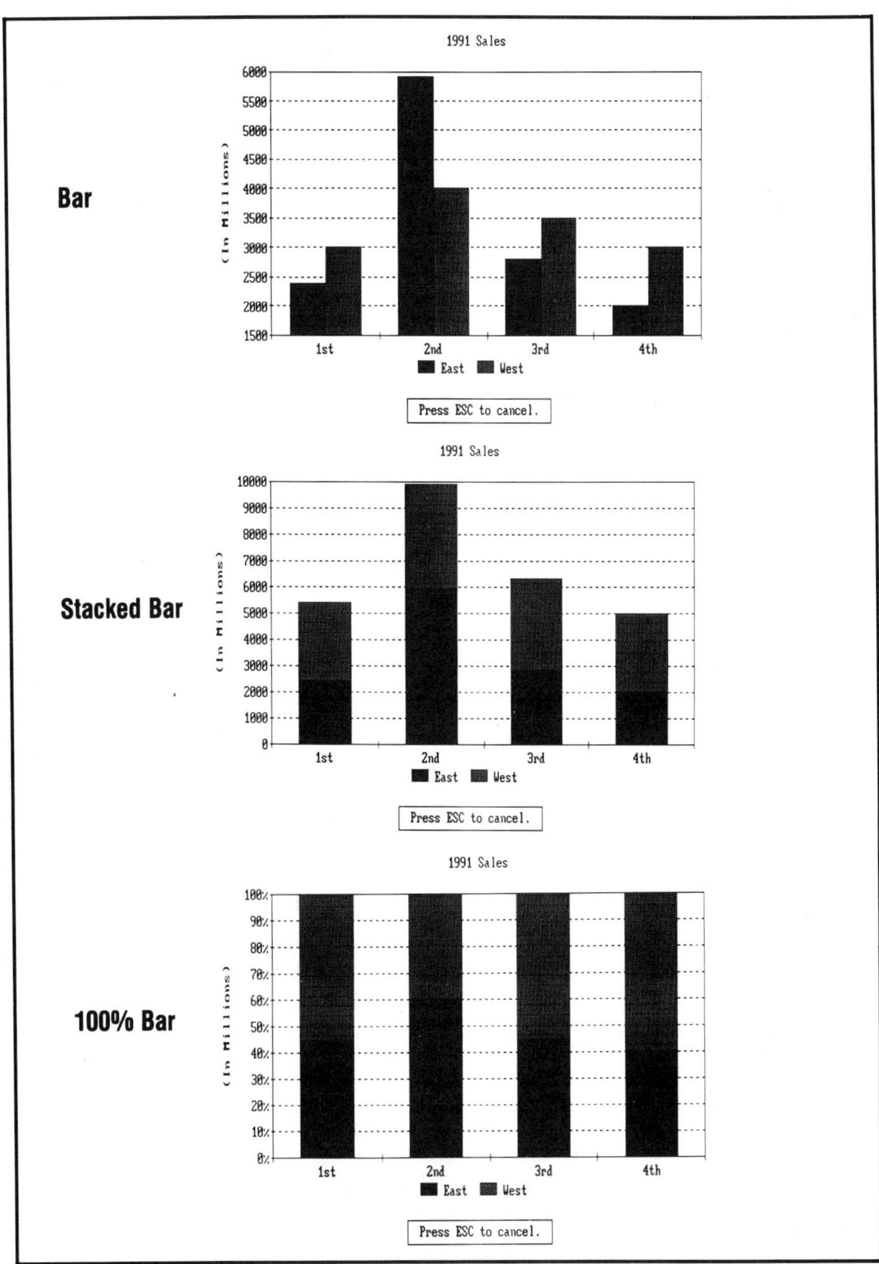

Figure 8.5: The eight basic graph types

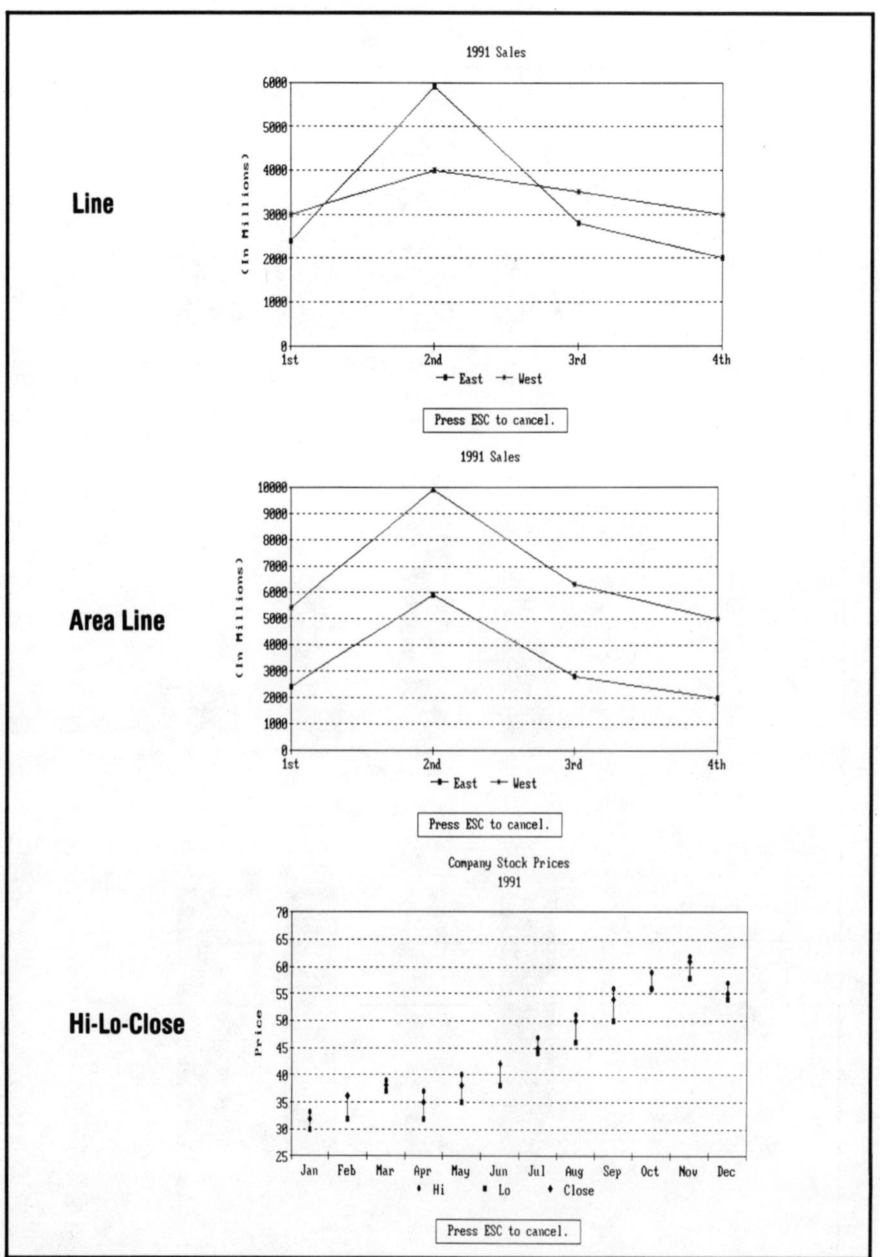

Figure 8.5: The eight basic graph types (continued)

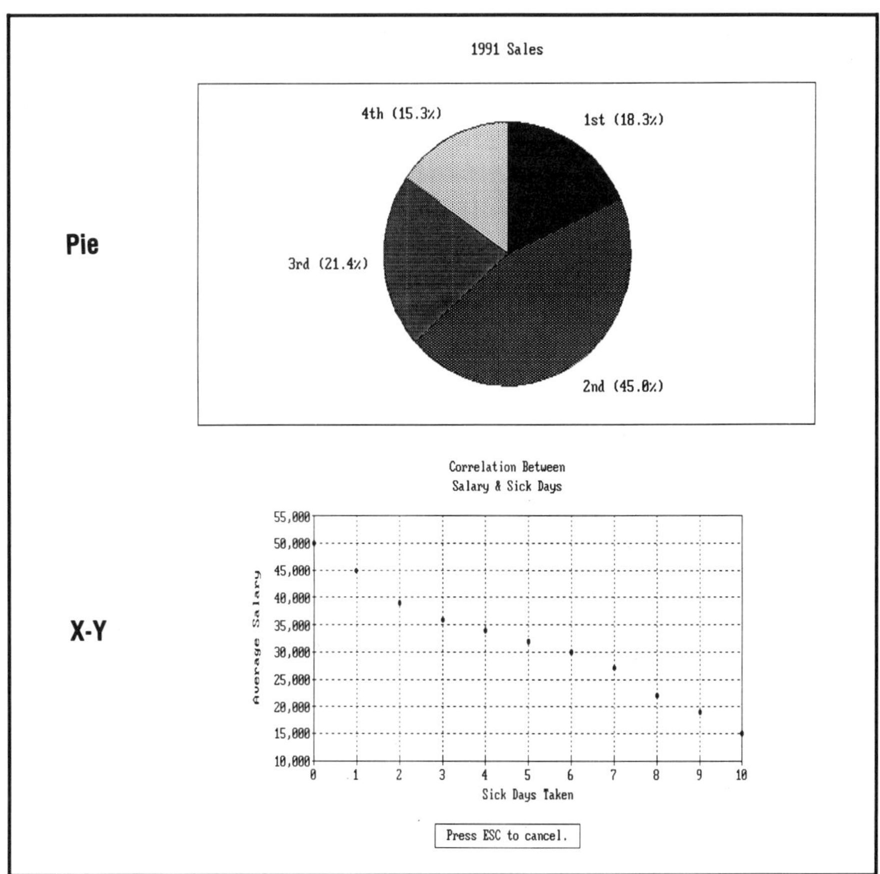

Figure 8.5: The eight basic graph types (continued)

Table 8.1: Graph Types

Bar	Bars are placed side by side to differentiate between the data series. Used with one or more data series.
Stacked Bar	Bars are placed on top of one another to show the total of the data series. Used with two or more data series only.

Table 8.1: Graph Types (continued)

100% Bar	Bars are placed on top of one another, with each series showing the proportion of the total. Used with two or more data series only.
Line	Data points are connected with lines to show a trend. Used with one or more data series.
Area Line	A line graph in which each line's values are added to those of the line below, like in a stacked bar. Used with two or more data series only.
Hi-Lo-Close	Used primarily for graphing stock-market data. Each increment on the x-axis has a mark representing a high, a low, and a closing value. Used with one or more data series.
Pie	Each pie slice represents a proportion of the total. Used with a single data series only.
X-Y	Has numbers on both the x- and y-axis. Shows whether a correlation exists between the x and y values. Used with one or more series.

Change the type to Stacked Bar by selecting Stacked Bar on the Format menu. You do not see the revised graph until you do one of the following:

- Press Shift-F10.
- Choose Chart1 on the View menu.

Chart1 is the default name Works assigns to the graph. If you were to create another graph for this same spreadsheet, Works would call it Chart2. Later on, you learn how to change graph names.

View the graph using one of the above methods. Notice that each pair of bars is now stacked on top of one another instead of side by side. Also, Works automatically rescaled the y-axis: It now ranges from 0 to 10,000. Press Esc to remove the graph from the screen.

Now select a 100% Bar graph from the Format menu, and press Shift-F10 to view the chart. In this graph type, the scale always ranges from 0 to 100%, and the bars are stacked on top of one another. Each piece of the bar represents a proportion of the total. For example, in the first quarter, the

East Coast division had about 45% of the total sales and the West Coast had about 55%.

Press Esc to remove the graph from the screen, and experiment with some of the other graph types if you like.

An additional graph type displays a combination of lines and bars in one graph. To see it, do the following:

1. Select the Bar graph type on the Format menu (you could also choose Line).
2. Choose Mixed Line & Bar on the Options menu. When the dialog box is displayed, both series are presently bars. (Notice the mark next to *Bar* in each series.)
3. To change the 2nd Y-Series to Line, click before Line C with the mouse or press **C**.
4. Choose OK and press Shift-F10 to view the graph. It should now look similar to Figure 8.6.
5. Press Esc to return to the chart worksheet.

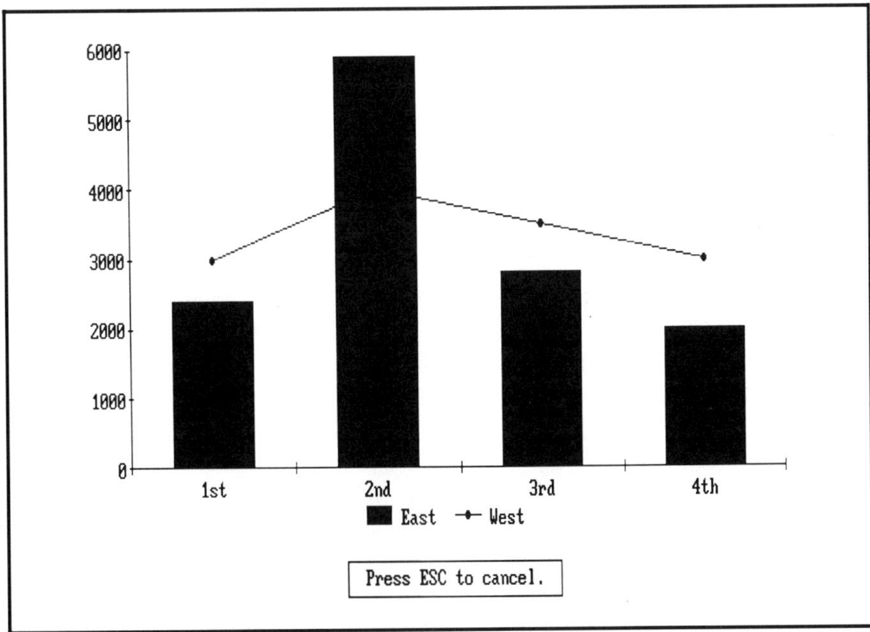

Figure 8.6: A Mixed Line & Bar graph

6. Redisplay the Mixed Line & Bar dialog box.
7. Make both series bars again by choosing option D.
8. Choose OK and view the graph. Your graph is now a regular side-by-side bar chart.

CHANGING DATA

As mentioned earlier, you can enter and edit data in either spreadsheet or chart view. Let's say you discovered a data-entry mistake in your spreadsheet: The second-quarter West Coast sales were actually 4400 instead of 4000.

1. Place the highlight on cell C3.
2. Type **4400**.
3. Press Enter.
4. Press Shift-F10 to view the graph; the graph automatically reflects the change in data.

ADDING TITLES, LEGENDS, AND DATA LABELS

A good graph should not require a human interpreter. As your graph now stands, it's not apparent what data you are graphing—it desperately needs some titles. The automatic graph does have legends at the bottom, but they could more descriptive. And sometimes it is important to know the exact values associated with each data point. The Data Labels command adds this information to a graph.

Creating Graph Titles

Using the Titles command on the Data menu, you can place two titles at the top of the graph and one title on each of the axes. Fill in the Titles dialog box like the one in Figure 8.7. When you add information in the dialog box, use the arrow keys or the mouse to position the cursor. Pressing the Enter key enters the current line of information and returns you to the chart

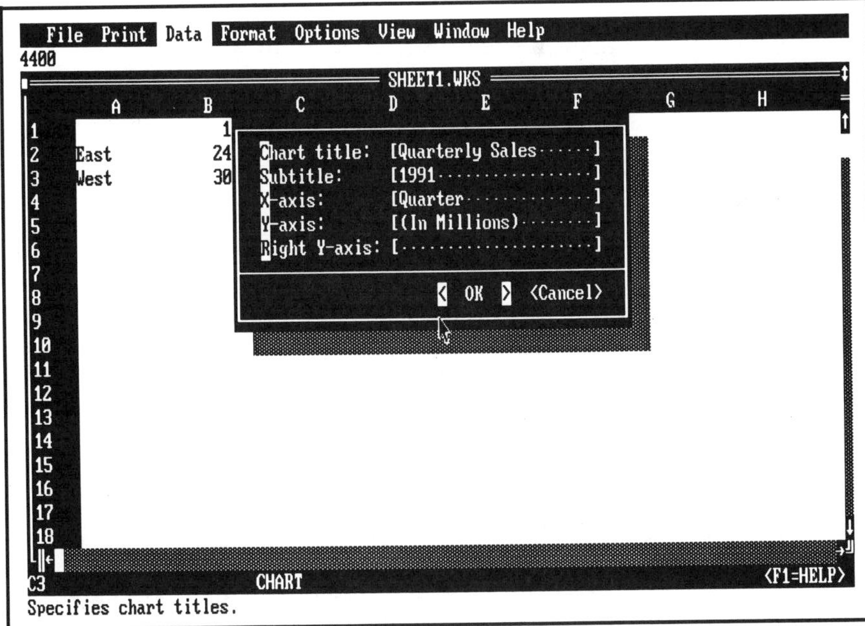

Figure 8.7: The Titles dialog box

worksheet. If you press Enter prematurely, you will not be able to finish filling the titles. When you're done, view the chart with its new titles.

If a spreadsheet cell contains text you'd like to use as a title, you can reference the cell rather than type the title. For example, if you typed the title *Quarterly Sales* in cell A1 in the spreadsheet, you could type *A1* next to *Chart Title.*

Modifying Your Legends

Works determined your legends (*East* and *West*) from the range you selected when you created the graph. Sometimes these cell labels work fine as graph legends. Other times, you may want to abbreviate them or expand upon them. The Legends command on the Data menu allows you to modify your legends.

1. Display the Legends dialog box, and notice that A2 (the cell containing East) appears next to *Legend* at the bottom of the dialog box. This legend corresponds to the first Y-series.

2. Highlight *2nd Y*; A3 (the cell containing West) is the legend.
3. Highlight *1st Y* again and choose Legend (or press Alt-L).
4. To make the legend more descriptive, type **East Coast Division** (the characters are scrolled as you type), and press Enter.
5. Highlight *2nd Y*, choose Legend, type **West Coast Division,** and press Enter.
6. Choose Done and view your graph with its new legends.

You can hide the legends if you don't want them on the graph. For example, if the graph has only one data series, you don't really need a legend. To hide the legends, you turn off the Show Legends command on the Options menu. When this option is turned off, a mark does *not* appear next to Show Legends on the menu.

Displaying Data Values

The purpose of a spreadsheet is to give you precise numbers and to do precise calculations. The purpose of a graph, on the other hand, is to give you an overall picture of the relationship between different series of data or to illustrate trends and correlations. But a graph can give you precise data, too, if you use *data labels.* Data labels are cell contents (usually your data series) that can be placed right above the data points on a graph.

Before you choose the Data Labels option, select the range of data you want placed on the graph. You must identify each series separately. To try it, follow these steps:

1. Select B2:E2.
2. Choose Data Labels on the Data menu.
3. *1st Y* should already be highlighted, so press Enter to select Create.
4. For the second series, select B3:E3.
5. Choose Data Labels on the Data menu.
6. Highlight *2nd Y*, and press Enter to choose Create.

View your graph. It should now look similar to Figure 8.8.

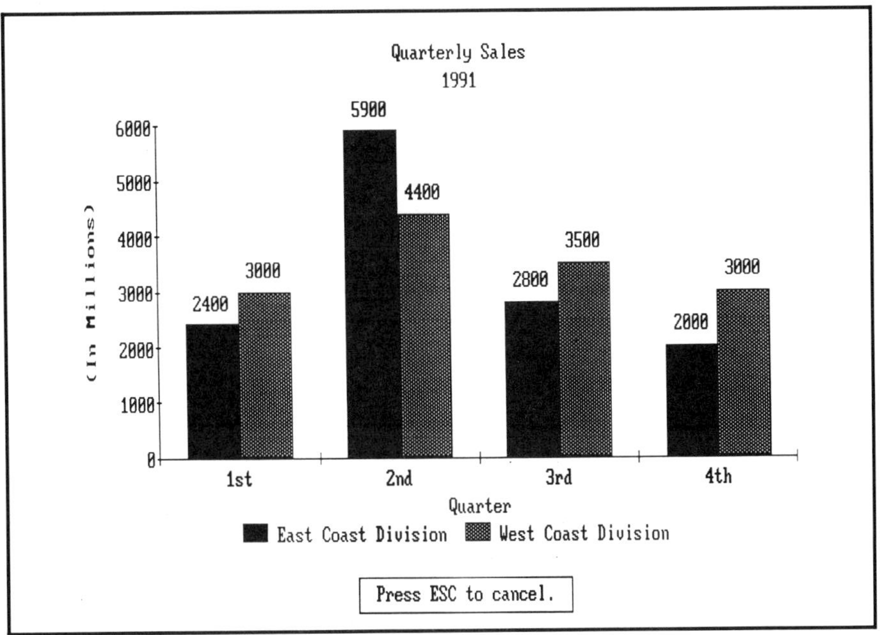

Figure 8.8: A chart with data labels

SWITCHING TO SPREADSHEET VIEW

As you may have noticed, the numbers on the y-axis scale and the data labels are not formatted with any punctuation. Since the chart view does not provide a way to format the spreadsheet, you must switch back to the spreadsheet view. Works offers two ways to switch from the chart view to the spreadsheet view:

- Press F10.
- Choose Spreadsheet on the View menu.

If you choose one of the above commands, all your regular spreadsheet formatting and editing commands become available.

1. Select the entire spreadsheet (choose All on the Select menu) and then format to Comma with zero decimal places.

2. To see if this formatting is reflected in the graph, view your chart by pressing Shift-F10. Now all the numbers in the y-axis scale and all the data labels contain commas.
3. Press Esc to remove the graph from the screen. What view are you in? Since the bottom window border does not display the word CHART, you are still in spreadsheet view. The Shift-F10 command does not actually take you into chart view; all it does is display the current chart.
4. To display the chart *and* go into chart view, choose Chart1 on the View menu. Remember, Chart1 is the name Works automatically assigned to the chart.

Regardless of whether you save the file in spreadsheet or chart view, when you open the file you are always in spreadsheet view. To go into chart view, choose the chart name on the View menu.

Congratulations, you are finished with your first graph. Save the file with the name EASTWEST, and close the file.

CHARTING IN AN IMPERFECT WORLD

You created the previous chart by selecting the spreadsheet range and then issuing the New Chart command. Works was able to accurately identify and assign the individual data series (X-Series, 1st Y-Series, and 2nd Y-Series) because the data you wanted to graph were in consecutive rows and columns.

But what if the spreadsheet is not laid out so perfectly? What if there are blank rows between the legends or the data series? What if there are columns in the middle that you don't want in the graph? The solution to all these problems is to define each series individually. This is remarkably easy to do.

Figure 8.9 is a prime example of a spreadsheet that is not ideally designed to be a chart. First, it contains a blank row between the column headings (the legends) and the data. Second, it has a column that you don't want in the graph (column B—First Name). You could redesign the spreadsheet by deleting the blank row and moving the unwanted column elsewhere. But let's assume you like your current layout, so redesigning is out of the question. Create this spreadsheet, and save the file as Q1SALES.

```
 File  Edit  Print  Select  Format  Options  View  Window  Help

=========================== Q1SALES.WKS ===========================
        A               B            C         D         E         F          G
1   1st Quarter Sales
2
3   Last Name     First Name       Jan       Feb       Mar     Total
4
5   Andrews       John          36,000    39,000    45,000   120,000
6   Cauldwell     George        65,000    45,000    52,000   162,000
7   Goldstein     Barbara       10,000    15,000    20,000    45,000
8   Jackson       Robert        45,000    52,000    56,000   153,000
9   Pauley        Mary         120,000   140,000   130,000   390,000
10  Smith         Ann           75,000    65,000    67,000   207,000
11  Smith         Jackson       24,000    23,000    29,000    76,000
12
13  Total                      375,000   379,000   399,000 1,153,000
14
15
16
17
18
A16                                                              <F1=HELP>
Press ALT to choose commands, or F2 to edit.
```

Figure 8.9: A spreadsheet with noncontiguous graph ranges

The chart you want to create is shown in Figure 8.10. Notice that the last names are on the x-axis, and each month (January, February, March) is a data series for the y-axis. To create this graph, do not select a range—just go directly to the New Chart command on the View menu. Instead of a graph, you see the following message: "Series not selected." Since you intentionally did not select a series, choose OK; you are now in chart view.

Defining Individual Data Series

The top part of the Data menu contains the options for defining your data series.

1. Display the Data menu. You can see the options for 1st Y-Series, 2nd Y-Series, etc. Before you can select these options, you must select the appropriate range.

2. Press Esc to clear the menu.

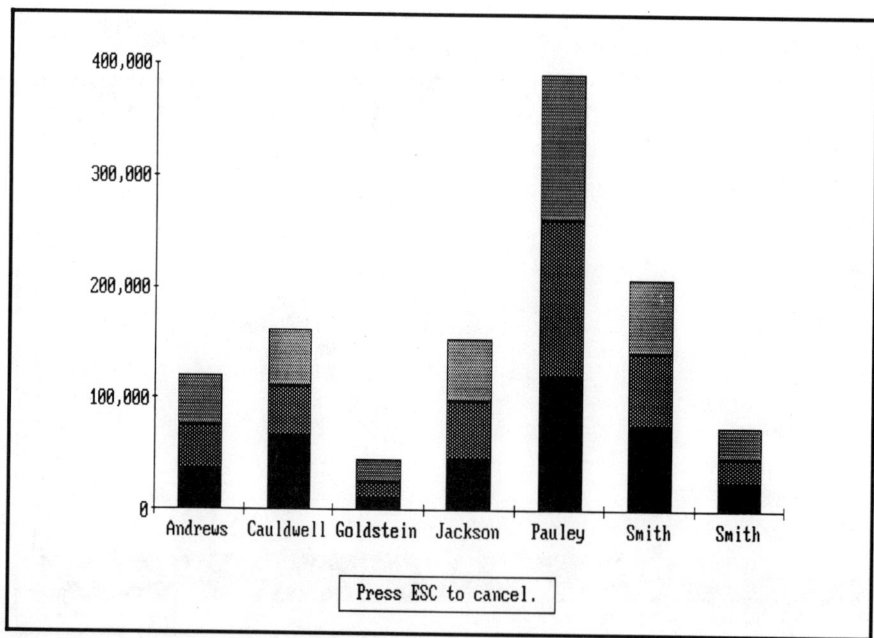

Figure 8.10: A stacked bar chart

3. Select the range of last names, A5:A11.
4. You want this range to go along the x-axis, so choose X-Series on the Data menu.
5. This graph has three Y-Series, one for each month. Select the January data, C5:C11.
6. Choose 1st Y-Series on the Data menu.
7. Assign the February data, D5:D11, to the 2nd Y-Series.
8. Assign the March data, E5:E11, to the 3rd Y-Series.
9. Because you are interested in seeing each salesperson's total sales for the quarter, a stacked bar graph would be more appropriate. Select Stacked Bar on the Format menu.

10. Press Shift-F10 to view your chart. It should look like Figure 8.10. Some monitors may truncate the labels on the x-axis. However, the labels will not print this way.

To review the current series ranges in a chart, use the Series command on the Data menu. It lists the range associated with each series. This command also allows you to go to or delete a series.

Finishing the Graph

This graph is missing a very important element: the legends. Without legends, the chart doesn't indicate what the three bar patterns signify. You already know how to define legends because you modified the legends in your first chart. Follow these steps to create legends:

1. Choose Legends on the Data menu. *1st Y* should be highlighted.
2. Press Alt-L or click next to Legend, and type **January.**
3. Press Enter to choose Create.
4. Highlight *2nd Y.*
5. Choose Legend and type **February.**
6. Press Enter to choose Create.
7. Repeat steps 4–6 to assign the legend *March* to the third series.
8. Choose Done and view your graph with the legends.

If you don't see the legends, it's possible that the Show Legends option is disabled. Display the Options menu and look to the left of Show Legends. If you *don't* see a mark, choose Show Legends to activate the option.

You can also type a cell coordinate for the legend, and Works will use the contents of this cell. For example, for the 1st Y-Series legend, you can type *C3* and *Jan* appears as the legend.

The chart also needs titles. Figure 8.11 displays the titles (chart title, subtitle, and y-axis title) for the chart. Enter these descriptions in the Titles dialog box on the Data menu. Save the file with the same name, Q1SALES.

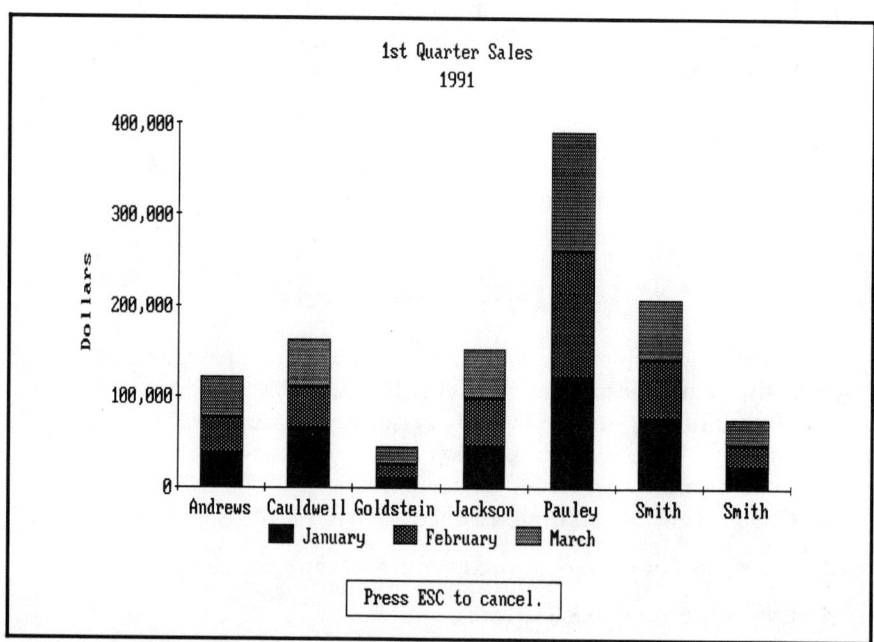

Figure 8.11: A chart with titles

CHANGING FONTS IN YOUR CHART

You've already explored part of the Format menu; you've used this menu to assign the chart type (for example, Line, Stacked Bar, Pie). Now in this section, you use the Format menu to change fonts in the chart.

In the word processor and the spreadsheet, you can only select fonts your printer has available. However, in the chart view, you can use *soft fonts* that are included with the Works program. Soft fonts are not built into or plugged into your printer; they are software files (with the extension .RFT or .SFT) that tell your printer what typeface to use. You can use these soft fonts in any printer capable of producing graphics (like laser and dot-matrix printers).

Works allows two fonts per chart. The main chart title is in one font, and all other text (legends, scale numbers, axis titles, subtitle, and data labels) is in the second font. Thus, you could choose a large, bold font for the title and a smaller font for everything else.

By default you do not see your chosen fonts on the screen. However, by choosing Show Printer Fonts on the Options menu, you see a fairly good representation of the printed font. Sometimes printer fonts are difficult to read on the screen and take longer to display. If so, turn off Show Printer Fonts. If you can't remember whether you turned the option on, check the Options menu. If you see a mark next to Show Printer Fonts, the option is turned on.

Turn on Show Printer Fonts if you haven't already. To take a look at the available fonts, choose Title Font on the Format menu. The dialog box that appears is similar to the one you see in the spreadsheet except it lists a different set of font names.

Two types of soft fonts are on the list: *raster* and *stroke*. Table 8.2 lists what font type each font is. *Raster* gives you the best print quality, but each font comes in only three sizes. The stroke or *bit-mapped* fonts, on the other hand, offer a wide selection of type sizes, from 6- to 126-point (even-numbered point sizes only). Keep in mind, though, that the stroke font's quality is inferior to the raster font's. Notice that all the stroke fonts have the letter *B* in their names (the B stands for bit-mapped).

Table 8.2: Soft Fonts Included with Works

RASTER FONTS (HIGHEST QUALITY)
Screen Modern C Bold Modern C Italic Modern C Decor A
STROKE FONTS (MORE SIZES)
Modern B Bold Modern B Roman B Bold Roman B Italic Roman B Bold Italic Roman B Script B

The raster fonts are not available in very small point sizes. When the x-axis labels or legends do not fit across the screen, you must choose a screen font or a small point size for one of the stroke fonts. (Six-point is the smallest.)

Just for fun, choose a "wild" font. Follow these steps:

1. Highlight Decor A.
2. Go over to the Sizes list (press Alt-S).
3. Select the largest point size available, and choose OK in the dialog box.
4. Press Shift-F10 to view the graph.

Assuming you turned on the Show Printer Fonts option, you should see a fancy-looking title. Your chart should look similar to Figure 8.12. This font would not be appropriate for a professional business graph, but it's OK for practice.

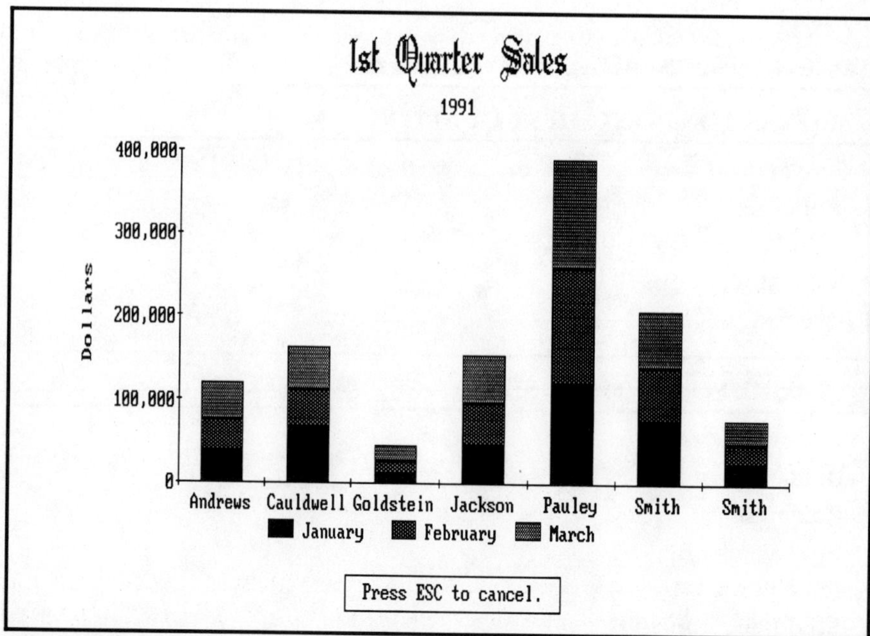

Figure 8.12: The title with a fancy font (Decor A)

The Other Font should be smaller than the Title Font, but not so small, of course, that the text is illegible. For this chart, keep the default screen font. Even the smallest raster font is too big for this graph, causing some of the x-axis labels to be truncated. You could choose a small point size in one of the stroke fonts, but you would sacrifice print quality.

When changing the Other Font, keep an eye on the x-axis labels and legends to make sure they completely fit on the screen. Choose a stroke or screen font and reduce the point size until all the text fits.

ADDING GRID LINES

Grid lines are light dotted lines behind a chart that help you tell which data point corresponds to which axis label. If you turn on the grid-line option for the x-axis, vertical lines are placed at each x-axis label. If you turn on the option for the y-axis, horizontal lines are placed across from each scale increment, allowing you to interpret the actual value of the data. It is rare to have only x-axis grid lines; more commonly, x-axis grid lines are used in combination with y-axis grid lines, or y-axis grid lines are used alone.

Follow these steps to place horizontal grid lines on your practice graph:

1. Choose Y-Axis on the Options menu.
2. Select *Grid lines* (Alt-G). An *X* should appear next to the option.
3. Choose OK.
4. Press Shift-F10 to view the graph with the grid lines. The graph should look similar to Figure 8.13.

ADDING A BORDER

Notice that on the right side of the chart (see Figure 8.13), the grid lines stop at the end of the x-axis. Because there is no vertical line on the right side, the grid lines look like they are hanging in outer space. By enclosing the graph in a border, you can eliminate the feeling that the graph is somehow incomplete.

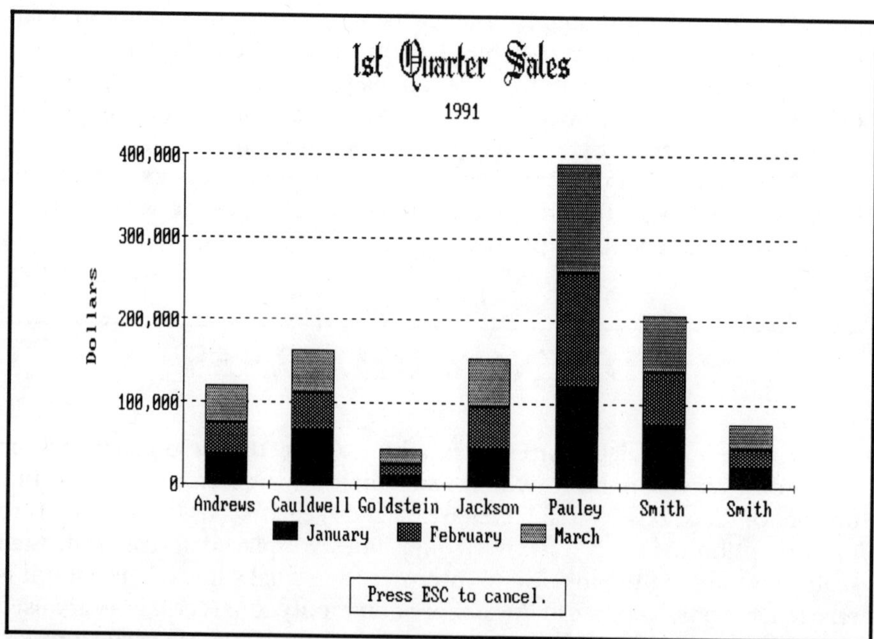

Figure 8.13: A chart with horizontal grid lines

If you turn on the Show Border command on the Options menu, solid lines extend from the ends of the x and y axes to form a rectangle around the chart. Turn on this option and view the chart. (If you specify Show Border for a pie chart, the pie is enclosed in a box; the titles appear above the border.)

PRINTING A CHART

To print a graph in chart view, choose the Print command on the Print menu. The graph will print full-page in landscape mode (sideways) and will be of medium quality. Figure 8.14 shows a chart printed on a Hewlett-Packard LaserJet Series II printer using the default settings. To indicate a different size, orientation, or print quality, you must specify print options as described in this section. This section also describes how to print a chart inside a document.

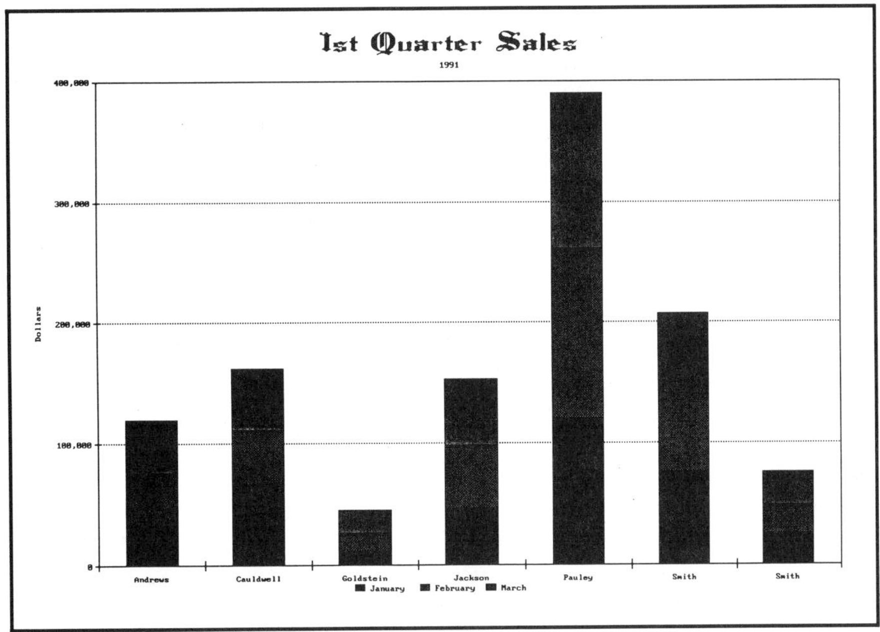

Figure 8.14: A chart printed on a LaserJet Series II

SIZING A CHART

You define the size of your chart using the Page Setup & Margins command on the Print menu. (You must be in chart view.) The dialog box you get in chart view is a bit different from the one you saw in the word processor and the spreadsheet. The first thing you may notice is that it has an option box for Orientation (landscape or portrait). Remember, if you choose landscape orientation, the chart prints horizontally and if you choose portrait, it prints vertically. In the spreadsheet or word processor, you have to go into Printer Setup to select a landscape printer. This step is not necessary when you print a chart; you can choose the orientation (landscape is the default) when defining the margins.

If you leave the margins and chart dimensions at their default settings, the chart prints horizontally across the entire page. To change the default settings, you must first know how to interpret them.

The margins, chart, and page size are defined according to a *vertical* page layout. Regardless of whether you choose portrait or landscape, the dimensions are measured as if the orientation were portrait. Therefore, none of the settings are what you might think they should be when you choose landscape orientation! Figure 8.15 illustrates the page measurements in portrait and landscape. (Note: Page 170 of the Works reference manual incorrectly illustrates how landscape dimensions are measured. The chart is rotated in the wrong direction.) To translate the measurements for landscape orientation, refer to Table 8.3.

As you can see from Table 8.3 and Figure 8.15, the landscape dimensions are the reverse of the portrait dimensions. For example, the value you enter for chart ***height*** on a portrait page is chart ***width*** on a landscape page. Likewise, the portrait chart width is the landscape chart height. The nice thing about this role reversal is that you don't have to change the page length and width when you change orientations. However, you might want to change the chart dimensions; if you don't, the chart's height will be greater than its width.

The chart height, in either landscape or portrait orientation, is measured along the length (the longest side) of the page. The chart width is measured across the width (the shortest side). These measurements include the titles and legends. Be careful with your chart dimensions so that the graph doesn't get stretched out of proportion. If possible, keep a width-to-height ratio of approximately 3:2.

To create a portrait chart on the top half of the page, use these settings:

Top margin	0.5″
Left margin	2″
Chart height	3″
Chart width	4.5″
Page length	11″
Page width	8.5″

To create a half-size landscape chart in the middle of the page, use these settings:

Top margin	3.5″
Left margin	2.5″
Chart height	4.5″

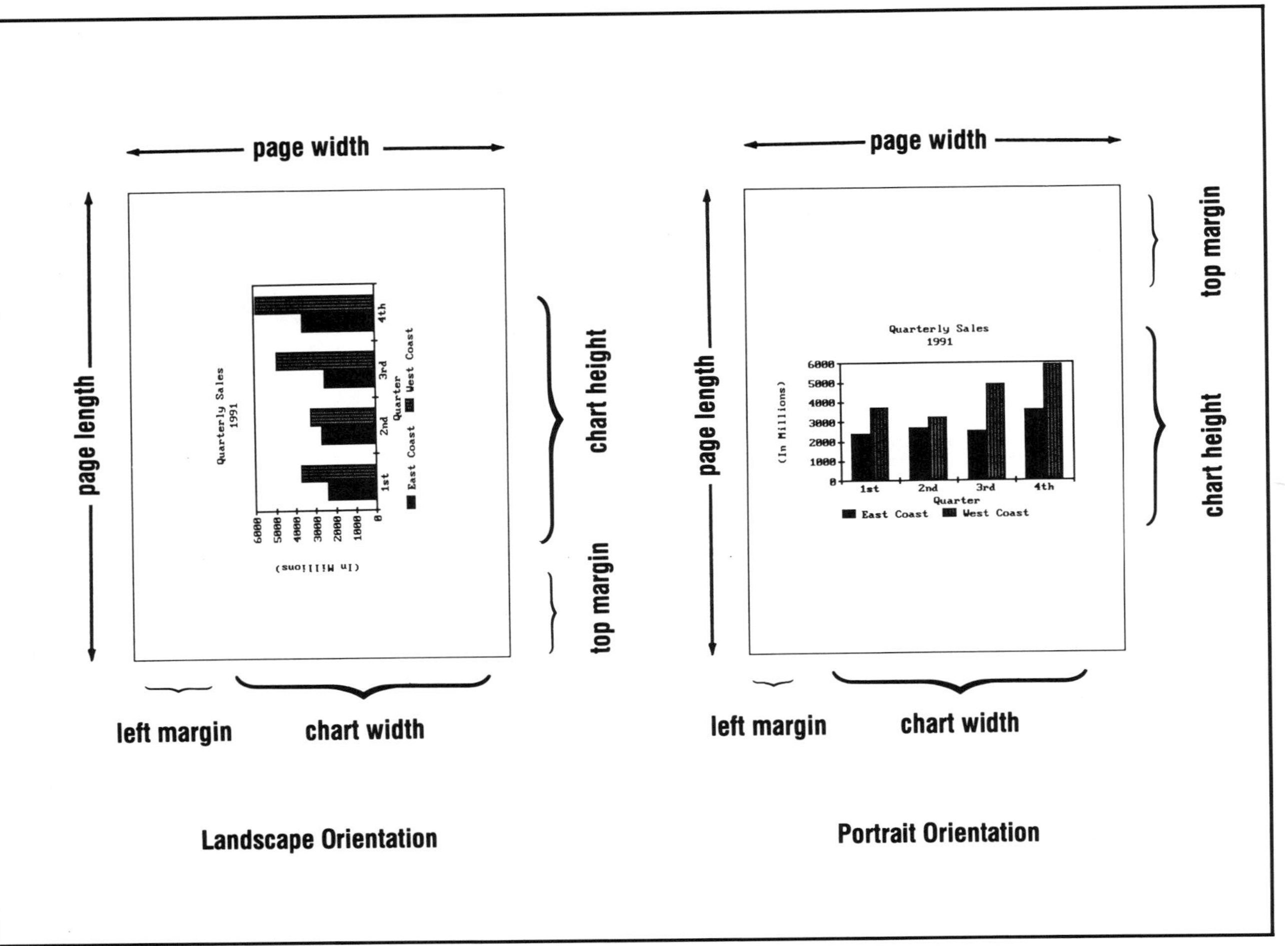

Figure 8.15: Portrait vs. landscape page measurements

Table 8.3: Converting Page Dimensions for Landscape Mode

PORTRAIT	LANDSCAPE	DEFAULT SETTING
Top margin	Left margin	1.3″
Left margin	Top margin	1″
Chart height	Chart width	6″
Chart width	Chart height	9″
Page length	Page width	11″
Page width	Page length	8.5″

Chart width	3″
Page length	11″
Page width	8.5″

PREVIEWING A CHART

Entering dimensions for a landscape page is confusing because all the values are switched around from what you think they should be. Consequently, it is all too easy to enter the wrong values. Because charts take a few minutes to print, it is wise to first preview the chart on the screen to ascertain whether you have entered the correct page setup. Follow these general steps:

- Choose Preview on the Print menu.
- Select the Preview command to view a screen representation of the printed chart. You cannot clearly see the labels or scale values, but you do get a good idea of where the chart is positioned on the page.
- If the margins and chart size look acceptable, press P to print.
- If the dimensions do not look correct, press Esc to cancel, then go back into the Page Setup & Margins option and adjust the settings.

ADJUSTING A CHART'S PRINT QUALITY

Print quality, or *resolution,* is measured in numbers of dots printed per inch, or *dpi.* The more dots that are printed, the better the print quality. The Hewlett-Packard LaserJet prints at 75, 150, or 300 dpi, and the Epson FX-80 prints at 60, 120, or 240 dpi. (On a laser printer, higher resolutions require more printer memory than lower resolutions do. If you get an error message when you print, try choosing a lower print resolution.)

You can change the print resolution by using the Printer Setup command on the Print menu. The Graphics list in the dialog box displays the resolution choices for your printer. The default resolution is 150 dpi (medium) on a LaserJet, 240 dpi (high) on an FX-80. If you want a rough draft of a chart, change to the lowest resolution, because printing is several times faster. When you are sure the graph is perfect, choose a higher (either medium or high) resolution and take a coffee break. A medium resolution chart takes about four minutes to print; a high resolution chart takes about fifteen minutes.

While the chart is printing, Works displays a progress report in the bottom window border (lower-left corner) to let you know how much of the graph has printed. For example, if *35%* is displayed, that indicates that 35 percent of the graph has printed. This information is especially useful when printing with a laser printer because you don't see the graph until it is completely finished.

The higher the resolution, the smaller the size of the printed characters. Depending on the chart's size, you may not always want the highest resolution; the characters may print so small they become illegible. Adjust the resolution until you get the size and quality you prefer. Surprisingly, the clearest resolution on the LaserJet is medium (150 dpi). On other printers, though, the highest resolution produces the best quality.

Those who are lucky enough to have access to a plotter can produce beautiful color charts. Because plotters draw graphs with pens, not dots, the dpi resolution measurement does not apply. You can create a higher quality chart by turning on the *Slow pen speed* option in the Print dialog box. If your plotter pens get dry, you can slow the pen speed to darken the ink.

PRINTING A CHART IN A DOCUMENT

Works offers a way to insert charts in your word processor documents. This feature is useful when you want to put written text on the same page as your chart or want to put a graph in the middle of a report. Figure 8.16 shows a chart printed on the same page as a memo. By inserting a chart *placeholder* in a document, you indicate where the chart should print. You

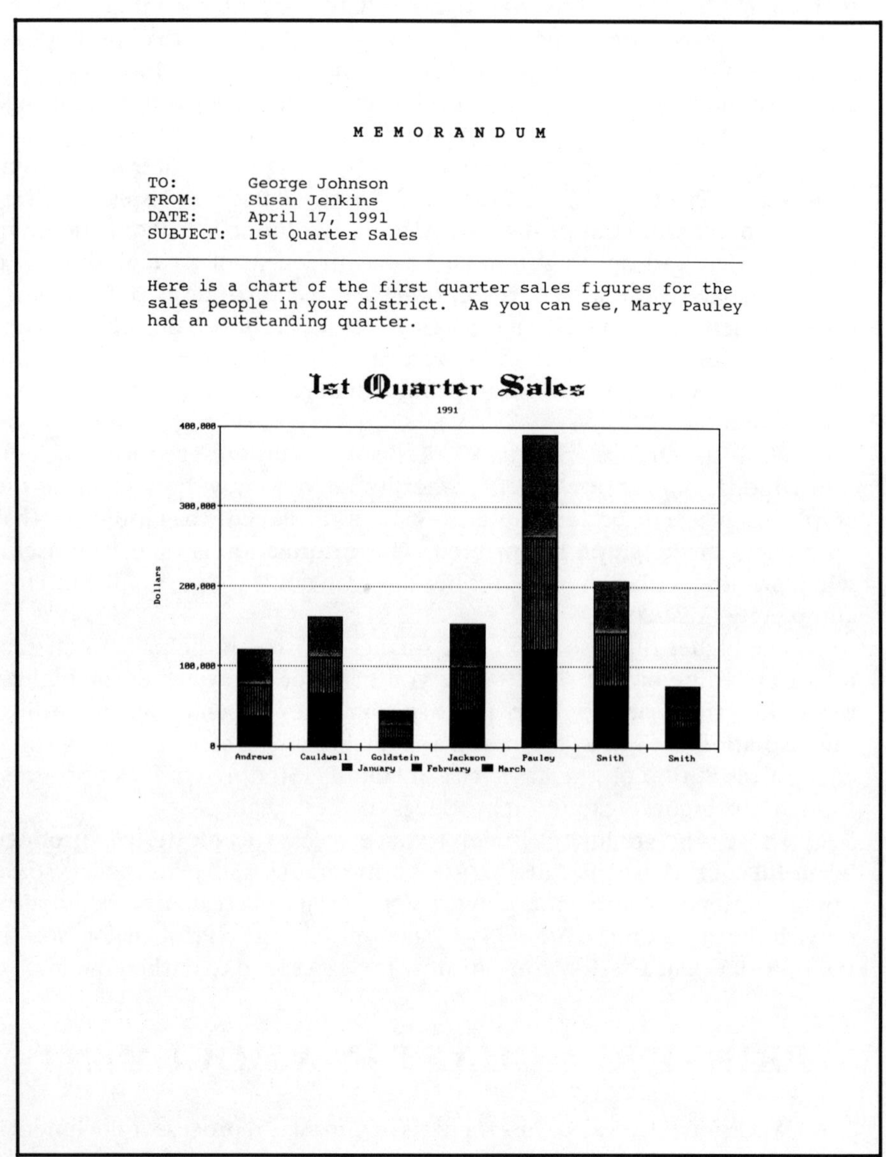

M E M O R A N D U M

TO: George Johnson
FROM: Susan Jenkins
DATE: April 17, 1991
SUBJECT: 1st Quarter Sales

Here is a chart of the first quarter sales figures for the sales people in your district. As you can see, Mary Pauley had an outstanding quarter.

Figure 8.16: A chart printed in a document

do not actually see the chart in the document; you see something like this:

chart Q1SALES.WKS:Chart1

In the above example, *Q1SALES.WKS* is the name of the spreadsheet file containing the chart, and *Chart1* is the name of the chart. (In the next section you will learn how to give your charts more meaningful names.)

The Q1SALES spreadsheet should still be on your screen. Follow these steps to insert your chart in a memo:

1. Create a new word processor file.
2. Type the memo shown in the top half of Figure 8.16.
3. At the end of the document, press Enter several times to put space between the memo and the chart you are going to insert.
4. Choose Insert Chart on the Edit menu.
5. In the Spreadsheets list, highlight Q1SALES.WKS. (Note: If no file names appear in the Spreadsheets list, you do not have any spreadsheets in memory. Press Esc to cancel the command, open Q1SALES, and repeat the steps for inserting a chart.)
6. Move the cursor over to the Charts list (press Alt-C), and highlight Chart1. If you have a mouse, you don't need to press Alt-C; just click on Chart1.
7. Choose OK and the placeholder is inserted in the document.
8. Save the file with the name Q1MEMO.

To adjust the size and orientation of the chart, you do not use the Page Setup & Margins command, as you did in chart view. Instead, you place the cursor on the chart placeholder and choose Indents & Spacing on the Format menu. This dialog box has different options than it usually does. Figure 8.17 displays the default settings.

You control the chart width by setting left and right indents. By default, the chart spans the width of the document text. To make the chart less wide, you set left and/or right indents. With the *Chart height* option, you can specify the chart's vertical dimension. To get more white space between the document text and the chart, you can enter higher values for

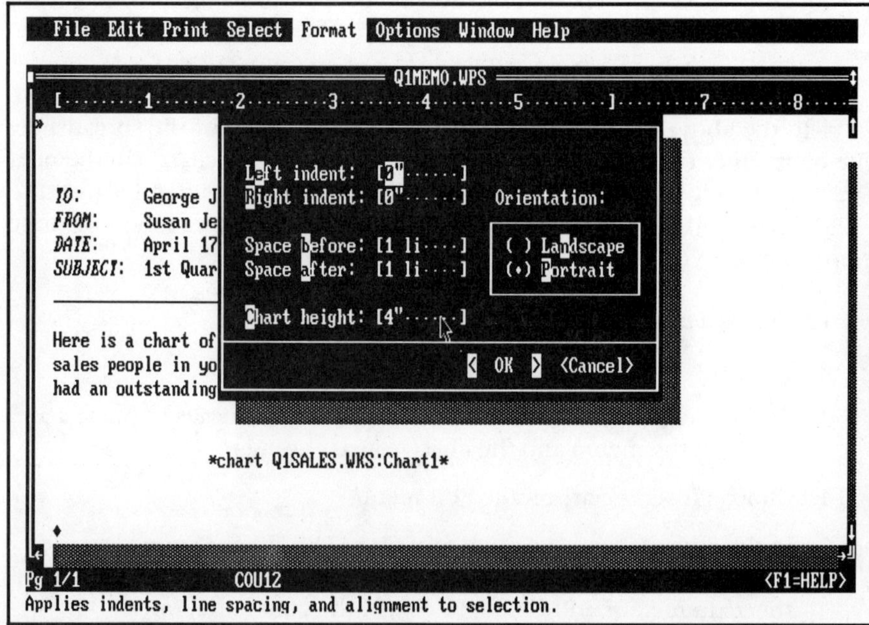

Figure 8.17: The Indents & Spacing dialog box for an inserted chart

Space before and *Space after.* For example, you can get a half-inch (three lines) between the text and the chart by specifying *3* for *Space before* and *3* for *Space after.*

A chart should probably be in portrait orientation 99 percent of the time. Even if you are printing the document in landscape orientation, you should specify portrait for the chart. The landscape setting tells Works to print the chart sideways—it rotates the chart 90 degrees from the text on the page. The only time you want to specify landscape is if the chart is on a page of its own. (To get the chart on its own page, you insert page breaks before and after the chart placeholder. See Chapter 5 for information on creating page breaks.)

You can move or delete chart placeholders. To move a chart placeholder to another position in the document, select the line and use the Move command as you normally do. To delete a placeholder, you don't even need to select the entire line—just place the cursor at the beginning of the line and press Del.

When you print the document, the spreadsheet containing the chart must be open. If it's not, Works displays the error message ''Spreadsheet not open: continue printing?'' You can choose OK to print everything except for the page containing the chart, or you can select Cancel to discontinue printing. A similar error message, ''Cannot find chart: continue printing?'', is displayed if Works cannot find the chart in the spreadsheet file. You see this message when you rename or delete the chart after inserting the placeholder. If you get this message, delete the existing placeholder and insert one with the correct chart name. Alternatively, you can rename the chart to match the one indicated in the placeholder (see the section ''Renaming Charts'').

Oddly enough, you cannot insert a chart in a spreadsheet. To print a chart and a spreadsheet on the same page, you have to copy the spreadsheet into a document and insert a placeholder for the chart.

Save and close Q1MEMO. Q1SALES should still be on your screen.

MANAGING YOUR CHARTS

As you have seen so far, Works automatically assigns a nondescript name, *Chart1,* to your graph. This name is fine if you only have one chart per spreadsheet, but if you create several graphs it becomes hard to remember what's what. In this section, you learn how to create multiple charts within a spreadsheet, how to give your charts more descriptive names, and how to delete and copy charts.

CREATING MULTIPLE CHARTS

The Q1SALES spreadsheet has only one chart so far. Let's create another graph—a pie chart of the quarterly totals of each salesperson (see Figure 8.18). Because this graph is completely different from the one you already created, you should create a new chart. When you choose the New Chart option, Works clears all existing settings—series, titles, formats, fonts, and options. Actually, the general procedure for creating a second chart (or third or fourth; the limit is eight per spreadsheet file) is the same as for creating the first one:

- If the data are laid out in consecutive rows and columns, select the range. If not, proceed to the next step.

- Choose New Chart on the View menu. (It doesn't matter whether you are in spreadsheet or chart view.)
- If you skipped the first step, select each range and assign each one to the appropriate series on the Data menu.

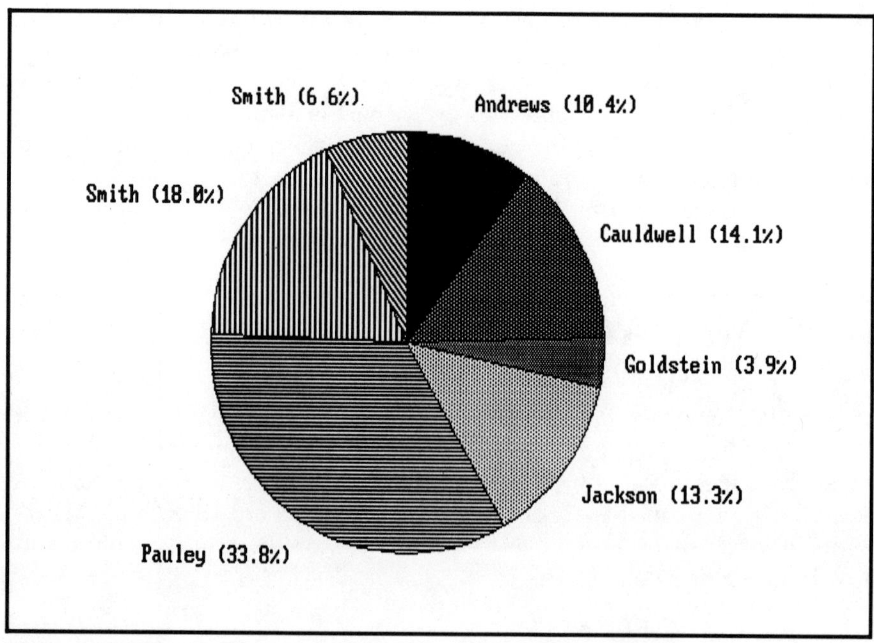

Figure 8.18: A second graph in the Q1SALES spreadsheet

Since the data series for the pie chart are not in contiguous columns (they are in columns A and F), you must select the ranges *after* creating the chart. Follow these steps to create the pie chart:

1. Choose New Chart on the View menu.
2. Choose OK for the message about the series not being selected.
3. Select the range A5:A11.
4. Choose X-Series on the Data menu.
5. Select the range F5:F11.
6. Choose 1st Y-Series on the Data menu.

7. Choose the Pie graph type on the Format menu.
8. Press Shift-F10 to view the graph. Your screen should look similar to Figure 8.18.

The Shift-F10 command displays the current chart. When you have more than one chart in a spreadsheet, use the View menu to choose a different chart. The bottom of the View menu lists the graphs in the file, in this case Chart1 and Chart2. The current graph, Chart2, has a mark next to its name.

To view Chart1 now, type **1** or select Chart1 on the View menu. The graph is displayed.

If you need to view this same chart later, you can press Shift-F10; you only need to choose the chart from the View menu when you want to see a different chart.

RENAMING CHARTS

Because these chart names are so generic (Chart1, Chart2), you may not remember which chart is the pie and which chart is the stacked bar a month from now (make that two hours from now if your memory is running on low power). Therefore, it's a good idea to assign more meaningful names to your charts. The Charts option on the View menu is the gateway to renaming charts. Choose this option now.

The Charts list displays the existing chart names. To rename a chart, follow these general steps:

- Highlight the existing name in the Charts list.
- Move the cursor next to Name (press Alt-N).
- Type the new name (up to 15 characters; spaces are allowed).
- Press Enter to choose Rename. The new name now appears in the Charts list.
- Repeat the above steps for each name.
- Select Done.

Using the steps above, rename Chart1 *Stacked Bar* and rename Chart2 *Pie*. Once you do this, the View menu displays more descriptive chart names—you won't have to play guessing games any longer to determine what type of graph is contained in each chart.

DELETING CHARTS

As a beginning chart maker, you may tend to make too many graphs. Each time you choose New Chart, another numbered chart is listed in the View menu. Thus, if you make a mistake defining the chart ranges and you start over, your previous attempts (Chart1, Chart2, etc.) are still listed. Fortunately, you can remove all the incriminating evidence of your mistake: You can delete the charts.

You don't want to delete the Stacked Bar or Pie charts in this spreadsheet, but if you have a chart you want to delete, follow these general steps:

- Choose Charts on the View menu.
- Highlight the name in the Charts list.
- Choose Delete (press Alt-T).
- Choose OK to confirm your intention to delete.
- Select Done when you are finished.

If you aren't sure what's in a chart, don't delete it. Instead, press Esc to cancel the Charts command. To see what the chart looks like, select the name from the View menu. If you determine that the chart is expendable, return to the Charts dialog box and finish your housecleaning.

DUPLICATING CHARTS

Before creating a new chart, stop and think for a minute. Will the new chart be completely different from one you already have? Or is it similar to one you have previously created, except for a few minor changes? When a new chart has more similarities than differences to an existing one, you should make a *copy* of the original chart and then modify it.

To copy a chart, follow these general steps:

- Choose Charts on the View menu.
- In the Charts list, highlight the name of the chart you want to copy.
- Move the cursor next to Name (press Alt-N).
- Type the name of the new copy.

- Choose Copy. The new name appears on the list.
- Select Done.

If you accidentally press Enter after typing the name for a copied chart, you choose the default command, Rename, instead of Copy. If you forget to type a new name, the chart is given a default name (like Chart1).

Once you create the copy, you can select the copy's name from the View menu and make any necessary modifications.

SUMMARY

In this chapter, you learned how to use the spreadsheet tool's second view, the chart view. Because the spreadsheet and charting features are packaged in one tool, you can quickly and easily create graphs of your spreadsheet data. If the data changes, the chart automatically changes as well. That's what integration is all about.

Using the chart view, you modified, formatted, and printed your charts. You also saw how you could include a chart in the middle of a word processor document.

This chapter concludes our study of the spreadsheet tool. Now we move on to the database tool.

EXERCISES

In the following exercises you will design a chart for the 89VS90 spreadsheet you created in the Chapter 6 Exercises, as shown in Figure 8.19. This chart will compare 1989 and 1990 sales for each salesperson. While you are doing the exercises below, refer to Figure 8.20 to see what the final graph should look like. If you get stuck, refer to the sections indicated inside parentheses.

1. Open the 89VS90 spreadsheet that you created in the Chapter 6 Exercises. The spreadsheet should look similar to Figure 8.19.
2. Select the range A6:C9, and create a new chart (see "Defining a Chart Range," page 195).
3. Change the type of graph to Stacked Bar (see "Changing the Graph Type," page 198).

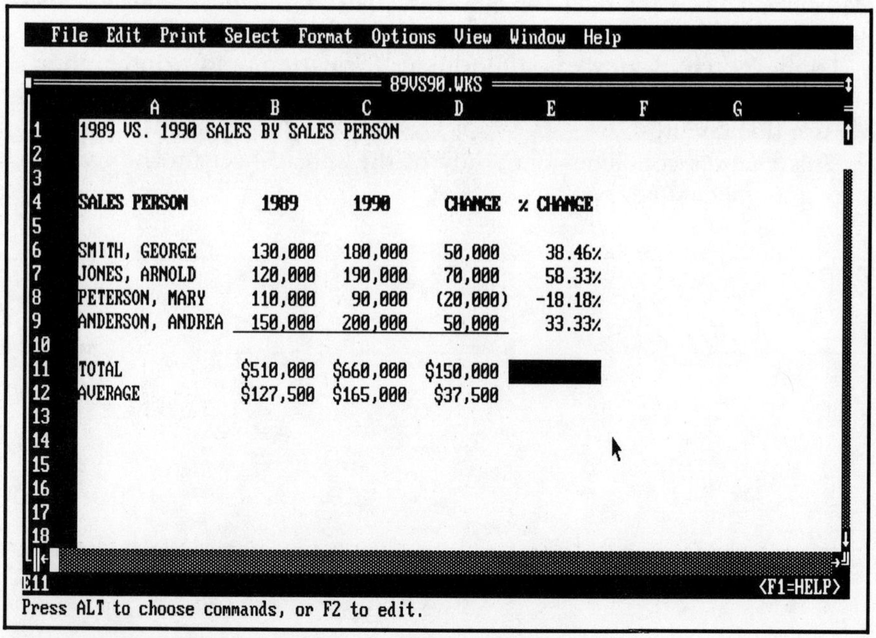

File Edit Print Select Format Options View Window Help

89VS90.WKS

	A	B	C	D	E	F	G
1	1989 VS. 1990 SALES BY SALES PERSON						
2							
3							
4	SALES PERSON	1989	1990	CHANGE	% CHANGE		
5							
6	SMITH, GEORGE	130,000	180,000	50,000	38.46%		
7	JONES, ARNOLD	120,000	190,000	70,000	58.33%		
8	PETERSON, MARY	110,000	90,000	(20,000)	-18.18%		
9	ANDERSON, ANDREA	150,000	200,000	50,000	33.33%		
10							
11	TOTAL	$510,000	$660,000	$150,000			
12	AVERAGE	$127,500	$165,000	$37,500			
13							
14							
15							
16							
17							
18							

E11 <F1=HELP>

Press ALT to choose commands, or F2 to edit.

Figure 8.19: The spreadsheet created in Chapter 6

4. Add the legends and titles shown in Figure 8.20 (see "Adding Titles, Legends, and Data Labels," page 204).
5. Add y-axis grid lines (see "Adding Grid Lines" page 215), and add a border (see "Adding a Border," page 215).
6. Turn on the Show Printer Fonts option, and try different fonts for the title and the rest of the text (see "Changing Fonts in Your Chart," page 212). Figure 8.20 uses 17-point Bold Modern B for Title Font and 7-point Screen for Other Font; you can select whatever fonts you think look best.
7. Save the file with the same name.
8. Print the chart (see "Printing a Chart," page 216).
9. Close the file.

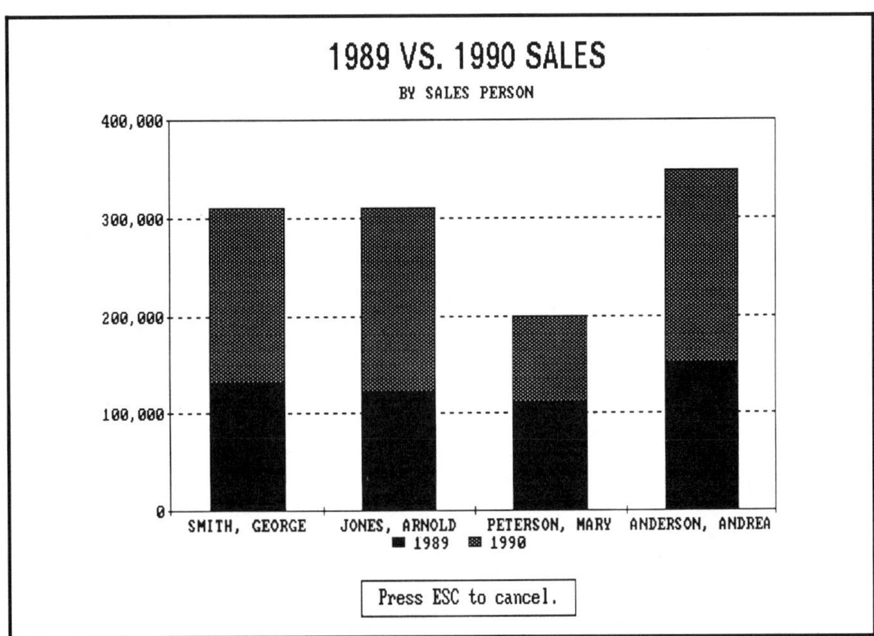

Figure 8.20: The final chart

part four

THE DATABASE TOOL

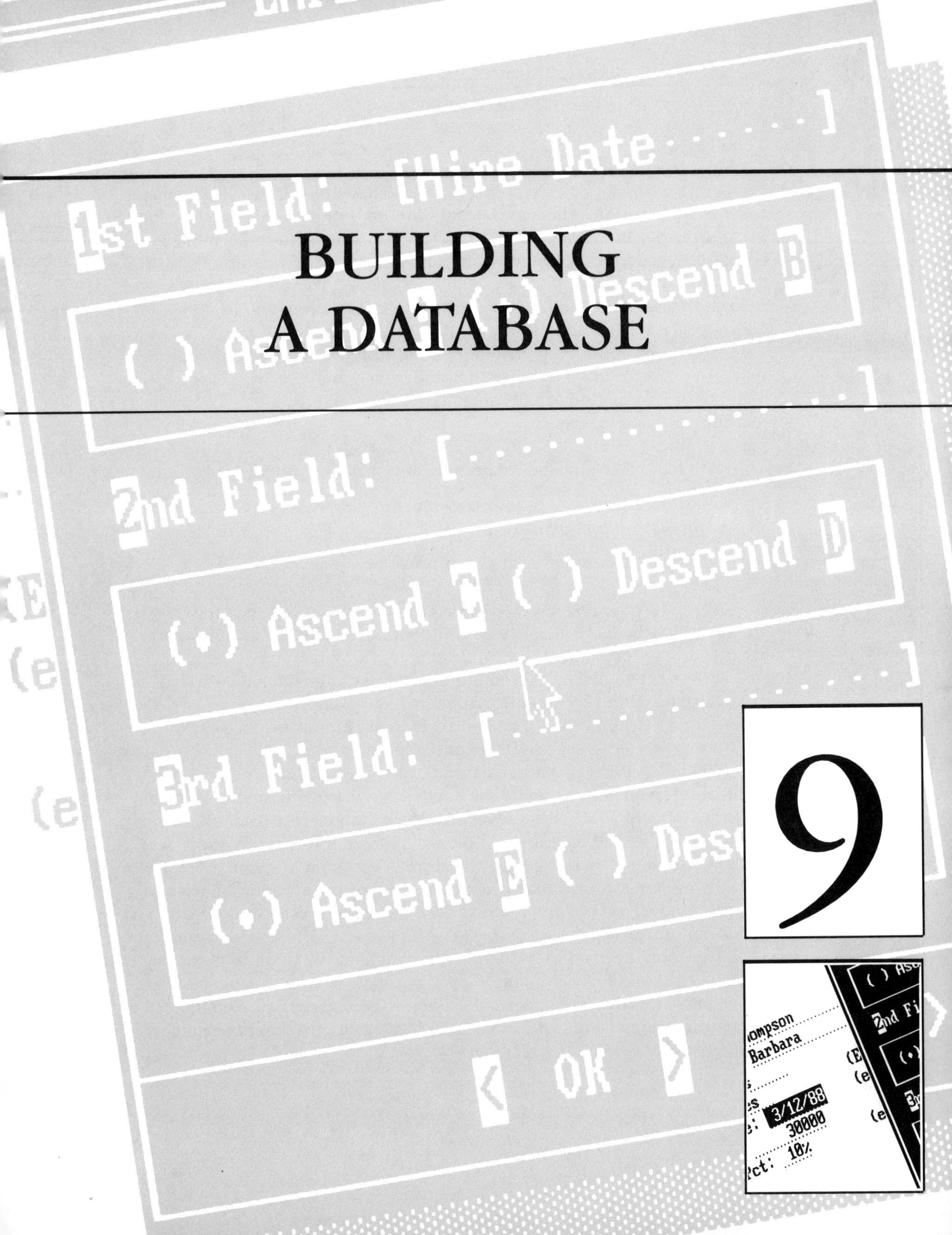

BUILDING A DATABASE

9

The database tool allows you to keep track of information. Think about the different types of information you manage in your home or business. At work you may need to keep track of customers, vendors, inventory, sales leads, invoices, and employees. At home you may keep a phone and address list of friends and relatives, records of your assets and debts, credit-card information, and lists of your collectibles (cassette tapes, stamps, coins, baseball cards, etc.).

Now think about your current methods for keeping track of information. You probably use file folders, a Rolodex, and index cards. These paper methods of information management have several disadvantages compared to a computerized system:

- It's tedious to alphabetize or otherwise order the folders or cards.
- It's time consuming to look up something (especially if it's not where it's supposed to be).
- It's difficult to summarize the information.

A computerized database solves all these problems. To sort the information in alphabetical order, you issue the Sort command and an entire database is quickly organized. To look up something (such as a particular customer's account balance), you use the Search command and Works displays the data within seconds. To summarize the data (for example, to produce a list of customers by city and their total amount of purchases in a certain year), you can use the Query and Report features.

What does the term database mean exactly? A database is a collection of information on one particular subject that is organized in such a way that it can be quickly and easily retrieved. One example of a database is the telephone book. The telephone book is a collection of names, addresses, and phone numbers in one geographical area. The book is organized alphabetically by last name so that you can easily look up a phone number or address. A novel, on the other hand, is not a database because the information is not organized for easy retrieval.

The computerized equivalent of your telephone book is Directory Assistance, like 411. The operator does not have to thumb through telephone books to find a phone number; he or she searches a computerized database for the city and name and usually locates the correct phone number within seconds.

An electronic database is organized into fields and records. A *field* is a piece of data that has a descriptive name assigned to it. For example, a customer database might have the following fields: Company, Contact, Telephone, Street, City, State, and Zip. An inventory database might have these fields: Part Number, Description, Quantity, Price, etc. A *record* contains all the information (fields) about one particular item or person in the database. In a customer database, each customer is in a different record. In an inventory database, each part or product is in a different record. In Works each record can hold up to 256 different fields, and a database can contain up to 4096 records. (The actual maximum depends on your hard disk capacity.) Figure 9.1 illustrates fields and records in a customer database.

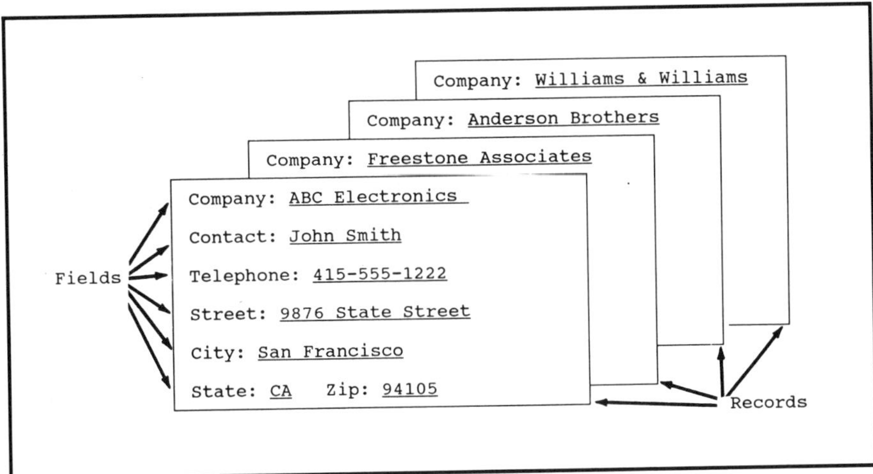

Figure 9.1: Fields and records in a database

The database tool has four different views: Form, List, Query, and Report. Each view provides a unique way of looking at your data. This chapter concentrates on Form view, where you see one record at a time in a fill-in-the-blank form. You use this view to create the database and to enter, look up, and update data. You can also print the data on preprinted forms. Chapter 10 explains List view (data are displayed in a spreadsheet format) and Query view (only specified records are displayed). In Chapter 11 you learn how to create and display reports in Report view.

CREATING A DATABASE FILE

The first step in creating a database is to get out an old-fashioned piece of paper and a pencil—don't turn on your computer yet. In this planning stage you need to decide which type of information you want the database to track and then write down descriptive names for the information. These descriptive names are your *field names.* You should also write down the maximum number of characters that will be entered in each field. This is your *field width.* Works uses the field width to determine how long a line to place next to the field name in the form (see Figure 9.1). For example, in a last-name field, the field width might be 15 characters. If you later discover someone with a longer name, such as "Martinez-Montgomery," you can widen the field. (The maximum field width is 256 characters.) But you should come up with rough estimates at this planning and design stage.

When designing your database, your fields should be as specific as possible and should contain only one piece of information. For example, don't create a single field called Address that contains the street address, city, state, and zip code. Instead, create four separate fields (Street, City, State, and Zip Code). When the information is in separate fields you have a lot more flexibility in searching, sorting, and reporting.

The example database in this and the following chapters is an employee data file. For the sake of brevity, this database has fewer fields and records than an actual database would probably have. The employee data file contains the following field names: Last Name, First Name, Dept, Exempt, Hire Date, Salary, and Raise Pct.

Let's create a database file now.

1. Choose Create New File on the File menu.
2. Select New Database.

The database window appears in Form view. Figure 9.2 points out the different parts of the Form view window, and the next section explains the window in detail.

EXPLORING THE SCREEN

Because you haven't created your database form yet, your window doesn't have much in it. Therefore, for this section, refer to Figure 9.2

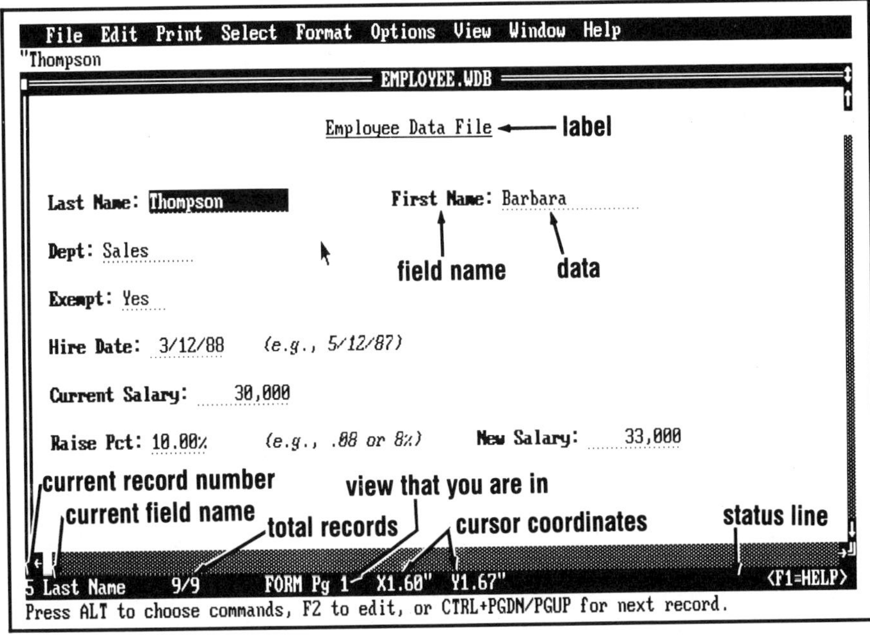

Figure 9.2: The Form view window

rather than your screen. This figure displays the form you will be creating in this chapter. Notice that the form consists of field names, dotted lines where data are entered, the data, and labels that give general, descriptive information. You can see that each of the field names has a colon and the labels do not. For example, *Last Name:* and *First Name:* are field names, and *Employee Data File* and *(e.g., 5/12/87)* are labels. The data are the specific pieces of information (like *Thompson* and *Barbara*) that appear on the dotted line.

The top border of the window is the title bar—it displays the name of your database. Right now your screen displays the default name, DATA1.WDB. In Figure 9.2, the file name is EMPLOYEE.WDB.

The bottom window border is the *status line* and contains information about your database. The first number in the status line is your current record number (record 5 in Figure 9.2). Next to the record number is the current field name. Since the cursor is highlighting the Last Name field, *Last Name* appears in the status line.

The next piece of information, *9/9,* tells you the number of records in the database. The number before the slash indicates the number of records you can browse through, and the second number indicates the total number of records in the database. The two numbers are the same unless you have a query in use or have hidden records (see Chapter 10).

FORM indicates that you are in Form view; this indicator changes according to the view you are in. The page number tells you which page number of the form your cursor is in (*Pg 1* unless you have inserted page breaks for a multipage form).

The X and Y coordinates indicate where the cursor is on the screen. The X value is the distance from the left edge of the page to the cursor (including the left margin), and the Y value is the distance from the top edge of the page (including the top margin). These values help you line up the fields on the screen. The X and Y coordinates are essential if you are trying to design your screen form to match an actual printed form (such as an invoice). For example, if your preprinted invoice form requires that the customer name be printed two inches down from the top of the page and three inches from the left, you place the Customer Name field at X2.00" and Y3.00".

At the very bottom of your screen, Works gives you a *Reader's Digest* condensed version of how to create a form:

> Press ALT to choose commands; type text followed by colon (:) to create field.

Once you have created the form, you can see in Figure 9.2 that this line changes to

> Press ALT to choose commands, F2 to edit, or
> CTRL + PGDN/PGUP for next record.

These abbreviated instructions are discussed in further detail later in this chapter.

DESIGNING A FORM

Right now your screen should be displaying an empty database window in Form view. Think of this window as your drawing pad, on which you design your form. The labels and field names can go anywhere on the screen. Works does not have any strict rules about where you must position your fields and labels on the screen, but you should still give careful consideration to their placement and consider several factors:

- If you are designing a screen form to match a printed form, you should lay out the fields in the same locations as they appear on the printed form. Use a ruler to measure the field positions on the printed form, and then watch the X and Y coordinates on the screen so that you can position the fields in the same location.
- If you are entering data from filled-in forms or slips of paper, try to position the fields in the same order; it will make data entry easier. The exact X and Y coordinates are not important.
- If neither of the above restrictions apply, the first field should be your ***key field,*** the field that makes the record unique. For example, the key field in a personnel database is *Last Name,* the key field in an inventory database is *Part Number,* and the key field in a customer database is *Company Name.*
- All other fields should be in an order that makes sense for either data entry or for viewing the data.

Figure 9.3 displays the form you will design in this chapter. The following are general rules for designing a form:

- To move the cursor around, use the arrow keys or the mouse. (The Enter key does not move the cursor.) Press Home to move to the beginning of a line.
- To create a field, type a colon after the field name and press Enter. Enter the field width and choose OK.
- You can type labels anywhere (just don't put a colon in them).

To begin creating this form, type a label at the top of the screen by following these steps:

1. Use the arrow keys or the mouse to position the cursor on the second line of the form, at about the center. It's not necessary to get the label in the exact same position as shown in Figure 9.3. However, if you want to position the label precisely, watch the X and Y coordinates in the status line and position the cursor at X4.30″ and Y1.17″.

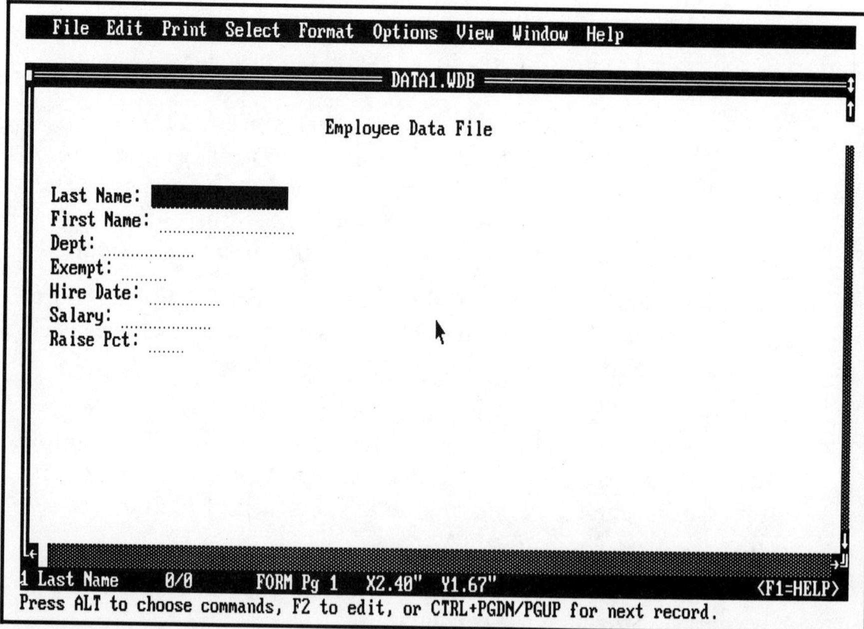

Figure 9.3: The employee data entry form

2. Type the label **Employee Data File.** As you type, the label appears both in the formula bar (the line between the menu bar and the window) and inside the window. Each character in the label is shaded.

3. Press Enter.

To enter your first field name, do the following:

1. Place the cursor at the beginning of the line, a couple of rows below the title you just entered.

2. Type **Last Name:** and press Enter. From the colon, Works recognizes that you entered a field name and displays a dialog box. A Width of 20 and Height of 1 are suggested in the dialog box.

3. Type **15** for the Width. Leave the Height value at 1. (Height refers to the number of lines in the field. Multiline fields are discussed later in this chapter.)

4. Choose OK to close the dialog box. A dotted line appears next to the field name, and the cursor automatically moves down to the next line. (If you don't see a dotted line next to the field name, you may be in Text mode. Use the Works Settings command on the Options menu to switch to Graphics mode.)
5. Enter the remaining field names, each one on a separate line (make sure you type the colons):

FIELD NAME	FIELD WIDTH
First Name:	15
Dept:	10
Exempt:	5
Hire Date:	8
Salary:	10
Raise Pct:	4

If you forget to type the colon in one of the field names, the text is considered to be a label, not a field. To correct this mistake, move the cursor back to that line (the entire label should be highlighted) and retype the field name. This time, remember the colon!

It's helpful to enter descriptive labels next to your fields so that you know what kind of data should be entered in the field. Figure 9.4 has several of these descriptive labels. The *(Enter Yes or No)* label lets you know the responses that should go in the Exempt field; the *(e.g., 5/12/87)* label indicates the appropriate format for entering the date; and the *(e.g., .08 or 8%)* label specifies the acceptable ways of entering data in the Raise Pct field. Enter these three labels as shown in Figure 9.4.

ENTERING DATA

Once you have designed your form, you can start entering data in it. Figure 9.5 lists the data for six records. The records are shown in List view so that you can see all of them at once; however, you should enter the data in

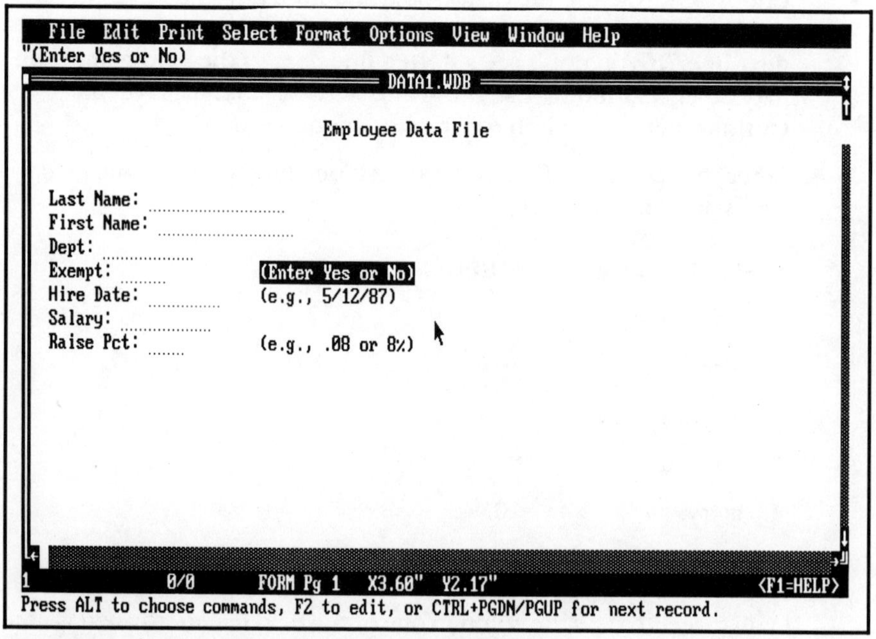

```
 File  Edit  Print  Select  Format  Options  View  Window  Help
"(Enter Yes or No)
                              DATA1.WDB

                         Employee Data File

 Last Name: ..................
 First Name: ..................
 Dept: ............
 Exempt: ......       (Enter Yes or No)
 Hire Date: ........  (e.g., 5/12/87)
 Salary: ............
 Raise Pct: .....     (e.g., .08 or 8%)

1          0/0       FORM Pg 1   X3.60"  Y2.17"                 <F1=HELP>
Press ALT to choose commands, F2 to edit, or CTRL+PGDN/PGUP for next record.
```

Figure 9.4: The form, with descriptive labels

Form view. Enter each record in a separate form, following these steps:

1. Place the cursor on the dotted line next to the first field (*Last Name* in this case). The cursor appears as a rectangular bar when it is on the dotted line.
2. Type the data. (Note: If two consecutive records contain the same data in a field, you can press Ctrl-' to copy the previous record's data.)
3. Press Tab to go to the next field. (Shift-Tab moves the cursor back to the previous field.)
4. Repeat steps 2 and 3 for each field. When you press Tab in the last field, a blank form appears for the next record. The cursor goes automatically to the dotted line next to the first field.
5. Repeat steps 2 through 4 for each record.

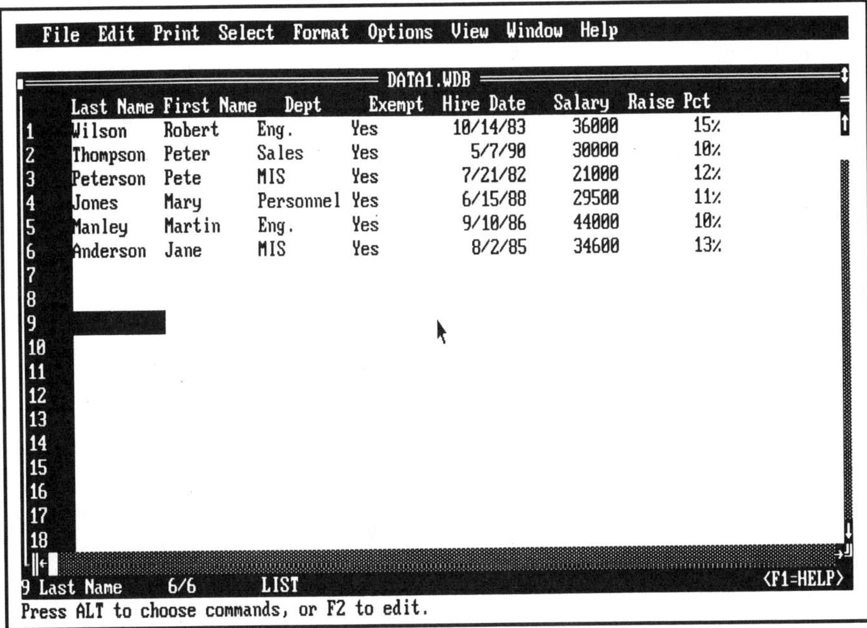

Figure 9.5: A list of records to enter

Save the file with the name EMPLOYEE. As shown at the top of the window, Works adds the extension .WDB to the file name.

EDITING IN FORM VIEW

Once you have entered your data, the next step is to look over the records to make sure you didn't make any typing errors. If you discover a mistake, Works offers a variety of ways to correct it. In this section you also learn how to insert, delete, copy, and sort records.

GETTING AROUND THE DATABASE

The bottom of the screen reminds you of one way to move between records: "CTRL + PGDN/PGUP for next record." Ctrl-PgUp displays the previous record, and Ctrl-PgDn displays the next record. I discovered that

Ctrl-↑ and Ctrl-↓ also move the cursor between records. The mouse offers yet another way to move between records: Click on the up and down arrows in the scroll bar.

To go to the top of the database, either press Ctrl-Home or place the mouse pointer on the scroll box at the top of the scroll bar and click the left button. The first record is displayed. To double-check that you are on the first record, look at the *1* at the beginning of the status line. To go to the end of the database, press Ctrl-End. This command actually does two things at once: It takes you to the end of the database, and it displays a blank form so that you can enter more records. To see the last record in the database, press Ctrl-PgUp after you press Ctrl-End.

You have already learned two ways to move the cursor between fields: The Tab key moves it to the next field, and Shift-Tab moves it to the previous field. But imagine that your form has dozens of fields. It would be quite tedious to press Tab or Shift-Tab to go to the field in which you want to make a change. If you have a mouse, simply click on the dotted line next to the field name you want to go to. If you don't have a mouse, you can use the Goto key, F5, to go directly to a field. The field names are displayed in the Go To dialog box so you can highlight the name and press Enter. It sure beats tabbing around the form!

Tables 9.1 and 9.2 summarize the different ways you can move around your database with the keyboard and with the mouse.

Table 9.1: Moving between Records and Fields with the Keyboard

MOVEMENT OF CURSOR	KEYSTROKE
Next record	Ctrl-PgDn or Ctrl-↓
Previous record	Ctrl-PgUp or Ctrl-↑
First record	Ctrl-Home
Blank form at end of database	Ctrl-End
Specific record number	F5 or Go To on the Select menu
Next screen of form	PgDn
Previous screen of form	PgUp
Next field	Tab
Previous field	Shift-Tab
Specific field	F5 or Go To on the Select menu

Table 9.2: Moving between Records and Fields with the Mouse

MOVEMENT OF CURSOR	MOUSE ACTION
Next record	Click on down arrow in scroll bar, or click in scroll bar
Previous record	Click on up arrow in scroll bar
First record	Click on scroll box at top of scroll bar
Specific field	Click on dotted line next to field name

EDITING DATA

Editing data in a field is similar to editing data in a spreadsheet cell. Place the cursor on the data you want to change, and then choose one of the following methods:

- Type over what's already there. Use this method if the new data are substantially different from the old data.
- Use the Edit key, F2, to modify the field contents. Use this technique to add to or delete from what's already there.

When you press F2, the contents of the field appear in the formula bar. As in the spreadsheet tool, the formula bar is the single line between the menu bar and the window. You can edit with any of the keys described in Table 9.3. To insert new text, position the cursor and start typing; the characters are automatically inserted to the left of the cursor. If you have a mouse, there is an alternative way to edit field contents. Instead of pressing F2, click the mouse pointer in the formula bar at the position where you want to edit.

Follow these steps to correct a typing mistake made in Mary Jones's Hire Date:

1. Display Mary Jones's record.
2. Place the cursor on the dotted line next to Hire Date.
3. Press F2.
4. Press Home to go to the beginning of the formula bar.

Table 9.3: Editing Keys

EDITING ACTION	KEYSTROKE
Left one character	←
Right one character	→
Beginning of entry	Home
End of entry	End
Select characters	Shift with arrow keys
Delete left	Backspace
Delete selection	Del

5. Press Del to delete the *6*.
6. Type **10.**
7. Press Enter.

To erase the data in a field, put the cursor on the data, and press Del or Backspace. Although the field contents disappear, you can press Esc to cancel the command and redisplay the data if you gave the command in error. Otherwise, you can press Enter or move the cursor to clear the contents permanently. You can also erase data with the Clear Field Contents command on the Edit menu.

INSERTING NEW RECORDS

After you have created a database and have entered data in it, you have several alternatives for inserting additional records:

- Press Ctrl-End to go to the end of the database; a blank form automatically appears.
- Use the Insert Record command on the Edit menu to insert a blank form at the beginning, or somewhere in the middle, of the database.
- Use the Copy Record command on the Edit menu to duplicate an existing record.

If you don't care where a new record appears, use the first technique (press Ctrl-End). You will use this technique most of the time because you can insert an infinite number of records without having to give a command for each new record. Simply by pressing Tab on the last field or by pressing Ctrl-PgDn, you get another blank form. The Insert Record command, on the other hand, only inserts one blank form at a time. It does have the advantage of allowing you to insert a record *anywhere* in the database, not just at the end.

If a new record has data similar to those in an existing record, you can copy the record and then modify the contents of the copied record. To duplicate Peter Thompson's record, follow these steps:

1. Place the cursor anywhere on Peter Thompson's record.
2. Choose Copy Record on the Edit menu. The message "Select new location and press ENTER." appears at the bottom of the screen.
3. Press Ctrl-End to copy the record into the blank form at the end of the database. (Note: If you specify an existing record as the new location, the record at the new location is replaced with the copy.)
4. Press Enter. The duplicated data appear in record 7 (look at the status line).
5. All the data in your duplicate record are the same except for *First Name* and *Hire Date*. Make the following changes:

First Name:	Barbara
Hire Date:	3/12/88

DELETING RECORDS

When you no longer need a record in a database, you can delete it. Deleting a record is easy—maybe too easy. To do it, you place the cursor anywhere on the record you want to delete and choose Delete Record on the Edit menu. You are *not* given a chance to confirm or cancel this command, and there is no Undo command in the database tool. Make sure you save the database file before you delete any records.

Do not delete any records in your employee data file.

ORGANIZING RECORDS

Records appear in the order you enter them, usually in a random order. Most likely, though, you will want to organize records alphabetically, numerically, or chronologically. Sorting records is similar to sorting rows in a spreadsheet (you learned the Sort Rows command in Chapter 7). But instead of specifying column(s) to sort by, you specify field(s).

You can sort by any field in the database, in either ascending or descending order. As you may remember from Chapter 7, ascending order is more common: It sorts text from A–Z, numbers from lowest to highest, and dates from earliest to latest. Choosing descending sorts data in the reverse order.

Follow these steps to sort the employee data so that the most recent hire dates appear first:

1. Choose Sort Records on the Select menu.
2. *Last Name* is filled in next to *1st Field* because Works automatically suggests the first field name in the form. Type **Hire Date** instead.
3. Press Alt-B to choose Descend (or click the mouse pointer next to Descend). Your dialog box should look similar to the one in Figure 9.6.
4. Choose OK.
5. Press Ctrl-PgDn (or click the mouse pointer on the downward-pointing scroll arrow) to look through the records one at a time. The records are now sorted by Hire Date, with the most recently hired employees at the beginning.

Next, follow these steps to sort the last names in alphabetical order:

1. Choose Sort Records on the Select menu.
2. Type **Last Name** next to 1st Field.
3. Press Alt-A to choose Ascend (or click the mouse pointer next to Ascend).
4. Choose OK.

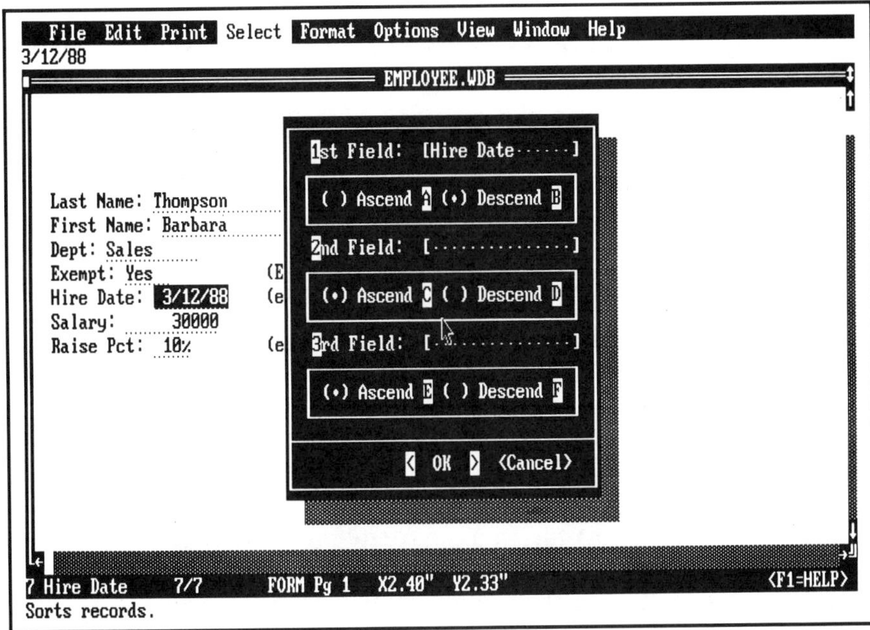

Figure 9.6: The Sort dialog box

5. Press Ctrl-PgDn (or click the mouse pointer on the downward-pointing scroll arrow) to look through the records one at a time. The records are now sorted alphabetically by last name.

When you have duplicate entries in your first sort field, you should specify an additional sort field to function as a "tiebreaker." In this example, two people have the last name Thompson, so you need to tell Works to sort by the First Name field when there is a duplicate entry (a "tie"). As the dialog box indicates, you can sort up to three fields at once.

1. Display the Sort Records dialog box. *Last Name* should still be indicated next to 1st Field.
2. Next to 2nd Field, type **First Name.**
3. Press Enter. The last names are sorted, and when a last name appears more than once, the first names are sorted. Barbara Thompson now appears before Peter Thompson.

CUSTOMIZING THE FORM

You can do several things to make the form easier to enter data in. First, you can create formulas that automatically fill in data for you. Second, you can format the fields, labels, and data to enhance the readability of the form.

CREATING CALCULATED FIELDS

The database tool offers all the calculating capabilities that you saw in the spreadsheet tool. What this means is that you can create fields that perform calculations on other fields. In an invoice database, for example, you can have a field called Total that is the product of the Price and Quantity fields. Or you can have a field called Tax that multiplies the Total field by 7 percent. You enter formulas on the dotted lines next to the field names.

In the employee data file, you can create a field called New Salary that calculates an employee's salary after a raise. This formula multiplies the Salary and Raise Pct fields and then adds that number to the original salary. Follow these steps:

1. Place the cursor on the line under the Raise Pct field. (It doesn't matter which record you put the cursor on.)
2. Type **New Salary:** (don't forget the colon), and press Enter.
3. In the dialog box that appears, type **10** for the Width and press Enter.
4. Move the cursor to the dotted line next to New Salary.
5. Type the formula **=SALARY*RAISE PCT+SALARY** and press Enter.
6. The result is automatically displayed for the current record. Browse through the database to see that the new field and formula were automatically added to every record.

Any new records you insert also have this new field and formula. Press Ctrl-End to go to a blank record, and type the record shown in Figure 9.7. Remember, use the Tab key to move from field to field. Do not type the New Salary value; it is automatically calculated as soon as you enter the Salary and Raise Pct.

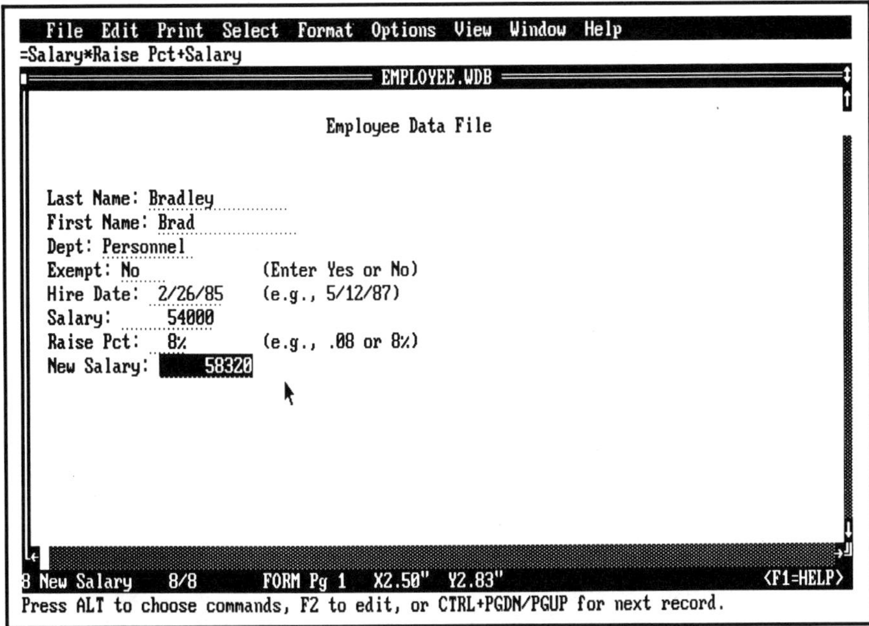

Figure 9.7: The form with New Salary calculated automatically

SPECIFYING A DEFAULT VALUE

Sometimes a database has a field that contains the same value from record to record. A state field in a database of local customers is a good example of a field that rarely changes values. Rather than typing the same value over and over again in each record, you can use either of two techniques:

- Press Ctrl-' to copy the field's data from the previous record.
- Specify a default value. This value will automatically appear in each new record.

To specify a default value, place the cursor on the dotted line next to the field name and type = (equal sign), followed by the default text or number. Default text must be preceded by a quotation mark. For example, to specify California as a default in a state field, you type = *"California.* Default numbers do not have a quotation mark. For example, to specify 10 as the default in a quantity field, you type = *10.*

The Exempt field in your employee data file is a good candidate for a default value since most of the employees are exempt. The default value in this case should be *Yes.*

1. Press Ctrl-End to move to the blank record at the end of the database.
2. Move the cursor next to Exempt.
3. Type ="**Yes**.
4. Press Enter. The formula seems to disappear until you enter data for the record.
5. Enter the data shown in Figure 9.8. As soon as you start entering data, *Yes* appears next to Exempt.
6. To accept the default value when you get to the Exempt field, press Tab to skip to the next field. When you do need to change the value, you can just type over the default.

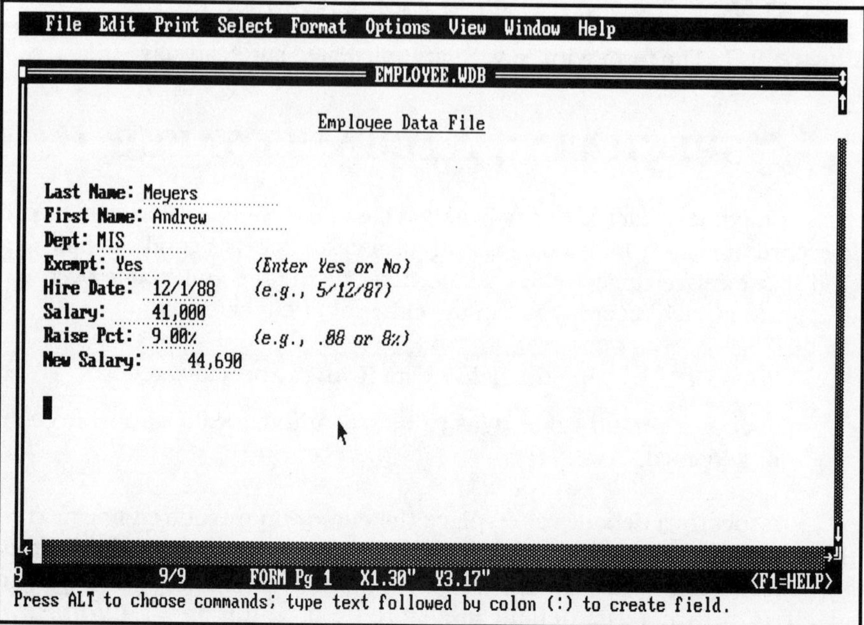

Figure 9.8: The form with Exempt displaying a default value

FORMATTING THE LABELS AND FIELD NAMES

To differentiate the labels and field names from the actual data, you can add character styles—bold, underline, and italic. First, let's underline the title at the top of your employee data file. Follow these steps:

1. Press Ctrl-End to move to the blank record at the end of the database.
2. Choose Style on the Format menu.
3. Press U or click next to Underline.
4. Choose OK. The label is now underlined. (If you are in Text mode, you will not see the underlining on the screen, but it will appear when it is printed.)

The field names will stand out better if they are in boldface, so follow these steps:

1. Highlight the first field name, Last Name.
2. Choose Style on the Format menu.
3. Press B or click next to Bold.
4. Choose OK.

Instead of going into the Style dialog box for each field name, you can tell Works to repeat the last format command you issued.

1. Place the cursor on the next field name, First Name.
2. Press Shift-F7 for Repeat Format.
3. Continue highlighting each field name and pressing Shift-F7 until all field names are formatted.

Specify an italic style for the remaining labels so that your form looks similar to Figure 9.9.

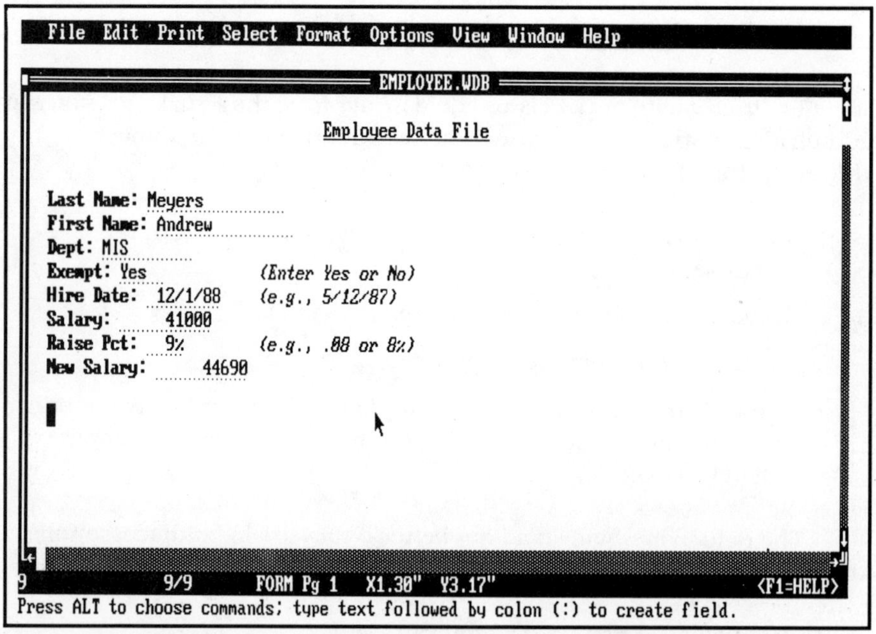

```
 File  Edit  Print  Select  Format  Options  View  Window  Help
 ═══════════════════════ EMPLOYEE.WDB ═══════════════════════
                         Employee Data File

 Last Name: Meyers
 First Name: Andrew
 Dept: MIS
 Exempt: Yes            (Enter Yes or No)
 Hire Date:  12/1/88    (e.g., 5/12/87)
 Salary:       41000
 Raise Pct:   9%        (e.g., .08 or 8%)
 New Salary:      44690

9          9/9       FORM Pg 1   X1.30"  Y3.17"              <F1=HELP>
Press ALT to choose commands; type text followed by colon (:) to create field.
```

Figure 9.9: The form with formatted labels and field names

FORMATTING THE NUMBERS

The numeric fields in the form could also use some formatting. The database tool offers the same types of numeric formats as the spreadsheet tool (Fixed, Currency, Comma, etc.) Figure 9.10 displays your form with formatted numbers. The Salary and New Salary fields have commas, and the Raise Pct field is formatted with percent signs and two decimal places. To add punctuation to your numeric fields, you place the cursor on the dotted line next to the field name (not on the field name) and choose the appropriate format on the Format menu. To add commas to the Salary field, follow these steps:

1. Highlight the dotted line next to Salary.
2. Choose Comma on the Format menu.
3. Type **0** for the number of decimal places.
4. Choose OK.

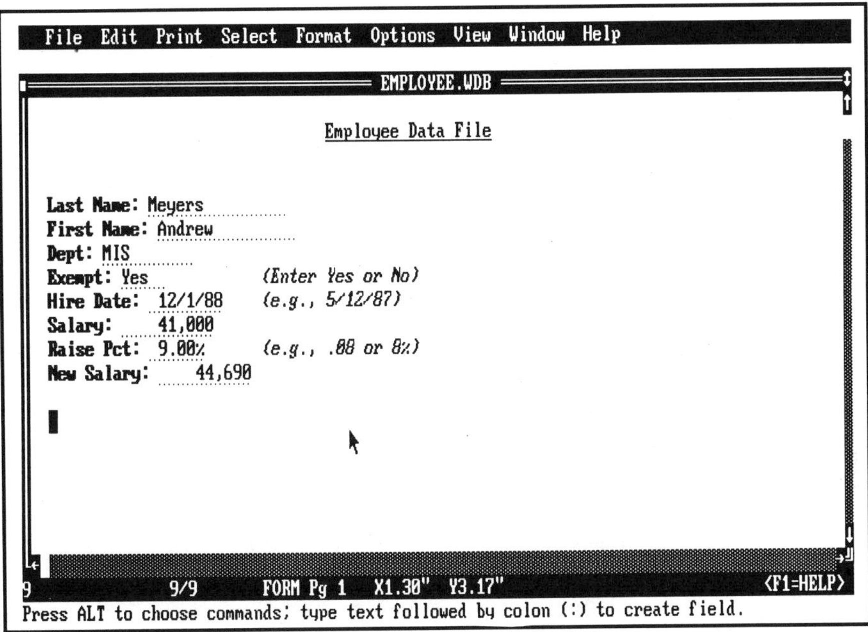

Figure 9.10: The form with formatted numbers

Look through the records to confirm that commas appear in all of them. Repeat the above steps to format the New Salary field (or use the Repeat Format command, Shift-F7).

Format the Raise Pct field to Percent with two decimal places. Look through the records—notice that some of the fields display number signs (####) and the remainder of the fields display two decimal places but no percent signs. Don't panic—you have not lost any data. As you may remember from the spreadsheet tool, the number signs indicate that the *column* is not wide enough. In the database tool, these symbols indicate that the *field* is not wide enough. To widen your Raise Pct field, do the following:

1. Choose Field Size on the Format menu (the cursor should be on the dotted line next to Raise Pct).
2. As shown in the dialog box, the current width of this field is *4.* To display the percentages with two decimal places, the width has to be *6.* Type **6**.

3. Press Enter. Browse through the records—notice that each Raise Pct field displays a percent sign with two decimal places.

MODIFYING THE FORM LAYOUT

The layout of the fields in your form is not set in stone. You can reposition fields and labels, insert new fields, delete fields and labels you no longer need, and assign different names to your fields.

The choices on the Edit menu vary depending on whether your cursor is highlighting a field (see Figure 9.11) or a label (see Figure 9.12). For example, when a field is highlighted, the Edit menu displays choices for Move Field and Delete Field. These choices are transformed into Move Label and Delete Label when you highlight a label.

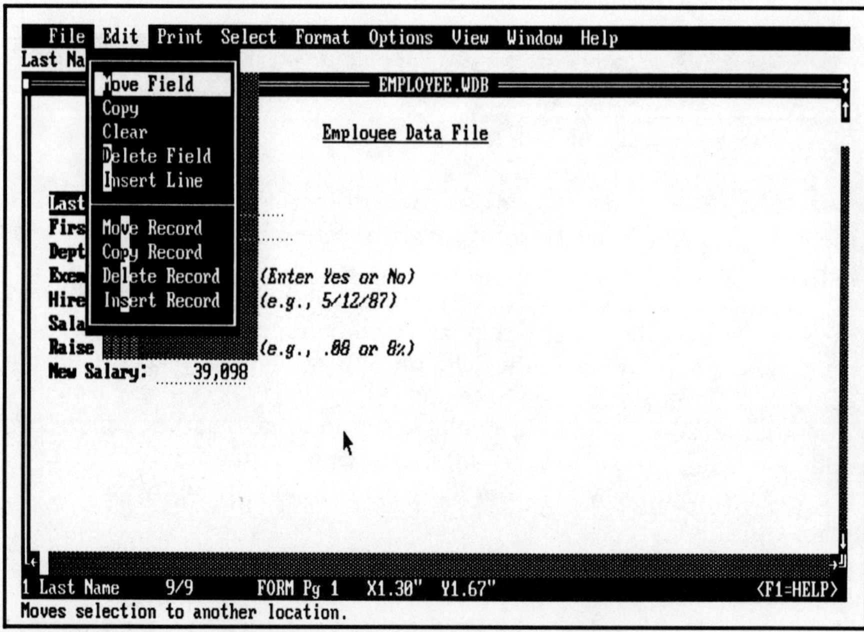

Figure 9.11: The Edit menu when a field is highlighted

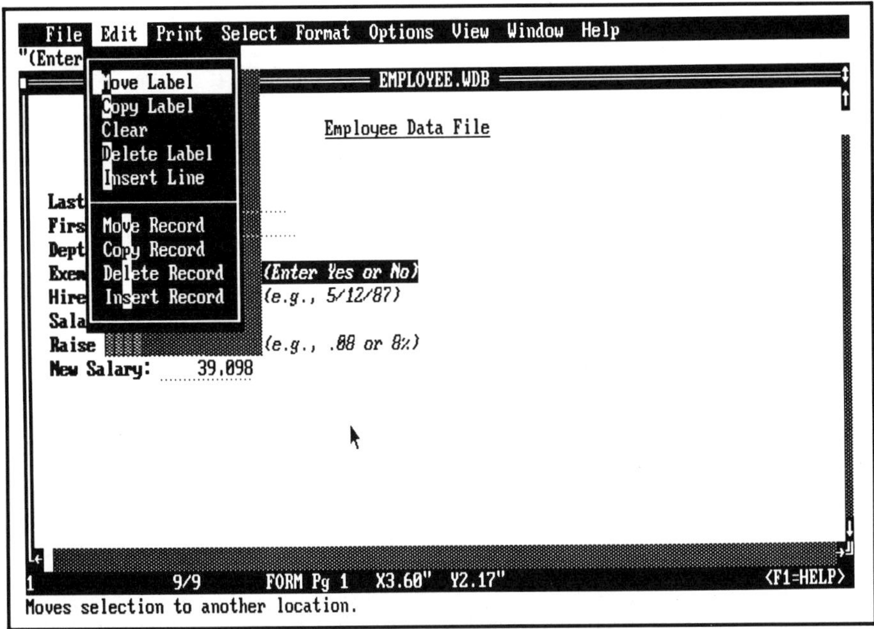

Figure 9.12: The Edit menu when a label is highlighted

INSERTING FIELDS

It doesn't matter whether you create fields before or after you enter data; the procedure for inserting fields is the same, regardless of when you do it. As you learned earlier, to insert a field, you position the cursor on the form, type the field name followed by a colon, and press Enter. At this point, a dialog box appears so that you can enter the field width and height.

Let's create a new field at the bottom of the form. This field will be called Comments and will be a multiline field. So far, you have created only single-line fields because you have accepted the default height of 1. By typing a different value for Height (such as 2 or 3), several rows of dotted lines appear next to the field name, as shown in the Comments field of Figure 9.13.

The main advantage of a multiline field is that the text word-wraps as you type—just as it does in the word processor tool. Consequently, these fields are perfect for long descriptions and comments. However, you *must*

```
 File  Edit  Print  Select  Format  Options  View  Window  Help
Comments:
                              EMPLOYEE.WDB

                           Employee Data File


  Last Name: Anderson
  First Name: Jane
  Dept: MIS
  Exempt: Yes             (Enter Yes or No)
  Hire Date:   8/2/85     (e.g., 5/12/87)
  Salary:     34,600
  Raise Pct: 13.00%       (e.g., .08 or 8%)
  New Salary:     39,098
  Comments:




1 Comments      9/9      FORM Pg 1   X1.30"  Y3.00"              <F1=HELP>
Press ALT to choose commands, F2 to edit, or CTRL+PGDN/PGUP for next record.
```

Figure 9.13: The form with a multiline field called Comments

let the text word-wrap in a multiline field; Works does not let you press Enter to move to the next line.

To create the Comments field, do the following:

1. Place the cursor on the line under New Salary.
2. Type **Comments:** and press Enter.
3. In the dialog box, type **25** for Width.
4. Type **3** for Height.
5. Choose OK.

When you create a field after you have already entered data in the database, the new fields are empty in each record. You must go back to the existing records and fill in the fields. To see how you enter data in a multiline field, follow these steps:

1. Press Ctrl-Home to move to the first record (Anderson).

2. Place the cursor next to Comments (all three dotted lines are highlighted).
3. Type **MS in Computer Science from Penn State**.
4. Press Enter. Notice how the text automatically word-wraps within the field.
5. Press Ctrl-PgDn to go to the next record. The same (empty) field is automatically highlighted in the next record. After entering data in a newly inserted field, do *not* press Tab as you normally do because you want to keep the cursor on the same field.

Don't bother entering any more comments because you are going to delete this field in the next exercise.

DELETING FIELDS AND LABELS

When you choose the Delete Field option on the Edit menu, you delete all the data that were entered in the field, in all records. If all you want to do is delete a field's data in one record, do not choose Delete Field; choose the Clear Field Contents command or press the Del key.

To delete the Comments field, follow these steps:

1. Highlight either the field name or the set of dotted lines next to it.
2. Choose Delete Field on the Edit menu.
3. Because the Delete Field command can result in the loss of data if you issue it accidentally, you are asked to confirm the command: "OK to delete data in this field?" Choose OK.

This field is now removed from the form, and all the data that were stored in the field go to computer heaven, never to be seen again.

Now let's remove a label. Follow these steps:

1. Highlight the label *(Enter Yes or No)*.
2. Display the Edit menu. Since your cursor is highlighting a label, the Edit menu displays the option Delete Label instead of Delete Field.

3. Choose Delete Label.
4. Choose OK.

Your form should look similar to Figure 9.14.

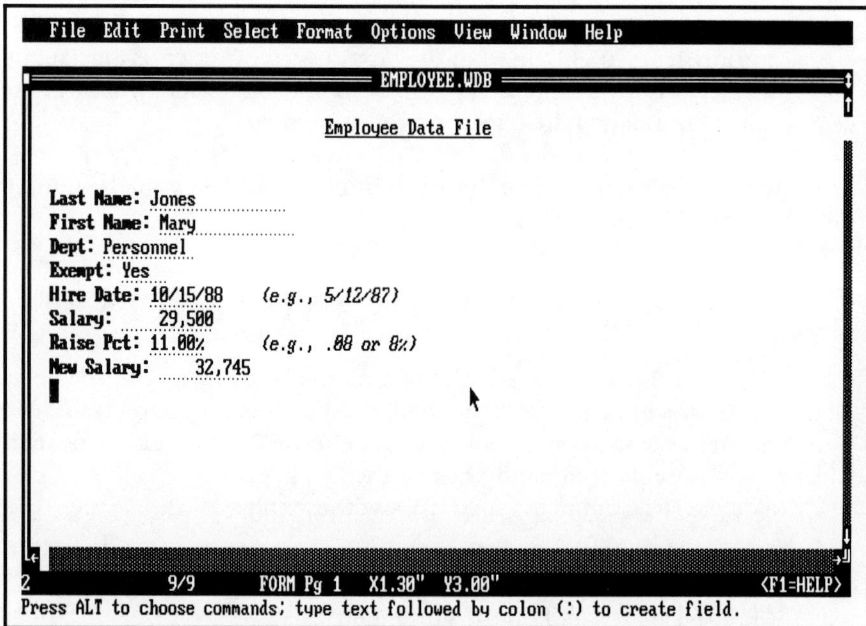

Figure 9.14: The form with a field and a label deleted

MOVING FIELDS AND LABELS

Your fields and labels can be repositioned anywhere on the form, as long as they don't overlap existing text—the new location must be empty. Depending on what you are moving, choose either the Move Label or Move Field command on the Edit menu.

All the fields on your form appear on separate lines. Sometimes, though, you may want to have several fields on a line. For example, in a mailing-list database, the City, State, and Zip Code fields can go on a single line. In your employee data file, it makes sense to place the Last Name and First Name fields on one line.

Follow these steps to move the First Name field:

1. Highlight the First Name field (either the name or the dotted line).
2. Choose Move Field on the Edit menu. The message "Select new location and press ENTER" appears at the bottom of the screen. Notice that the entire field (the name and the dotted line) is highlighted—this rectangular bar is the cursor that you move when you specify the new location. The bar is the size of the field name and the dotted line, enabling you to easily see if there is enough room for the field in the new location.
3. You can specify the new location with the arrow keys or with the the mouse:

   Using the arrow keys: As you press an arrow key, the highlighted rectangular bar moves in the arrow's direction. Position the bar to the right of the Last Name field, at around X5.00″ (check the status line at the bottom of the screen).

   Using the mouse: Click on the new location—to the right of the Last Name field, at around X5.00″.

4. When you have positioned the field in the new location, press Enter.

Follow these same steps to move the New Salary field on the same line as Raise Pct (see Figure 9.15).

You can move labels in the same way as you move fields. Because Works doesn't offer a way to center a label at the top of the form, you can use the Move Label command to position a title in the center. If any of the labels in your employee form aren't positioned properly, use the Move Label command now to put them in place.

INSERTING AND DELETING LINES

The form would be easier to read if it had blank lines between each row of fields. Since this form doesn't have very many fields, there's enough room to double-space the form and still fit everything on one screen. If adding blank lines caused the form to be displayed on two screens, you probably wouldn't want to do it; it's more convenient to work with a one-screen form.

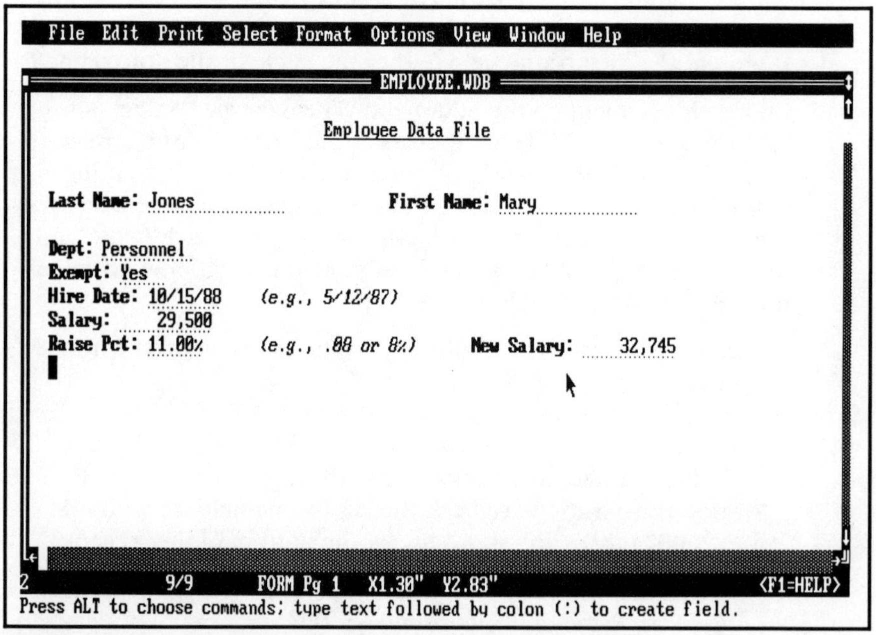

```
 File  Edit  Print  Select  Format  Options  View  Window  Help
                         EMPLOYEE.WDB
                       Employee Data File

 Last Name: Jones                   First Name: Mary

 Dept: Personnel
 Exempt: Yes
 Hire Date: 10/15/88    (e.g., 5/12/87)
 Salary:     29,500
 Raise Pct: 11.00%      (e.g., .08 or 8%)     New Salary:      32,745

2          9/9       FORM Pg 1   X1.30"  Y2.83"                  <F1=HELP>
Press ALT to choose commands; type text followed by colon (:) to create field.
```

Figure 9.15: The form after fields have been moved

Follow these steps to insert blank lines in your form:

1. To insert a line between Dept and Exempt, place the cursor anywhere on the Exempt line. (Lines are inserted above the cursor.)
2. Choose Insert Line on the Edit menu.
3. Repeat this process until you have double-spaced the entire form. Your form should look similar to Figure 9.16.

To remove extra blank lines, you use the Delete Line command on the Edit menu. However, you cannot delete lines containing fields or labels. You must first remove each field and label on the line using the Delete Field and Delete Label commands, and then use Delete Line.

REVISING FIELD NAMES AND LABELS

In the "Editing Data" section, you learned how to revise data with the Edit key, F2, and with the mouse. These techniques also work on your field

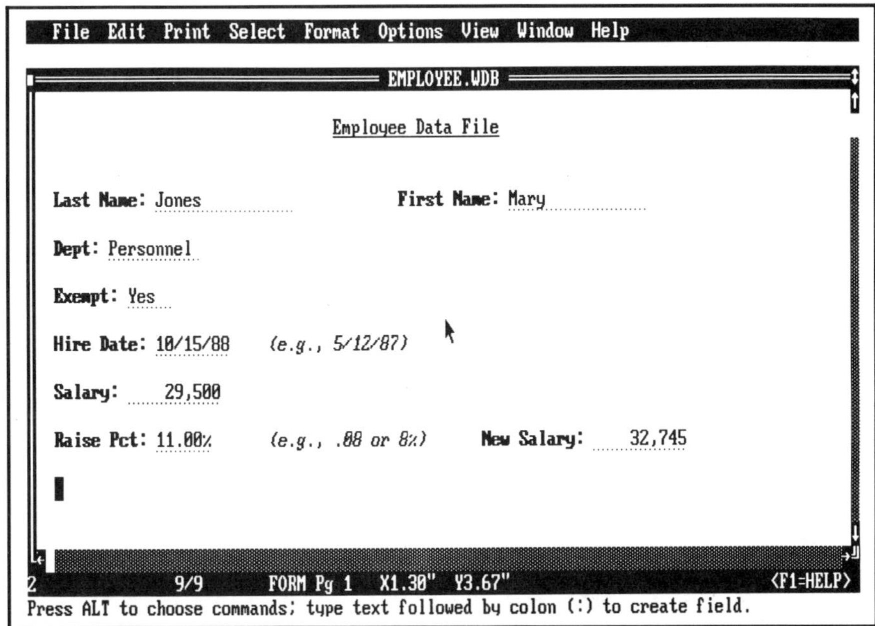

Figure 9.16: The form with inserted blank lines

names and labels. If you discover a typing mistake in a label, you can edit it. Or, if you decide your field name is not descriptive enough, you can rename the field.

Follow these steps to change the name of the Salary field to Current Salary:

1. Highlight the Salary field name.
2. Press F2 to edit the name. The cursor appears at the end of Salary in the formula bar.
3. Press Home to move to the beginning of the line.
4. Type **Current,** and press the spacebar.
5. Press Enter.

After you change the field name, the New Salary formula, which references the Salary field, also changes. Move the cursor next to New Salary and read the formula bar: *Current Salary*Raise Pct + Current Salary.*

When changing the name of a field, make sure the new name includes a colon. If you don't put in a colon, the field is replaced with a label and all the data for the field are lost. Fortunately, Works gives you a confirmation message when this happens.

PRINTING THE FORM

You will probably do most of your printing in the List and Report views so that you can produce reports with columns. When you print in Form view, each record prints in the format of the form—just as you see on the screen. You will want to print in Form view if your form is one that replaces a preprinted form. For example, you may want to print out the form and its data to use the form as an invoice or a purchase order. You can also print the data directly on a preprinted form. Another reason to print in Form view is so you can print a blank form that can be used for data entry.

PRINTING RECORDS IN A FORM

Let's say you want to print out the form exactly as it appears on the screen—with the descriptive labels, field names, and data that appear next to the field names.

Because your form is spread out over all the screen, it probably is too wide to fit on the printed page, unless you change the margins. As in all Works tools, the default margins are large (1.3″ for the left margin and 1.2″ for the right). Follow these steps to change the margins and print a record:

1. Choose Page Setup & Margins on the Print menu.
2. Type **.5** for the Left margin.
3. Type **.5** for the Right margin.
4. Choose OK.

Follow these steps to print a record:

1. Display the record you want to print (choose any record).

2. Choose Print on the Print menu. All the options in the dialog box are correct for printing the form and data for the current record. Notice that *Current record only* is selected in the *Print which records* box and that *All items* is chosen for *Print which items.* The *All items* option prints the entire form—the field names, labels, and data.
3. Make sure your printer is turned on.
4. Choose Print. Your printed form should look similar to Figure 9.17.

Employee Data File

Last Name: Anderson **First Name:** Jane

Dept: MIS

Exempt: Yes

Hire Date: 8/2/85 *(e.g., 5/12/87)*

Current Salary: 34,600

Raise Pct: 13.00% *(e.g., .08 or 8%)* **New Salary:** 39,098

Figure 9.17: The printed form

To print all the records, choose *All records* in the Print dialog box. Each record prints on a separate page. If you want a selected group of records to print (for example, all employees in the sales department), see Chapter 10.

PRINTING A BLANK FORM

You may also want to print a blank form that displays the field names and labels, but no data. You can then make photocopies of this form and enter data in them when you aren't near a computer. Because the printed form is exactly like your screen form, you can easily transfer the data from paper to computer.

The only problem with the printed blank form is that the dotted lines do not print. You can get around this problem by specifying an underline style for each of the fields. You should consider this change to be temporary; if you leave the fields underlined, each piece of data is underlined in the List and Report views.

Follow these steps to underline the dotted lines:

1. Save the file.
2. Highlight the dotted line next to the Last Name field in any record.
3. Choose Style on the Format menu.
4. Press U or click next to Underline.
5. Choose OK.
6. Press Tab to go to the next field and use the Repeat Format command, Shift-F7.
7. Repeat step 6 for each field.

To print out a blank form, follow these steps:

1. Press Ctrl-End to display a blank form.
2. Choose Print on the Print menu.
3. Make sure *All items* is chosen for the *Print which items* option (otherwise the field names won't print).
4. Make sure *Current record only* is chosen in the *Print which records* box.
5. Choose Print. Your blank form should look similar to Figure 9.18.

Now close the file without saving it.

1. Choose Close on the File menu.
2. Press N or click on No to close without saving.

If you save the file with the underlined fields, all the field contents are underlined in other views. If you accidentally save the underlines, you can remove them by turning off Underline in the Style dialog box for each field.

Employee Data File

Last Name: ________ First Name: ________

Dept: ______

Exempt: ___

Hire Date: _____ *(e.g., 5/12/87)*

Current Salary: ______

Raise Pct: ____ *(e.g., .08 or 8%)* New Salary: ______

Figure 9.18: A printed blank form

PRINTING THE DATA ON PREPRINTED FORMS

If your database tracks customer invoices, purchase orders, or tax information, you might want to print the data on preprinted forms. The employee data file you have been working with in this chapter is probably not a database you would want to print on a preprinted form. But because the capability to print on preprinted forms is so useful and powerful, this section explains the procedures involved. The instructions included here are general and apply to any database. If you want to, you can pretend you have a preprinted form for your employee data file and follow along with the exercises. Open the EMPLOYEE.WDB file now. Otherwise, you can skip this section and return to it later when you need it.

There are two main concerns when printing data on a preprinted form, such as an invoice. First, you do not want the field names on the screen form to print. Second, you want the data to print on the preprinted form's blank lines. The first requirement is simple to meet—it's an option in the Print dialog box. Meeting the second requirement takes more effort on your part.

To get the data to print in the right locations, the fields on your screen form must be laid out in precisely the same positions as on the printed form.

The first step is to specify the page size and margins.

- Bring up the Page Setup & Margins dialog box.
- Set the appropriate top, bottom, left, and right margins.
- If your form is not the standard letter size (8½″ × 11″), change the page length and page width.

Next, you need to use a ruler to measure where each field appears on the printed form, and then position the fields in the corresponding places on the screen. To position the fields, refer to the X and Y coordinates on the status line, and use the Move Field command. Though it takes time and effort to position the fields, once you get it right you won't need to do it again.

After you have positioned all the fields, you should test-print one record. You probably don't want to waste your printed forms during the testing stage; print on a regular piece of paper and then lay it over a form to see if the data prints on the lines next to the fields. Follow these steps to print one record:

1. Display any record that you want to print.
2. Turn on your printer and insert the preprinted form (or a blank piece of paper the size of your form) so that the top of the form lines up with the print head.

The print head contains the mechanism that prints characters on the paper. If you aren't sure where the print head is, it may take several attempts to find the correct position for the form. If you are using a laser printer, you don't need to worry about finding the print head since it doesn't have one; you can place the form in the paper tray or between the manual-feed paper guides.

3. Choose Print on the Print menu.
4. To print only the data (and not the field names and labels), press Alt-L or click next to *Field contents only.*
5. Make sure *Current record only* is chosen in the *Print which records* box. Press Alt-U if necessary.
6. Choose Print.

If every field prints in exactly the right location, consider yourself lucky. More often than not, you will need to move a few fields until they are just right. When the form is perfect, you can print all the records. If you want to manually insert each form in the printer, go into the Printer Setup dialog box and specify Manual page feed (press Alt-A). To print all the records on forms, follow the above steps, except in step 5 choose *All records* (press Alt-A).

Save and close your file.

SUMMARY

In this chapter you learned the fundamentals of building a database. You learned how to use Form view to design and modify a database form, enter and edit data, search for a specific record, and print the data on a form. But the database tool offers several more ways to look at your data. In the next chapter, you will learn two more views: *List* and *Query*.

EXERCISES

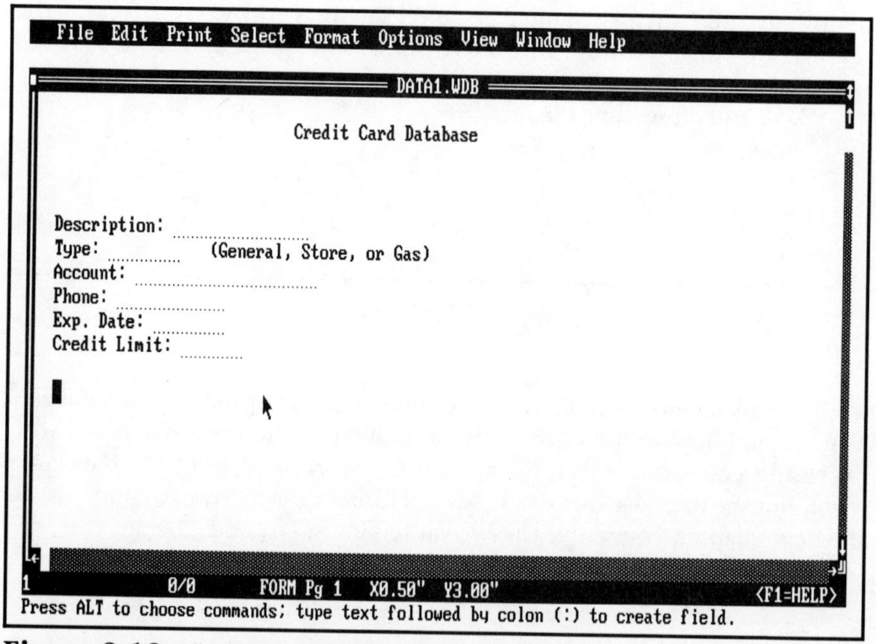

File Edit Print Select Format Options View Window Help

DATA1.WDB

Credit Card Database

Description:
Type: (General, Store, or Gas)
Account:
Phone:
Exp. Date:
Credit Limit:

1 0/0 FORM Pg 1 X0.50" Y3.00" <F1=HELP>
Press ALT to choose commands; type text followed by colon (:) to create field.

Figure 9.19: The credit-card data-entry form

In the following exercises you will create a database to keep track of your credit cards. This database will be useful if your wallet ever gets stolen, because it keeps track of the card description, the account number, the phone number to call in case of theft, and the expiration date. If you need help, refer to the appropriate sections indicated inside parentheses.

1. Create a new database file, and design a form with the following fields (see "Designing a Form," page 240):

FIELD NAME	**FIELD WIDTH**
Description:	15

FIELD NAME	FIELD WIDTH
Type:	8
Account:	20
Phone:	12
Exp. Date:	8
Credit Limit:	7

Your form should look similar to Figure 9.19.

2. Format the form, following these steps:
   - Boldface the field names and italicize the labels (see "Formatting the Labels and Field Names," page 255).
   - Format the Credit Limit field to Comma with zero decimal places (see "Formatting the Numbers," page 256).
3. Get out your credit cards and enter a separate record for each credit card. You may need to refer to a monthly statement for some of the information. (See "Entering Data," page 243.)
4. Refer to Figure 9.20, and redesign the form as follows:
   - Move the Phone field to the bottom of the form (see "Moving Fields and Labels," page 262).
   - Insert a line between each field (see "Inserting and Deleting Lines," page 263).
5. Save the file with the name CRCARDS.
6. Print a copy of your blank form (see "Printing a Blank Form," page 267).
7. Close the file without saving.

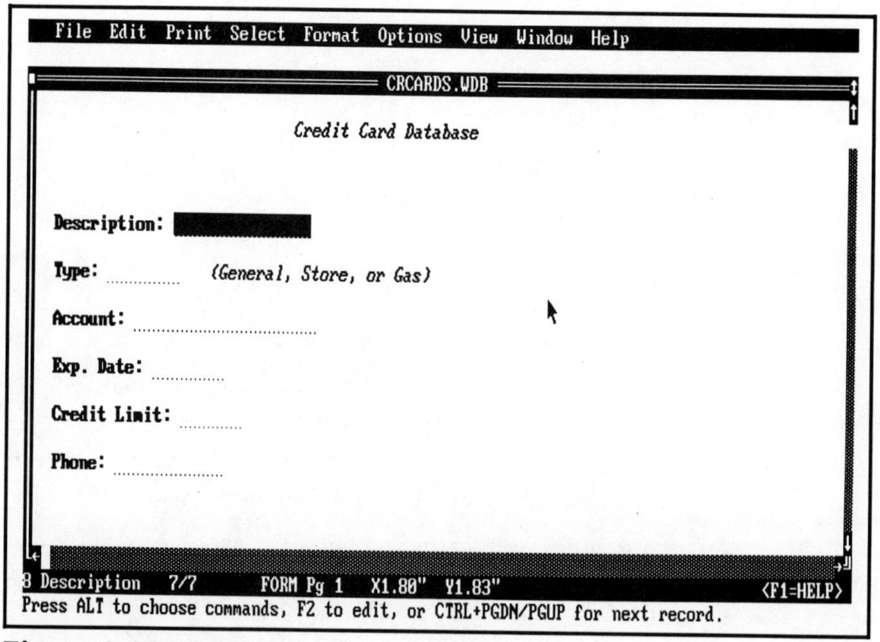

File Edit Print Select Format Options View Window Help

CRCARDS.WDB

Credit Card Database

Description:

Type: (General, Store, or Gas)

Account:

Exp. Date:

Credit Limit:

Phone:

8 Description 7/7 FORM Pg 1 X1.80" Y1.83" <F1=HELP>

Press ALT to choose commands, F2 to edit, or CTRL+PGDN/PGUP for next record.

Figure 9.20: The revised data-entry form

10

OTHER WAYS OF VIEWING THE DATABASE

Although Form view works well for creating the database and entering and editing data, it's not ideal for all tasks. The problem with Form view is that you can only see one record at a time. If you want to simultaneously look at a group of records so that you can compare or print the data, List view is more appropriate. In List view, you see the data in a spreadsheet format of rows and columns. Most commands and operations you can do in Form view you can do in List view. The only difference is that the data appear in a layout with columns.

Query view is another view available in the database tool. With this view you can specify which records you want to be displayed when you are in Form or List view. For example, you may want to display or print a list of only the employees in the sales department. You do not actually see your data when you are in Query view; instead, you tell Works which data you want to see and switch to List or Form view to see the data.

LIST VIEW

Use the Open Existing File command on the File menu to open EMPLOYEE.WDB, the employee data file that you created in Chapter 9. As you saw in the last chapter, Form view is the default view when you create a database file.

To see your database in a spreadsheet format, switch to List view: Choose List on the View menu. Your screen should look similar to Figure 10.1. If you don't see all the records, press Ctrl-Home to go to the top of the file. (Note: On some monitors, you may not be able to see the last column, New Salary.)

Working in the database tool's List view is almost identical to working in the spreadsheet tool. First, the screen layout is similar: You see a spreadsheet grid of rows and columns. Second, the commands for moving the highlight, scrolling the screen, selecting cells, and editing are the same. Because of this similarity, this chapter does not go into as much detail on these topics as the spreadsheet chapters did. If you need additional details on any of the spreadsheet commands, refer back to chapters 6 and 7.

EXPLORING THE SCREEN

As you can see on your screen and in Figure 10.1, the database is displayed in a row-and-column format, allowing you to see 18 records at a

File Edit Print Select Format Options View Window Help

"Anderson

EMPLOYEE.WDB

	Last Name	First Name	Dept	Exempt	Hire Date	Current Sa	Raise Pct	New Salary
1	Anderson	Jane	MIS	Yes	8/2/85	34,600	13.00%	39,098
2	Jones	Mary	Personnel	Yes	10/15/88	29,500	11.00%	32,745
3	Manley	Martin	Eng.	Yes	9/10/86	44,000	10.00%	48,400
4	Peterson	Pete	MIS	Yes	7/21/82	21,000	12.00%	23,520
5	Thompson	Barbara	Sales	Yes	3/12/88	30,000	10.00%	33,000
6	Thompson	Peter	Sales	Yes	5/7/90	30,000	10.00%	33,000
7	Wilson	Robert	Eng.	Yes	10/14/83	36,000	15.00%	41,400
8	Bradley	Brad	Personnel	No	2/26/85	54,000	8.00%	58,320
9	Meyers	Andrew	MIS	Yes	12/1/88	41,000	9.00%	44,690
10								
11								
12								
13								
14								
15								
16								
17								
18								

1 Last Name 9/9 LIST <F1=HELP>

Press ALT to choose commands, or F2 to edit.

Figure 10.1: The employee data file in List view

time. Each record is entered in a spreadsheet row, and each field is entered in a different column. The numbers on the left side of the window represent record numbers. Instead of seeing letters labeling each column, you see field names. Each piece of data is entered in a separate cell. The cursor is a rectangular bar called the highlight (just like in the spreadsheet tool). In Figure 10.1 the highlight is on record 1, in the Last Name field.

The status line in the bottom window border is similar to the one in Form view. This line lets you know where the highlight is in the database (the record and the field). For example, in Figure 10.1, the status line indicates *1 Last Name,* which means the highlight is on record 1 in the Last Name field. Use your arrow keys now to move the highlight around to different cells, and notice how the status line changes. The status line also lets you know how many records are in your database (*9/9*) and that you are in List view.

EDITING IN LIST VIEW

The Edit pull-down menu is virtually identical to the one you have seen in the spreadsheet tool. The only difference is that List view uses the terms *records* and *fields,* while the spreadsheet tool uses the terms *rows* and *columns.* For example, instead of Insert Row/Column, the List view Edit menu has the option Insert Record/Field. Although the terms are different, the functions are the same.

You can edit your database in either Form or List view. List view offers these advantages:

- You can see more than one record at a time.
- You can copy data down a column.
- You can delete multiple records at once.

List view also has these disadvantages:

- Depending on the size of your database, you may not be able to see all your fields on the screen at once.
- You may find it hard to concentrate on the individual record you are editing because the screen displays other records.

Both views are useful, so you will probably want to use the view most appropriate for your task. Generally, if your editing affects consecutive records, use List view. If you are editing an isolated record, use Form view.

Getting Around

List view uses the same commands to move the highlight and scroll the database as the spreadsheet tool. You learned these commands in Chapter 7, but Tables 10.1 and 10.2 are included here to refresh your memory. Take a few minutes now to practice moving around your database.

The fastest way to get to a particular record in a large database is to use the Search command. Follow these steps to find the record for Mary Jones:

1. Select Search on the Select menu.
2. Type **jones**.
3. Press Enter.

The highlight moves directly to her record. (If the database contained more than one person with the last name Jones, you could press F7, the Repeat Search key, to go to the next occurrence.) The reason why you want

Table 10.1: Moving the Highlight in List View

MOVEMENT OF HIGHLIGHT	KEYSTROKE
Beginning of record	Home
End of record	End
Beginning of file	Ctrl-Home
End of file	Ctrl-End
Next screen	PgDn
Previous screen	PgUp
Screen right	Ctrl-PgDn
Screen left	Ctrl-PgUp
Next block down	Ctrl-↓
Previous block up	Ctrl-↑
Block to the right	Ctrl-→
Block to the left	Ctrl-←
Field	F5

Table 10.2: Mouse Scrolling Commands

SCROLLING MOVEMENT	MOUSE ACTION
Down one record	Click on down arrow in vertical scroll bar
Down continuously	Click on down arrow in vertical scroll bar, and hold the button down
Up one record	Click on up arrow in vertical scroll bar
Up continuously	Click on up arrow in vertical scroll bar, and hold the button down
Right one field	Click on right arrow in horizontal scroll bar
Right continuously	Click on right arrow in horizontal scroll bar, and hold the button down
Left one column	Click on left arrow in horizontal scroll bar
Left continuously	Click on left arrow in horizontal scroll bar, and hold the button down
Down one screen	Click on vertical scroll bar underneath the scroll box

Table 10.2: Mouse Scrolling Commands (continued)

SCROLLING MOVEMENT	MOUSE ACTION
Right one screen	Click on horizontal scroll bar to the right of the scroll box
To record 1	Click and drag scroll box to top of vertical scroll bar, or click on scroll box when it's at the top of the scroll bar
To first field	Click and drag scroll box to left of horizontal scroll bar

to go to Jones's record is so that you can correct a mistake; she should *not* be exempt.

1. To go to the Exempt field in this record, either press the Tab key or →, or click on the cell.
2. Type **No**.
3. Press Enter to replace the cell contents.

Inserting New Records

Most of the time, you will probably use Form view to enter new records because it's easier to enter data in a fill-in-the-blank form. However, you can also insert new records in List view. Maybe you are already in List view and don't feel like switching to Form view to enter a record. Or perhaps you work with a lot of spreadsheets and feel more at home in List view.

To enter new records in List view, you have three choices, just as you had in Form view:

- You can go to the first blank line at the end of the database.
- You can use the Insert Record/Field command on the Edit menu to insert a blank row.
- You can use the Copy command on the Edit menu to duplicate an existing record.

The Insert Record/Field command inserts a blank row *above* the highlight. Follow these steps to insert a record above Wilson:

1. Place the highlight anywhere in Wilson's record.
2. Select Insert Record/Field on the Edit menu.
3. In the dialog box that appears, Record should already be selected. Choose OK. A blank row is inserted at row 7.
4. Type the data shown in record 7 of Figure 10.2. Row 7 is selected in this figure to identify the new record for you; it should not be highlighted on your screen. Notice that the default value for Exempt (*Yes*) and the result for the New Salary formula automatically fill into their respective fields.
5. Press the Tab key or → to move from field to field.

If your new record is similar to an existing one, you can use the Copy command. Before you can copy a record, you must select the record.

```
 File  Edit  Print  Select  Format  Options  View  Window  Help
"Bradford
                             EMPLOYEE.WDB
    Last Name First Name  Dept    Exempt  Hire Date Current SaRaise Pct New Salary
1   Anderson  Jane      MIS        Yes       8/2/85    34,600     13.00%   39,098
2   Jones     Mary      Personnel  No      10/15/88    29,500     11.00%   32,745
3   Manley    Martin    Eng.       Yes      9/10/86    44,000     10.00%   48,400
4   Peterson  Pete      MIS        Yes      7/21/82    21,000     12.00%   23,520
5   Thompson  Barbara   Sales      Yes      3/12/88    30,000     10.00%   33,000
6   Thompson  Peter     Sales      Yes       5/7/90    30,000     10.00%   33,000
7   Bradford  William   Personnel  Yes       3/9/91    60,000      7.00%   64,200
8   Wilson    Robert    Eng.       Yes     10/14/83    36,000     15.00%   41,400
9   Bradley   Brad      Personnel  No       2/26/85    54,000      8.00%   58,320
10  Meyers    Andrew    MIS        Yes      12/1/88    41,000      9.00%   44,690
11
12
13
14
15
16
17
18
7 Last Name     10/10     LIST                                         <F1=HELP>
Press ALT to choose commands, or F2 to edit.
```

Figure 10.2: A new record inserted in row 7

Table 10.3 lists the ways you can select cells in List view. These commands are identical to the ones you use in the spreadsheet tool.

Deleting Records

One of the advantages of working in List view is that you can delete multiple records at once. If you have a group of consecutive records you want to delete, you can select them and then issue the Delete Record/Field command. When selecting the records to delete, you only need to select one cell in each record. However, if you select an entire record using one of the record-selection commands in Table 10.3, the Delete Record/Field command automatically knows you want to delete a record and does not stop to ask you what you want to delete.

Table 10.3: Selecting Data

WITH THE KEYBOARD	
Extend selection	Press F8 once, or choose Cells on Select menu, or hold down Shift with arrow keys
Record	Press Ctrl-F8, or choose Record on Select menu
Field	Press Shift-F8, or choose Field on Select menu
Database	Press Ctrl-Shift-F8, or choose All on Select menu
WITH THE MOUSE	
Extend selection	Click-and-drag, or shift-and-click
Record	Click on record number
Field	Click on field name
Database	Click on intersection of record numbers and field names

Follow these steps to delete two records (Barbara and Peter Thompson) in your employee data file:

1. Place the highlight anywhere on record 5.
2. Select the records to delete.

   Using the keyboard: Press F8 to extend the selection (*EXT* is displayed on the status line), and move the highlight down to record 6. One cell in each record (5 and 6) should be highlighted as shown in Figure 10.3.

   Using the mouse: Click-and-drag from record 5 to record 6 (one cell in each record is sufficient).
3. Choose Delete Record/Field on the Edit menu.
4. Press R to choose Record or click next to Record.
5. Choose OK.

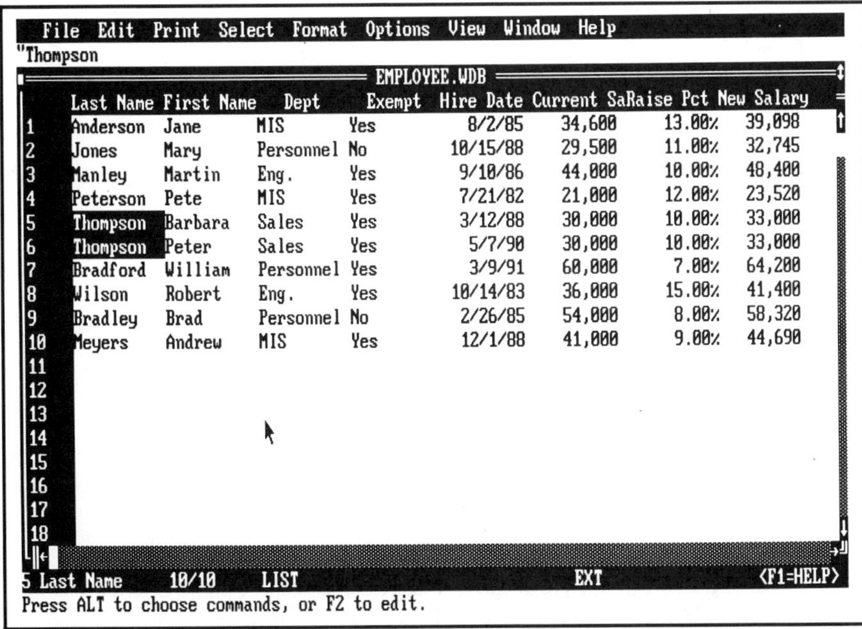

Figure 10.3: Selecting two records to delete

Inserting a Field

There are two steps to inserting a new field in your database while you are in List view. First, you insert a column with the Insert Record/Field command, and then you assign a field name to the column with the Field Name command. If you want to place a new field at the end of the database, you do not need to insert a column—just use the empty column after the last field.

Follow these steps to insert a new field for employee identification numbers before the Dept field:

1. Place the highlight anywhere in the Dept field (new fields are inserted to the left of the highlight).
2. Choose Insert Record/Field on the Edit menu.
3. Press F or click next to Field.
4. Choose OK. A blank column is inserted between the First Name and Dept fields.
5. Choose Field Name on the Edit menu.
6. Type **ID** and press Enter. The column is now labeled with the field name, ID.

Regardless of where you insert a field in List view, the field is placed at the end of the form in Form view. The same thing happens when you insert a field in the form; the new field appears as the last column in List view.

Choose Form on the View menu now. Notice that the ID field is sitting at the bottom of the form.

If you want your fields to be in the same position in both List and Form views, you must move the field. Follow these steps to revise your form:

1. Use the Move Field command in Form view to put the ID field above the Dept field.
2. Insert lines above and below the field so that it looks like Figure 10.4.
3. Since all the other field names are boldfaced, use the Style command on the Format menu to bold the ID field name. Your form should look similar to Figure 10.4.
4. Choose List on the View menu, and press Ctrl-Home.

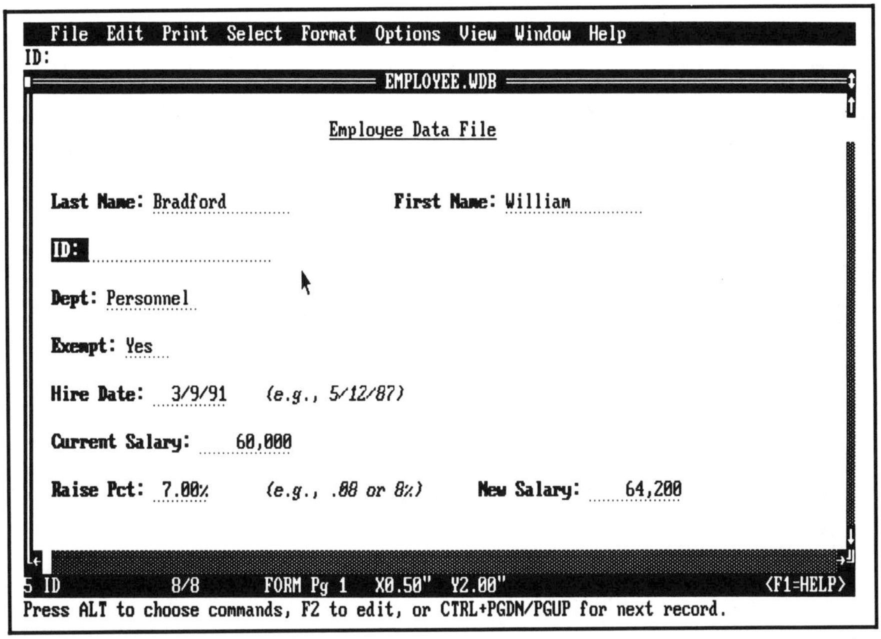

```
 File  Edit  Print  Select  Format  Options  View  Window  Help
ID:
                         EMPLOYEE.WDB

                       Employee Data File

 Last Name: Bradford                First Name: William

 ID:

 Dept: Personnel

 Exempt: Yes

 Hire Date:  3/9/91    (e.g., 5/12/87)

 Current Salary:   60,000

 Raise Pct:  7.00%     (e.g., .08 or 8%)    New Salary:   64,200

5 ID          8/8      FORM Pg 1   X0.50"  Y2.00"              <F1=HELP>
Press ALT to choose commands, F2 to edit, or CTRL+PGDN/PGUP for next record.
```

Figure 10.4: The revised form

Entering Data in a New Field

It's easy to enter data in an inserted field when you are in List view: You type in the data and press ↓ to go to the next record. If several consecutive records contain the same data as the new field, you can copy the data with the Fill Down command or press Ctrl-' to copy the data from the record above.

The data for your ID field appear in Figure 10.5. Notice that the identification numbers start with 1000 and go up by increments of 1 for each employee. Rather than typing in the data yourself, you can have Works fill it in for you.

The Fill Series command on the Edit menu lets you automatically fill in a range of numbers that have even increments (it's also available in the spreadsheet tool). Before you use this command, you must type in the starting value and select the range you want to fill. Follow these steps to fill in the

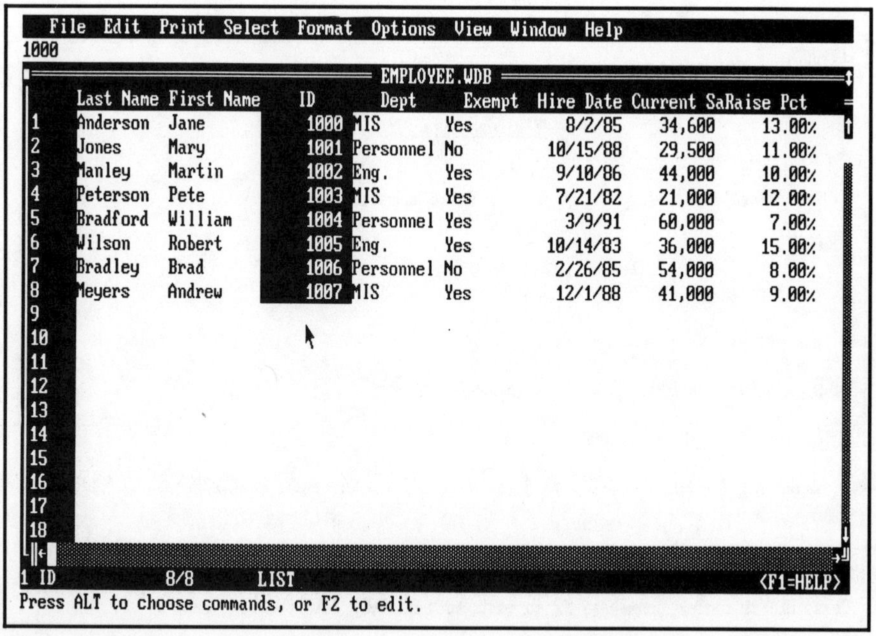

File Edit Print Select Format Options View Window Help
1000

EMPLOYEE.WDB

	Last Name	First Name	ID	Dept	Exempt	Hire Date	Current Sa	Raise Pct
1	Anderson	Jane	1000	MIS	Yes	8/2/85	34,600	13.00%
2	Jones	Mary	1001	Personnel	No	10/15/88	29,500	11.00%
3	Manley	Martin	1002	Eng.	Yes	9/10/86	44,000	10.00%
4	Peterson	Pete	1003	MIS	Yes	7/21/82	21,000	12.00%
5	Bradford	William	1004	Personnel	Yes	3/9/91	60,000	7.00%
6	Wilson	Robert	1005	Eng.	Yes	10/14/83	36,000	15.00%
7	Bradley	Brad	1006	Personnel	No	2/26/85	54,000	8.00%
8	Meyers	Andrew	1007	MIS	Yes	12/1/88	41,000	9.00%
9								
10								
11								
12								
13								
14								
15								
16								
17								
18								

1 ID 8/8 LIST <F1=HELP>
Press ALT to choose commands, or F2 to edit.

Figure 10.5: A series in the ID field filled in automatically

data for the ID field:

1. Place the highlight in record 1 of the ID field.
2. Type **1000** and press Enter.
3. Select the range shown in Figure 10.5.

   Using the keyboard: Press F8 and then ↓.

   Using the mouse: Click-and-drag.
4. Select Fill Series on the Edit menu.
5. *Number* is selected in the Units box, and *1* is filled in next to *Step by.* With these defaults, the numbers go up by increments of 1 in each cell of the range. Both of these settings are correct, so choose OK.

The numbers are automatically entered in the range. This automatic-numbering technique is a big time-saver. It is not available in Form view.

Changing a Field Name

The Field Name command that you used to name the new ID field also renames an existing field. If you look at the field names above each column, you can see that the Current Salary name is too long. You could widen the field to see more of the name, but then fewer fields would fit on the screen. An alternative is to shorten the name. Follow these steps to shorten the Current Salary field name:

1. Place the cursor anywhere in the Current Salary field.
2. Choose Field Name on the Edit menu.
3. Type **Salary** and press Enter. The field name at the top of the column is now completely visible.

Follow the same steps to change the name of the Raise Pct field to *Raise.*

FORMATTING THE LIST

The Format menu offers options for adjusting the field (column) width, changing the numeric formats, and specifying the style and alignment of the data. Unlike in Form view, you cannot format your field names. Because they are embedded in the window border, they are "untouchable."

Changing the Field Widths

The column widths in List view do not correspond to the field widths you set in Form view. Each column in the list has the default width of 10 characters. This standard width is not appropriate for all fields, though. It may be too narrow for some and too wide for others. Generally, you will want to make the column widths as narrow as possible so that you can squeeze more fields on the screen.

Now that you have inserted a new field in your employee database, the last field, New Salary, no longer fits on the screen. By narrowing some of the columns, you can see more fields. Follow these steps to change the field width of the ID field:

1. Place the highlight anywhere in the ID field.

2. Choose Field Width on the Format menu.
3. Type 7.
4. Press Enter.

Repeat the above steps to change the width of the Exempt field to 7 and the Raise field to *6*. All fields should now fit on the screen, as shown in Figure 10.6. (Note: On some monitors you may still have to scroll to see the New Salary column.)

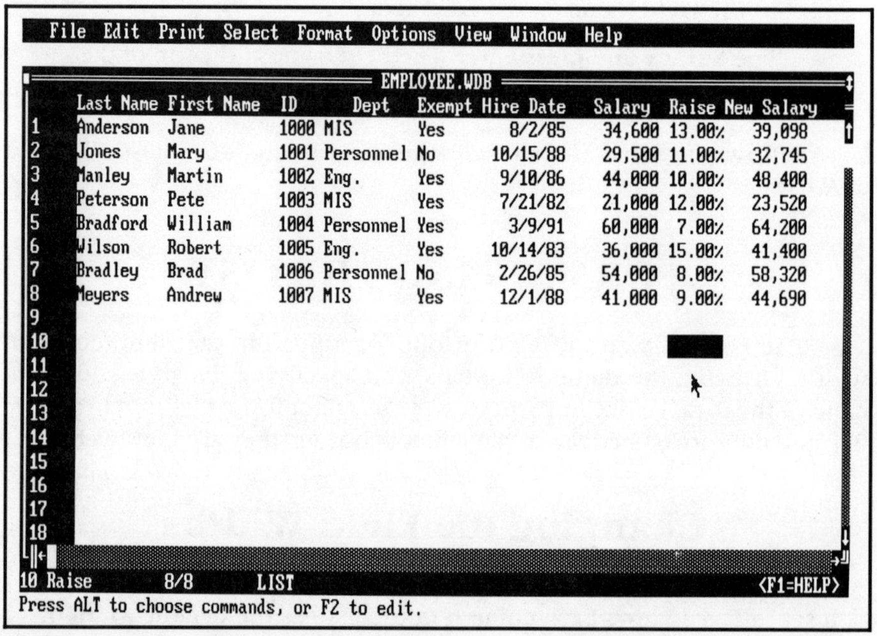

```
 File  Edit  Print  Select  Format  Options  View  Window  Help
                         EMPLOYEE.WDB
    Last Name First Name  ID      Dept   Exempt Hire Date   Salary  Raise New Salary
1   Anderson  Jane       1000 MIS        Yes       8/2/85   34,600 13.00%   39,098
2   Jones     Mary       1001 Personnel  No      10/15/88   29,500 11.00%   32,745
3   Manley    Martin     1002 Eng.       Yes      9/10/86   44,000 10.00%   48,400
4   Peterson  Pete       1003 MIS        Yes      7/21/82   21,000 12.00%   23,520
5   Bradford  William    1004 Personnel  Yes       3/9/91   60,000  7.00%   64,200
6   Wilson    Robert     1005 Eng.       Yes     10/14/83   36,000 15.00%   41,400
7   Bradley   Brad       1006 Personnel  No       2/26/85   54,000  8.00%   58,320
8   Meyers    Andrew     1007 MIS        Yes      12/1/88   41,000  9.00%   44,690
9
10
11
12
13
14
15
16
17
18
10 Raise      8/8     LIST                                              <F1=HELP>
Press ALT to choose commands, or F2 to edit.
```

Figure 10.6: Narrowing field widths to see more fields on the screen

The Field Width command can also be used to hide entire fields. By specifying a width of zero, the field does not appear in the list. You can use this technique to temporarily remove fields you don't need to see so that you can fit additional fields on the screen. Follow these steps to hide the Exempt field:

1. Place the highlight in the Exempt field.
2. Choose Field Width on the Format menu.

3. Type **0**.
4. Press Enter. The column disappears, as shown in Figure 10.7.

To redisplay a hidden field, you must move to the field and then specify a wider field width. But how do you move to a hidden field? The only way you can is to use the Go To command on the Select menu or the Goto key, F5. Follow these steps to bring back the Exempt field:

1. Press the Goto key, F5.
2. Type **Exempt** next to *Go to* or select Exempt on the Names list.
3. Press Enter. The status line indicates you are in the Exempt field. Notice that when you are in a hidden field, the highlight disappears from the screen.
4. Choose Field Width on the Format menu.
5. Type **7**.
6. Press Enter. The field is displayed again.

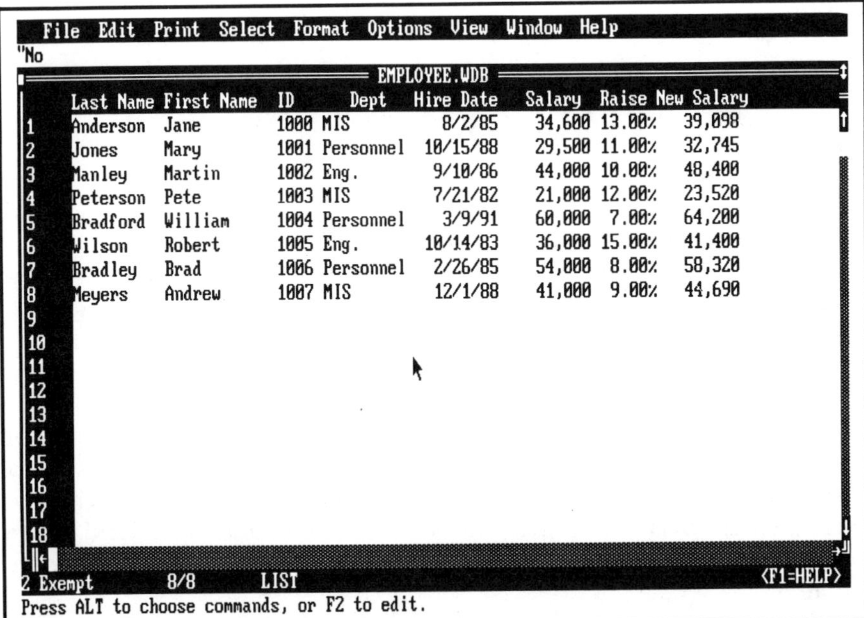

Figure 10.7: The list with the Exempt field hidden

Formatting the Numbers

Although the field widths in Form and List views are independent of each other, the numeric formats correspond exactly. Whatever format you specify in Form view is displayed in List view and vice versa. Notice that the formats you set in your form are used in your list: The Raise field displays Percent format with two decimal places, and the Salary and New Salary fields display Comma format without decimal places.

To change the format in List view, you simply place the highlight anywhere in the field and set the appropriate numeric format. Unlike in the spreadsheet tool, you do *not* have to select the range to change the format; the entire column is automatically formatted. Follow these steps to change the format of the Raise field to Percent with zero decimal places:

1. Place the highlight in the Raise field.
2. Choose Percent on the Format menu.
3. Type **0** for the number of decimal places.
4. Press Enter. All the numbers in the field change to this new format.

If you switch to Form view now, you can see that the Raise field in the form also has zero decimal places. Be sure to switch back to List view.

Specifying Style and Alignment

In the Form view, you can change the style of your field names, labels, and data. In Chapter 9, you underlined and italicized the labels and boldfaced the field names. In the List view, you can only change the style of the data. Unless you want to make the data in a particular field stand out from the rest, you probably won't use the bold, underline, and italic styles in List view.

The Style dialog box also offers alignment options, a useful feature for columns of data. As you remember from the spreadsheet tool, the default alignment places text on the left side of the cell and dates and numbers on the right. But sometimes this alignment causes columns of data to be too close together. For example, notice how close the ID and Dept fields are. Because of the default alignment of each field (ID is right-aligned and Dept is left-aligned), widening the fields would not create more space between the columns.

By aligning the ID field on the left side of the cell, however, you can create more space between the ID and Dept fields. Follow these steps to left-align the ID field:

1. Place the highlight anywhere in the ID field.
2. Choose Style on the Format menu.
3. Press L or click next to Left.
4. Choose OK. Your screen should look similar to Figure 10.8.

```
 File  Edit  Print  Select  Format  Options  View  Window  Help
1000
                              EMPLOYEE.WDB
     Last Name First Name  ID      Dept    Exempt Hire Date   Salary  Raise New Salary
1    Anderson  Jane       1000  MIS        Yes      8/2/85    34,600   13%   39,098
2    Jones     Mary       1001  Personnel  No      10/15/88   29,500   11%   32,745
3    Manley    Martin     1002  Eng.       Yes      9/10/86   44,000   10%   48,400
4    Peterson  Pete       1003  MIS        Yes      7/21/82   21,000   12%   23,520
5    Bradford  William    1004  Personnel  Yes      3/9/91    60,000    7%   64,200
6    Wilson    Robert     1005  Eng.       Yes     10/14/83   36,000   15%   41,400
7    Bradley   Brad       1006  Personnel  No       2/26/85   54,000    8%   58,320
8    Meyers    Andrew     1007  MIS        Yes     12/1/88    41,000    9%   44,690
9
10
11
12
13
14
15
16
17
18
1 ID           8/8        LIST                                               <F1=HELP>
Press ALT to choose commands, or F2 to edit.
```

Figure 10.8: The list with the ID field left-aligned

SORTING RECORDS

By sorting records in List view (as opposed to Form view), you can immediately see that the records are sorted. In Form view, you have to browse through the records one at a time to see if they are sorted correctly. Because you can see many records in List view, you do not need to browse through the database.

Sorting records in List view is identical to sorting rows in a spreadsheet and to sorting records in Form view. Let's see who has the highest salary in the employee database. By sorting the Salary field in descending order, the largest salary appears at the top of the list. Follow these steps:

1. Choose Sort Records on the Select menu.
2. Type **Salary** next to 1st Field.
3. Press Alt-B or click next to Descend.
4. Choose OK. Your list should be in the same order as Figure 10.9. As the sorted list indicates, Bradford is the top breadwinner.

Follow the same steps to sort the database by last name in ascending order.

File Edit Print Select Format Options View Window Help

EMPLOYEE.WDB

	Last Name	First Name	ID	Dept	Exempt	Hire Date	Salary	Raise	New Salary
1	Bradford	William	1004	Personnel	Yes	3/9/91	60,000	7%	64,200
2	Bradley	Brad	1006	Personnel	No	2/26/85	54,000	8%	58,320
3	Manley	Martin	1002	Eng.	Yes	9/10/86	44,000	10%	48,400
4	Meyers	Andrew	1007	MIS	Yes	12/1/88	41,000	9%	44,690
5	Wilson	Robert	1005	Eng.	Yes	10/14/83	36,000	15%	41,400
6	Anderson	Jane	1000	MIS	Yes	8/2/85	34,600	13%	39,098
7	Jones	Mary	1001	Personnel	No	10/15/88	29,500	11%	32,745
8	Peterson	Pete	1003	MIS	Yes	7/21/82	21,000	12%	23,520
9									
10									
11									
12									
13									
14									
15									
16									
17									
18									

10 Salary 8/8 LIST <F1=HELP>

Press ALT to choose commands, or F2 to edit.

Figure 10.9: The list sorted by salary in descending order

PRINTING A LIST

There is not a lot involved in printing a list; it's quite similar to printing a spreadsheet. Before printing, consider the following:

- Choose a font using the Font command on the Format menu. Only one font is allowed per list. Do not choose a proportionally spaced font—the columns will not line up properly.
- To print in landscape orientation, choose a landscape printer (for example, HPLASLAN) in the Printer Setup dialog box.
- Set your margins using the Page Setup & Margins command on the Print menu. If you are printing in landscape, change the page length and page width.

To print your employee database list, make sure your printer is turned on, and follow these steps:

1. Choose Page Setup & Margins on the Print menu.
2. Check your left and right margins. If necessary, set them to 0.5″ each.
3. Choose OK.
4. Choose Preview on the Print menu.
5. Press Alt-L to turn on the *Print record and field labels* option. Choosing this option prints the field names and record numbers on each page.
6. Choose Preview. Notice that the last field (New Salary) doesn't show on page 1. Press PgDn to see that it appears on the next page.
7. Press P to print the list. The first page should look similar to Figure 10.10.

You have several options for getting the New Salary column to print on page 1:

- Change to a smaller font.
- Narrow some of the field widths.
- Hide some of the fields (by setting the field width to zero).
- Turn off the *Print record and field labels* option.

	Last Name	First Name	ID	Dept	Exempt	Hire Date	Salary	Raise
1	Anderson	Jane	1000	MIS	Yes	8/2/85	34,600	13%
2	Bradford	William	1004	Personnel	Yes	3/9/91	60,000	7%
3	Bradley	Brad	1006	Personnel	No	2/26/85	54,000	8%
4	Jones	Mary	1001	Personnel	No	10/15/88	29,500	11%
5	Manley	Martin	1002	Eng.	Yes	9/10/86	44,000	10%
6	Meyers	Andrew	1007	MIS	Yes	12/1/88	41,000	9%
7	Peterson	Pete	1003	MIS	Yes	7/21/82	21,000	12%
8	Wilson	Robert	1005	Eng.	Yes	10/14/83	36,000	15%

Figure 10.10: The database printed in List view

You can experiment with any of the above options and then use the Preview command to see if you can print everything on a single page. If you hide any of the fields, be sure to redisplay them before you continue.

This list probably suits you fine if you are the only one looking at it. But if you had to submit it to someone else, you would most likely not be very proud of it. The headings do not line up over the columns of data, there is no space between the headings and the first record, the report has no title, and the numeric fields are not totaled or averaged.

As you can see, the report you print in List view is not nicely formatted, nor can you change it. You are stuck with field names for the column headings, and you cannot boldface them or change their alignment. You cannot specify a range to print; you must print out all fields, unless you hide the fields you don't want to print (and then you have to redisplay them after printing). You can, however, specify which records you want to print by creating a *query*—this is explained in the next section.

Before you get too miserable about this unformatted report, don't despair: The database tool offers a Report view, which allows great flexibility in report design. The next chapter explains how to create beautiful reports in Report view.

QUERY VIEW

The Query view allows you to display a subset of your database. Using this view, you can tell Works which records to display. For example, you may want to print out a list of only the employees in the sales department or a list of all the employees who are exempt from overtime. You specify these *conditions* in a query form. A condition is a formula that has only two possible answers: true or false. If the condition is true, then Works displays the record. If the condition is false, Works temporarily hides the record. The result is a list of records that matches your condition. You can then edit, delete, sort, or print this list.

CREATING A QUERY

To specify which records you want to display, you must go into Query view. Choose Query on the View menu now. Your database form appears on the screen, and *QUERY* appears on the status line (see Figure 10.11). Your menu bar displays fewer choices than it does in other views because the only thing you can do in Query view is type conditions on a single form.

Display the Edit pull-down menu now; you can see that only a couple of options are available: Clear and Delete Query. You will use these options later. Press Esc to cancel the menu.

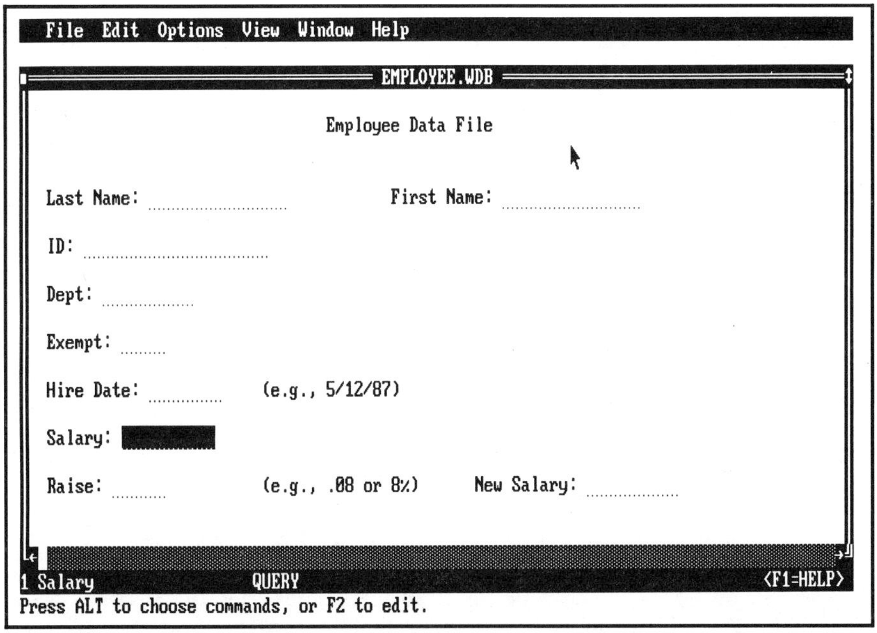

```
 File  Edit  Options  View  Window  Help
                         EMPLOYEE.WDB
                      Employee Data File

 Last Name: ..........          First Name: ..........
 ID: ..........
 Dept: ..........
 Exempt: ....
 Hire Date: ......     (e.g., 5/12/87)
 Salary:
 Raise: ....           (e.g., .08 or 8%)     New Salary: ......

1 Salary                  QUERY                          <F1=HELP>
Press ALT to choose commands, or F2 to edit.
```

Figure 10.11: The employee data file in Query view

To create a query, follow these general steps:

- Go into Query view.
- Type a condition.
- Return to List or Form view to see the results of your query.

For your first query, follow these steps to display a list of all the employees in the MIS department:

1. Move the cursor to the dotted line next to the Dept field. To move the cursor from field to field, you can press Tab or Shift-Tab. If you have a mouse, click on the dotted line next to Dept.
2. Type **MIS**. As you type, the characters appear in the field and in the formula bar. You can type the text in upper- or lowercase but make sure you spell the word correctly; the query text must match the database text, character for character.
3. Press Enter.
4. Choose List on the View menu, or press F10. The list of matching records—only employees in the MIS department—is displayed (see Figure 10.12). You can view the matching records in either Form or List view, but List view lets you see more records at once. The F10 key takes you to the last view you were in (Form or List).

The status line indicates the number of records displayed out of the total number of records in the database. Right now the status line displays *3/8*—3 records are displayed out of a total of 8 records.

You could now edit, delete, sort, or print this partial list. In the rest of this chapter, you are going to perform many different queries, one after the other, so that you can see how this view operates. In your actual work, though, you would probably do a single query and then print a report, do another query and then print, etc.

Querying Numeric Fields

Each type of field (numeric, text, and date) has specific rules for how you must enter conditions. Table 10.4 gives a list of these rules. This section covers the rules you must follow for numeric fields.

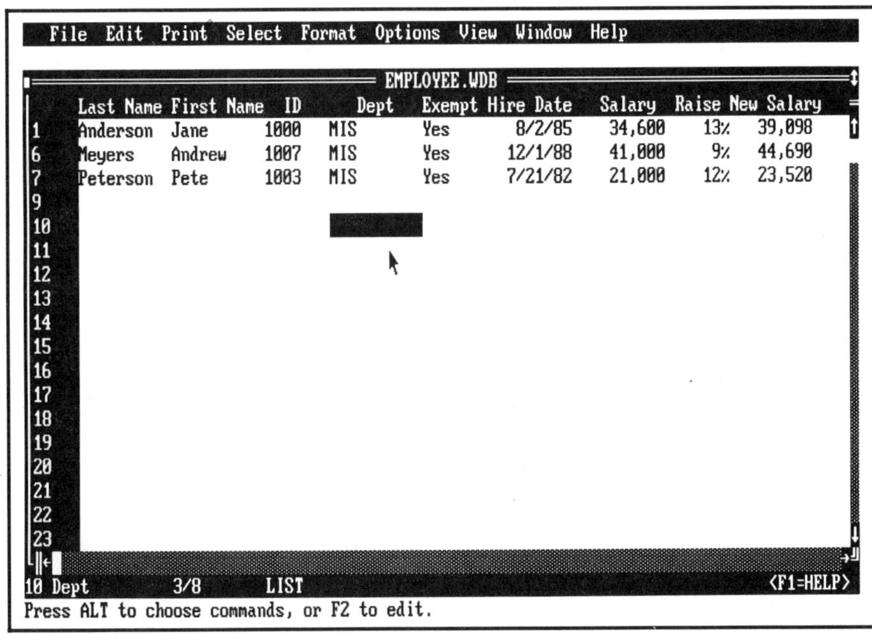

File Edit Print Select Format Options View Window Help
EMPLOYEE.WDB
Last Name First Name ID Dept Exempt Hire Date Salary Raise New Salary
1 Anderson Jane 1000 MIS Yes 8/2/85 34,600 13% 39,098
6 Meyers Andrew 1007 MIS Yes 12/1/88 41,000 9% 44,690
7 Peterson Pete 1003 MIS Yes 7/21/82 21,000 12% 23,520
9
10
11
12
13
14
15
16
17
18
19
20
21
22
23
10 Dept 3/8 LIST <F1=HELP>
Press ALT to choose commands, or F2 to edit.

Figure 10.12: A list of employees in the MIS department

Table 10.4: Query Rules

FIELD TYPE	RULE	EXAMPLE
Numeric	No quotes	> = 30000
Text	Double quotes	> = "M"
	Wildcards (*,?)	T*, Thomps?n
Date	Single quotes	< = '1/1/87'
	Date functions	= YEAR() = 88, = MONTH() = 4

Entering Comparison Formulas

When you queried the Dept field in the previous example, you performed an *exact-match* query. The condition had to exactly match the data in the database. With numeric fields, you rarely do exact-match queries; more often, you display a range of values. For example, you may want to display everyone whose salary is greater than $40,000. To enter this kind of condition, you must type a *comparison formula* that uses any of the following relational operators:

SYMBOL	DESCRIPTION
>	Greater than
<	Less than
=	Equal to
> =	Greater than or equal to
< =	Less than or equal to
<>	Not equal to

Thus, to display everyone who makes $40,000 or more, the comparison formula is > = *40000.* Follow these steps to enter this condition in a query form:

1. Choose Query on the View menu. Your last query (*MIS*) appears in the form.
2. Choose Delete Query on the Edit menu. (You could also move the cursor to the condition and press Del; use whichever method is faster for you.)
3. Move the cursor to the dotted line next to the Salary field.
4. Type **> = 40000** and press Enter.
5. Press F10 to display the matching records. As the list indicates, four employees make more than $40,000 (see Figure 10.13).

Linking Comparison Formulas in Numeric Fields

Let's say you want to display the employees who are in the $30,000 to $40,000 salary range. This query actually comprises two conditions: salary greater than $30,000 and salary less than $40,000. To specify multiple conditions in a single field, you can link the conditions with the following

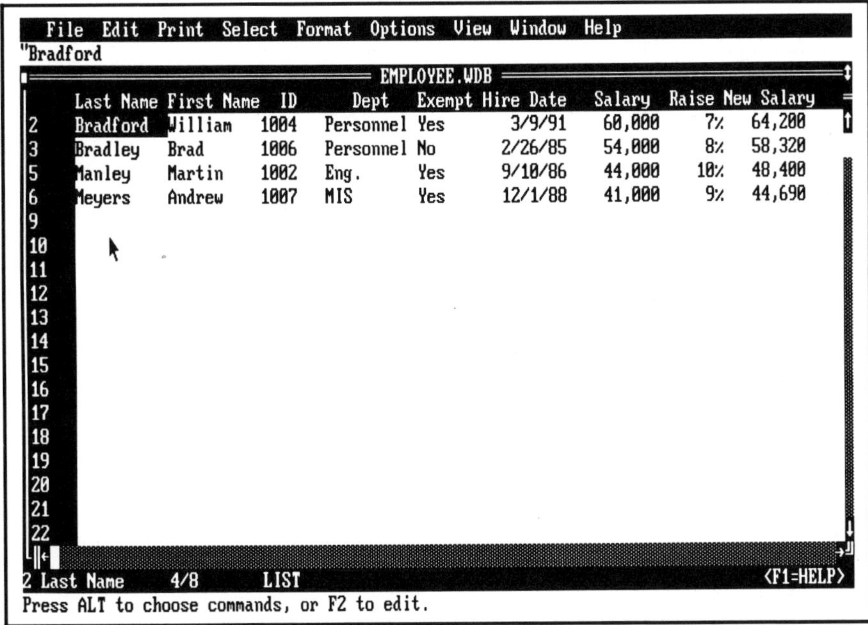

Figure 10.13: A list of employees who make more than $40,000

logical operators:

SYMBOL	DESCRIPTION
& (ampersand)	AND
¦ (broken vertical bar)	OR
˜ (tilde)	NOT

The query formula you use to find a range of salaries between $30,000 and $40,000 is *> = 30000&< = 40000.* When the & (ampersand) operator is used, both conditions must be met in order for the record to be displayed. In this example, a record is displayed only if the salary is greater than or equal to $30,000 ***and*** less than or equal to $40,000. This condition matches two records (Anderson and Wilson).

With the OR operator, ¦ (vertical bar), only one of the conditions has to be met for the record to be selected. You can use this operator to find values at the lower or upper end of a scale. For example, *<30000¦>50000* would display a list of the employees who make less than $30,000 or more than

$50,000. This condition matches four records (Bradford, Bradley, Jones, and Peterson).

If you want to, try each of the queries mentioned above, or make up some of your own.

Querying Text Fields

The first query you performed in this chapter was on the Dept field, a text field. The condition you entered (*MIS*) had to exactly match the data in the database in order for the record to be displayed. However, when you can't be so exact, you can use wildcards and comparison formulas to make partial matches.

Using Wildcards

If you aren't sure how a word is entered in the database, you can use wildcards to take the place of the characters you aren't sure of. Chapter 7 discussed how to use the asterisk and question mark wildcards in the spreadsheet tool's Search command. These same two wildcards are available in your queries.

Use wildcards in your conditions when you do not know (or don't feel like typing) the complete, exact contents of a field. The asterisk matches any group of characters in the position where you type it; the question mark matches a single character. Here are a few examples:

- The condition *t** matches all words that start with the letter *t*.
- The condition **computer** displays all records containing the word *computer* anywhere in the field.
- The condition *T*son* in the Last Name field lists all the people whose last names start with *T* and end in *son* (like Tyson and Thompson).
- The condition *Thomps?n* lists all names that have a single character in the position of the question mark (like Thompsen and Thompson).

One way of using the wildcard is as a shortcut for entering your conditions. For example, if you know that each of your departments begins with a unique letter, you can simply type *s** to match *sales* and *p** to match *personnel*. Remember, this only works if each department name begins with a different letter. Follow these steps to use a wildcard to list the employees in the personnel department:

1. Choose Query on the View menu. Your last query appears in the form.
2. Choose Delete Query on the Edit menu.
3. Move the cursor to the dotted line next to the Dept field.
4. Type **p*** and press Enter.
5. Press F10 to display the matching records (Bradford, Bradley, and Jones).

Follow the same steps to get a list of employees whose last names end in *son*. (Hint: The condition is **son.*) Your list should match Figure 10.14.

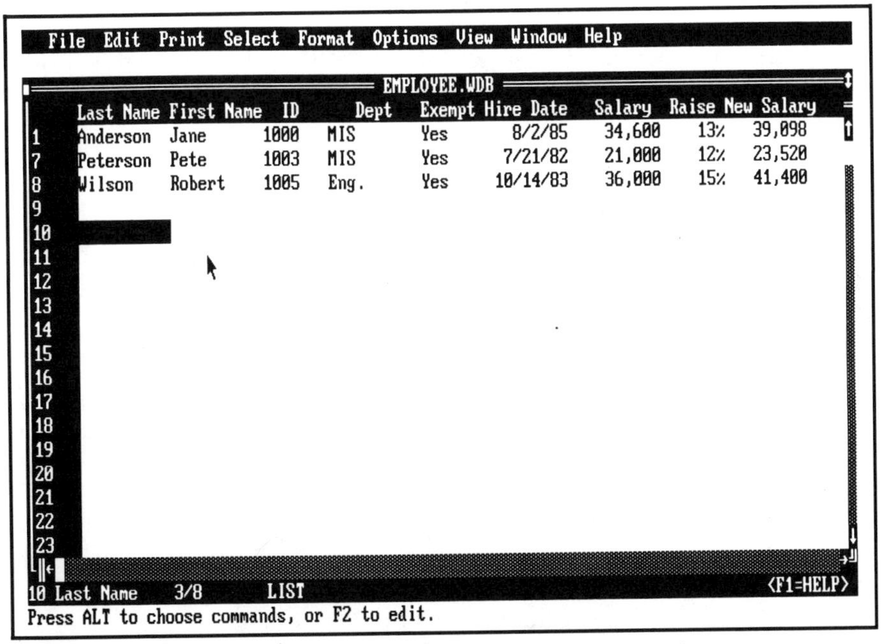
File Edit Print Select Format Options View Window Help
EMPLOYEE.WDB
Last Name First Name ID Dept Exempt Hire Date Salary Raise New Salary
1 Anderson Jane 1000 MIS Yes 8/2/85 34,600 13% 39,098
7 Peterson Pete 1003 MIS Yes 7/21/82 21,000 12% 23,520
8 Wilson Robert 1005 Eng. Yes 10/14/83 36,000 15% 41,400
9
10
11
12
13
14
15
16
17
18
19
20
21
22
23
10 Last Name 3/8 LIST <F1=HELP>
Press ALT to choose commands, or F2 to edit.

Figure 10.14: A list of employees whose last names end in *son*

Entering Comparison Formulas

Comparison formulas for text fields are similar to those for numeric fields. The only difference is that the comparison data must be enclosed in quotation marks. For example, to display the last names that begin with a letter after M (that is, M through Z), the comparison formula is > = *"M"*. (Again, it doesn't matter whether you type in upper- or lowercase). Follow these steps:

1. Choose Query on the View menu.
2. Choose Delete Query on the Edit menu.
3. Move the cursor to the dotted line next to the Last Name field.
4. Type **> = "M"** and press Enter.
5. Press F10 to display the matching records.

You can also link comparison formulas, like you did with numeric fields. For example, to display the last names that start with a letter between J and R, the query formula is > = *"J"&< = "R"*. If you like, enter this condition and display the matching records.

Linking Conditions in Text Fields

Sometimes you may want to enter two conditions in a single text field. For example, you may want a list of all the employees in the MIS and engineering departments. Because the conditions are testing the same field, you must link them together. As you saw earlier, you link conditions with the following operators: & (AND), ¦ (OR), ~ (NOT).

The condition you use to list everyone in the MIS and Eng. departments is = = *"MIS"*¦ = *"Eng."*. Notice the two equal signs at the beginning of the condition. The first equal sign begins the formula; the second one is the relational operator (= , as opposed to > = or < >). Also note that this condition contains the OR operator (¦), not AND (&) as you might think. Remember, both conditions have to be true for a record to be selected if you use the AND operator; only one condition has to be true with the OR operator. If the AND operator were used in this example, no records would be selected, because a person cannot be in two departments.

Now enter the condition to list all the employees in the MIS and personnel departments. Your list should match the one in Figure 10.15.

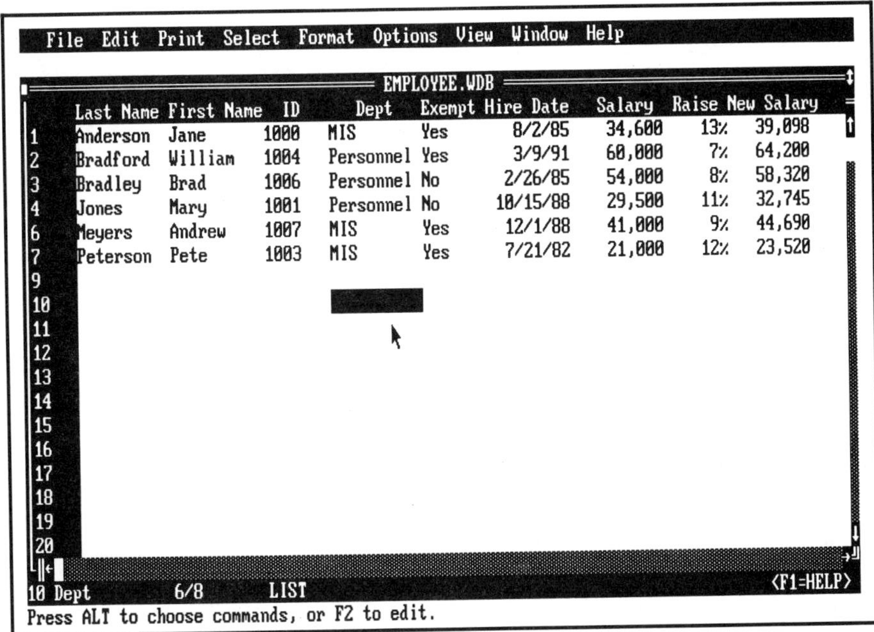

Figure 10.15: A list of employees in the MIS and personnel departments

Querying Date Fields

Usually with date field queries, you want to match a range of dates. For example, you may want to see all records before a certain date, or in a certain year or month. Thus, most of your date queries will be comparison formulas. The date in your comparison formula must be enclosed in single quotes. For example, *<'3/1/91'* lists all dates before March 1, 1991.

Follow these steps to list all employees who were hired before January 1, 1986:

1. Choose Query on the View menu.
2. Choose Delete Query on the Edit menu.
3. Move the cursor to the dotted line next to the Hire Date field.
4. Type **<'1/1/86'** and press Enter.
5. Press F10 to display the matching records. Your list should look similar to Figure 10.16.

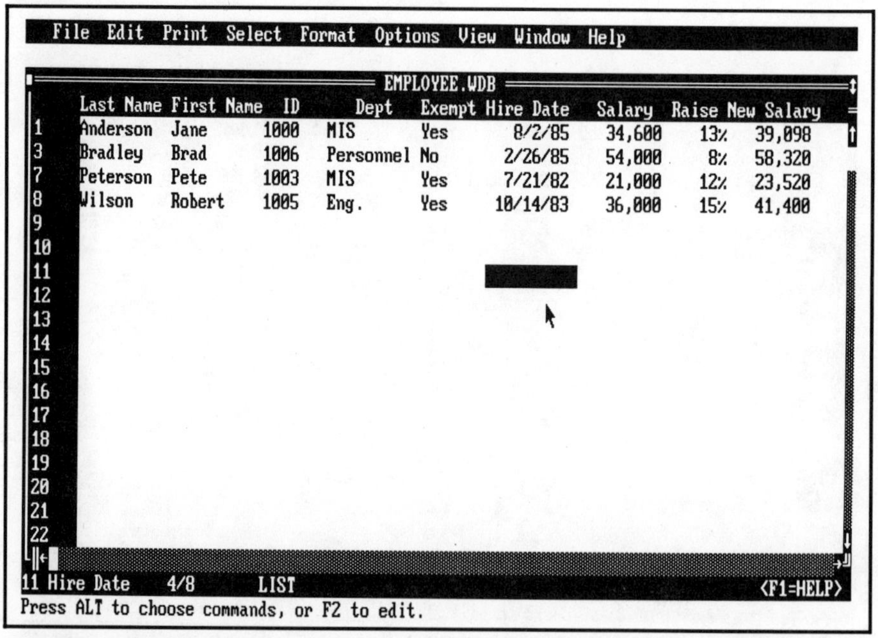

```
 File  Edit  Print  Select  Format  Options  View  Window  Help
═══════════════════════════ EMPLOYEE.WDB ═══════════════════════════
    Last Name First Name  ID      Dept    Exempt Hire Date   Salary  Raise New Salary
1   Anderson  Jane       1000   MIS       Yes       8/2/85   34,600   13%   39,098
3   Bradley   Brad       1006   Personnel No       2/26/85   54,000    8%   58,320
7   Peterson  Pete       1003   MIS       Yes      7/21/82   21,000   12%   23,520
8   Wilson    Robert     1005   Eng.      Yes     10/14/83   36,000   15%   41,400
9
10
11
12
13
14
15
16
17
18
19
20
21
22
11 Hire Date    4/8        LIST                                        <F1=HELP>
Press ALT to choose commands, or F2 to edit.
```

Figure 10.16: A list of employees hired before January 1, 1986

Works comes with several functions that you can use with dates in your spreadsheets and databases. (These functions are listed in Appendix C.) The two most useful ones in a database query are *MONTH()* and *YEAR()*. These functions allow you to display all dates within a specific month or year. For example, *=MONTH()=5* lists all the dates in the fifth month (May). Notice that you do not type single quotes when using the date functions.

Follow these steps to list all the employees hired in 1988:

1. Choose Query on the View menu.
2. Choose Delete Query on the Edit menu.
3. Move the cursor to the dotted line next to the Hire Date field.
4. Type **=YEAR()=88** and press Enter.
5. Press F10 to display the matching records. As the list indicates, two employees were hired in 1988 (Jones and Meyers).

SPECIFYING MULTIPLE CONDITIONS

Sometimes you will want to enter several different conditions as part of a single query. For example, you may want to get a list of all people hired before January 1, 1987, who make $40,000 or more. When you enter multiple conditions in a single query form, all conditions must be met in order for the record to be selected. Enter each condition next to the appropriate field, as follows:

1. Choose Query on the View menu.
2. Choose Delete Query on the Edit menu.
3. Move the cursor to the dotted line next to the Hire Date field.
4. Type **<'1/1/87'** and press Enter.
5. Move the cursor next to the Salary field.
6. Type **> = 40000** and press Enter.
7. Press F10 to display the matching records. As shown in Figure 10.17, two records match the two conditions (Bradley and Manley).

SELECTING RECORDS

The Select menu in the Form and List views offers several different ways to select the records you want to display. You can see a list of the following:

- All records in the database. (In essence, this cancels the query.)
- Only the records hidden by the query.
- The records matching the last query.

Redisplaying All the Records

After you enter a query, only the records that match the condition(s) are displayed in List and Form views. What do you do when you want to see all the records in the database again? You have two options. You can go back into Query view, delete your query, and then switch back to List or Form view. It is faster, however, to simply choose the Show All Records command

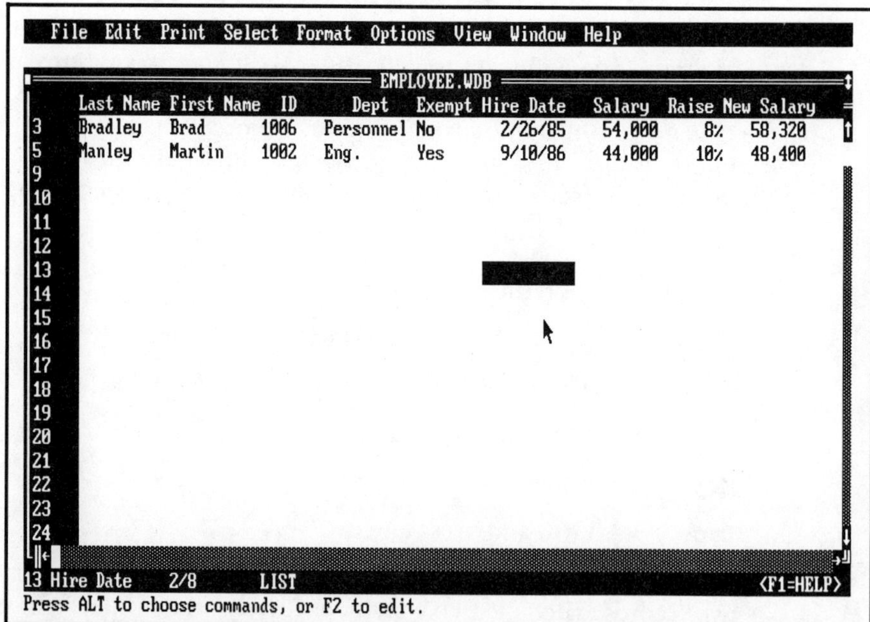

Figure 10.17: A list of employees hired before 1987 who make $40,000 or more

on the Select menu. Give this command now and all records are displayed. Check the status line to see that the record counter indicates *8/8*.

Reactivating a Query

Both the List view and the Form view offer a way to reactivate the last query that you entered, without your having to switch to Query view. The Apply Query command on the Select menu tells Works to display all the records that match the last condition you entered in the query form.

Select the Apply Query command now. You now see the list of employees hired before 1987 who make $40,000 or more (your last query).

Seeing the Hidden Records

When you activate a query, Works displays the records that match your condition and hides all the other records. Using the Switch Hidden Records command on the Select menu, you can see only the records that do *not* match your condition. There are several reasons why you might want to use this command.

First, you may have intentionally entered the query in such a way that you want to see the hidden records, not the selected records. For example, let's say you want a list of the employees in all departments except for Personnel. One way of getting this list is to enter a condition that lists only the personnel department and then use Switch Hidden Records to view all the other departments.

Second, you may want to see the hidden records because of idle curiosity. You may want to check out which records are hidden. Once you have looked at them, you can choose Switch Hidden Records again to go back to the original selection.

Before proceeding to the next chapter, choose Show All Records on the Select menu. The status line should show *8/8*. Now, save and close the file.

SUMMARY

In this chapter you explored two more views in the database tool: List and Query. With List view you can display, edit, and print your database in a row-and-column format. This view has one main advantage over Form view: You can see more than one record at a time. The Query view is not actually a view of your database. It allows you to specify which records you want displayed. You can then edit or print these selected records in Form or List view.

The fourth and final database view is *Report* view. In the next chapter, you will learn how to use this view to design and print formatted reports of your database.

EXERCISES

```
 File  Edit  Print  Select  Format  Options  View  Window  Help

                         CRCARDS.WDB
    Description   Type     Account      Phone    Exp. Date Credit Lim
 1  Emporium     Store    1-200-100-213-555-80none            1,000
 2  Macys        Store    50-100-20-415-555-09none            1,500
 3  Nordstrom    Store    400-900-10415-555-54none            2,000
 4  Am Express   General  4000-90000800-555-90    1/92  none
 5  B of A Visa  General  5000-1000-800-555-10    9/92        5,000
 6  Exxon        Gas      800-1000  800-555-40    6/92  none
 7  Shell        Gas      400-500-30800-555-43    3/93  none
 8
 9
 10
 11
 12
 13
 14
 15
 16
 17
 18
9 Description   7/7        LIST                                 <F1=HELP>
Press ALT to choose commands, or F2 to edit.
```

Figure 10.18: The credit-card database in List view

The exercises in this chapter use the credit-card database you created in Chapter 9. In the following exercises you will view and format the database in List view and then perform a number of queries. If you need help, refer to the appropriate sections indicated inside parentheses.

1. Open the CRCARDS file you created in Chapter 9, and switch to List view (see "List View," page 276). Your screen should look similar to Figure 10.18, except it should have your own credit-card data.
2. Adjust the column widths so that they match the Form view's field widths (see "Changing the Field Widths," page 287):

FIELD NAME	FIELD WIDTH
Description	15
Type	8

FIELD NAME	FIELD WIDTH
Account	20
Phone	12
Exp. Date	8
Credit Limit	7

3. Right-align the Exp. Date and Credit Limit fields (see "Specifying Style and Alignment," page 290).
4. Hide the Account field.
5. Sort the records alphabetically by Description (see "Sorting Records," page 291). Print this list.
6. Create and print queries to list the credit cards that
    - are gasoline credit cards (see "Creating a Query," page 295)
    - expire this year (see "Querying Date Fields," page 303)

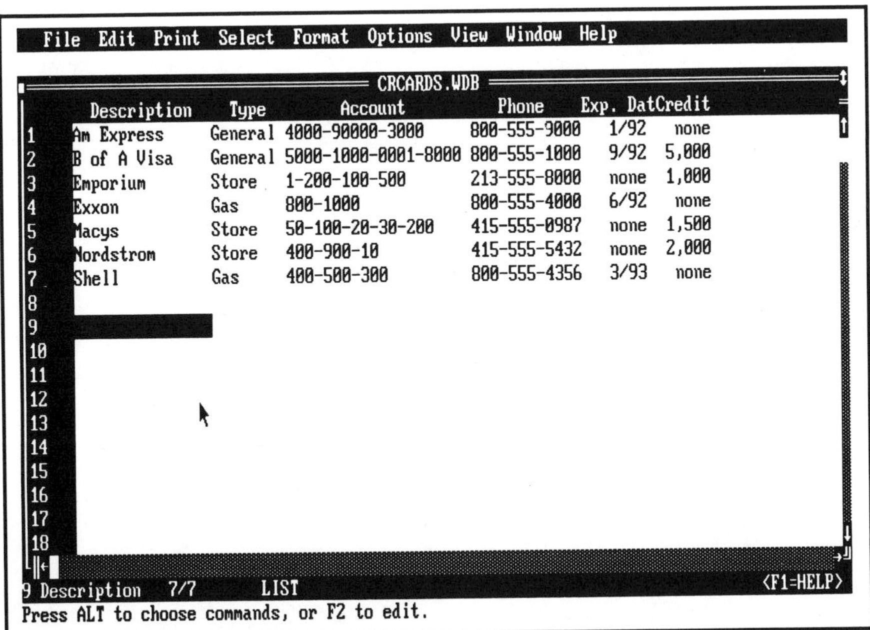

Figure 10.19: The formatted list

- have a credit limit over $2,000 (see ''Entering Comparison Formulas,'' page 302)
- have a credit limit between $1,000 and $3,000 (see ''Linking Comparison Formulas in Numeric Fields,'' page 298)
- are gasoline or department-store credit cards (see ''Linking Conditions in Text Fields,'' page 302)
- are general credit cards with a credit limit over $2,000 (see ''Specifying Multiple Conditions,'' page 305)

7. Display all the records (see ''Redisplaying All the Records,'' page 305).
8. Save and close the file.

CREATING REPORTS

11

In the preceding two chapters, you displayed and printed your data in a data-entry form (Form view) and in a columnar table (List view). Another way to see your data is in a formatted report (Report view).

The initial report that you produce in Report view is similar to the report you print in List view. The field names appear at the top of each column, all fields are included, and each record is printed on a different line. The advantage of Report view, though, is that almost every aspect of the report can be *customized;* you can specify the fields, labels, and formatting that you want in the report. Here are a few of the things you can do in Report view:

- You can format the style and alignment of the column headings.
- You can modify the text in the column headings.
- You can summarize (for example, total and average) the numeric fields.
- You can choose which fields to include in the report and print them in any order.
- You can print a title at the top of the report.

Like Query view, Report view does not actually contain your data. Instead, this view contains the layout or design of your report, called the *report definition.* Once you have created the report, you can press Shift-F10 to see the data in the report you designed.

CREATING THE AUTOMATIC REPORT

You do not need to create a report from scratch in Works. When you choose New Report on the View menu, Works creates a default report that lists all your fields with field names as column headings.

VIEWING THE AUTOMATIC REPORT

Open the EMPLOYEE database file that you have been working with in the last two chapters, and follow these steps to view the automatic report:

1. Choose New Report on the View menu. The report shown in Figure 11.1 is displayed on your screen.

2. The message "Press ENTER to continue, ESC to cancel" appears at the bottom of the screen. Press Enter and the next page of the report is displayed. (The bottom window border displays *Page 2.*) As you can see, the last three columns do not fit on the first page.

3. Press Enter again, and the Report view window is displayed.

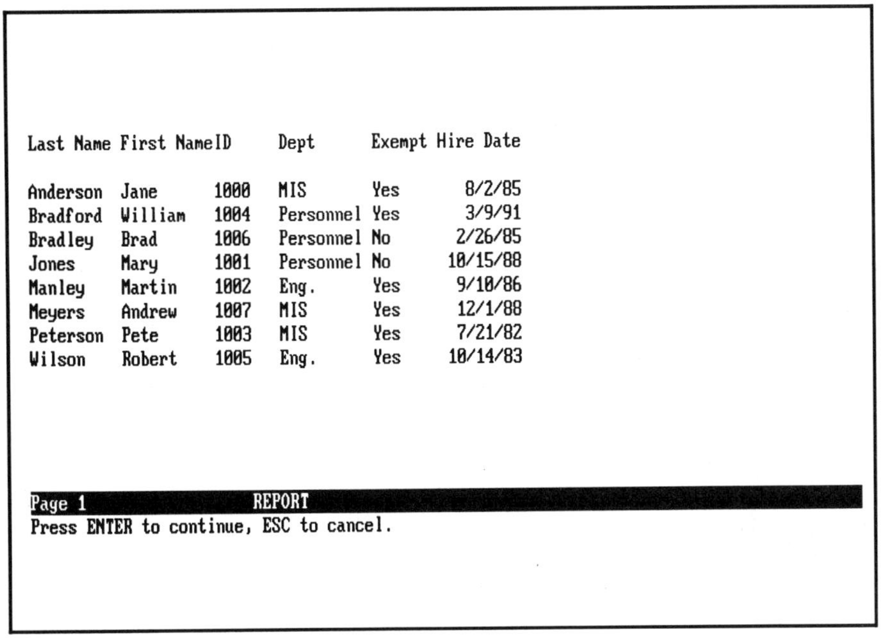

```
Last Name First NameID      Dept       Exempt Hire Date

Anderson  Jane       1000   MIS        Yes        8/2/85
Bradford  William    1004   Personnel  Yes        3/9/91
Bradley   Brad       1006   Personnel  No        2/26/85
Jones     Mary       1001   Personnel  No       10/15/88
Manley    Martin     1002   Eng.       Yes       9/10/86
Meyers    Andrew     1007   MIS        Yes       12/1/88
Peterson  Pete       1003   MIS        Yes       7/21/82
Wilson    Robert     1005   Eng.       Yes      10/14/83


Page 1                          REPORT
Press ENTER to continue, ESC to cancel.
```

Figure 11.1: The automatic report

If you felt that this automatic report was acceptable, you could use the Print command to print it on paper. Most likely, though, you will want to fine-tune the report before you print it. The rest of this chapter explains how to customize the automatic report.

EXPLORING THE SCREEN

Figure 11.2 points out the various parts of the Report view window. The top window border displays the name of your database file (EMPLOYEE.WDB), and the bottom border contains the word REPORT to let you know what view you are in. Like in the spreadsheet tool, the columns are labeled with letters (A, B, C, etc.). However, instead of row numbers, report *row types* appear in the left window border. Table 11.1 describes each of the row types. These row types will be explained in more detail as you modify the report.

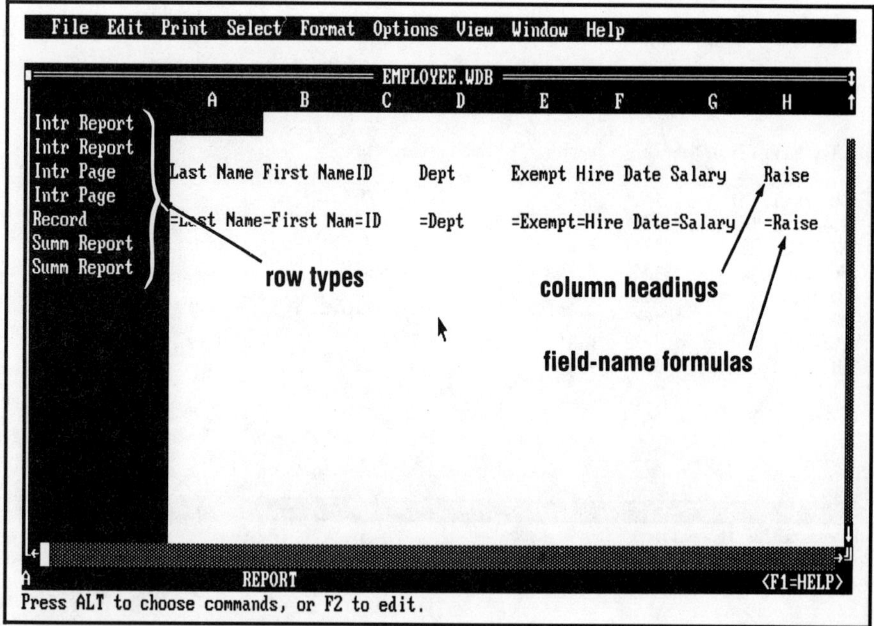

Figure 11.2: The Report view window

Table 11.1: Row Types

TYPE	DESCRIPTION	EXAMPLE
Intr Report	Prints at the top of first page	Report title
Intr Page	Prints at the top of each page	Column headings
Record	Prints once for each record	Field contents
Summ Report	Prints at the end of last page	Field totals

CHOOSING YOUR FIELDS

The automatic report prints all the fields, in the order they appear in List view. However, you can delete the fields you don't want in the report and move the remaining fields around so that they are positioned in the order you desire.

DELETING A FIELD

When you delete a field from the report, you are *not* deleting it from the database; you needn't be concerned that the data will be lost. When you remove a field column in Report view, you are simply indicating that you don't want the field included in the report.

The report you will be creating in this chapter will list employee names and salary information. Consequently, the ID, Dept, Exempt, and Hire Date fields are not necessary for this report and can be deleted.

First, follow these steps to delete the ID column from the report:

1. Move the highlight to the ID column (column C).
2. Choose Delete Row/Column on the Edit menu.
3. Press C or click next to Column.
4. Choose OK.

Repeat the above steps to delete the Dept, Exempt, and Hire Date fields. Your report definition should look similar to Figure 11.3. To view the modified report, press Shift-F10. Because you eliminated four columns, the entire report now fits on one page. Press Enter to continue, and you are brought back to the report definition.

MOVING A FIELD

You can easily reposition your fields by using the Move command on the Edit menu or by pressing the Move function key, F3. Before you invoke the Move command, *you must select the entire column.* If you only select a

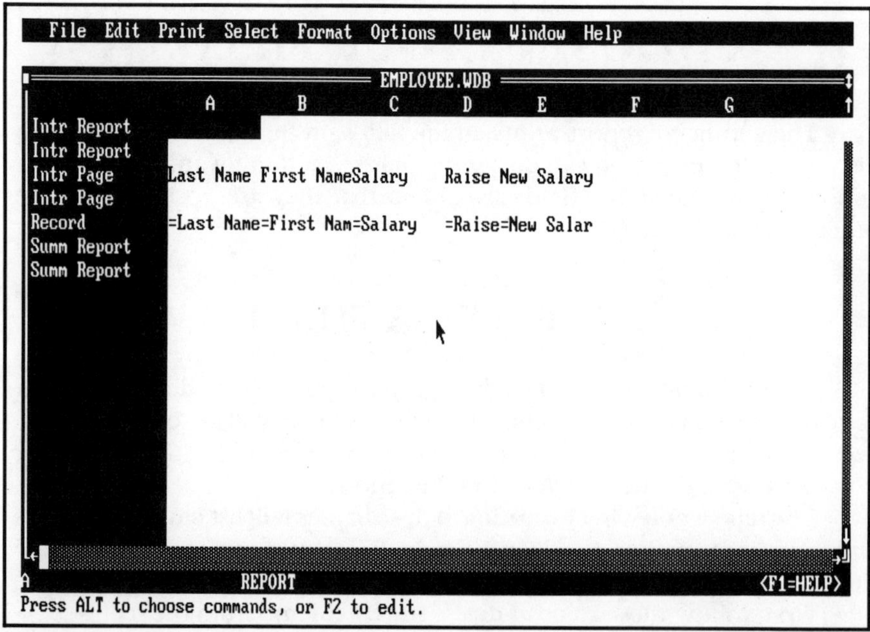

Figure 11.3: The report-definition screen after deletion of four fields

range, you will lose data in the new location. As you learned in Chapter 6, you can use any of the following methods to select a column:

- Choose Column on the Select menu.
- Press Shift-F8.
- Click on the column letter.

In your employee salary report, follow these steps to move the First Name field before the Last Name field:

1. Move the highlight to the First Name column (column B).
2. Select the column.
3. Press F3 for Move. The message "Select new location and press ENTER" appears at the bottom of the screen.
4. Because moved columns are inserted to the *left* of the highlight, place the highlight in column A.

5. Press Enter. *First Name* is now the first field in the report, as shown in Figure 11.4.

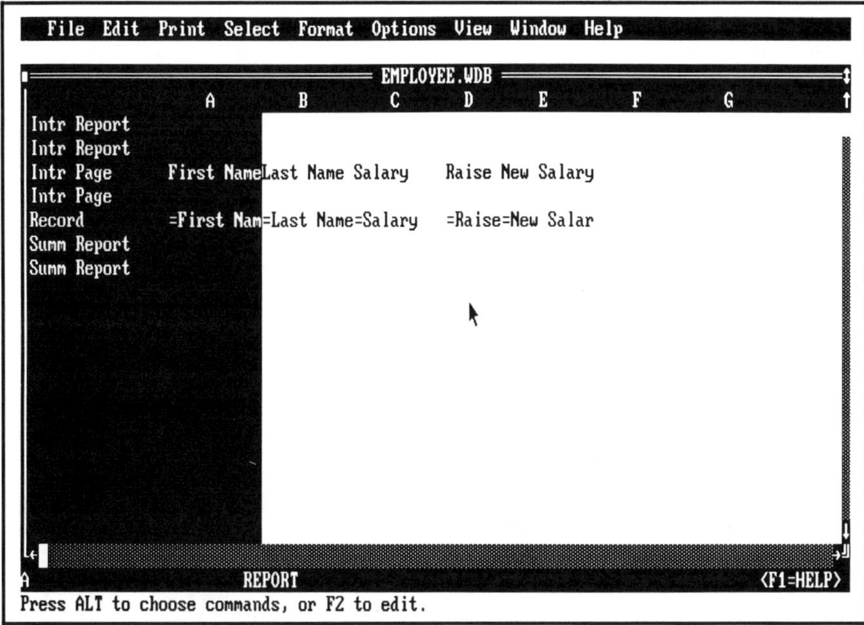

Figure 11.4: The report-definition screen after the First Name field has been moved before the Last Name field

INSERTING A FIELD

If you accidentally delete a field or you change your mind about a field you deleted, you can insert the field back in your report. (There is no Undo command.) Several steps are required to insert a field:

- Insert a column where you want the new field to go.
- Type a column heading in the Intr Page row.
- Insert a formula in the Record row.

To understand what is involved in inserting a field, take a closer look at the Intr Page and Record rows. In your automatic report, Works automatically placed your field names in each column of the Intr Page row. However, you can type *any* column headings you like in this row. You can either type over the field name or use the Edit function key, F2, to modify the contents. You can also create multiline column headings. (You will do this later in the chapter.)

Now take a look at the Record row. Each cell contains a formula that starts with an equal sign (as all spreadsheet formulas do) and is followed by the field name. This formula tells Works where to insert the contents of a specific field.

Now that you understand (I hope) what should go into a new field, follow these steps to insert the Dept field before Salary:

1. Place the highlight in the Salary column (column C).
2. Choose Insert Row/Column on the Edit menu.
3. Press C or click next to Column.
4. Choose OK. A blank column is inserted at column C.
5. Move the highlight to the first Intr Page row in column C.
6. Choose Insert Field Name on the Edit menu.
7. Select Dept from the list of field names and choose OK. The column heading, *Dept,* is displayed in the cell.
8. Move the highlight to the Record row in column C.
9. Choose Insert Field Contents on the Edit menu.
10. Select Dept from the list of field names and choose OK. The formula, *=Dept,* appears in the cell, as shown in Figure 11.5.

An alternative to using the Insert Field Name command is to simply type the field name, or any column heading, yourself. Likewise, instead of using the Insert Field Contents command, you can type the formula.

To see your modified report, press Shift-F10. To return to the report-definition window, press Enter or Esc.

FORMATTING THE REPORT

Formatting your report is similar to formatting a spreadsheet. You can adjust column widths, change the alignment of your column headings, add boldface and underlining, and format the numbers.

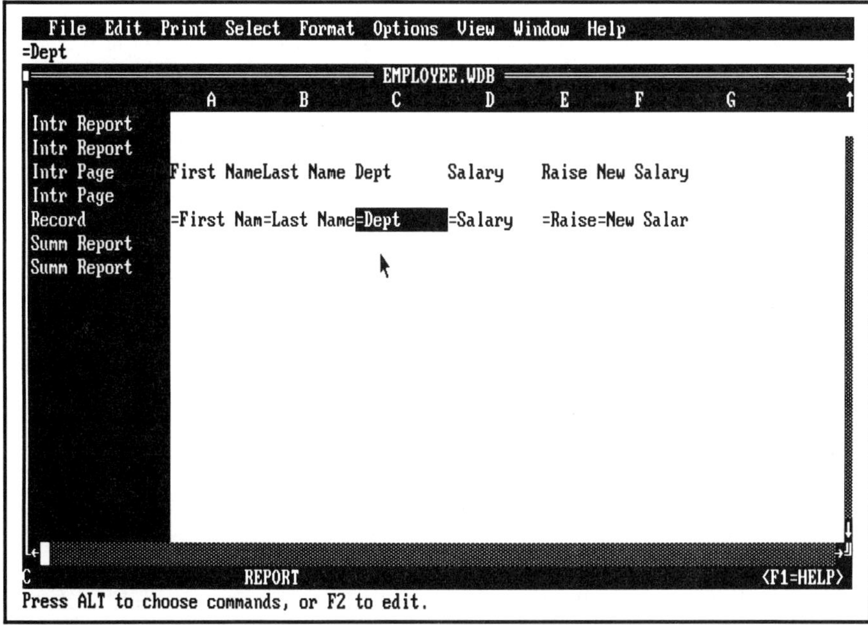

Figure 11.5: The report-definition screen after insertion of the Dept field

CHANGING COLUMN WIDTHS

The column widths in your report currently correspond to the List-view field widths. As you learned in Chapter 10, column widths are set to 10 characters in List view unless you change them; in the last chapter you narrowed several of the columns so that you could fit more columns on the screen. If you are trying to maximize the number of fields on a report page, you want to decrease the column widths. Changing the column widths in Report view does not affect the field widths in List view or Form view.

In your employee salary report, the six fields fit on one page, but some of the columns are too close together. Follow these steps to widen the First Name and Last Name columns to 12 characters each:

1. Move the highlight to the First Name column (column A).
2. Select columns A and B. (A single cell in each column is sufficient.)
3. Choose Column Width on the Format menu.

4. Type **12** and press Enter.
5. Press Shift-F10 to view the report. (Press Enter or Esc to exit to the report-definition window.)

FORMATTING THE COLUMN HEADINGS

Your column headings would look better if they were properly aligned over the data below them, and they would stand out more if they were emphasized in some way (for example, with boldface, underlining, or italic). The Style dialog box offers options for alignment and character styles.

Aligning the Column Headings

Notice that the Salary heading does not line up over the numbers in the column. This misalignment happens because, by default, text lines up on the left side of the cell and numbers line up on the right. Consequently, you frequently need to change the alignment of your numeric field column headings. Follow these steps to center the Salary heading:

1. Move the highlight to Salary in the Intr Page row.
2. Choose Style on the Format menu.
3. Press C or click next to Center.
4. Choose OK.
5. Press Shift-F10 to see how the centered heading looks. Your report should look similar to the one in Figure 11.6.

Boldfacing the Column Headings

One of the deficiencies of the List view report is that you can't format the column headings. In Report view you can use the Style command to add boldface, underlining, and italic to any part of your report. Follow these steps to boldface the column headings:

1. Select the Intr Page row that contains the column headings. (Put the highlight anywhere in the Intr Page row, and choose Row on the Select menu.)

```
First Name  Last Name   Dept        Salary  Raise New Salary

Jane        Anderson    MIS          34,600   13%   39,098
William     Bradford    Personnel    60,000    7%   64,200
Brad        Bradley     Personnel    54,000    8%   58,320
Mary        Jones       Personnel    29,500   11%   32,745
Martin      Manley      Eng.         44,000   10%   48,400
Andrew      Meyers      MIS          41,000    9%   44,690
Pete        Peterson    MIS          21,000   12%   23,520
Robert      Wilson      Eng.         36,000   15%   41,400



Page 1                  REPORT
Press ENTER to continue, ESC to cancel.
```

Figure 11.6: The formatted report

2. Choose Style on the Format menu.
3. Press B or click next to Bold.
4. Choose OK. If you are in Graphics mode, the field names are displayed in bold on your screen. If you are in Text mode, you will only see the bold when you print.

Press Shift-F10 to view the report. Notice that the column headings are *not* displayed in bold. Styles (bold, underline, and italic) do not appear on the screen when you view the report, though they will appear on the report-definition screen and when you print on paper.

ADDING A TITLE

To place a title at the top of your report, you need to make an entry in one of the Intr Report rows. This row type prints on the first page of the report. Notice that the default report gives you two blank Intr Report rows. Let's type a title on the first row and then underline it.

1. Move the highlight to column C in the first Intr Report row.
2. Type **Employee Salaries** and press Enter.
3. Choose Style on the Format menu.
4. Press U or click next to Underline.
5. Choose OK.
6. Press Shift-F10 to view the report (see Figure 11.7). Again, notice that the style (underline) is not displayed here.

```
                        Employee Salaries

First Name Last Name  Dept        Salary  Raise New Salary

Jane       Anderson   MIS         34,600    13%   39,098
William    Bradford   Personnel   60,000     7%   64,200
Brad       Bradley    Personnel   54,000     8%   58,320
Mary       Jones      Personnel   29,500    11%   32,745
Martin     Manley     Eng.        44,000    10%   48,400
Andrew     Meyers     MIS         41,000     9%   44,690
Pete       Peterson   MIS         21,000    12%   23,520
Robert     Wilson     Eng.        36,000    15%   41,400




Page 1                REPORT
Press ENTER to continue, ESC to cancel.
```

Figure 11.7: The report with a title in the Intr Report row

INSERTING NEW LINES

The automatic report has two rows each for Intr Report, Intr Page, and Summ Report and one row for the Record row type. Using the Insert Row/Column command on the Edit menu, you can insert more rows of any type. For example, you may want additional space between the report title and the column headings, or you may want to put your column headings on two lines.

When you use the Insert Row/Column command, Works first asks you whether you want to insert a row or column. If you choose Row, you see a list of row types from which you can select the type you want to insert. Follow these steps to insert a line under the report title so that there is more space between the title and the column headings:

1. Move the highlight to the second Intr Report row. (Rows are inserted *above* the highlight.)
2. Choose Insert Row/Column on the Edit menu.
3. *Row* is already selected, so choose OK.
4. From the list of row types, choose Intr Report.
5. Choose OK. A blank row is inserted, and it is labeled with the row type *Intr Report.*

Because you want to place some of the column headings over two rows, you need to insert another Intr Page row. Follow the steps above to insert an Intr Page row under the column headings. Revise and format the headings so that they match Figure 11.8.

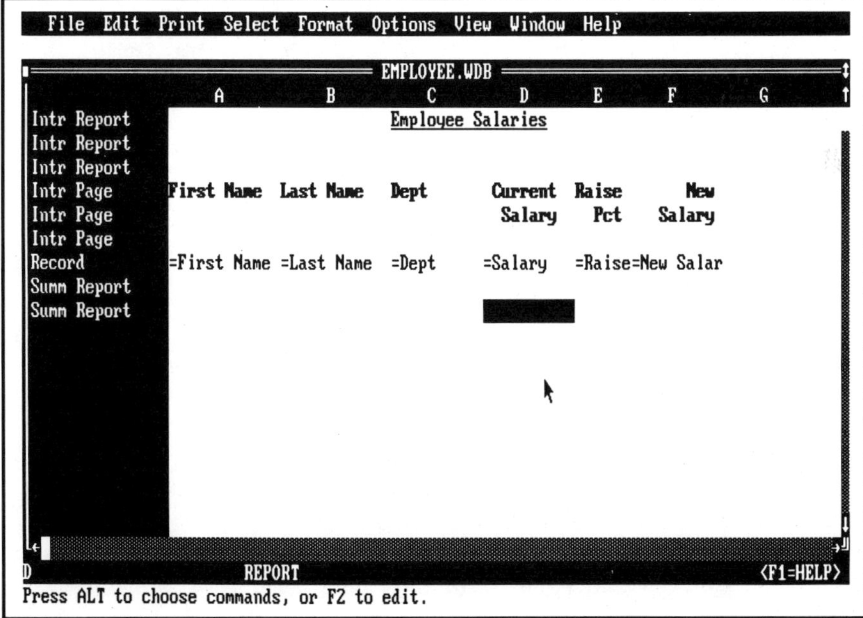

Figure 11.8: The report-definition screen with multiline column headings

FORMATTING THE NUMBERS

The numeric formatting in your report corresponds to the formatting you defined in either Form or List view. Thus, you see commas in the Salary and New Salary fields and percent signs in the Raise field. However, the Report view allows you to set different formats from what you see in other database views.

Because you do not actually see your data in Report view, it may not be immediately obvious what cell(s) you are formatting. To format the data in your report, you format the appropriate cell in the Record row (that is, the cell containing the formula).

Follow these steps to format the Raise field to Percent with one decimal place:

1. Place the highlight in column E, the Record row. Your highlight should be on the formula *=Raise.*
2. Choose Percent on the Format menu.
3. Type **1** for the number of decimal places.
4. Choose OK.
5. Press Shift-F10 to display the report. Your report should look similar to Figure 11.9.

SUMMARIZING A FIELD

Your report is starting to look more professional, now that it is formatted. However, the report is missing one important element: column totals. The totals go in the last row type, *Summ Report.* This row type prints at the end of the report. Besides totals, your summary rows can contain the following statistical functions:

FUNCTION	DESCRIPTION
AVG	Averages the values in the field
COUNT	Counts the number of records that contain an entry in the field

Employee Salaries

First Name	Last Name	Dept	Current Salary	Raise Pct	New Salary
Jane	Anderson	MIS	34,600	13.0%	39,098
William	Bradford	Personnel	60,000	7.0%	64,200
Brad	Bradley	Personnel	54,000	8.0%	58,320
Mary	Jones	Personnel	29,500	11.0%	32,745
Martin	Manley	Eng.	44,000	10.0%	48,400
Andrew	Meyers	MIS	41,000	9.0%	44,690
Pete	Peterson	MIS	21,000	12.0%	23,520
Robert	Wilson	Eng.	36,000	15.0%	41,400

Page 1 REPORT
Press ENTER to continue, ESC to cancel.

Figure 11.9: The report with the Raise column formatted to Percent with one decimal place

MAX	Maximum value in the field
MIN	Minimum value in the field
STD	Standard deviation of the field (square root of the variance)
VAR	Variance of the field (how much the field values vary)

There are two ways you can enter a statistical formula in the summary row: You can type it yourself, or you can use the Insert Field Summary command. You will have an opportunity to try both techniques in the upcoming exercise.

For the first formula, let Works build the formula for you.

1. Move the highlight to the second Summ Report row in the Salary column (column D).

2. Choose Insert Field Summary on the Edit menu. The dialog box shown in Figure 11.10 is displayed.
3. Highlight the name Salary in the Fields list box.
4. By default, SUM is selected in the Statistics list. Choose OK.

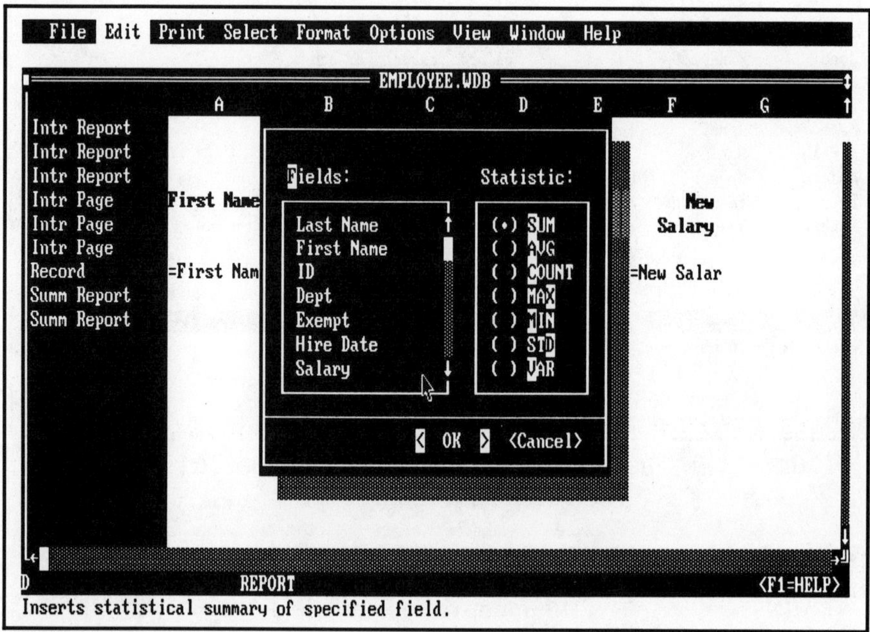

Figure 11.10: The Insert Field Summary dialog box

The formula, = *SUM(Salary)*, appears in the cell. This formula is similar to the SUM function in the spreadsheet tool except that a field name, instead of a range, appears inside parentheses. Also notice that the formula, not the result, is in the cell. To see the result, you must display the report. (We'll display it after we do another formula.)

For the New Salary total, use the alternative method of entering a summary formula (that is, type it yourself).

1. Move the highlight to the New Salary column (column F) in the Summ Report row.
2. Type **= SUM(New Salary)** and press Enter.
3. Press Shift-F10 to display the report.

Notice that these totals are not formatted. Format these cells to Comma with zero decimal places, and type the word **Total** at the beginning of the row. Your report should look similar to Figure 11.11.

```
                    Employee Salaries

First Name  Last Name   Dept        Current  Raise      New
                                     Salary    Pct   Salary

Jane        Anderson    MIS          34,600  13.0%   39,098
William     Bradford    Personnel    60,000   7.0%   64,200
Brad        Bradley     Personnel    54,000   8.0%   58,320
Mary        Jones       Personnel    29,500  11.0%   32,745
Martin      Manley      Eng.         44,000  10.0%   48,400
Andrew      Meyers      MIS          41,000   9.0%   44,690
Pete        Peterson    MIS          21,000  12.0%   23,520
Robert      Wilson      Eng.         36,000  15.0%   41,400

Total                               320,100         352,373

Page 1                  REPORT
Press ENTER to continue, ESC to cancel.
```

Figure 11.11: The report with totals for the Salary and New Salary fields

To include averages in your report summary rows, you need an additional row. Because this row is at the end of the report, you do not have to use the Insert Row/Column command. Simply move the highlight to the row underneath your totals and start typing; Summ Report is automatically filled in as the row type. Follow these steps to average the Salary and New Salary fields:

1. In column A, underneath *Total,* type **Average** and press Enter. Summ Report appears as the row type.
2. In column D, type **=AVG(Salary)** and press Enter.
3. In column F, type **=AVG(New Salary)** and press Enter.
4. Format these cells to Comma with zero decimal places.

5. Press Shift-F10 to display the report. It should look similar to Figure 11.12.

```
                    Employee Salaries

First Name  Last Name  Dept       Current  Raise      New
                                   Salary   Pct    Salary

Jane        Anderson   MIS         34,600  13.0%   39,098
William     Bradford   Personnel   60,000   7.0%   64,200
Brad        Bradley    Personnel   54,000   8.0%   58,320
Mary        Jones      Personnel   29,500  11.0%   32,745
Martin      Manley     Eng.        44,000  10.0%   48,400
Andrew      Meyers     MIS         41,000   9.0%   44,690
Pete        Peterson   MIS         21,000  12.0%   23,520
Robert      Wilson     Eng.        36,000  15.0%   41,400

Total                             320,100         352,373
Average                            40,013          44,047
Page 1                 REPORT
Press ENTER to continue, ESC to cancel.
```

Figure 11.12: The report with averages for the Salary and New Salary fields

SORTING THE REPORT

Your report automatically appears in the order you last sorted it in Form or List view. As part of the report definition, you can include instructions to sort the current database by a certain field. The Sort Records command in the Report view is more powerful than its counterpart in List and Form views. In the other views, you must reissue the sort command after you add new records to the database. In Report view, every time you display the report, the data will be sorted properly.

For the employee salary report, let's say that you want it sorted primarily by the Dept field, and within each department, you want the last names to be alphabetized. Thus, the first sort field is Dept, and the second sort field is Last Name. Follow these steps to record this information in the report definition:

1. Choose Sort Records on the Select menu.
2. Next to 1st Field, type **Dept**.
3. Next to 2nd Field, type **Last Name**.
4. Choose OK.
5. Display the report (press Shift-F10) to see that the report is sorted properly (see Figure 11.13).

```
                    Employee Salaries

First Name  Last Name  Dept       Current  Raise      New
                                   Salary    Pct   Salary

Martin      Manley     Eng.        44,000  10.0%   48,400
Robert      Wilson     Eng.        36,000  15.0%   41,400
Jane        Anderson   MIS         34,600  13.0%   39,098
Andrew      Meyers     MIS         41,000   9.0%   44,690
Pete        Peterson   MIS         21,000  12.0%   23,520
William     Bradford   Personnel   60,000   7.0%   64,200
Brad        Bradley    Personnel   54,000   8.0%   58,320
Mary        Jones      Personnel   29,500  11.0%   32,745

Total                             320,100         352,373
Average                            40,013          44,047
Page 1                 REPORT
Press ENTER to continue, ESC to cancel.
```

Figure 11.13: The report sorted by Dept and Last Name

Let's make sure that new records automatically appear in the proper sort order in the report. To enter a new record, you have to go to List view or Form view. To go to the last view you were in, you can either press F10 or choose the view (the Form or List option) from the View menu. However, you can only go to the last view you were in before you went to Report view. Since you invoked Report view from List view, you must return to List view. From there, you can go into Form view if you want.

Press F10 now to go to List view, and notice that your records are sorted in the order you specified in your report definition. Enter record 9 as it is displayed in Figure 11.14.

```
 File  Edit  Print  Select  Format  Options  View  Window  Help
"Smith
                              EMPLOYEE.WDB
   Last Name First Name  ID     Dept    Exempt Hire Date   Salary  Raise New Salary
1  Manley    Martin    1002  Eng.       Yes     9/10/86   44,000    10%   48,400
2  Wilson    Robert    1005  Eng.       Yes    10/14/83   36,000    15%   41,400
3  Anderson  Jane      1000  MIS        Yes      8/2/85   34,600    13%   39,098
4  Meyers    Andrew    1007  MIS        Yes     12/1/88   41,000     9%   44,690
5  Peterson  Pete      1003  MIS        Yes     7/21/82   21,000    12%   23,520
6  Bradford  William   1004  Personnel  Yes      3/9/91   60,000     7%   64,200
7  Bradley   Brad      1006  Personnel  No      2/26/85   54,000     8%   58,320
8  Jones     Mary      1001  Personnel  No     10/15/88   29,500    11%   32,745
9  Smith     Sally     1008  Eng.       Yes     6/12/91   36,500     6%   38,690
10
11
12
13
14
15
16
17
18
9 Last Name     9/9        LIST                                        <F1=HELP>
Press ALT to choose commands, or F2 to edit.
```

Figure 11.14: The employee-raise spreadsheet in List view

To display your report when you are in List view, you have two alternatives:

- Press Shift-F10.
- Choose Report1 on the View menu. (*Report1* is the default name assigned to your first report. In the section "Renaming a Report," you will learn how to assign more descriptive names to your reports.)

Although both these commands display your report, they take you to different views after the report is displayed. Using the Shift-F10 command in Form or List view displays the report and then returns you to the view you were in; it doesn't take you into Report view, where you could redesign or print the report. By choosing Report1 on the View menu, however, you go directly to Report view. Consequently, the method you should choose depends on what you want to do next. If you want to continue editing or entering records, press Shift-F10. If you want to modify or print the report, use the View menu.

Since you want to display the report and then go back to Report view, choose Report1 on the View menu. The new record you inserted was sorted correctly and is in the correct position in the report.

COMBINING QUERIES WITH REPORTS

When you view a report, it lists whichever records are currently selected and displayed in List view or Form view. If you create a query, only the records that match the condition in the query are listed in the report. For example, if you use Query view to enter a condition to display only the employees in the personnel department, only these records are printed in the report. Therefore, to produce a report that prints a range of records in your database, you follow these basic steps:

- Enter your condition(s) in Query view.
- Go to Report view (choose Report1 on the View menu).
- Display and/or print the report.

Let's say you want to print a report of the employees in the MIS department. You need to create a query for this condition.

1. Choose Query on the View menu. The query form is displayed.
2. Delete any existing conditions.
3. Next to the Dept field name, type **MIS** and press Enter.
4. Choose Report1 on the View menu.
5. Press Shift-F10 to display the report. Your report should only list the MIS employees, as shown in Figure 11.15.

To print this report now, use the Print command. For details on printing, refer to the next section, "Printing a Report."

```
                     Employee Salaries

First Name  Last Name  Dept      Current  Raise      New
                                  Salary    Pct   Salary

Jane        Anderson   MIS        34,600  13.0%   39,098
Andrew      Meyers     MIS        41,000   9.0%   44,690
Pete        Peterson   MIS        21,000  12.0%   23,520

Total                             96,600         107,308
Average                           32,200          35,769



Page 1                 REPORT
Press ENTER to continue, ESC to cancel.
```

Figure 11.15: The report with a query activated

Before going on, turn off the query so that all records are displayed. The quickest way to do this is to choose the Show All Records command in List view or Form view. Follow these steps:

1. Press F10 to switch to List view.
2. Choose Show All Records on the Select menu.
3. Switch back to Report view. All records are now shown in the report.

PRINTING A REPORT

To print your employee salary report, choose the Print command on the Print menu. The Print dialog box has one new option: *Print all but record rows.* This option prints only the summary lines (your totals and averages), not the records themselves. Figure 11.16 gives an example of this type of report. For your salary report, you don't need to choose this option. Choose Print; your report should look similar to Figure 11.17.

Employee Salaries

First Name	Last Name	Dept	Current Salary	Raise Pct	New Salary
Total			356,600		391,063
Average			39,622		43,451

Figure 11.16: The report without record rows printed

Employee Salaries

First Name	Last Name	Dept	Current Salary	Raise Pct	New Salary
Martin	Manley	Eng.	44,000	10.0%	48,400
Sally	Smith	Eng.	36,500	6.0%	38,690
Robert	Wilson	Eng.	36,000	15.0%	41,400
Jane	Anderson	MIS	34,600	13.0%	39,098
Andrew	Meyers	MIS	41,000	9.0%	44,690
Pete	Peterson	MIS	21,000	12.0%	23,520
William	Bradford	Personnel	60,000	7.0%	64,200
Brad	Bradley	Personnel	54,000	8.0%	58,320
Mary	Jones	Personnel	29,500	11.0%	32,745
Total			356,600		391,063
Average			39,622		43,451

Figure 11.17: The final employee-salary report

This particular report is small and easily fits on a single page. If you want to print wider and longer reports, read the following two sections.

PRINTING WIDE REPORTS

As with your spreadsheets and lists, you should consider how the report fits horizontally on the page. The report you display by pressing Shift-F10 reflects your current margins, font, and printer orientation (portrait or landscape). If all the columns fit on one page when you press Shift-F10, they will fit across the printed page.

For wide reports, try any of the following techniques to fit more columns on the page:

- Narrow the left and right margins using the Page Setup & Margins command on the Print menu.
- Assign a smaller font size using the Font command on the Format menu.
- Specify a landscape printer (like HPLASLAN) in the Printer Setup dialog box.

PRINTING LONG REPORTS

If your database has many records, the report will automatically be printed on multiple pages. Because your column headings are typed in the Intr Page row, they will be displayed at the top of every page when you print. However, your report title appears only at the top of page 1 because it is in the Intr Report row. If you want a title or page number to appear on every page, you should use headers and footers. For additional information on creating headers and footers, refer to Chapter 5.

CREATING ADDITIONAL REPORTS

Each time you choose New Report on the View menu, Works creates an automatic report that contains all fields with the field names as column headings. The reports are assigned names according to the order in which you created them. The first report is called *Report1,* the second report is called *Report2,* etc. Because these names are so generic, you may have a hard time keeping track of multiple reports. The Reports command on the View menu offers a way to manage your reports—you can rename, copy, and delete reports.

RENAMING A REPORT

When working with multiple reports in a database file, you should assign more descriptive names to the reports. A month from now it's doubtful that you will remember the difference between reports named Report1, Report2, and Report3. Follow these steps to give your employee salary report a more meaningful name:

1. Choose Reports on the View menu.
2. Report1 should be highlighted in the Reports list box, and Rename should be selected at the bottom of the dialog box.
3. Move the cursor next to Name.
4. Type **Salary** and press Enter to choose Rename. *Salary* now appears in the Reports list box in the place of Report1.
5. Choose Done.

Now when you display the View pull-down menu, *Salary* appears on the menu instead of Report1.

COPYING A REPORT

If a new report is more similar to an existing report than to the automatic report, you should duplicate the report you have already created. Modifying a copy of an existing report is sometimes faster than working from the automatic report.

To duplicate your Salary report, follow these steps:

1. Choose Reports on the View menu. (Salary should be highlighted in the Reports list box.)
2. Move the cursor next to Name.
3. Type **Salary2**. (Do not press Enter or you will rename the chart.)
4. Choose Copy. Salary and Salary2 now appear in the Reports list box.
5. Choose Done.

To modify the duplicate report, choose Salary2 on the View menu. The report that is displayed is identical to the salary report you created in this chapter. Save your file before you close it.

SUMMARY

In this chapter you learned how to create, modify, and print columnar reports. These reports are similar to the ones you see in List view except that the layout and format are flexible and can be customized.

The next chapter explains how to print two other kinds of report. You can merge the data from your database with documents in the word processor tool to create form letters and mailing labels.

EXERCISES

In this chapter's exercises, you will continue using the credit-card database you created in Chapter 9. You will create a report that you can keep handy in case your credit cards get stolen. This report lists the card description, account number, phone number, and expiration date. If you need help, refer to the appropriate sections indicated inside parentheses.

1. Open your CRCARDS file, and create an automatic report (see "Creating the Automatic Report," page 312). The first page of your report should look similar to Figure 11.18.
2. Delete the Type and Credit Limit fields (see "Deleting a Field," page 315).

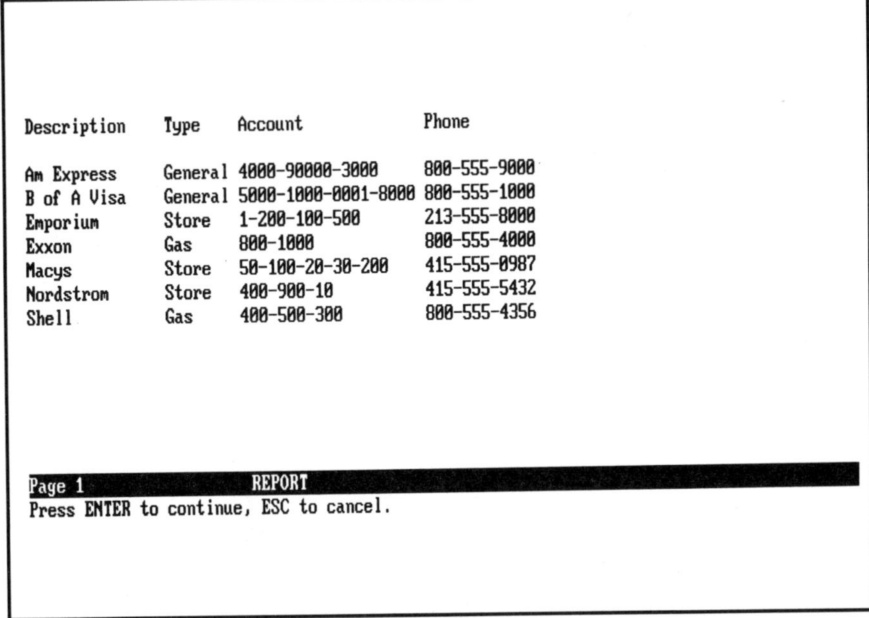

Description	Type	Account	Phone
Am Express	General	4000-90000-3000	800-555-9000
B of A Visa	General	5000-1000-0001-8000	800-555-1000
Emporium	Store	1-200-100-500	213-555-8000
Exxon	Gas	800-1000	800-555-4000
Macys	Store	50-100-20-30-200	415-555-0987
Nordstrom	Store	400-900-10	415-555-5432
Shell	Gas	400-500-300	800-555-4356

Page 1 REPORT
Press ENTER to continue, ESC to cancel.

Figure 11.18: The automatic report

3. Format the report as follows:
    - Widen the Exp. Date field to 9 (see "Changing Column Widths," page 319).
    - Boldface the column headings (see "Boldfacing the Column Headings," page 320).
4. Create the title *Credit Card List* and underline it.
5. Print the report. It should look similar to Figure 11.19.
6. Save and close the file.

```
                    Credit Card List

Description    Account              Phone          Exp. Date

Am Express     4000-90000-3000      800-555-9000     1/92
B of A Visa    5000-1000-0001-8000  800-555-1000     9/92
Emporium       1-200-100-500        213-555-8000     none
Exxon          800-1000             800-555-4000     6/92
Macys          50-100-20-30-200     415-555-0987     none
Nordstrom      400-900-10           415-555-5432     none
Shell          400-500-300          800-555-4356     3/93
```

Figure 11.19: The formatted, printed report

FORM LETTERS AND MAILING LABELS

12

Before the advent of the word processor, in order to send the same letter to 50 people, you had to individually type 50 different letters so that each person had a personalized letter with his or her name and address on it. Or, in some cases, you could make photocopies of the body of the letter and then type the individual's name and address on each photocopy. Furthermore, to mail all these letters, you had to retype the names and addresses on envelopes or mailing labels.

With Works, you can use the form letter and mailing label features to eliminate the wasted time and tedious work involved in doing mass mailings. You use the database tool to enter the names and addresses, and the word processor tool to type the form letter. Then, when you print, each name and address from the database is inserted in the letter, giving you an individualized letter for each person on your mailing list.

The process of inserting names and addresses in a form letter is sometimes called a *mail merge.* One of the advantages of doing a merge is that you only have to enter the names and addresses once; you can then include them in different letters and print them on envelopes or mailing labels. To perform a mail merge, you must follow these basic steps:

- Create the database and enter the names and addresses in it.
- Create the form-letter document. Type the standard text (the body of the letter), and insert *placeholders* where you want the field data to be printed.
- Merge the names and addresses into the form letter using the Print Form Letters command.

This chapter will show you how to create a mailing-list database and will then cover the steps you need to know to produce form letters, envelopes, and mailing labels.

CREATING THE DATABASE

Because you learned how to create a data-entry form in Chapter 9, this section provides minimal information on creating the mailing-list database. Refer back to Chapter 9 if you need additional help.

Before you design the data-entry form, you should think about what fields you need. The rule you learned in Chapter 9 applies here: Create separate fields for each piece of data. First, do not lump the parts of the address into one field. Create separate fields for the street address, the city, the state, and the zip code. That way, you have the greatest flexibility in sorting and printing. You may even want two fields for the street address (for example, Street1 and Street2) if some of the people on your mailing list have long addresses. You will also need two fields for the name—one that contains the complete name (for example, Mr. Herbert Hoolihan) and another for the salutation. The salutation is the greeting that comes after the word "Dear" in the letter (Mr. Hoolihan or Herbert).

Figure 12.1 contains the data-entry form for your mailing list. Use this figure as a guide for laying out your form. Create a new database file and then specify the field names and widths listed below. Be sure to type a colon after each field name.

FIELD NAME	WIDTH
Company:	25
Contact:	20
Salutation:	15

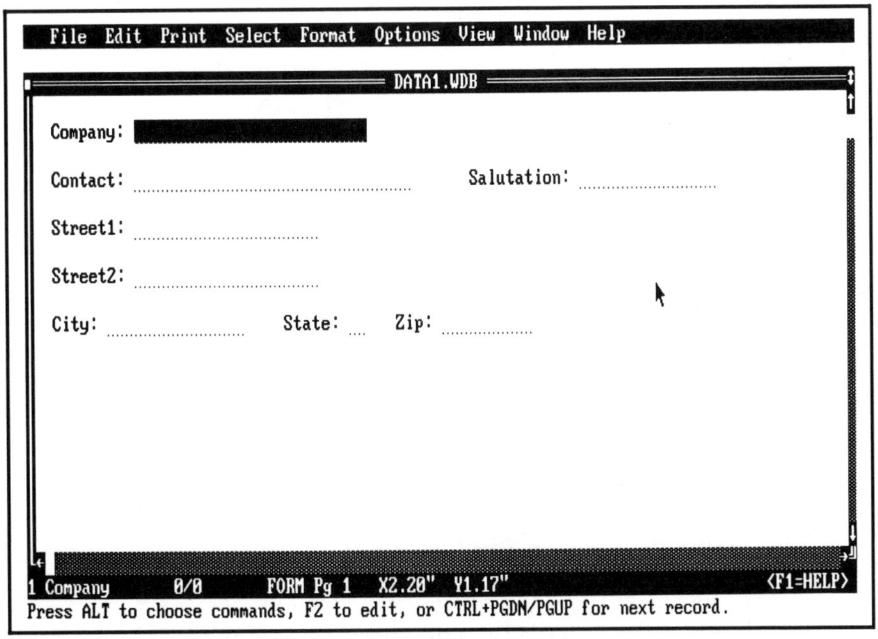

```
File  Edit  Print  Select  Format  Options  View  Window  Help
DATA1.WDB
Company:
Contact:                              Salutation:
Street1:
Street2:
City:             State:    Zip:
1 Company      0/0      FORM Pg 1   X2.20"  Y1.17"          <F1=HELP>
Press ALT to choose commands, F2 to edit, or CTRL+PGDN/PGUP for next record.
```

Figure 12.1: The mailing-list data-entry form

FIELD NAME	WIDTH
Street1:	20
Street2:	20
City:	15
State:	2
Zip:	10

To differentiate the names from the data, format each field name to the bold style.

Figure 12.2 lists the records for your mailing-list database. Each record should be entered in a separate form; use the Tab key to move from field to field. When you press Tab on the last field in the form, a blank form is automatically displayed so that you can enter the next record. After you have entered all seven records, save the file with the name CUSTDATA. Do not close this file, because in order to create and print the form letters, the database file must be open.

Company	Contact	Salutation	Street1	Street2	City	State	Zip
Smith Electronics	Mr. William Smith	Mr. Smith	P.O. Box 9002		Menlo Park	CA	94025
Anderson Appliances	Ms. Mary Anderson	Ms. Anderson	4523 State Street	Suite 199	Palo Alto	CA	94303
Johnson Electric	Mr. John Johnson	Mr. Johnson	1666 First Street	Suite 10	Los Altos	CA	94022
Thompson & Thompson	Ms. Jane Thompson	Ms. Thompson	P.O. Box 1234		Palo Alto	CA	94303
Carlyle, Inc.	Mr. Steven Benson	Mr. Benson	9876 Second Street	Suite 206	Los Altos	CA	94022
Galveston Industries	Mr. Robert Jackson	Mr. Jackson	19201 Main Street	Suite 7	Palo Alto	CA	94306
HIB Associates	Ms. Janet Jones	Ms. Jones	6655 University Ave.	Suite 23	Menlo Park	CA	94025

Figure 12.2: The mailing-list data

CREATING FORM LETTERS

The form letter you will be sending to all your customers is an announcement of the grand opening of a new store. You will type the form letter and then print a letter to each person in your customer database.

TYPING THE FORM LETTER

The body of the letter is the same for each customer; only the name and address change from letter to letter. Instead of typing specific names and addresses in your letter, you insert *placeholders* that specify field names. During the printing process, the data are inserted in the placeholders.

You insert placeholders using the Insert Field command on the Edit menu. Your placeholders can appear anywhere in your letter. Keep the following points in mind:

- You can insert the placeholders in any order; the order *does not* have to correspond to the order in which the fields are entered in the database form. Rather, the position of a placeholder should correspond to where you want that field to appear in the letter.
- You don't have to insert placeholders for every field—only the ones you want to use in the letter. For example, your database may contain telephone numbers or comment fields that you don't want in the letter.
- You can insert the same field more than once in the letter. If you want to print a name in the address block and in the body of the letter, you can insert the placeholder in two different places.

Figure 12.3 displays the top part of your letter. Create a new word processor file. (The CUSTDATA file should still be open.) Type the date at the top of the file, and press Enter four times to get several blank lines. To insert the placeholder for the Company field, follow these steps:

1. Choose Insert Field on the Edit menu. The Insert Field dialog box is displayed.
2. The box on the left lists the database files that are currently open (CUSTDATA.WDB). Press ↓ or click on CUSTDATA.WDB. The Fields box now displays a list of fields in the CUSTDATA file.
3. Go to the Fields box (press Alt-F, or click in the box).
4. Highlight the name Company in the list. *Company* should appear next to *Field name* at the bottom of the dialog box.
5. Press Enter or click on OK. Your letter now contains a placeholder for the Company field.

Notice that the cursor is to the right of the placeholder. You could insert another placeholder on the same line, type text next to the placeholder, or press Enter to type on the next line.

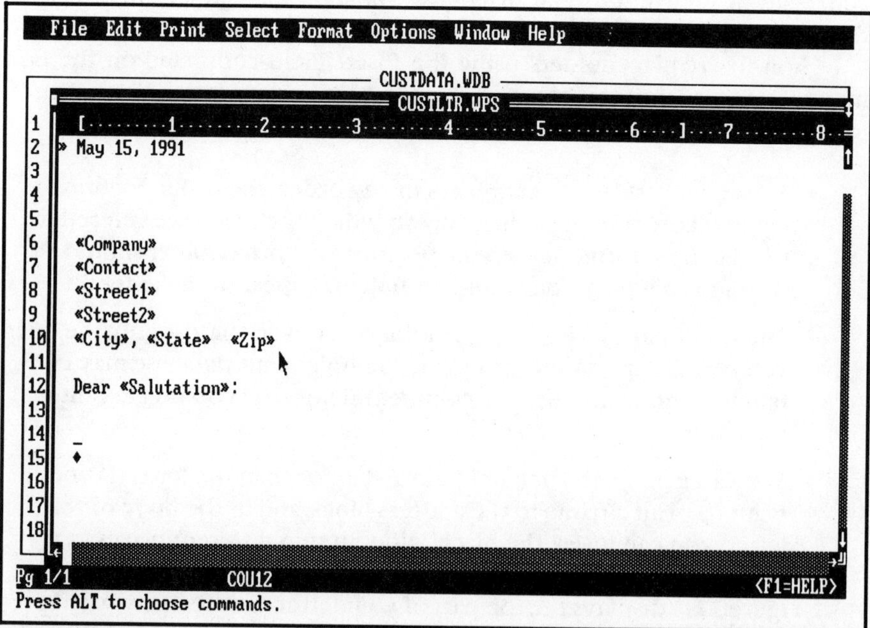

Figure 12.3: The placeholders in the form letter

1. Since the next placeholder, Contact, belongs on its own line, press Enter.
2. Display the Insert Field dialog box again; this time the database file name is already highlighted. All you need to do is highlight the name in the Fields list.
3. Choose Contact.
4. Choose OK.
5. Insert placeholders for the Street1 and Street2 fields, putting each placeholder on a separate line.

The City, State, and Zip fields all belong on the same line. In Figure 12.3, notice that a comma and a space appear after the City placeholder, and two spaces appear between the State and Zip placeholders. Make sure you insert this punctuation, or the address will not be spaced properly.

Enter the salutation underneath the address block, following these steps:

1. Press Enter twice after the last address line. There should be one blank line between the address and the salutation.
2. Type **Dear** and press the spacebar.
3. Insert the Salutation placeholder.
4. Type **:** (colon) and press Enter twice. Make sure your salutation line matches Figure 12.3.

Now that you have finished inserting your placeholders, you can type the body of the form letter as shown in Figure 12.4. Read the letter, and correct any typing errors you find. Also run the document through the spelling checker. You want to make sure your letter is *absolutely perfect* before you print it. You don't want to print 50 letters and then notice you made a typo. Save the file with the name CUSTLTR.

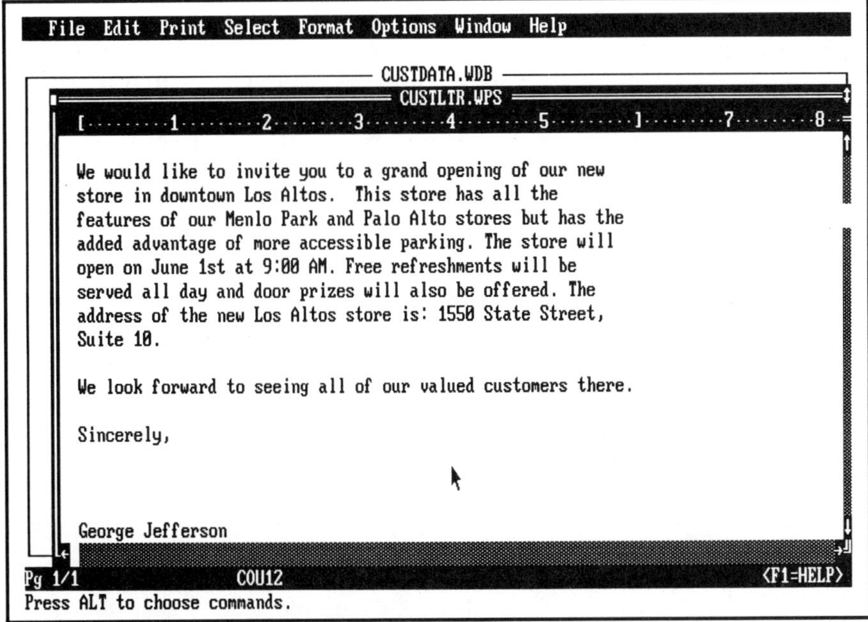

Figure 12.4: The body of the form letter

PRINTING THE FORM LETTERS

To print your form letters, the following conditions must be met:

- The database file must be open.
- The form-letter file must be open.
- The window containing the form letter must be active.

If you have followed the instructions in this chapter, the above conditions should already be satisfied. CUSTLTR.WPS should be your current window, and CUSTDATA.WDB should be open behind this window. Remember, you can move between open windows with Ctrl-F6. (For further information on windows, see Chapter 15.)

Previewing the Letter

It's important to get the margins exactly right before you merge-print; otherwise, you will print many letters with the wrong margins and waste a lot of paper. The accuracy of the top margin is crucial for getting the letter vertically centered on the page. If you don't set a large enough top margin, the letter will sit too high on the page. The best way to find the correct top margin is to use the print preview feature. You enter an estimated top margin and view it on the screen with the Print Preview command. If necessary, you can repeat these steps until the page looks nicely centered on the page. (As an alternative to setting a top margin, you can press Enter a number of times at the top of the page.)

In the Page Setup & Margins dialog box, enter the following margins:

Top	3″
Bottom	1″
Left	1″
Right	1″

Now choose Preview on the Print menu, and look at the overall page layout. The letter should look comfortably centered on the page, so press P to print a draft copy. This printout is for proofreading only; it contains the placeholders instead of the data. After you have made sure that the letter's margins and text are precise, you are ready to merge the record data with the form letter.

Merge Printing

Because each form letter prints on a separate page, you should consider what method you are going to use to feed paper into the printer. If your printer cannot feed paper continuously, make sure you indicate manual page feed in the Printer Setup dialog box.

To merge your database records with your letter, *do not* choose the Print command on the Print menu. (This command only prints a copy of the letter—it does not perform the merge.) Instead, choose the command specific for form letters: Print Form Letters. When you select this command, Works displays a list of database files currently open. Press Enter to select CUSTDATA.WDB, and the familiar Print dialog box appears.

Please note that the *Print specific pages* option refers to the pages in the form letter (in this case, page 1), *not* to the records in the database. You might think that to print the letter for the third record in the database, you could fill in the Print dialog box so that only page 3 is printed. This would not work. To print the letter for one record, you need to select this record in the database tool. (See the next section, "Printing Letters for Part of the Database," for further information on this topic.)

Make sure your printer is turned on, and choose Print. Works prints a letter for each record in your database. Figure 12.5 displays a sample of the letter to Smith Electronics. Notice that Works does not leave a blank line when the record does not have a second line for the street address (for example, Thompson & Thompson); it automatically closes up the space.

Printing Letters for Part of the Database

Works prints a letter for each record *displayed* in the database. If all the records are displayed, a letter is printed for each and every record in the database. In Chapter 10, though, you learned how to create a query to limit the number of records that are displayed. Thus, by creating a query before you merge-print the form letters, you can limit the number of letters you

```
May 15, 1991


Smith Electronics
Mr. William Smith
P.O. Box 9002
Menlo Park, CA  94002

Dear Mr. Smith:

We would like to invite you to a grand opening of our new store
in downtown Los Altos.  This store has all the features of our
Menlo Park and Palo Alto stores but has the added advantage of
more accessible parking. The store will open on June 1st at 9:00
AM. Free refreshments will be served all day and door prizes will
also be offered. The address of the new Los Altos store is: 1550
State Street, Suite 10.

We look forward to seeing all of our valued customers there.

Sincerely,



George Jefferson
```

Figure 12.5: A printed form letter

print. For example, if you want to send the letter to only the customers in Los Altos, you can specify a query condition in the database tool. Let's do this now.

1. Press Ctrl-F6 to switch to the database window.
2. Go to Query view.
3. Next to the City field, type **Los Altos** and press Enter.
4. Press F10 (or select Form on the View menu) to display the matching records. The status line indicates *2/7,* meaning two records out of seven total records are displayed.
5. Press Ctrl-PgDn to see the other matching record.
6. Press Ctrl-F6 to switch back to the word processor window.
7. Print the form letters using the Print Form Letters command on the Print menu. This time, Works only prints letters for the two customers in Los Altos.

Frequently you want to print only one letter—perhaps the paper jammed in the printer and you need to reprint the letter, or you discovered a typing mistake in the name and address of one letter. There are several ways you can display a single record in the database tool:

- Hide the record with the Hide Record command, and then choose the Switch Hidden Records command to display the hidden record.
- Create a query to display the record.
- Use the Search command.

The Search command has an option that we didn't explore in Chapter 9. Normally when you do a search, Works moves the cursor to the first matching record, and then you press F7 to see the next matching record. However, the search works a little differently if you turn on the *All records* option: Works displays only the records containing the search text. Thus, to print a letter for only one record, you search for that record using the *All records* option. Only that record will be displayed.

Let's search for and display the Galveston record.

1. Press Ctrl-F6 to switch to the database window.
2. Choose Search on the Select menu.
3. Next to *Search for,* type **Galveston**.
4. Press Alt-A or click next to *All records.*
5. Choose OK.

The record for Galveston Industries is displayed and the status line displays *1/7,* indicating that only one record is selected.

1. Press Ctrl-F6 to switch back to the word processor window.
2. Choose the Print Form Letters command on the Print menu.
   The only letter that is printed is the one addressed to Galveston Industries.
3. Before you continue, go back to the database window.
4. Choose Show All Records on the Select menu to display all the records. You can remain in this window.

SORTING THE LETTERS

The letters are printed in the same order as the records in the database. If you sort the database records before you print, the printed letters will be sorted. The most common way of sorting a mass mailing is by zip code so that you can get a postage discount. Follow these steps to sort your customer database by zip code:

1. If necessary, switch to the database window (press Ctrl-F6).
2. Switch to List view, and press Ctrl-Home so that you can see all the records.
3. Choose Sort Records on the Select menu.
4. Next to 1st Field, type **Zip**.
5. Choose OK. The records are now sorted by zip code, as shown in Figure 12.6. (The column widths in the figure were changed to enhance readability; your column widths will be 10 characters each.)

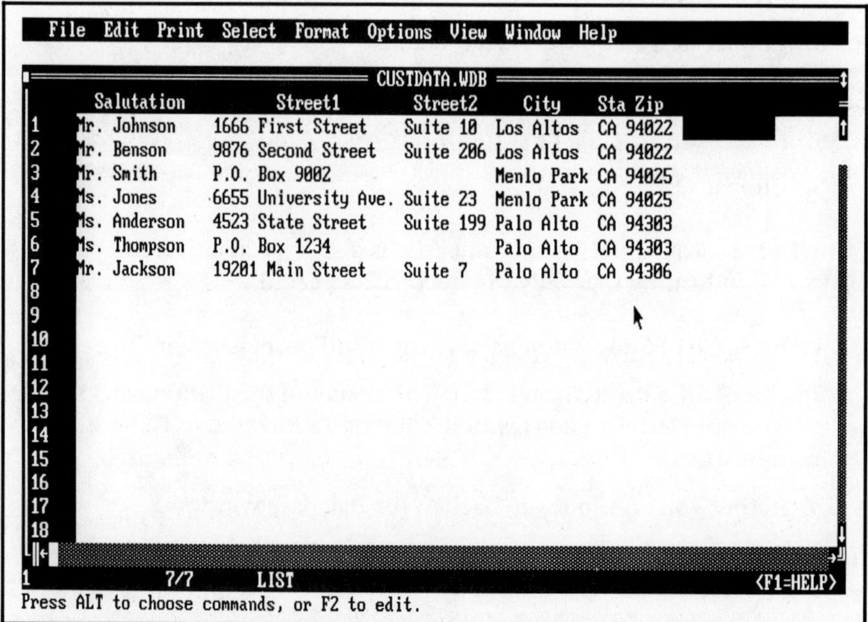

Figure 12.6: The database sorted by zip code

6. Switch back to the word processor window (press Ctrl-F6).

We're not going to reprint all the letters, but if we did, they would be printed in zip-code order. In the next section, you will print the names and addresses on envelopes and mailing labels, and you will see that the records are printed in zip-code order.

ENVELOPES VS. MAILING LABELS

There are two ways you can put addresses on your envelopes:

- Use the Print Form Letters command to print directly on the envelopes.
- Use the Print Labels command to print on mailing labels, which you can affix to the envelopes.

Printing on envelopes requires more effort than printing on mailing labels because you have to manually insert each envelope in the printer (unless your printer has an automatic envelope-feeder). Mailing labels, on the other hand, require little "babysitting" because you can print on a continuous roll of labels or on sheets of 20, 30, or 40 labels each.

The advantage of envelopes is that they look more personal; it's more obvious that mailing labels were created on a computer. You will learn how to print on both envelopes and labels in this section, and then you can decide which method is most appropriate for the kinds of mailings you do.

PRINTING ON ENVELOPES

To print the name and address on an envelope, you must first create a form-letter file that contains placeholders for the fields you want printed on the envelope. The envelope file is the address block in your form letter (containing name, street address, city, state, and zip code) printed with different margins. Rather than creating your envelope file from scratch, it's easier to simply delete the body of your form letter and then save the file with a new name. Follow these steps to create your envelope file:

1. Make sure your form letter is displayed on the screen.

2. Delete the date and the blank lines at the top of the file so that the Company placeholder is on the first line.
3. Delete all the text underneath the address block. (Refer to Figure 12.7 if you aren't sure what to delete.)
4. Save the file with the name CUSTENV.

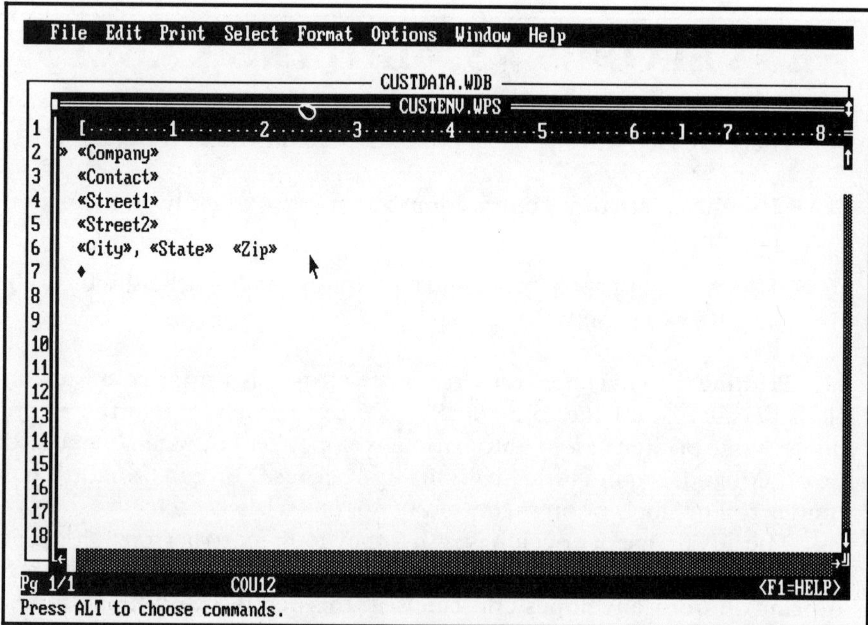

Figure 12.7: The envelope form-letter file

Setting Margins

To position the address block in the current position on the envelope, you must enter precise margins *and* align the envelope in the printer in the correct location. The standard business envelope is 4 1/8″ long by 9 1/2″ wide. If you are using a different-size envelope, you will need to adjust your margins and page size accordingly. The following margins and page size work well on most printers:

Top	2″
Bottom	1″

Left	4″
Right	1.2″
Page length	4.25″
Page width	9.5″

The bottom and right margins are not as crucial as the other settings; you can usually leave these margins at their default values. If the address block isn't positioned properly on the envelope, adjust the top and left margins.

Unless you have a laser printer, enter the above values in the Page Setup & Margins dialog box. If you have a laser printer, the values are quite different because you must print in landscape orientation. On my Hewlett-Packard LaserJet Series II, I use the following settings:

Top	4.25″
Bottom	1″
Left	5.5″
Right	1.2″
Page length	8.5″
Page width	11″

To make sense of these settings, you must first understand how envelopes are fed into the laser printer. The following procedure works for the LaserJet Series II:

- Slide the paper guides on the front of the printer together so that the distance between them is approximately the width of an envelope.
- Hold the envelope so that the return address is in the lower-left corner (face up).
- Insert the envelope between the paper guides as far as it will go.

Because the envelope is positioned in the *middle* of a normal-size (8½″ × 11″) page, the page length is 8.5″ and the width is 11″. (Remember, you are printing in landscape, so the width and length are reversed.)

Figure 12.8 illustrates how the envelope margins are calculated. To calculate the margins when you are using a laser printer, you must imagine that

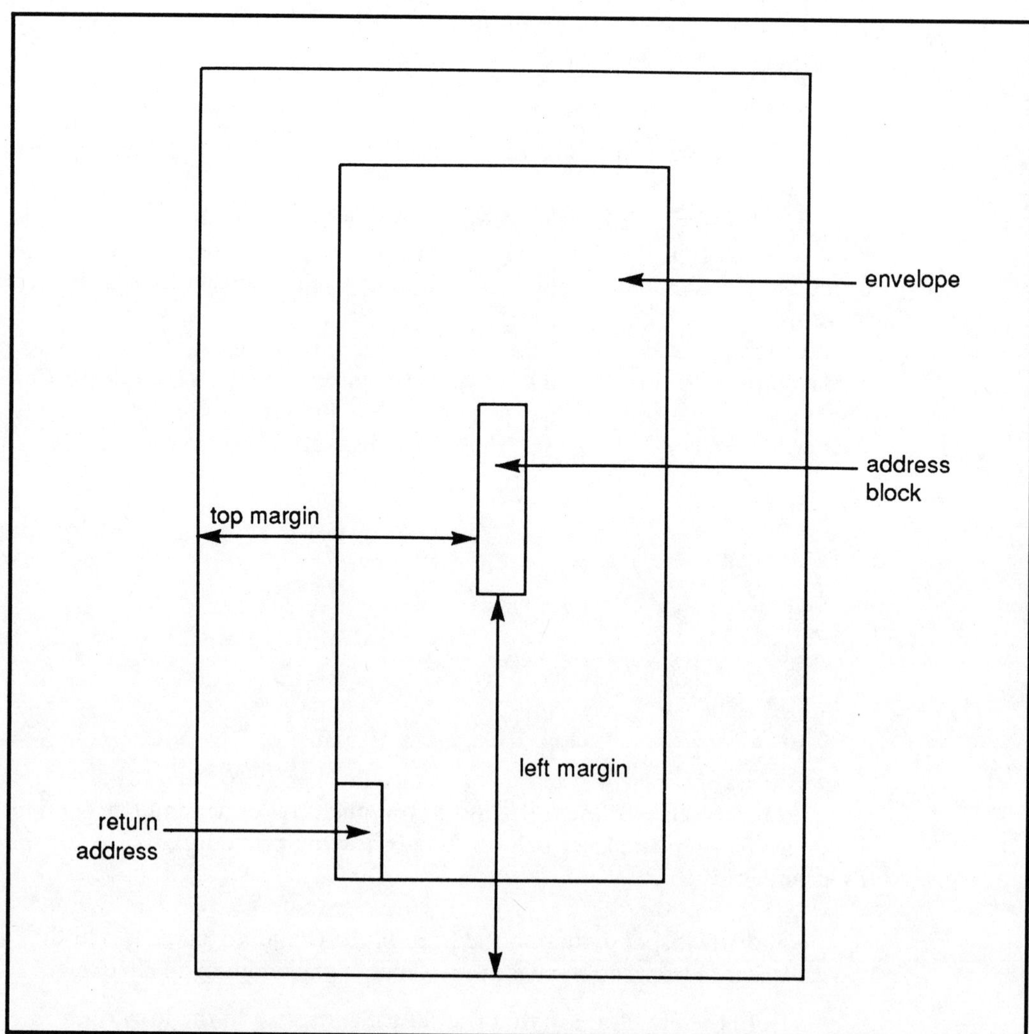

Figure 12.8: Envelope margins

the envelope is placed in the center of a piece of paper. The top margin is measured, not from the top of the envelope, but from the top of a regular page. Thus, the 4.25″ top margin centers the address block on the page. The left margin doesn't really make much sense, but through trial and error I found that the 5.5″ inch setting gives about a 4″ margin. If all this sounds convoluted, it's because it *is*. In most cases, you can use the above settings without having to understand how they were derived. Enter these settings now in your Page Setup & Margins dialog box.

Printing the Addresses on Envelopes

Unless your printer has an envelope-feeding mechanism, you will need to manually insert each envelope in the printer.

To print the envelopes, follow these steps:

1. Choose Printer Setup on the Print menu.
2. Make sure your *Page feed* setting is Manual.
3. If you are using a laser printer, choose a landscape printer name (for example, HPLASLAN) from the Printers list.
4. Choose OK.
5. Make sure the CUSTDATA window is behind the CUSTENV window.
6. Choose Print Form Letters on the Print menu.
7. Choose OK to select the CUSTDATA database.
8. Choose Print.
9. A box containing the message "Choose OK after loading paper" pops up on the screen. Insert your envelope in the printer (or between the paper guides on a laser printer). Line up the top of the envelope with the print head—you should probably *not* put the paper bail down. If you roll the envelope high enough to fit under the paper bail, the address block will probably be printed too low on the envelope. Placing the envelope correctly may take some practice.
10. Choose OK and the address block prints on the envelope. If the address block is not aligned in the center of the envelope, either you placed the top of the envelope in the wrong position, or you entered the wrong top and left margins.
11. If the address block was printed in the correct place, repeat steps 9 and 10 for each envelope. Otherwise, press Esc twice to cancel printing, adjust your margins, and try again.

Notice that the envelopes were printed in zip-code order since that was how you sorted the records in the database tool.

Before you print mailing labels, go back to the Printer Setup dialog box and reset any of the options you changed for envelope printing. You may need to switch from manual to continuous page feed. If you have a laser printer, change from a landscape printer name to your regular printer (for example, HPLASER1).

CREATING MAILING LABELS

If you don't have an aversion to computerized mailing labels, using labels will save you a lot of time and effort in the printing process. You can load a continuous roll of labels into your printer's tractor feed or place sheets of labels into your printer's paper bin and let the labels print on their own, while you have a cup of coffee, make a phone call, or work on another project.

The mailing-label file is very similar to your envelope document. The only differences are the margins and indents. Because of this similarity, you can use your CUSTENV.WPS file for your mailing labels and then set new margins. Your envelope should still be open on the screen. Use the Save As command to name the file CUSTLBL.

Normally, you will want to set a left indent for your mailing labels. This indent is the amount of space each label is indented from the left edge of the label. The left margin, on the other hand, is the amount of space from the left edge of the page. In most cases, you will want to indent labels a quarter- or a half-inch. Follow these steps to indent your labels:

1. Select all the text.
2. Choose Indents & Spacing on the Format menu.
3. Next to *Left indent,* type **0.5**.
4. Press Enter.

Printing the Labels

Labels come in many different configurations and sizes. Probably the most common label size is one inch long by approximately three to four inches wide (depending on how many labels there are across the page). My experience has shown that printing two labels across the page works the best. Twenty labels can fit on a sheet, and the labels are wide enough (3.75″ each) to fit most addresses comfortably. If you use three- or four-across labels, you may have trouble fitting some of the longer address lines. If you are printing labels on a laser printer, make sure you get labels that are specially designed for laser printers because you cannot print on the top or bottom half-inch of the page. I use Avery two-across labels (model 5121).

This example exercise assumes that you are using two-across labels that are 1″ × 3.75″. If you have already purchased different-size labels, you can print the sample labels on regular paper or adjust the settings to match your label size and configuration.

To get the text in the right place, you must pay close attention to your margins, page setup, and indents. Because the settings are so important to printing the label in the right spot, Works automatically displays several dialog boxes, including the Page Setup & Margins dialog box, after you issue the Print Labels command.

You should be in the CUSTLBL window now, and the CUSTDATA database file should be open in the background. Choose Print Labels on the Print menu—you see the first of three dialog boxes.

The diagram in Figure 12.9 illustrates the different measurements for mailing labels. The values refer to the spacing between labels. The vertical spacing value refers to the height of each label, from the beginning of one label to the beginning of the next. As previously mentioned, 1″ is the standard and therefore is the default value. The horizontal spacing value is measured from the left edge of the first label to the left edge of the second label. Get out your ruler and measure this distance on your labels. For the two-across labels in this example, the horizontal spacing value is 4.25″.

To enter a value for the number of labels that will be printed across the page, type **2** and press Enter. (Works can handle up to four labels across.) The second dialog box—actually your Page Setup & Margins dialog box—now appears. If you are using a continuous roll of labels or sheets of labels that start right at the top of the page, you should specify 0″ top and bottom margins. If you are using sheets of labels in a laser printer, you cannot print on the top or the bottom half-inch of the page, so you must specify 0.5″ top and bottom margins.

Setting the left and right margins is not so straightforward. The easiest thing to do is set 0″ left and right margins and control the label placement with indents, as you have already done. If you do not set 0″ left and right margins, you are likely to encounter the following message when you try to choose OK in the dialog box: "Label wider than margins." Works does not let you print until you narrow your margins.

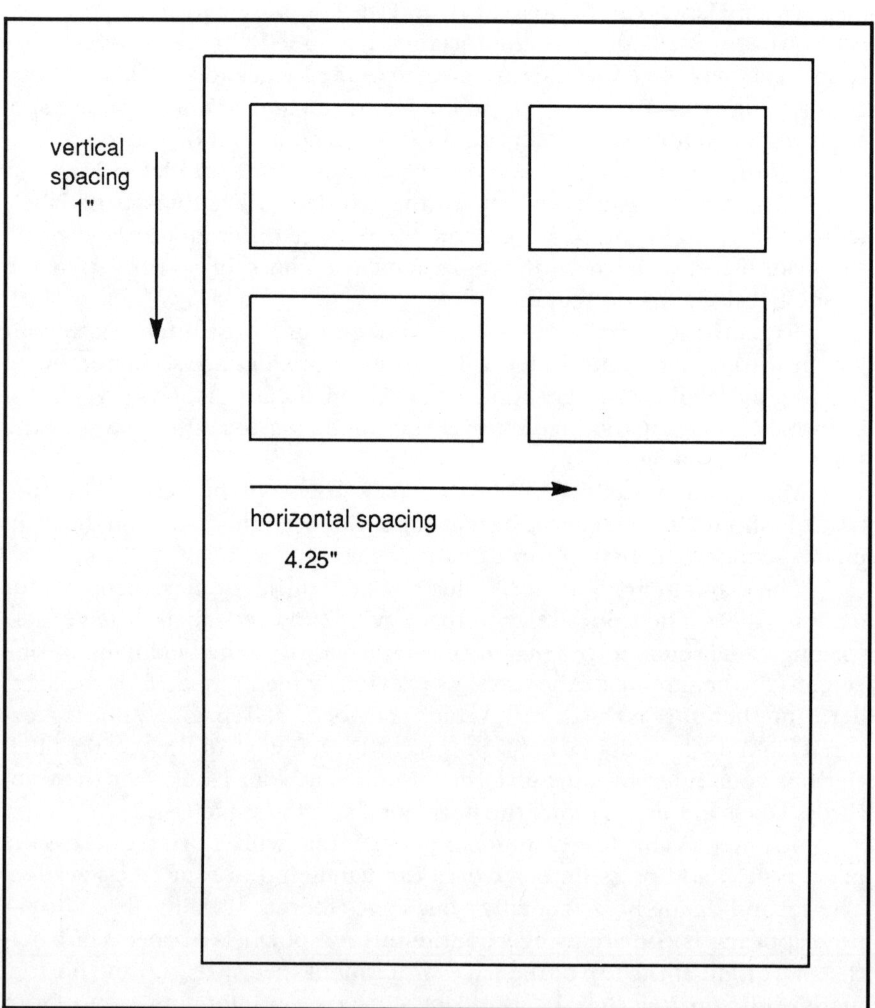

Figure 12.9: Mailing-label measurements

Here is the rule to follow: The page width must be greater than the left and right margins added to the horizontal spacing times the number of labels across. Thus, in this example, the horizontal spacing (*4.25″*) times the number of labels across (*2*) equals *8.5″*, the page width. These settings do not leave room for any left and right margins, so you must set them to 0″. Remember, even though you are setting a 0″ left margin, the label information will not be printed at the edge of the label because of the left indent you set in the previous section.

To summarize, your margins should be set as follows:

Top	0″ (0.5″ for a laser printer)
Bottom	0″ (0.5″ for a laser printer)
Left	0″
Right	0″
Page length	11″
Page width	8.5″

Choose OK. If you get the message "Label wider than margins," you must decrease the left and right margins and/or the horizontal label spacing before you can continue. If Works finds your margins to be acceptable, the final dialog box appears—your regular Print dialog box. Choose Print; the labels should be printed as shown in Figure 12.10.

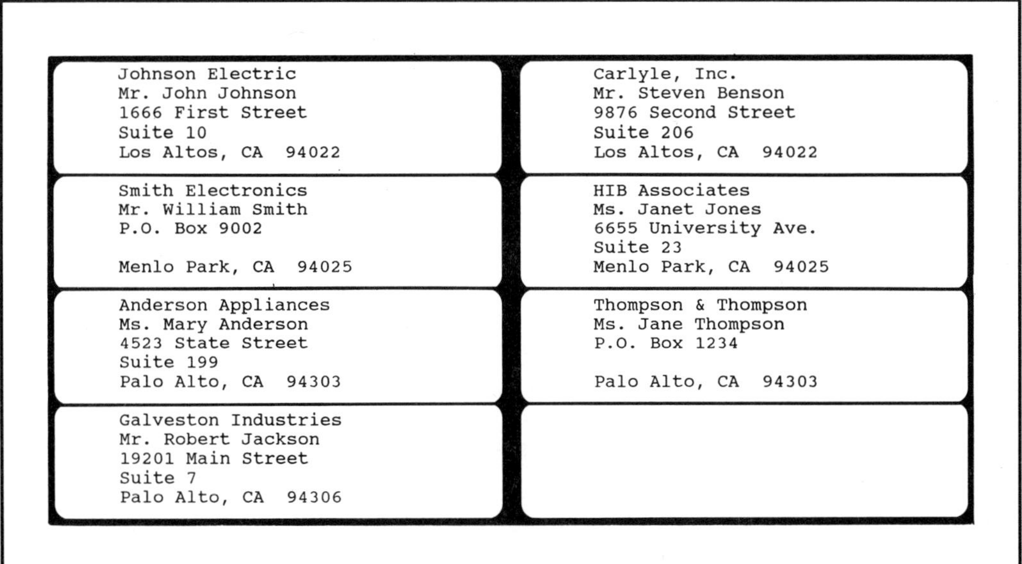

Figure 12.10: The printed mailing labels

If you are using a laser printer, you may see the following message:

Your printer cannot print at edge of page. If text is cut off, adjust margins and label size and print again.

This message appears because you set 0″ left and right margins, and the laser cannot print in this area. However, because you set a left indent, you should not have the problem described in the message. Choose OK to have the labels printed out.

Notice that, unlike form letters, labels leave a blank line when a field is empty. Unfortunately, there is no easy way around this. If this blank line bothers you, you can create a longer Street1 address field and eliminate the Street2 field. You have to make sure your labels are wide enough to accommodate the longer fields or use a smaller font size.

Printing a Test

Before printing labels for a large database, it's a good idea to print out a few labels to make sure you have the correct margins and that you have placed the labels in the proper location in the printer. You wouldn't want to print all your labels and then discover that the address block isn't in the right place!

If you choose Test instead of Print in the first Print Labels dialog box, Works prints only the first two labels. After it prints the test labels, you see the following message:

Print all labels or reprint test labels?

You have three choices at this point:

- Cancel the Print command and reset your margins.
- Adjust the labels in the printer, and choose Test to print out another set of test labels.
- If the test labels were printed in the proper locations, choose Print to print all your labels.

This test feature can be very helpful when you aren't sure about your margins or label placement in the printer.

Save and close the CUSTBL and CUSTDATA files.

SUMMARY

In this chapter you learned all the steps involved in doing a mass mailing. First, you have to create a database containing your mailing list information. Next, you must create a form-letter file. Finally, you print the individualized letters using the Print Form Letters command. You also learned how to print the address block on mailing labels and envelopes.

This chapter completes our study of the database tool. In the next chapter, you will learn how to use the final Works tool, communications. If you don't have a modem and don't think you will need to use communications, you may want to skip Part V and turn to Part VI, which discusses windows and macros.

EXERCISES

The exercises in this chapter use the credit-card database that you created in Chapter 9. In the following exercises, you will create a form letter that you will merge with your credit-card database. If you need help, refer to the appropriate sections indicated inside parentheses.

1. Open your CRCARDS file.
2. Create a new word-processor file, and type the form letter displayed in Figure 12.11 (see ''Typing the Form Letter,'' page 342).
3. Set your margins, and preview the letter to make sure the letter is centered on the page (see ''Previewing the Letter,'' page 346).
4. Merge your credit-card database with the form letter (see ''Merge Printing,'' page 347).
5. Save the file with the name CREDLTR.
6. Close all files.

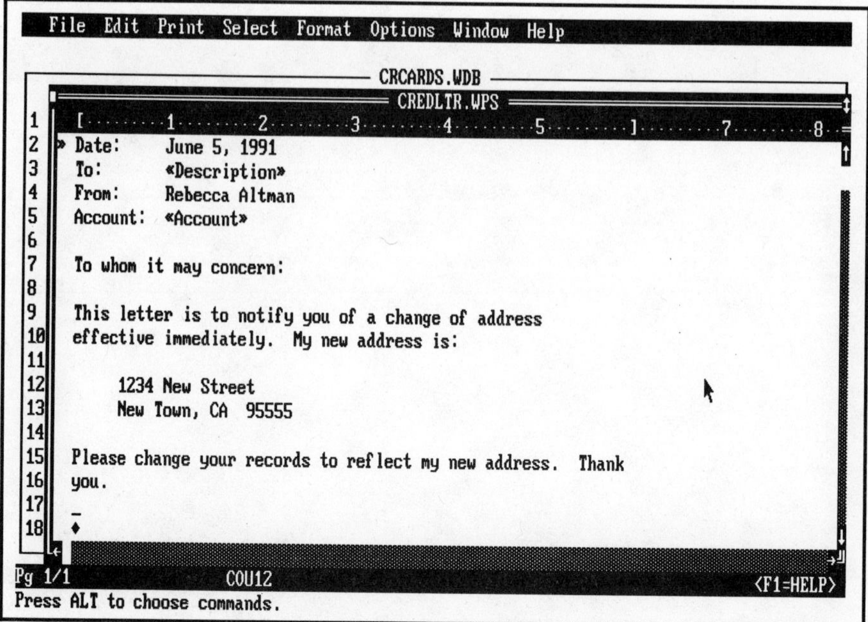

Figure 12.11: The form letter

part five

THE COMMUNICATIONS TOOL

COMMUNICATING ELECTRONICALLY

13

The communications tool allows you to use your computer to send and receive information over the telephone lines. Because the telephone lines are used to transmit data, this type of communication is sometimes called *telecommunication.* If you need to send someone a file you have created in Works (or in any software program), you don't have to use mail delivery services. Instead, you can use the communications tool to transmit the file electronically; the person will receive the file immediately—not in a day or two—and at a fraction of the cost.

The communications tool provides access to many other useful services and procedures. Here are a few of them:

Information Services: Two of the more popular services accessible through the communications tool are CompuServe and MCI Mail. The following are among the tasks you can do with these services:

- Look up current and historical stock prices.
- Browse through and search news stories.
- Send and read messages.
- Play games.
- Copy free software.
- Do your shopping.
- Plan a vacation or business trip.

Any information you see on your screen while you are connected to an information service can be saved to a file in Works. For a brief description of the major information services and how to use them, see Chapter 14.

Home Banking: With services like Bank of America's HomeBanking, you can pay your bills, transfer funds between accounts, look up your current balance, and see whether a check has cleared. I have used this service for several years; it works reliably and it's even fun. I actually look forward to paying bills.

Bulletin Board Systems (BBS): A BBS is the electronic equivalent of the cork bulletin board hanging on your wall. You can send and receive messages as well as make copies of free programs. The free software you find on a BBS is called *public domain software.* Many computer user groups offer BBSs to their members.

Direct Connection: Instead of using the telephone lines to transfer data, you can directly connect two computers with a cable. You can use this technique if you need to transfer a lot of data between two computers (for example, between a desktop computer and a portable computer), assuming you can get the computers in the same room.

Because there are so many variables in telecommunications, and so many different ways to use telecommunications, this chapter does not guide you through communicating with a specific computer. The information here is reference material rather than a hands-on tutorial. It introduces communications terminology and concepts, and explains the Works communications commands. Consequently, you should read the entire chapter before attempting electronic communications. Put paper clips or bookmarks on the pages you will need to refer to during your first communications session. For example, if you are going to receive a file, earmark the ''Receiving a File'' page so that you can easily refer to the procedure if you need to.

The exercises at the end of this chapter lead you through the general steps for communicating with another personal computer user. The next chapter gives hints and information on connecting to CompuServe, MCI Mail, HomeBanking, and an electronic bulletin board.

HOW DOES TELECOMMUNICATIONS WORK?

To connect your computer to the telephone lines, you need a *modem*. A modem is a hardware device that translates your computer data to a format that can be sent over the telephone lines. A modem is also needed at the computer you are connecting to, because the telephone data has to be translated back into computer data. The diagram in Figure 13.1 illustrates all the elements of this connection.

Two types of modems are available: internal and external. An internal modem is placed in a slot inside your computer. An external modem sits on your desk, and a cable connects it to a *serial port* at the back of your computer. The serial port is the type of ''outlet'' that an external modem is plugged into. The internal modem has the advantage of not taking up precious desktop space. The external modem, on the other hand, does not consume a potentially valuable slot inside your computer, plus it can be easily transported to other computers. Furthermore, you can see the indicator lights on the external modem, letting you know the status of your communications.

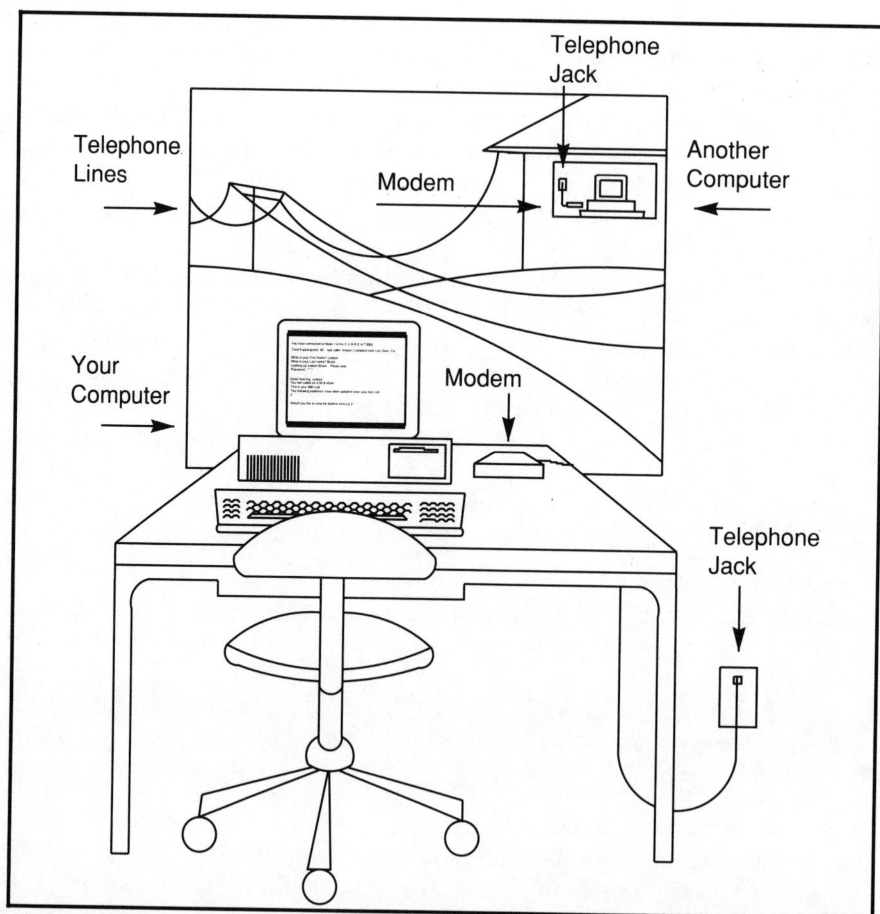

Figure 13.1: Connecting two computers using the telephone lines

Regardless of which type of modem you have, you need to plug the modem's telephone cable into the telephone jack in the wall. This cable is identical to the one connected to your telephone. You need to unplug your telephone's cable or get a T-adapter that allows you to connect two cables into a single jack.

Like your computer and printer, external modems have a power cord that you must plug into your power strip. Also, make sure you turn on the modem's power switch.

Many different manufacturers make modems, but Works will work only with a Hayes modem or a modem that uses the same commands as Hayes. Make sure your modem says that it is Hayes-compatible.

Once your modem is set up, you can instruct the communications tool to use the modem to dial the other computer. Assuming the other computer's modem answers your call, you will get a "Connect" message on your screen. When you do, you can say that you have successfully *connected* to a *remote computer.*

USING A MODEM

Before you get into the communications tool, practice using your modem with the phone dialer accessory. If you remember what you learned in Chapter 2, you know that the Options menu contains a command that uses your modem to dial a telephone number typed in a word processor document, spreadsheet, or database file. Thus, you can create a phone list in any of these three tools and have Works place a personal or business call for you. Since each of the tools offers a search feature, you can search for the name of the person you want to call, highlight the telephone number, and tell Works to dial that number. Please note that the phone dialer is *not* for communicating with another computer; it's for communicating with another person.

To use the phone dialer, you should check your communications settings in the Works Settings dialog box.

1. Choose Works Settings on the Options menu.
2. Locate the dialog box options *Modem port* and *Dial type.*

As mentioned earlier, the external modem's cable is connected to the serial port at the back of your computer. This port is nicknamed *COM1* or *COM2.* Because internal modems are not connected to a serial port, they have a switch that you can set to indicate which communications port (COM1, COM2, etc.) to assign to the modem. If you aren't sure which port your modem is connected to or assigned to, leave the setting at COM1, the default. You will know you have chosen the incorrect port if you see the message "Cannot find COM port" when you try to use your modem to dial. If you see this error message, go back into the Works Settings dialog box and set a different modem port.

If you have a pulse telephone, change the dial type from Tone to Pulse, and then choose OK in the dialog box.

Now you are ready to test out the phone dialing feature. Follow these steps:

1. Create a new word processor file.
2. Type a friend's name and phone number. Figure 13.2 gives several examples of how to enter the phone number. The phone number you enter should correspond to what you normally punch on the telephone keypad. Thus, if you have to dial 1 before the area code, or 9 to get an outside line, be sure to enter these numbers as part of the phone number. The commas after the 9 in Figure 13.2 are pause instructions. (When you dial the number manually, you have to pause for a dial tone after pressing the 9.) Each comma you enter allows for a two-second pause. Enter as many commas as necessary.
3. Select the telephone number. (In the spreadsheet or database tool, put the highlight on the telephone number.)
4. Choose Dial This Number on the Options menu. You should hear the modem dialing the phone number, followed by a ring or a busy signal. The message "Pick up phone and press OK to answer" appears on the screen.
5. You can pick up the phone receiver while the number is being dialed, after the phone starts ringing, or even after someone answers the phone.
6. Choose OK.
7. When you are done with the call (or if you get a busy signal), hang up the receiver.

If you were successful in dialing the number, you can be assured that your modem is connected properly and that you have specified the correct modem port. Close the word processor file before continuing (you don't need to save it).

CREATING A COMMUNICATIONS FILE

To use the communications tool, you must create a communications file. This file is a little different from the other files you have created in

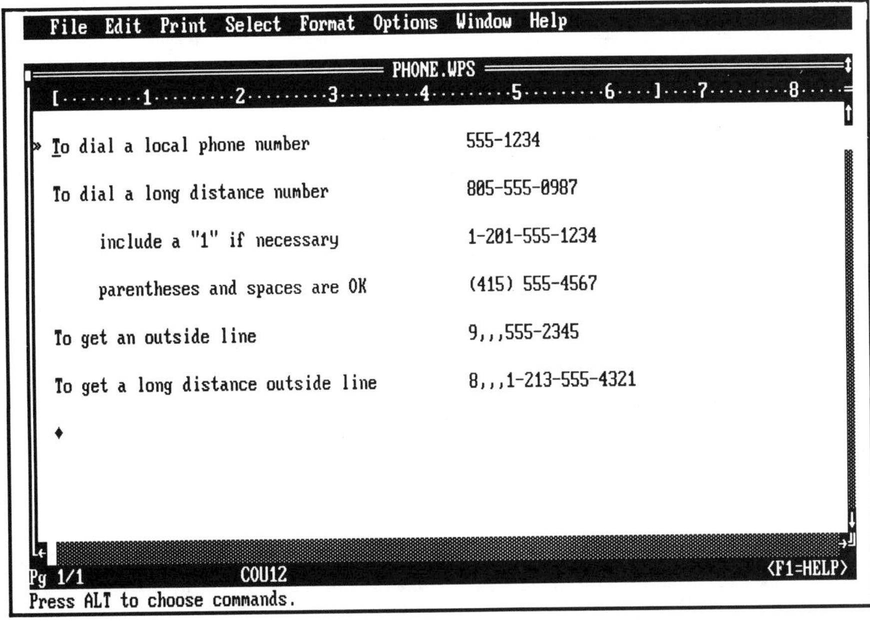
File Edit Print Select Format Options Window Help
PHONE.WPS
To dial a local phone number 555-1234
To dial a long distance number 805-555-0987
include a "1" if necessary 1-201-555-1234
parentheses and spaces are OK (415) 555-4567
To get an outside line 9,,,555-2345
To get a long distance outside line 8,,,1-213-555-4321
Pg 1/1 COU12 <F1=HELP>
Press ALT to choose commands.

Figure 13.2: Examples of acceptable phone numbers

Works. It doesn't contain the kind of data that you have worked with so far; it contains communications settings. As you will soon see, successful communication requires precise settings. So once you get the correct settings, you save the file so that you don't have to remember and reenter all the settings.

1. Choose Create New File on the File menu.
2. Select New Communications. The communications window appears as shown in Figure 13.3.

The initial file name is COMM1.WCM; all communications files have the extension .WCM. The left-hand portion of the bottom window border currently displays the word OFFLINE. *Offline* means you are not connected to another computer. Once you do connect, you are *online,* and the amount of time that you have been connected appears in place of OFFLINE. The window is blank now, but later on when you connect to a computer, you will see menus and messages inside the window.

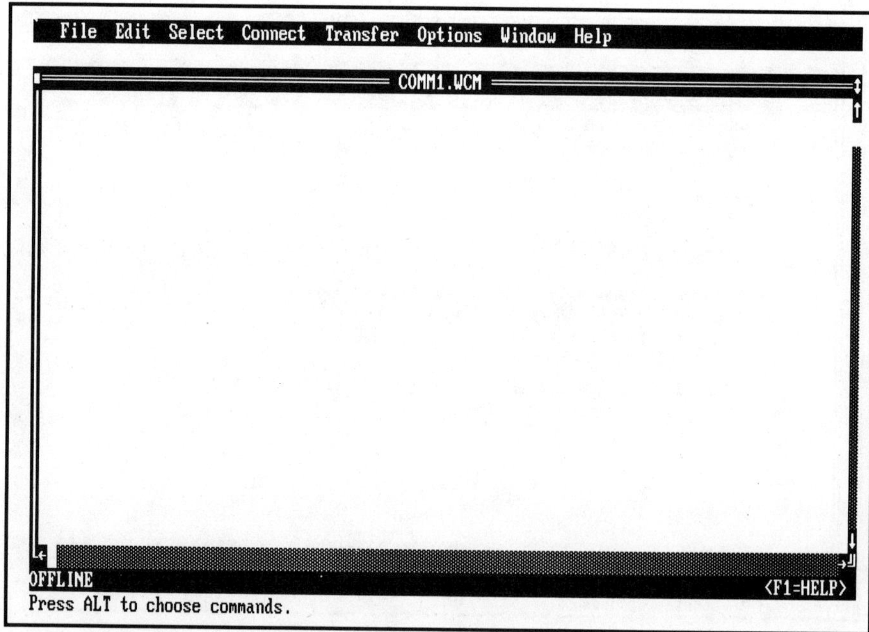

Figure 13.3: The communications window

ADJUSTING YOUR COMMUNICATIONS SETTINGS

Communications settings are located in two different dialog boxes: Terminal and Communication. The Terminal dialog box contains options that allow you to determine how your keyboard and screen operate when connected to a remote computer. (The word *terminal* refers to your keyboard and monitor.) The Communication dialog box contains options that are essential for connecting to the remote computer and successfully transferring data between the computers. The options in each of these dialog boxes are discussed in the upcoming sections.

COMMUNICATION DIALOG BOX SETTINGS

Choose Communication on the Options menu, and the dialog box shown in Figure 13.4 appears.

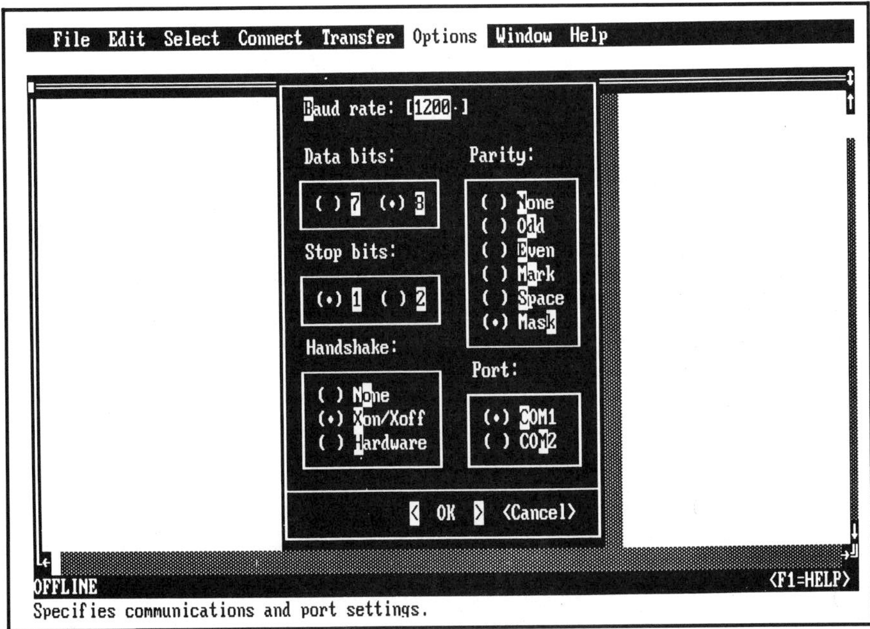

Figure 13.4: The Communication dialog box

Baud Rate

The *baud rate* is the speed at which data is sent or received over the modem. Typical baud rates are 300, 1200, and 2400. The baud rate you enter in the dialog box must match the speed of your modem *and* the remote computer's modem; if the baud rates don't match, you will not be able to connect to the other computer. Therefore, you will need to find out the remote computer's baud rate before you connect. If your modem's maximum speed is 1200 baud and the remote computer's modem can work at up to 2400 baud, both computers must be set for 1200 baud (the lowest common denominator).

Data Bits and Stop Bits

First of all, what is a bit? *Bit* is actually an abbreviation for ***binary digit.*** Computers use the binary counting system for storing data; in this system, zero and one are the only numbers used. When you type something on your keyboard, the computer translates each character into a code made up of zeros and ones. It is these bits that are manipulated and stored, not characters. Fortunately, *you* don't have to know the bit assignments for each character; it's your computer's job to do this translation.

When you send information by modem, a continuous stream of bits is sent. To convert this stream into usable data, the receiving computer counts off a certain number of bits (the *data bits*) and looks for a signal that the complete character has been sent (the *stop bits*). ***Data bits*** are the bits in each transmitted character, and ***stop bits*** are the bits that signal the end of each character.

Your choice for the data-bit setting is 7 or 8, and your choice for the stop-bit setting is 1 or 2. If your settings don't match the settings on the remote computer, the receiving computer will try to form a character out of the wrong number of bits. The result will be garbage data.

Handshake

The friendly-sounding Handshake option makes sure that no data gets lost during transmission. The Xon/Xoff (short for Transfer On/Transfer Off) option is like a traffic cop regulating the flow of data between two computers. When the receiving computer is ready, willing, and able to receive, the traffic cop waves the data through (Xon). When the receiving computer's memory is temporarily full, the traffic cop halts the flow of data (Xoff). This process of starting and stopping data transfer happens automatically and transparently when the Xon/Xoff option is selected.

The other two handshaking methods are None and Hardware. If you find out that the other computer doesn't use handshaking, select None. The Hardware handshaking method is used when two computers' serial ports are connected with a cable.

Parity

Parity is an error-checking mechanism used in telecommunications. The parity setting determines how the last bit of each transmitted character is checked for errors. Works offers the following types of parities: None, Odd, Even, Mark, Space, and Mask. It's not important to understand what each of the parity options means, but it is imperative that your parity matches the remote computer's parity.

Works's default option is Mask. With this setting, you can successfully transfer information without knowing the other computer's parity setting.

Port

The Port option should look familiar: Earlier in this chapter you specified the modem port in the Works Settings dialog box. However, the Works Settings apply only to the phone dialer feature, not to telecommunications in the communications tool. Consequently, you see a Port option again in the Communication dialog box. If you determined in the phone dialing exercise that your modem was connected to COM2, change it now. Keep in mind that this setting (as are all settings) is changed for the *current* communications file only. If your modem is connected to COM2, you will need to adjust this setting in every communications file you create. (See Appendix E for a way to permanently change your settings.)

TERMINAL DIALOG BOX SETTINGS

Choose Terminal on the Options menu to display the dialog box shown in Figure 13.5. Most of the Terminal options cannot be set before you connect to another computer because you don't know whether or not you need to change the settings. Once you see the incoming data on your screen and type something at your keyboard, you can go into the Terminal dialog box and make any necessary changes.

Terminal

If you have a mainframe or minicomputer at work, you can access it at home with your personal computer. Using your PC as a terminal for a larger computer is called *terminal emulation.* You can use the Terminal option to specify the type of terminal you have at work. The options *Keypad alternate* and *Cursor alternate* are also specific to terminal emulation; you will not use these options in normal telecommunications.

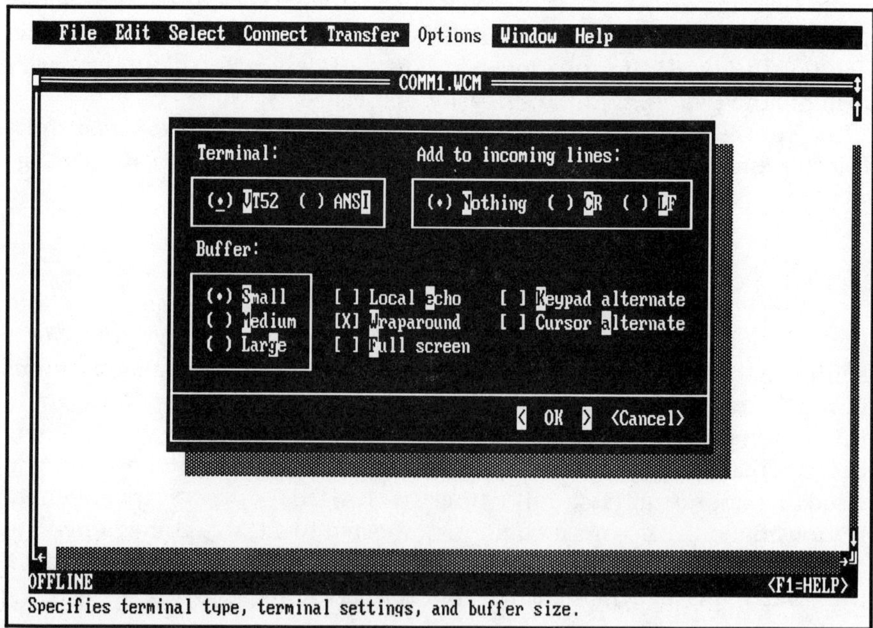

Figure 13.5: The Terminal dialog box

Add to Incoming Lines

With the *Add to incoming lines* option, you choose what should be added to each incoming line of data: Nothing (the default), CR (a carriage return), or LF (a line feed). If each line of incoming data starts at the beginning of a new line, you can leave the option at its default setting, Nothing. If each incoming line overwrites the previous line, turn on the line feed option. If line feed is turned on when it shouldn't be, the lines will be double-spaced on the screen. If the lines do not begin at the left edge of the screen, turn on the carriage return option.

Local Echo

Echo, in telecommunications lingo, refers to whether the characters that you type are displayed on the screen. If you and the remote computer have echo turned on, you will have double vision: You will see two characters for every one that you type. For example, you see *tthhiiss*. If you and the remote computer have the echo turned off, you will be blind: You won't see anything on the screen when you type.

Usually, you don't know beforehand whether the remote computer has echo turned on or off. By default, Works has echo turned off. If you can't see what you type, turn echo on.

Wraparound

By default, Works automatically word-wraps an incoming line of text to the next line if it has more than 80 characters (80 is the width of the screen). If you turn off this option, long lines are truncated after 80 characters.

Full Screen

With the Full Screen option turned on, the menu bar, status line, and window borders are removed from the screen during your communications session. Even though your menu bar doesn't show, you can still access it with the Alt key.

Buffer

The data you see on your screen during the communications session is temporarily stored in a *buffer*. The buffer is similar to a word processing document. After your communications session, you can move the cursor in the text and scroll the screen.

There are several important differences between the buffer and a word processing document: 1) You can't edit the buffer, and 2) when you save the communications file, the buffer is not saved. If you want to save the contents of the buffer, you can copy it into a word processing document or a spreadsheet when you are through with the communications session. Or, alternatively, you can save the incoming information to a disk file as it is received. For details, see "Capturing Incoming Data."

The Buffer option controls the size of your buffer. A *Small* buffer stores the most recent 100 lines that were displayed on the screen, a *Medium* buffer stores 300 lines, and a *Large* buffer stores 750 lines. If you receive more lines than the buffer can hold, the oldest data is thrown out of the buffer as new lines are received. If you want to create a larger buffer, set the buffer size before you connect to another computer. If you wait until you are in the middle of a session, you may lose the lines at the beginning of the session.

The larger the buffer, the less memory you will have available for other open files. If you don't have any other files open, set a large buffer so that you can review/save more of your communications session if you need to.

CONNECTING TO A REMOTE COMPUTER

Once you have specified your Terminal and Communication settings, you are ready to call the remote computer. You do not pick up the handset on your telephone and punch in the number yourself; Works and the modem do this for you. Three steps are required:

- Enter the phone number in the Phone dialog box.
- Make sure your modem is turned on.
- Choose Connect on the Connect menu to get Works to dial the number for you.

ENTERING THE PHONE NUMBER

You enter the phone number in the Phone dialog box. Choose Phone on the Options menu now. The rules for entering phone numbers in the communications tool are the same as for the phone dialer accessory. Be sure to include all the numbers you must normally dial manually (for example, *1* for long distance, *9* for an outside line), and type commas to pause the dialing process (for example, *9,,,555-0877*). You can type hyphens, parentheses, or spaces in the telephone number, but they are optional.

If you have the Call Waiting telephone feature, you should disable it before dialing another computer. If you don't, and another call comes in while you are online, your connection will be lost. Check with your local telephone company for the method to disable Call Waiting.

Like the Works Settings dialog box, the Phone dialog box has an option for dial type. Choose Pulse if you have a rotary telephone.

DIALING THE NUMBER

To dial the number you entered in the Phone dialog box, first make sure your modem is plugged in and turned on. Choose Connect on the Connect menu. Once you choose this command, several things happen almost simultaneously:

- Your communications window displays *ATDT* and the remote computer's telephone number.
- You hear the modem dial the number.
- You hear the telephone ring or a busy signal.
- The OFFLINE message in the window border disappears and is replaced with a counter that displays the amount of time you have been online.

If you get a busy signal, you have two options:

- You can hang up the phone by choosing Connect on the Connect menu, then choose OK to disconnect. Wait a few minutes and try connecting again.
- Choose Dial Again on the Connect menu. The modem automatically redials the number without your having to disconnect.

When the remote computer answers, you hear a high-pitched tone followed by a lower, fuzzy-sounding tone when the two computers establish a connection. The word CONNECT appears in the window. Success!

Depending on what type of computer you are communicating with, your screen displays different things after you connect. If you dial an information service, HomeBanking, or an electronic bulletin board system (BBS), you are asked to enter your name or account number, along with a password. This process is called *logging on.* Figure 13.6 displays a BBS log-on screen. Chapter 14 explains how to automate your log-on responses so that you don't have to type in your name and password every time you connect to another computer. Once you get by the security measures, you will see a menu of choices inside your communications window. Figure 13.7 displays a menu of a BBS called SPARC.

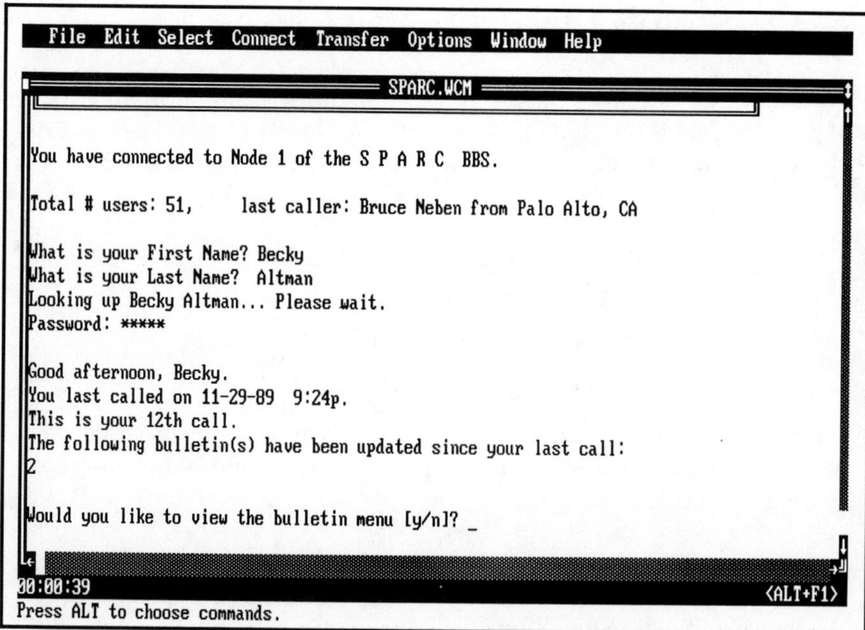

Figure 13.6: A BBS log-on screen

If you are dialing another personal computer with a human being at the keyboard, you don't have to enter any passwords, and you don't see any menus. You can simply start "chatting" with the other user. Instead of talking, though, you type what you want to say. Once you have chatted about how happy you are that you have been able to establish a connection, you can send or receive files.

As soon as you start typing, you will know whether you need to change any of your terminal settings. If necessary, go to the Terminal dialog box and adjust the echo or add a carriage return or a line feed.

MAKING AN AUTOMATIC CONNECTION

After you have created and saved a communications file, you don't ever again need to enter the phone number (it's already in the Phone dialog box) or choose the Connect command to dial another computer. Whenever

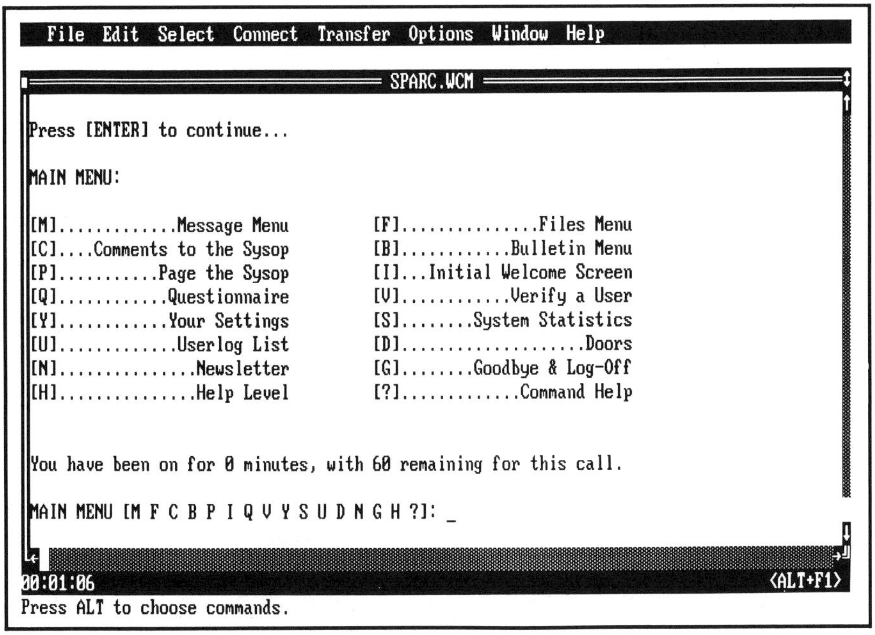

```
 File  Edit  Select  Connect  Transfer  Options  Window  Help
                              SPARC.WCM
Press [ENTER] to continue...

MAIN MENU:

[M]............Message Menu         [F]..............Files Menu
[C]....Comments to the Sysop        [B]...........Bulletin Menu
[P]..........Page the Sysop         [I]...Initial Welcome Screen
[Q]...........Questionnaire         [V]...........Verify a User
[Y]...........Your Settings         [S].......System Statistics
[U]............Userlog List         [D]...................Doors
[N]..............Newsletter         [G].......Goodbye & Log-Off
[H]..............Help Level         [?]............Command Help

You have been on for 0 minutes, with 60 remaining for this call.

MAIN MENU [M F C B P I Q V Y S U D N G H ?]: _

00:01:06                                                  <ALT+F1>
Press ALT to choose commands.
```

Figure 13.7: A BBS menu

you open a communications file, Works asks you whether you want to connect to the other computer. If you choose OK, Works automatically dials the number in the Phone dialog box.

ANSWERING AN INCOMING CALL

If you are transferring a file to or from another personal computer user, either of you can initiate the call. One disadvantage of answering the call is that you cannot disable Call Waiting; only the person making the call can disable Call Waiting. Therefore, you should discuss this issue with your communications partner before you connect; whoever has Call Waiting should initiate the call so that he or she can disable the feature. If both of you have Call Waiting, be prepared to be rudely interrupted at any time.

Follow these steps to get Works to automatically answer the call when the phone rings:

- Select Phone on the Options menu.

- Press Alt-A or click next to Automatic Answer.
- Choose OK.
- Choose Connect on the Connect menu. The message *ATS0 = 1* appears on the screen. The Connect command turns on the modem's automatic answer feature. Also, *ANSW* is displayed in the bottom window border to let you know that you are in auto-answer mode.

Most modems have an automatic answer switch on them. If you turn on this switch, you can eliminate the first three steps above. But be aware that as long as your modem is turned on, it will answer *all* your phone calls—computer and human. (Whoever calls you will hear a high-pitched tone as the modem answers the phone. It's not a welcoming sound, to say the least.) External modems can be switched off easily when not in use; but, unless you have a phone line dedicated to telecommunications, you do not want to turn on an internal modem's automatic answer switch.

Assuming the modem is in auto-answer mode *and* the Connect option is enabled, you see the message *RING* in your communications window as soon as the phone rings. If your communications settings match your partner's, you will then see the message *CONNECT* in the window. At this point you are online with your partner. You can type messages back and forth, and transmit files in either direction. Remember, if you have trouble reading what you type, go to your Terminal dialog box and adjust the echo, line feed, and carriage return options.

DISCONNECTING

Disconnecting is the equivalent of hanging up the phone when you have finished a call. Before disconnecting in Works, you should formally exit the information service or bulletin board. This exiting process is called *logging off.* You log off by either choosing a menu option or typing a command. From the BBS menu in Figure 13.7, you would type *G* to choose Goodbye & Log-Off. There is no formal way to log off when you are communicating with another personal computer user (just be polite and type *goodbye!*).

Even after you log off the other computer, the timer is still counting in the lower-left window border—as far as Works is concerned, you are still connected. Choose Connect on the Connect menu to disconnect, and then choose OK.

Be sure to save the file to store all your settings in the Communication and Terminal dialog boxes.

TRANSFERRING FILES

Receiving a file from another computer is synonymous with the communications term *downloading;* sending a file is called *uploading*. The Send File and Receive File options are both located on the Transfer menu.

Because data can be corrupted during transmission, Works automatically checks transferred data for accuracy. The method of error checking that Works uses is called *X-Modem protocol. Protocol* is the set of conventions governing the exchange of information. *X-Modem* is a commonly used protocol that sends and receives files in blocks of 128 bytes (a *byte* is the same thing as a character). After a block is sent, X-Modem checks to make sure all the data were received correctly. If an error is found, X-Modem automatically retransmits the block.

As with all communications settings, both computers must use the same protocol. When you are accessing an information service or a bulletin board, you are usually asked for the type of protocol you want for file transfer. You must choose X-Modem since it is the only protocol Works offers.

RECEIVING A FILE

Receiving a file is actually a two-step process:

1. Instruct the other computer to send the file. If you are connected to another personal computer, you can simply type a message that you are ready to receive the file. If you are connected to an information service or a bulletin board, you choose a menu option to download a file, and then type the name of the file you want to download. Figure 13.8 displays a file-download screen from a BBS. Notice that the system first asked for the file name to download and then summarized the transfer information: protocol, number of blocks, number of bytes, and estimated transfer time.

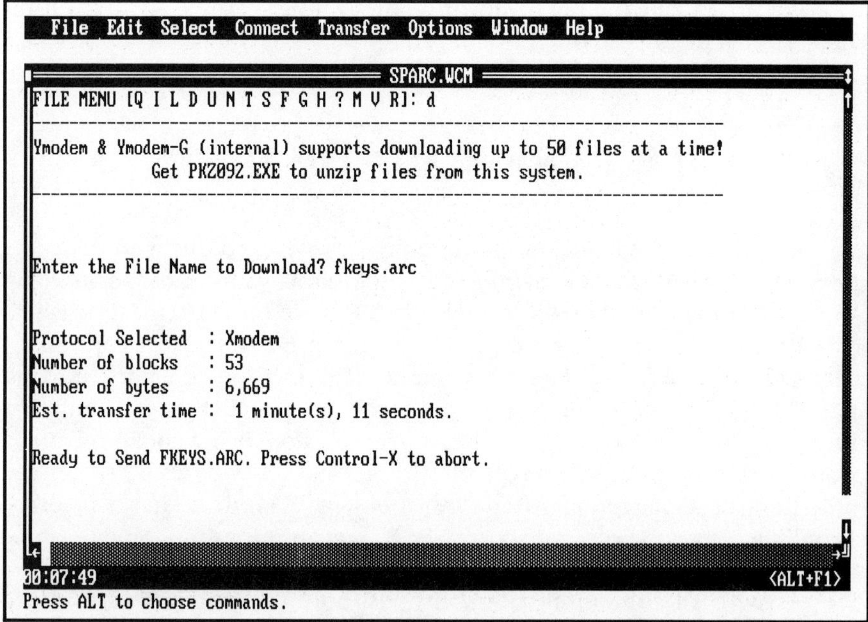
File Edit Select Connect Transfer Options Window Help
SPARC.WCM
FILE MENU [Q I L D U N T S F G H ? M V R]: d
Ymodem & Ymodem-G (internal) supports downloading up to 50 files at a time!
Get PKZ092.EXE to unzip files from this system.
Enter the File Name to Download? fkeys.arc
Protocol Selected : Xmodem
Number of blocks : 53
Number of bytes : 6,669
Est. transfer time : 1 minute(s), 11 seconds.
Ready to Send FKEYS.ARC. Press Control-X to abort.
00:07:49
<ALT+F1>
Press ALT to choose commands.

Figure 13.8: A bulletin board's file-download screen

2. Tell Works to receive the file. Choose Receive File on the Transfer menu and enter a file name. The name you enter here doesn't have to be the same name as the file being sent, but make sure it has the same extension. For example, if the file you are downloading has the extension .COM, you should save the received file with this same extension.

After you choose OK in the Receive File dialog box, a file-transfer status box appears on the screen as shown in Figure 13.9. This box lets you know how many bytes have been received. Because Works uses X-Modem protocol, the file is sent in 128-byte blocks, and each block is checked for errors. If an error is detected, the *Retries* number is increased by an increment of one, and X-Modem automatically resends the block. If a transmitted block contains more than ten errors, Works will cancel the transfer—either the file has something wrong with it or you have a bad telephone connection. Try disconnecting and starting over again. Sometimes switching to a lower baud rate helps, because the data are sent more slowly.

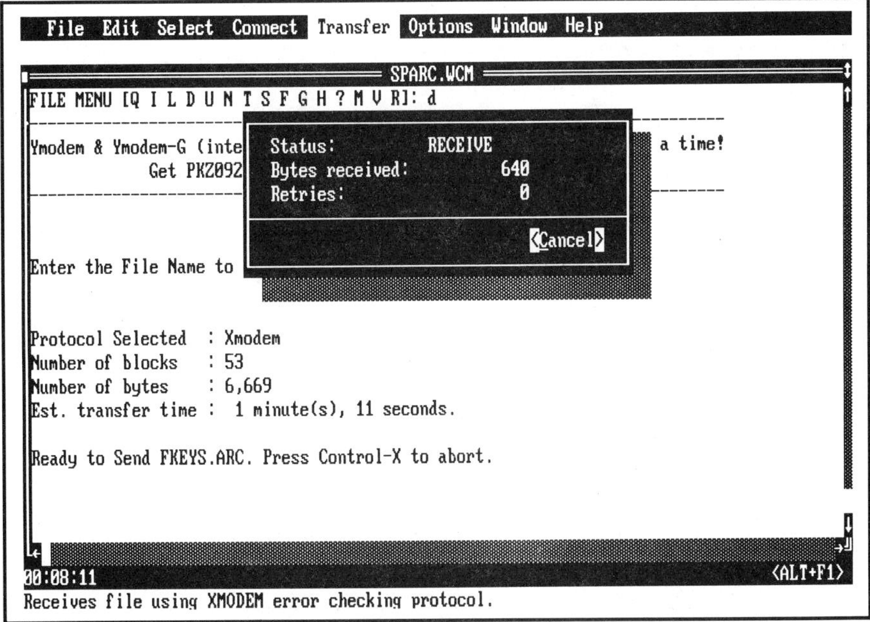

Figure 13.9: The Receive File status box

When the file transfer is finished, the message "Transfer successful" appears in the status box. Choose OK. You are still connected to the other computer, and you can either continue with your communications session or disconnect.

SENDING A FILE

You will most frequently use the Send File command when you are connected to a computer with a person on the other end. Here are a few examples of circumstances for sending a file:

- A writer can send articles to a publisher or editor.
- A traveling salesperson can send customer orders to the home office.
- An office in one city can send financial data to an office in another city.

You can also send files to an information service or a BBS, but you probably won't have an occasion to do so unless you discover that you possess a public domain program that the service doesn't have.

Before you send a large file or a set of files, consider *archiving* them. There are archive programs available in the public domain that can compress a file, or a group of files, into a single, smaller file with the extension .ARC. Archiving saves a lot of time when you transfer files. The person receiving the file must also have an archive program so that he or she can decompress the file into the original, regular-size file or files. Most people shorten the term archive to *arc.* To "arc a file" means to create a compressed file; to "de-arc a file" means to decompress it.

Just as in receiving a file, sending a file requires two steps:

1. Tell the other computer that you want to send a file. If you are sending the file to an information service or a BBS, choose a menu option to upload a file. Otherwise, type a message to your communications partner to let him or her know that you are ready to send a file.

2. Tell Works that you want to send a file. Choose the Send File command on the Transfer menu, and select the name of the file from the Files list. If the name is not in the current directory (for example, *C:\WORKS*), you can use the Directories list box to navigate to the directory containing the file.

After you choose OK in the Send File dialog box, a file-transfer status box appears on the screen as shown in Figure 13.10. When the file transfer is finished, choose OK. You are still connected to the other computer; you could continue with your communications session or disconnect.

CAPTURING INCOMING DATA

One of the reasons for using an information service is to look up and retrieve information. For example, you might want to get the closing stock prices for IBM for the last three months. Or you may want to read all the 1989 news stories about the fall of communism in Eastern Europe. Because information services charge you by the minute, you need a way to save the information so that you can read and analyze it on your own time, at no charge.

Works offers two ways to save the information that you look up:

- After the communications session, you can copy the buffer contents into a word processor, spreadsheet, or database file.
- At any point during the communications session, you can capture the incoming text in a disk file.

Let's look at each of these options in more detail.

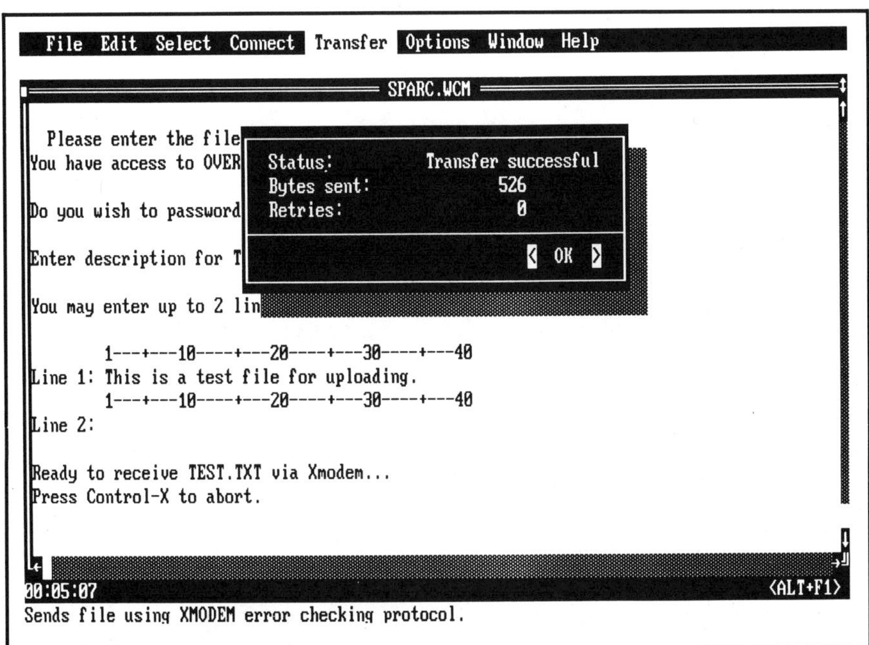

Figure 13.10: The Send File status box

SAVING THE BUFFER CONTENTS

As discussed earlier, incoming text is temporarily stored in your communications window in a *buffer*. The Terminal dialog box lets you control the size of the buffer. After you disconnect from the other computer (or if you choose Pause on the Connect menu), you can scroll through the communications buffer just as you would in a word processor document.

Table 13.1 lists the ways you can move the cursor around in the buffer. These keystrokes should look familiar because they are the same commands used in the word processor tool (though not all the word processor commands are available). If you have a mouse, you can also use the scroll bar. You cannot edit the text.

Table 13.1: Cursor Movement in the Buffer

MOVEMENT OF CURSOR	KEYSTROKE
Beginning of line	Home
End of line	End
Beginning of buffer	Ctrl-Home
End of buffer	Ctrl-End
Next screen	PgDn
Previous screen	PgUp

Although the communications buffer looks and feels like a word processor document, don't be fooled into thinking that it is saved with the communications file; by definition, a buffer is a temporary storage area. To save the buffer's contents, you must copy the text into another Works tool before you close the communications file. Copying text between different Works tools is easy; in fact, you did it in Chapter 7 when you copied a spreadsheet into a word processor document. The steps are as follows:

- Select the text to be copied. To select text, you can press F8 or use the options on the Select menu (Text or All). With the mouse, you can click-and-drag, shift-and-click, or press the right button to select a line.
- Press Shift-F3, or choose Copy on the Edit menu. The bottom of the screen displays "Select new location and press ENTER." Your new location can be a new or an existing file.
- Open or create the file you want to copy the buffer into. If you are creating a new file, select the type of file you want to copy the buffer into (word processor, spreadsheet, or database).
- Position the cursor at the new location and press Enter.

After you copy the buffer, you will probably want to clean up the file. Delete unwanted menus and messages so that your file contains only the data you want to save. If you paused your communications session so that you could copy the buffer, you will want to return to your session before you do any housekeeping in the file. Press Ctrl-F6 to return to your communications window, and then choose Pause on the Connect menu to continue your communications session where you left off.

CAPTURING TEXT

Because the buffer is limited in size (750 lines maximum), you may want to save the incoming text in a file. That way you don't have to worry about exceeding the size of the buffer. Remember, if your incoming text exceeds the buffer size, the oldest data are thrown away. When you capture text to a file, there is no limit to how much incoming text you can save.

When you are ready to begin capturing (after you are connected, of course), follow these steps:

- Choose Capture Text on the Transfer menu.
- Enter a file name and, if you want, an extension.
- Choose OK. *CAPTURE* appears in the bottom window border.
- When you no longer want to capture text, choose End Capture Text on the Transfer menu. The CAPTURE message disappears from the window border.

After your communications session, you can open this file, edit it, and print it. Because the captured text is stored in text format, not in Works format, you are asked which tool you want to use (word processor, spreadsheet, or database) when you open the file.

Rather than capturing every incoming line of data that is displayed in your communications session, you can turn capturing on and off as needed. All the captured text can be stored in the same file, or you can create different files for each block of captured text.

To store a subsequent block of text in an existing file of captured data, follow these steps:

- Choose Capture Text on the Transfer menu.
- Enter the same file name you gave before.

- Choose OK. Works asks you if you want to "Append to or replace existing file?"
- Choose Append to place the next block of captured text at the end of the existing file.
- When you no longer want to capture text, choose End Capture Text on the Transfer menu.

To append other blocks of captured text, you can repeat these steps as many times as is necessary.

SUMMARY

This chapter introduced you to the basics of telecommunications. It explained commonly used communications terminology and settings that are important to successful telecommunications. You learned how to connect to and disconnect from a remote computer, how to transfer files back and forth, and how to save a log of your communications session.

If you are going to use the communications tool to transfer files to and from another personal computer, do the exercises at the end of this chapter. If you are planning on connecting to an information service or to an electronic bulletin board, the next chapter explains how to log on and off these remote computers.

EXERCISES

In these exercises you will use the communications tool to connect to another personal computer. The first step is to find a communications partner—a friend, relative, or business associate who has a personal computer, modem, and communications software. Your partner does not need Works; any communications package will do. It's preferable, though, if your partner is experienced in communications so that he or she can help you out if you encounter problems.

In the following steps, you will enter your communications settings, initiate the call to connect to the other computer, send files back and forth, and save the buffer in a word processor file. If you need help while working on these exercises, refer to the sections indicated inside the parentheses.

1. Create a new communications file (see "Creating a Communications File," page 370).
2. Talk to your communications partner and agree on the settings both of you will use for
   - baud rate
   - parity
   - data bits
   - stop bits
3. Enter the settings in the Communication dialog box (see "Communication Dialog Box Settings," page 373). Change your modem port setting to COM2, if necessary.
4. Enter your partner's phone number in the Phone dialog box (see "Entering the Phone Number," page 378).
5. Specify a large buffer in the Terminal Settings dialog box (see "Buffer," page 377).
6. Connect to the other computer (see "Dialing the Number," page 379).
7. Type messages back and forth to your partner. If you have trouble reading what you or your partner types, adjust the appropriate settings in the Terminal dialog box (see "Terminal Dialog Box Settings," page 375).

8. Send a file to your partner (see ''Sending a File,'' page 385).
9. Receive a file from your partner (see ''Receiving a File,'' page 383).
10. Disconnect from the other computer (see ''Disconnecting,'' page 382).
11. Save the communications file.
12. Copy the buffer to a word processor file, and print out a log of your conversation (see ''Saving the Buffer Contents,'' page 387).
13. Save the word processor file.
14. Close both files.

SAMPLE COMMUNICATIONS SESSIONS

14

Chapter 13 introduced you to the world of telecommunications and many of its concepts and terms. While the previous chapter was more of a reference guide, this chapter gives step-by-step instructions on connecting to and disconnecting from a variety of remote computers:

- CompuServe
- MCI Mail
- HomeBanking
- An electronic bulletin board

This chapter contains a series of practice exercises similar to the ones normally found at the end of a chapter. Consequently, this chapter doesn't have any additional exercises after the Summary.

Before you can connect to an information service or bulletin board, you must first become a member. Once you sign up for the service, you will be given an information packet that includes your personal identification name or number, a password, and a local or toll-free telephone number for dialing the service's computer. You will need this information before you can try any of the sample communications sessions in this chapter.

You should read the next section, "Recording a Sign-On," and then turn to the appropriate section for the session you want to practice (CompuServe, MCI Mail, HomeBanking, Electronic Bulletin Boards). Before proceeding, make sure you are familiar with the communications terms discussed in Chapter 13. It's not imperative that you understand the terms thoroughly, but before you continue with this chapter, you should be familiar with the following: baud rate, data bits, stop bits, parity, echo, and line feed.

RECORDING A SIGN-ON

After you connect to an information service or an electronic bulletin board, you are asked a series of questions to verify your membership—usually you have to provide an identification code and a password. You must answer these questions each time you log on to the system. Works offers a way to *record* the process of signing on to another computer so that you do not have to answer the same questions every time you connect. Follow these general steps to record your sign-on:

- Connect to the other computer.
- After the phone starts to ring or after you get a CONNECT message, choose Record Sign-On on the Connect menu. *RECORD* appears in the bottom window border.
- Enter your user ID name or number, password, and any other information the remote computer requests.
- After completing your log-on responses, choose Record Sign-On on the Connect menu to turn off the recording.

When you save the communications file, your settings *and* your recorded sign-on are stored in the file. The next time you open this file, Works asks you if you want to connect to the other computer. If you choose OK, Works will dial the computer, connect, and log on for you—how's that for automation?

If you choose not to connect to the other computer when you open the communications file, you can still use your sign-on. When you are ready to connect and sign on, follow these steps:

- Connect to the remote computer by choosing Connect on the Connect menu.
- Choose Sign-On on the Connect menu. *PLAY* appears in the bottom window border when Works initiates your sign-on sequence.

COMPUSERVE

CompuServe is an information service that allows you to retrieve information, send and receive messages, make airline reservations, shop at an electronic mall, and play games. You can also peruse a variety of topics:

- National and international news
- Weather reports
- Sports

- Travel
- Current and historical stock prices
- Computers (Microsoft has its own area in CompuServe)

CompuServe charges by the minute. At press time, the rates were $6.00/hour for 300 baud and $12.50/hour for 1200 and 2400 baud. For additional information on CompuServe, call 800-848-8199.

COMPUSERVE SETTINGS

CompuServe uses the following communications settings (select them in the Communication dialog box):

SETTING	CHOICE
Baud	300, 1200, or 2400
Parity	Even
Data Bits	7
Stop Bits	1

If your modem port is COM2, be sure to adjust this setting as well. The default Terminal settings work fine, though you may want to increase the buffer size.

LOGGING ON TO COMPUSERVE

Before you can connect to CompuServe, you will need the following information:

- A local access telephone number (Note: If you have a 2400-baud modem, you must use a special telephone number reserved for 2400 baud.)
- Your user ID
- Your password

This information should be included in your packet from CompuServe.

Figure 14.1 displays CompuServe's complete sign-on screen. The circled items are what you need to enter; everything else is incoming text from CompuServe. Now, follow these steps to connect to CompuServe for the first time:

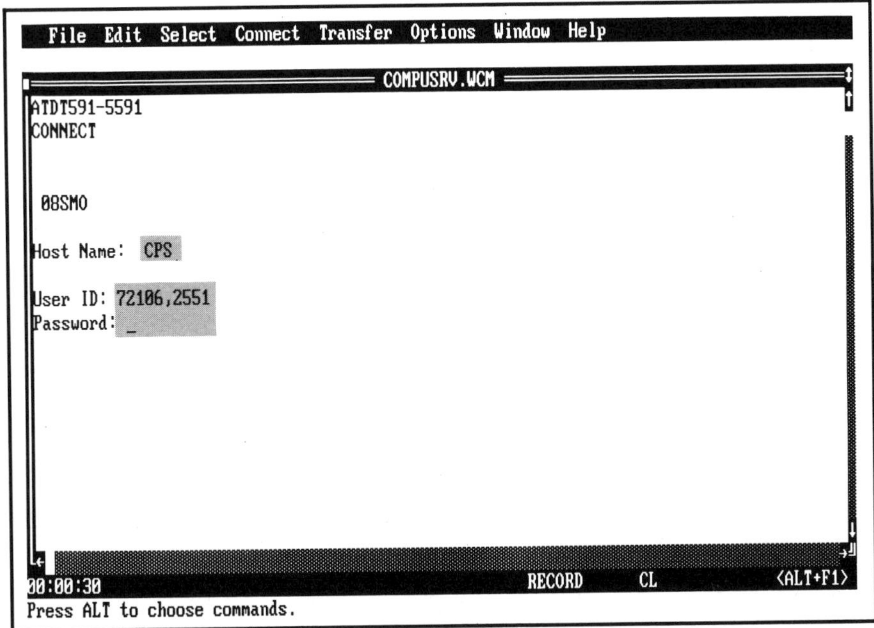

Figure 14.1: The CompuServe sign-on screen

1. Enter the local access number in the Phone dialog box.
2. Choose Connect on the Connect menu. Works dials the number for you.
3. When the phone starts to ring, choose Record Sign-On on the Connect menu.
4. After you get the CONNECT message, CompuServe waits for you to press Enter. Pressing Enter is how you get the computer's attention.
5. After the prompt *Host Name,* type **CPS** and press Enter.
6. After the prompt *User ID,* type your ID (an example of an ID is *72106,2551*) and press Enter.

7. After the prompt *Password,* type your password. For security reasons, the characters are not displayed as you type. Press Enter. A series of messages appears; press Enter and the main CompuServe menu appears as shown in Figure 14.2.
8. Turn off the recording of the sign-on by choosing Record Sign-On on the Connect menu.

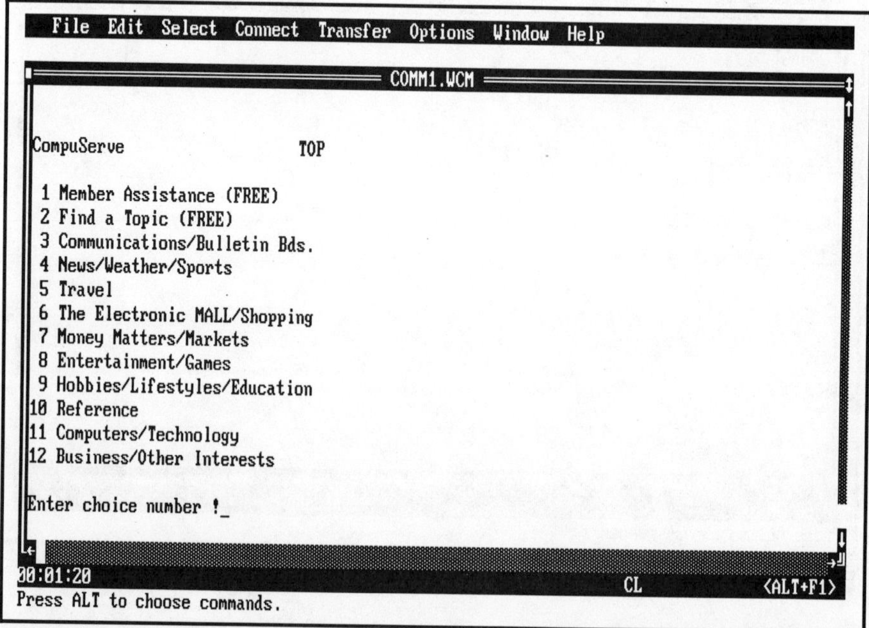

Figure 14.2: The CompuServe main menu

You can now use any of the functions displayed on the CompuServe menu.

LOGGING OFF COMPUSERVE

After you have finished your communications session, follow these steps to log off:

1. At CompuServe's ! prompt, type **bye** and press Enter.
2. Choose Connect on the Connect menu.

3. Choose OK to disconnect. The bottom window border should display *OFFLINE* to show that you have been disconnected.

If you want to save a record of your CompuServe session, you should copy the buffer to a word processor file. You can then save the document as it is, delete the unwanted text that was recorded (such as the menus), and/or print out the session. See "Saving the Buffer Contents" in Chapter 13 for complete information on copying the buffer.

Before you close the communications window, be sure to save the file with a descriptive name, such as *COMPUSRV*. The next time you open this file, Works will ask you if you want to connect to the other computer. If you choose OK, Works dials the number and signs on for you (assuming you recorded a sign-on).

MCI MAIL

With MCI Mail, you can send and receive information anywhere in the world. MCI Mail offers several avenues for sending your messages. You can do the following:

- Exchange electronic messages with other MCI Mail subscribers.
- Transmit messages to fax machines.
- Send messages to and receive messages from telex subscribers.
- Print letters and envelopes on an MCI laser printer and have the letters delivered by first-class mail or a courier service.

Furthermore, through MCI Mail, you have access to the Dow Jones News/Retrieval service, from which you can retrieve stock price quotes, financial information, airline schedules, sports reports, weather updates, movie reviews, and a wide variety of other information. MCI charges an annual subscription fee of $25. You are also charged for each message you send; the prices vary according to the length of the message and how you are sending the message—electronically to another MCI Mail user, by fax, by telex, or by paper mail. For additional information on MCI Mail, call 800-444-6245.

MCI MAIL SETTINGS

MCI Mail uses the following communications settings (select them in the Communication dialog box):

SETTING	CHOICE
Baud	300, 1200, or 2400
Parity	None (Even for 2400 baud)
Data Bits	8 (7 for 2400 baud)
Stop Bits	1

If your modem port is COM2, be sure to adjust this setting as well.

The default Terminal settings work fine, though you may want to increase the buffer size.

LOGGING ON TO MCI MAIL

Before you can connect to MCI Mail, you will need the following information:

- A local access or toll-free telephone number
- Your user name
- Your password

The above information should be included in your packet from MCI Mail.

Figure 14.3 displays MCI Mail's sign-on screen. The circled items are what you need to enter; everything else is incoming text from MCI Mail. Now, follow these steps to connect to MCI Mail for the first time:

1. Enter the local access or toll-free number in the Phone dialog box.
2. Choose Connect on the Connect menu. Works dials the number for you.
3. When the phone starts to ring, choose Record Sign-On on the Connect menu.

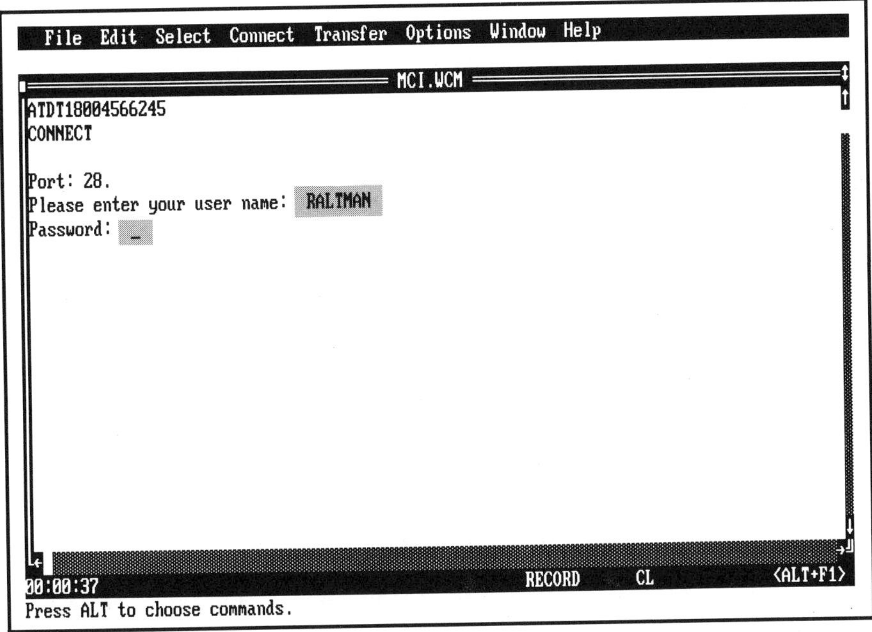

Figure 14.3: The MCI Mail sign-on screen

4. After the CONNECT message appears, MCI Mail waits for you to press Enter. Pressing Enter is how you get the computer's attention.
5. After the prompt *Please enter your user name,* type your user name and press Enter.
6. After the prompt *Password,* type your password. For security reasons, the characters are not displayed as you type. Press Enter. You then see a welcome message from MCI Mail; the COMMAND prompt appears.
7. Turn off the recording of the sign-on by choosing Record Sign-On on the Connect menu.

MCI Mail does not have a menu from which you can choose commands; you give instructions by typing command words. Table 14.1 lists the most commonly used commands in MCI Mail. In a typical communications session, you use the SCAN command to view a summary of your mail, the READ command to see your incoming mail, and the ANSWER, CREATE, and SEND commands to send messages. If you don't know the user name of the person you want to send a message to, you can use the FIND command.

Table 14.1: MCI Mail Commands

COMMAND	DESCRIPTION
ANSWER	Reply to a message you received
CREATE	Write an MCI letter
DOWJONES	Access the Dow Jones News/Retrieval service
FIND	Search for an MCI Mail subscriber's name
INDEX	List all available topics
READ	Read messages
SCAN	View a summary of your mail
SEND	Send a message

SENDING A WORKS DOCUMENT AS AN MCI MAIL MESSAGE

Instead of typing your letter or message while you are logged on to MCI, you can type the letter ahead of time in Works's word processor tool. To use a Works document as an MCI Mail message, you must save the document in *text* format, as opposed to *Works* format. A document saved in text format contains only text; it doesn't have any special formatting.

Follow these general steps to create a text file:

- Create your letter in the word processor tool. Do not use any special character formatting (for example, underlining, boldface, or special fonts), because the formatting will not be saved in text format.
- On the last line of the file, type / (slash) on a line by itself. This code lets MCI Mail know that this is the end of the message.
- Choose Save As on the File menu.
- Type the file name. (Note: By default, text files are not assigned an extension, so you can type your own three-character extension if you like.)
- Press Alt-T or click the left mouse button next to Text to save the file in text format.
- Choose OK.

- A message box warns you that you are saving the file without formatting. Choose OK.

Once you have created the text file, you can log on to MCI Mail and give the CREATE command. After you fill in the letter's heading information (who you are sending it to, who to send copies to, and the subject), you will get the following message:

Text: (Enter text or transmit file. Type / on a line by itself to end.)

Follow these steps to send your text file:

- Choose Send Text on the Transfer menu.
- Type the name of the text file you created earlier.
- Choose OK.

You then identify the "handling" of the message (electronic, fax, telex, or printed) and confirm that you want to send the message.

LOGGING OFF MCI MAIL

After you have finished your communications session, follow these steps to log off:

1. At MCI Mail's COMMAND prompt, type **exit** and press Enter.
2. Choose Connect on Works's Connect menu.
3. Choose OK to disconnect. The bottom window border will display *OFFLINE* to show that you have been disconnected.

If you want to save a record of your MCI Mail session, you should copy the buffer to a word processor file. You can then save the document as it is, delete the unwanted text that was recorded (such as the menus), and/or print out the session. See "Saving the Buffer Contents" in Chapter 13 for complete information on copying the buffer.

Before you close the communications window, be sure to save the file with a descriptive name, such as *MCI*. The next time you open this file, Works will ask you if you want to connect to the other computer. If you choose OK, Works dials the number and signs on for you (assuming you recorded a sign-on).

HOMEBANKING

With Bank of America's HomeBanking service you can manage your money electronically. Several major banks offer similar services.

Here are a few examples of what you can do in HomeBanking:

- Pay your bills.
- Transfer funds between accounts.
- Check current account-balances.
- Look at recent account transactions (for example, check payments, deposits, and transfers).
- Send electronic mail messages to bank employees.

Bank of America charges a flat monthly fee for HomeBanking. The fee at press time was $10/month. For more details on HomeBanking, call 800-792-0808.

HOMEBANKING SETTINGS

Because HomeBanking uses the same communications and terminal settings as the Works defaults (8 data bits and 1 stop bit), you do not need to change any of the settings before you connect. However, if you do not have a 1200-baud modem, you will want to change the baud setting in the Communication dialog box. If your modem port is COM2, be sure to adjust this setting as well. I also recommend changing the buffer size to Large so that you can save a complete record of your banking transactions. (Change the buffer size in the Terminal dialog box.)

LOGGING ON TO HOMEBANKING

Before you can connect to HomeBanking, you will need the following information:

- A local access telephone number

- Your ID code (the last nine digits on your Versatel card)
- Your HomeBanking password

This information should be included in your packet from Bank of America.

Figure 14.4 displays HomeBanking's sign-on screen. The circled items are what you need to enter; everything else is incoming text from HomeBanking. Now, follow these steps to connect to HomeBanking for the first time:

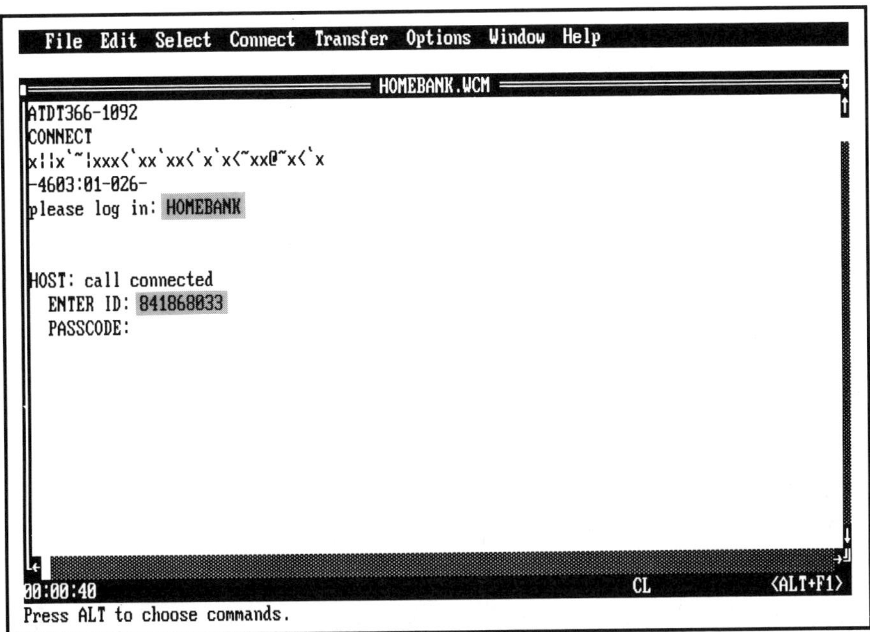

Figure 14.4: The HomeBanking sign-on screen

1. Enter the local access number in the Phone dialog box.
2. Choose Connect on the Connect menu. Works dials the number for you.
3. When the phone starts to ring, choose Record Sign-On on the Connect menu.
4. After the CONNECT message appears, you will see gibberish on the screen (see Figure 14.4). This is normal! Wait two seconds and type

the letter **A**. You do not actually see this letter, but typing it cancels the gibberish.

5. After the prompt *please log in,* type **HOMEBANK** and press Enter. You then see the message "HOST: call connected."
6. After the prompt *ENTER ID,* type the last nine digits on your Versatel card and press Enter. You are then prompted for your passcode.
7. Turn off the recording of the sign-on by choosing Record Sign-On on the Connect menu. For your own protection, you should not record your passcode into the sign-on. (If you record your passcode in the sign-on and someone else opens your HomeBanking communications file, the person will have complete access to all your bank accounts.)
8. After the prompt *PASSCODE,* type your password. For security reasons, the characters are not displayed as you type. Press Enter. The main HomeBanking menu appears as shown in Figure 14.5.

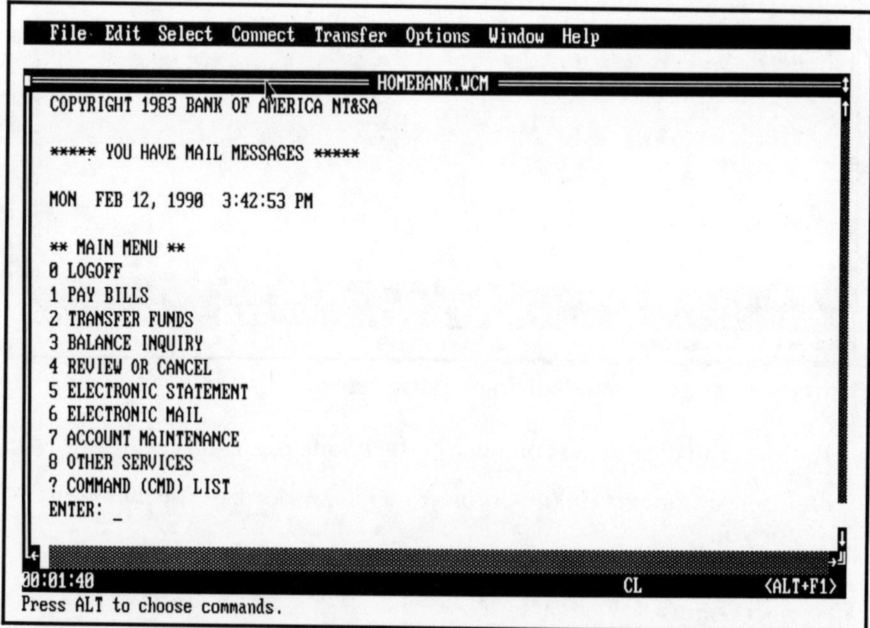

Figure 14.5: The HomeBanking main menu

You can now use any of the functions displayed on the HomeBanking menu.

LOGGING OFF HOMEBANKING

After you have finished your banking session, follow these steps to log off:

1. From the main HomeBanking menu, type **0** and press Enter.
2. Choose Connect on Works's Connect menu.
3. Choose OK to disconnect. The bottom window border will display *OFFLINE* to show that you have been disconnected.

If you want to save a record of your HomeBanking transactions, you should copy the buffer to a word processor file. You can then save the document as it is, delete the unwanted text that was recorded (such as the menus), and/or print out the session. See "Saving the Buffer Contents" in Chapter 13 for complete information on copying the buffer.

Before you close the communications window, be sure to save the file with a descriptive name, such as *HOMEBANK*. The next time you open this file, Works will ask you if you want to connect to another computer. If you choose OK, Works dials the number and signs on for you (assuming you recorded a sign-on). You will have to enter your password each time, since you purposely did not record it in your sign-on.

ELECTRONIC BULLETIN BOARDS

There are two main reasons for using an electronic bulletin board. First, you can download public domain software. There are many useful programs available free in the public domain. Here are a few examples of programs you can download:

- CED (command editor): Allows you to edit your commands in DOS.
- RENDIR: Renames a subdirectory.

- RED (redirect): Moves files to another subdirectory.
- STOCK: A stock-tracking program.
- TETRIS: A popular Russian game.

Second, you might want to use a bulletin board's message system. This allows you to exchange messages with other members of the bulletin board. If you have a computer-related problem, you can post your question and check back later for a response—someone is likely to know the answer or lead you to someone who might know.

Electronic bulletin boards are usually operated by computer user groups, businesses, or individuals and are located all over the world. You will want to find a bulletin board in your vicinity so that you won't have to pay long-distance charges while you are connected to the system. Since most computer user groups offer bulletin boards as a service to their members, you might want to consider joining a local group. Check the community calendar section of your newspaper for notifications of the next user-group meeting. Some computer magazines also list user groups and bulletin boards.

Bulletin boards do not usually charge a monthly or a by-the-minute fee, unlike the other services discussed in this chapter. The group or person running the BBS (Bulletin Board System) may require a yearly membership fee of $25 or so.

BULLETIN BOARD SETTINGS

The settings for each bulletin board vary—check with the bulletin board's contact person for the correct settings. The most common settings are the following:

SETTING	CHOICE
Baud	300, 1200, or 2400
Parity	None
Data Bits	8
Stop Bits	1

If your modem port is COM2, be sure to adjust this setting in the Communication dialog box.

LOGGING ON TO A BULLETIN BOARD

Before you can connect to a bulletin board, you will need the following information:

- The bulletin board's telephone number
- Your user ID
- Your password

The bulletin board that I am a member of uses the member's first and last name as an ID. Other boards may assign you a special user name or number.

Figure 14.6 displays the sign-on screen for a bulletin board called SPARC. The circled items are what you need to enter; everything else is incoming text from SPARC. Now, follow these steps to connect to the bulletin board for the first time:

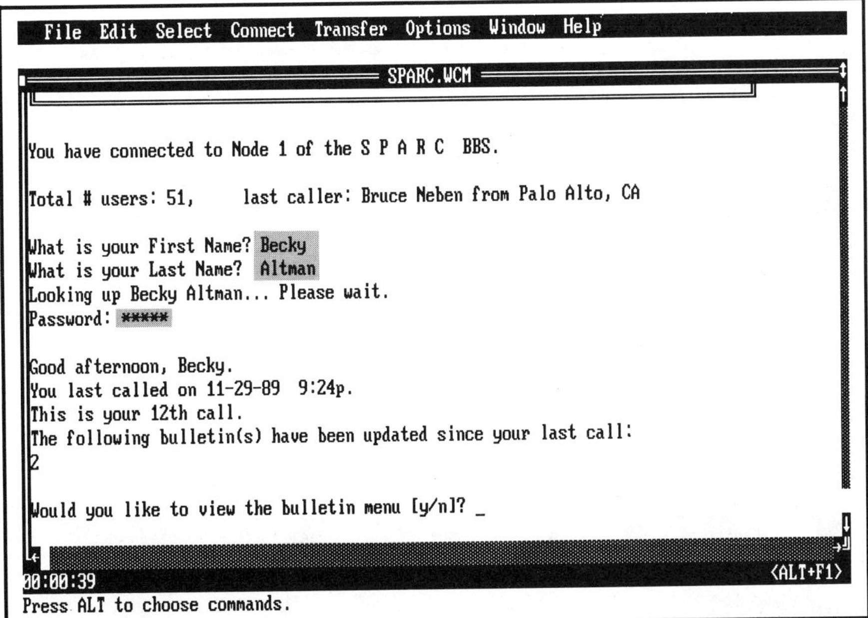

Figure 14.6: A BBS sign-on screen

1. Enter the telephone number in the Phone dialog box.
2. Choose Connect on the Connect menu. Works dials the number for you.
3. When the phone starts to ring, choose Record Sign-On on the Connect menu.
4. Respond to the bulletin board's prompts for your name (or user ID) and your password.
5. Turn off the recording of the sign-on by choosing Record Sign-On on the Connect menu.

You can now use any of the functions displayed on the bulletin board's menu. Figure 14.7 is an example of SPARC's main menu. If you want to download a file from the bulletin board, refer to ''Receiving a File'' in Chapter 13.

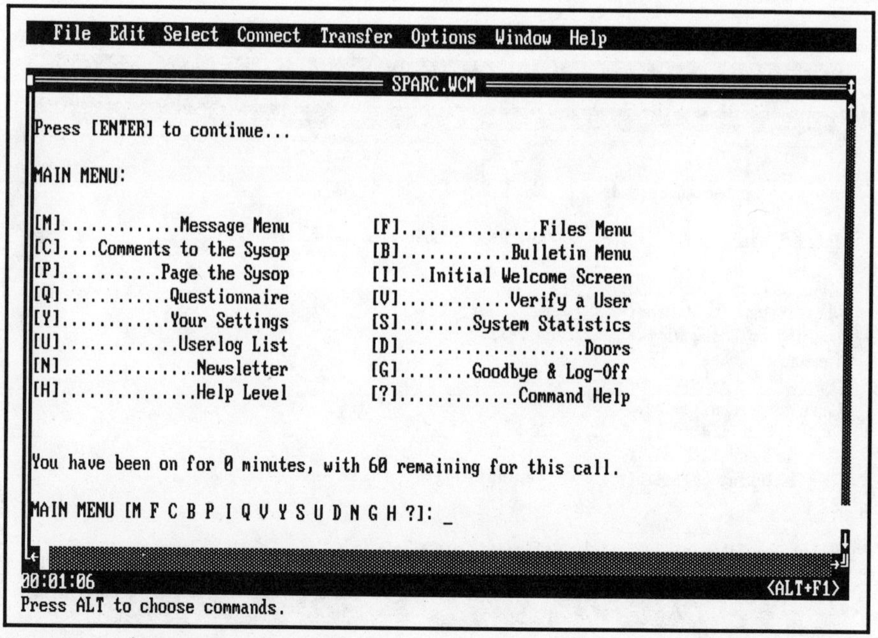

```
 File  Edit  Select  Connect  Transfer  Options  Window  Help
                         SPARC.WCM
Press [ENTER] to continue...

MAIN MENU:

[M]............Message Menu        [F]..............Files Menu
[C]....Comments to the Sysop       [B]...........Bulletin Menu
[P]..........Page the Sysop        [I]...Initial Welcome Screen
[Q]...........Questionnaire        [V]...........Verify a User
[Y]...........Your Settings        [S]........System Statistics
[U]............Userlog List        [D]....................Doors
[N]..............Newsletter        [G]........Goodbye & Log-Off
[H]..............Help Level        [?]............Command Help

You have been on for 0 minutes, with 60 remaining for this call.

MAIN MENU [M F C B P I Q V Y S U D N G H ?]: _
00:01:06                                                <ALT+F1>
Press ALT to choose commands.
```

Figure 14.7: A BBS main menu

LOGGING OFF A BULLETIN BOARD

After you have finished your communications session, follow these steps to log off:

1. Each bulletin board has its own way of logging off. If the bulletin board has a menu (most do), look at the menu for an option that will exit you from the system. For example, in Figure 14.7, typing *G* chooses the Goodbye & Log-Off option.
2. Choose Connect on Works's Connect menu.
3. Choose OK to disconnect. The bottom window border will display *OFFLINE* to show that you have been disconnected.

To save a record of your BBS session, you should copy the buffer to a word processor file. You can then save the document as it is, delete the unwanted text that was recorded (such as the menus), and/or print out the session. See "Saving the Buffer Contents" in Chapter 13 for complete information on copying the buffer.

Before you close the communications window, be sure to save the file with a descriptive name. The next time you open this file, Works will ask whether you want to connect to another computer. If you choose OK, Works dials the number and signs on for you (assuming you recorded a sign-on).

SUMMARY

This chapter showed you how to log on and off several remote computers: CompuServe, MCI Mail, HomeBanking, and an electronic bulletin board. For details on the actual use of one of these services, you have to consult the documentation that accompanies your membership packet. You may also need to refer to Chapter 13 for information on transferring files and capturing incoming data.

Because this chapter comprises four sample communications sessions that are very similar to the exercises normally found at the end of each chapter, no additional exercises are included here. You can immediately go on to Chapter 15 and learn how to manage your windows and files.

part six

WINDOWS AND MACROS

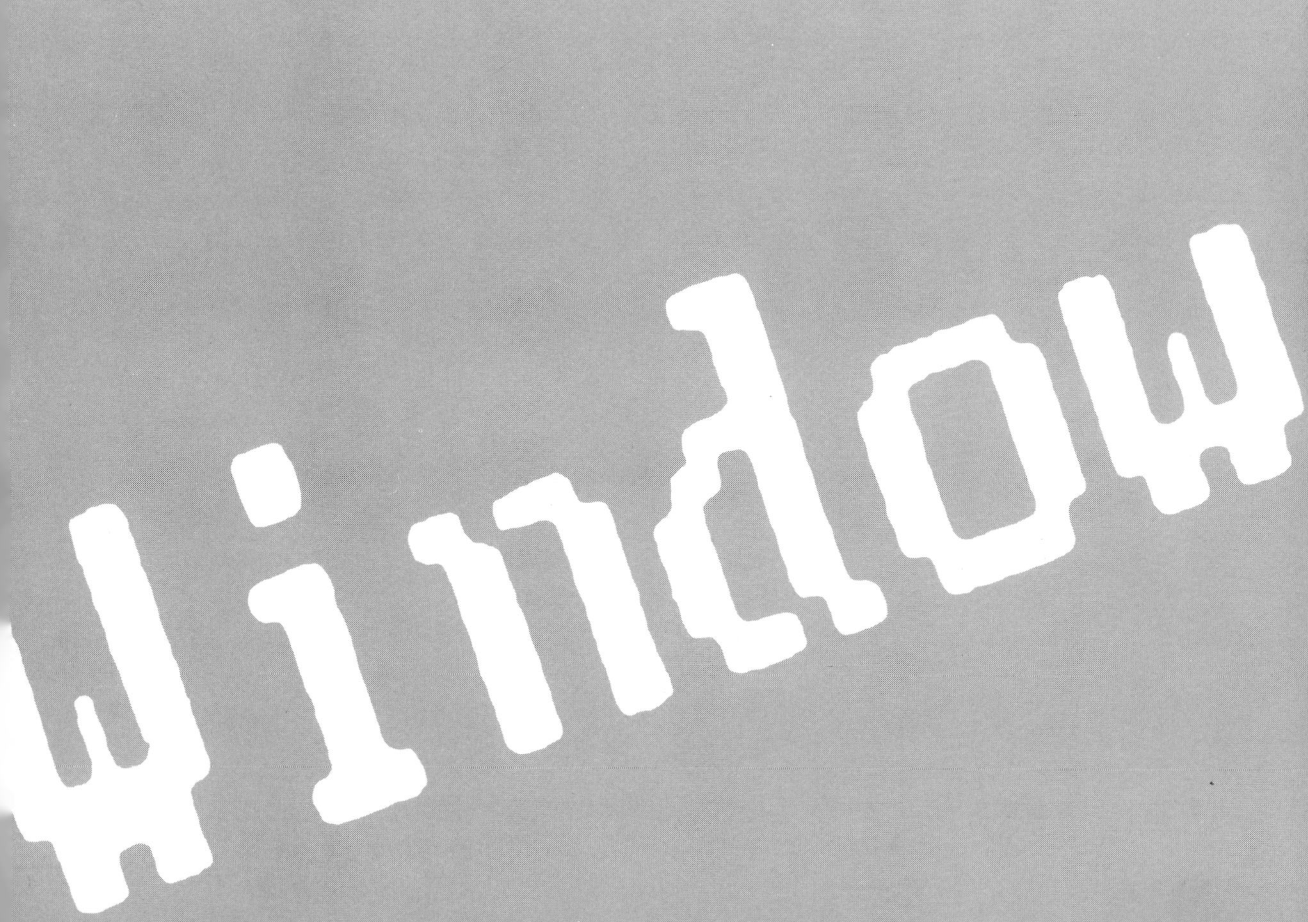

GETTING THE MOST FROM YOUR WINDOWS

15

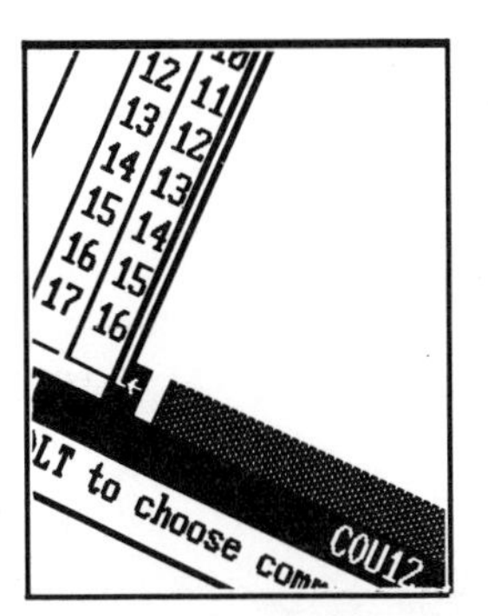

One of Works's most powerful features is its ability to have up to eight files open simultaneously, each in its own window. This capability allows you to easily transfer data from one file to another, or to look up a fact in a different file without having to close your current file. Several times throughout this book you have had two files open at the same time:

- In Chapter 7 you copied a spreadsheet into a word processor document.
- In Chapter 12 you merged a form letter with a database of names and addresses.
- In Chapter 13 you learned how to copy a communications buffer into a word processor document.

These previous chapters glossed over the specifics of working with multiple windows so as not to digress from the main task at hand. The details for working with Works's windowing feature have been reserved for this single chapter.

Works offers two ways to manipulate windows: You can use the Window menu, or you can click on window *icons* with the mouse. An icon is a graphic image or symbol. The window icons are marked in Figure 15.1. Although this figure shows the icons in a spreadsheet window, the same icons are available in any type of window.

In this chapter, you will learn how to move between open windows, change the size and position of windows, and simultaneously view different parts of a file.

Don't confuse Microsoft Works's windowing feature with the Microsoft Windows program. The techniques for window manipulation in the two programs are remarkably similar. Microsoft Windows, however, is an operating environment that allows you to simultaneously work with more than one software program at a time (sometimes called *multitasking*). There are programs (for example, Microsoft Excel) that are designed to run in the Windows operating environment, but Works is not one of them.

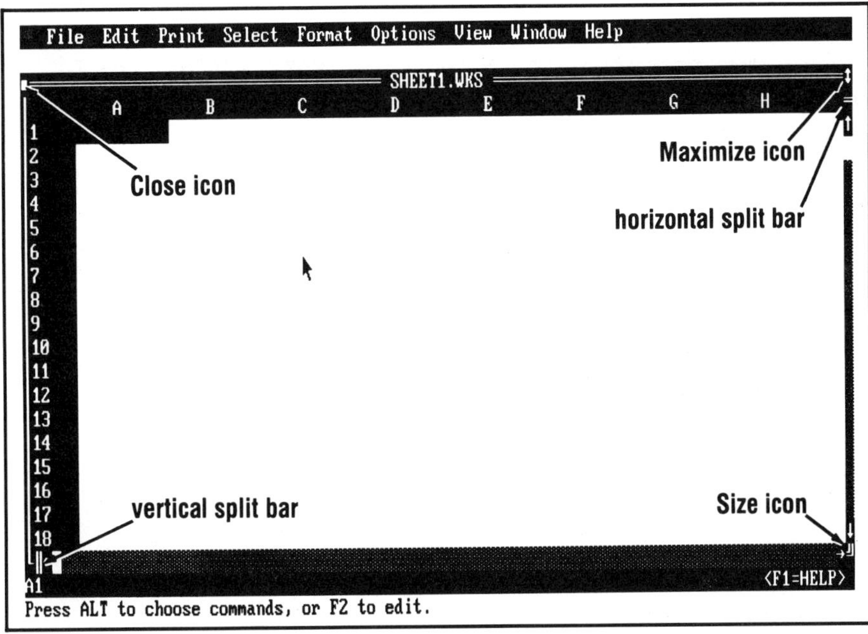

Figure 15.1: Window icons

OPENING MULTIPLE FILES

As you have previously seen, Works automatically lets you have multiple files open; if you don't close the current file before opening or creating a second one, both files remain open at the same time. The second file overlays the first one, though you can still see part of the first file's window border.

Let's open several files. If you can't find one of the files listed below, choose any Works file or create a new file; you do not need the exact files suggested in the exercises to practice the window commands. Just make sure you have the same number of files open that are specified in the exercises. Follow these steps to open files:

1. Choose the Open Existing File command on the File menu.
2. Choose the JOHNSON.WPS file.

3. Open the RAISE.WKS file. This file is now the *active window*; in other words, it is the window that the cursor is in. Notice that you can still see part of the other window's border, including the file name at the top. Your screen should look similar to Figure 15.2.

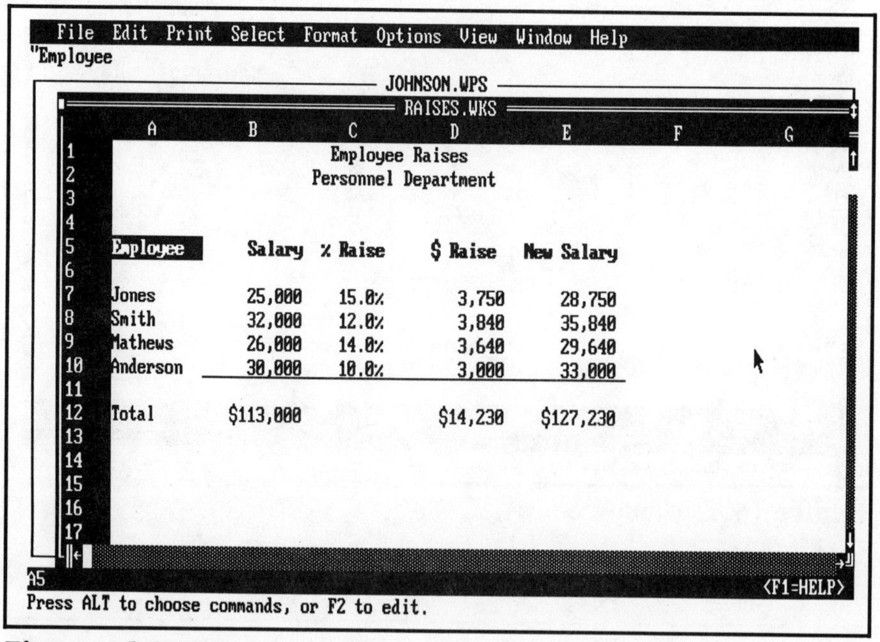

```
 File  Edit  Print  Select  Format  Options  View  Window  Help
"Employee
                        JOHNSON.WPS
                         RAISES.WKS
        A          B         C          D          E          F          G
1                          Employee Raises
2                        Personnel Department
3
4
5   Employee      Salary  % Raise    $ Raise  New Salary
6
7   Jones         25,000    15.0%      3,750      28,750
8   Smith         32,000    12.0%      3,840      35,840
9   Mathews       26,000    14.0%      3,640      29,640
10  Anderson      30,000    10.0%      3,000      33,000
11
12  Total       $113,000             $14,230    $127,230
13
14
15
16
17
A5                                                                  <F1=HELP>
Press ALT to choose commands, or F2 to edit.
```

Figure 15.2: Two open windows, with RAISE.WKS active

4. Open the EMPLOYEE.WDB file. EMPLOYEE.WDB is now the active window, and you can see the window borders for JOHNSON.WPS and RAISE.WKS.

5. Create a new word processor file. WORD1.WPS is the active window, and you can see the window borders for JOHNSON.WPS, RAISE.WKS, and EMPLOYEE.WDB. Your screen should resemble Figure 15.3.

Notice that as you open more windows, each new window is smaller than the previous one. If you want a window to fill the entire screen (the way the first window you opened did), you can *maximize* the window. When you maximize the current window, all open windows are enlarged to

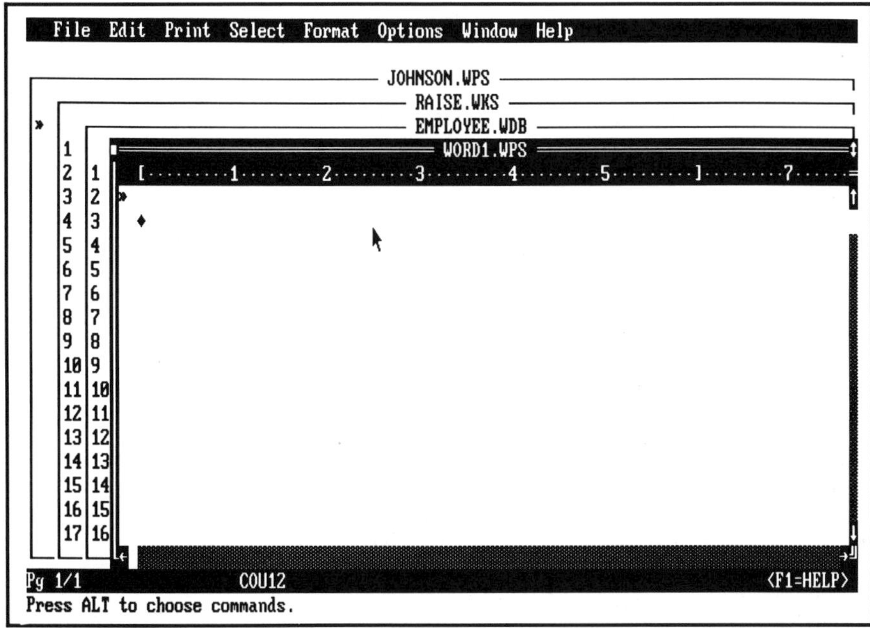

Figure 15.3: Four open windows

full-screen size. Works offers two ways to maximize windows:

- Choose the Maximize command on the Window menu.
- With the mouse, click on the double-headed arrow in the upper-right window corner. (This icon is circled in Figure 15.1.)

When the windows are maximized, a mark appears next to Maximize in the Window menu. The Maximize setting remains active until you exit Works or restore the windows to their previous sizes. To restore windows, reissue the same command you gave to maximize them: either choose the Maximize command again or click on the Maximize icon.

Make sure your windows are *not* maximized before you continue with this chapter's examples.

MOVING BETWEEN OPEN WINDOWS

The last window you have opened is always the active or current window. The active window contains the cursor and has highlighted window borders and mouse scroll bars. Works offers four ways to move the cursor to a different window:

- Press Ctrl-F6 to move to the next window.
- Press Ctrl-Shift-F6 to move to the previous window.
- Choose the file name from the Windows menu.
- Click inside the window with the mouse.

The first two methods, pressing Ctrl-F6 and Ctrl-Shift-F6, cycle you through the open windows in the order that you opened them. If you are in the last window and you issue the Next Window command (Ctrl-F6), you move to the first window you opened. Likewise, if you are in the first window and you issue the Previous Window command, you move to the last window. If you have only two files open, Ctrl-F6 will move you back and forth between the windows. Right now the current window is the last file you created, WORD1.WPS. Practice moving to the other open windows:

1. Issue the Previous Window command: Press Ctrl-Shift-F6. The EMPLOYEE.WDB file is now the current window. Notice that you no longer see WORD1.WPS. (See Figure 15.4.) With the default window sizes and positions, you can only see windows opened *before* the active window. Later on you will learn how to change the window layout so that you can see all windows, no matter which window you are in.
2. Press Ctrl-Shift-F6 again. You are now in the RAISE.WKS window.
3. Issue the Next Window command: Press Ctrl-F6. The file EMPLOYEE.WDB is now active.

If the window you want to go to is displayed on the screen, the fastest way to get to that window is to use the mouse. Simply place the mouse pointer in the part of the window that is exposed, and click the left

```
 File  Edit  Print  Select  Format  Options  View  Window  Help
1004
                              JOHNSON.WPS
                                 RAISE.WKS
»                               EMPLOYEE.WDB
 1          Last Name First Name  ID     Dept    Exempt Hire Date  Salary  Raise
 2  1       Bradford  William    1004  Personnel Yes      3/9/91  60,000     7%
 3  2       Bradley   Brad       1006  Personnel No      2/26/85  54,000     8%
 4  3       Manley    Martin     1002  Eng.      Yes     9/10/86  44,000    10%
 5  4       Meyers    Andrew     1007  MIS       Yes     12/1/88  41,000     9%
 6  5       Wilson    Robert     1005  Eng.      Yes    10/14/83  36,000    15%
 7  6       Anderson  Jane       1000  MIS       Yes      8/2/85  34,600    13%
 8  7       Jones     Mary       1001  Personnel No     10/15/88  29,500    11%
 9  8       Peterson  Pete       1003  MIS       Yes     7/21/82  21,000    12%
10  9
11  10
12  11
13  12
14  13
15  14
16  15
17  16
1 ID          8/8        LIST                                         <F1=HELP>
Press ALT to choose commands, or F2 to edit.
```

Figure 15.4: The active window, EMPLOYEE.WDB

mouse button. This technique doesn't work if you have maximized the windows, because other windows are not visible when the Maximize setting is active. Furthermore, you can only go to exposed windows. If you don't see part of a window on the screen, you can't click on it with the mouse.

When you have several files open, and not all of them are exposed, the best way to move between windows is to use the Window menu. Follow these general steps to use the menu to move to another window:

- Pull down the Window menu. The bottom of the menu lists the files that are currently open.
- To choose a particular window, highlight the file name and press Enter, or double-click on the name, or type the number next to the name. (The numbers correspond to the order in which you opened the files.)

Follow the above steps to move to the JOHNSON.WPS file.

CLOSING WINDOWS

To close an open window, you simply go to that window and close the file. Throughout this book you have been closing files by using the File menu's Close option. However, if you have a mouse, there is a shortcut for closing a file: Click on the icon in the upper-left corner of the window. (This icon is circled in Figure 15.1.)

Close the WORD1.WPS file, following these steps:

1. Move to the WORD1.WPS file.
2. Choose the Close command on the File menu, or, if you have a mouse, click on the Close icon in the upper-left window border. The window is now closed.

Both of the file-closing commands will ask you whether you want to save the file, if you have made any changes since you last saved. If you choose Yes, the file is saved before the window is closed.

SIZING AND MOVING WINDOWS

You have already learned one way to change the size of a window: Use the Maximize command. With this command, each open window consumes the entire screen (except for the menu bar, of course). The Maximize command is a toggle, and choosing it a second time returns the windows to their previous sizes. But what if you want to control the size and position of each window on the screen? The Window menu offers three options: Move, Size, and Arrange All.

The size and screen position of a window are temporary and not saved with the file. If you change a window's attributes and then save and close the file, the next time you open the file, the window is displayed at its normal size and in its normal position.

ARRANGING THE WINDOWS AUTOMATICALLY

The easiest way to position your open windows is to use the Arrange All command on the Window menu. This command arranges your windows so that they are all visible and positioned side by side. Figure 15.5 displays three open files after the Arrange All command was selected. The window that is active before you issue this command is always placed on the left side of the screen and remains active. The other windows are stacked in the order they were opened. Choose Arrange All on the Window menu now.

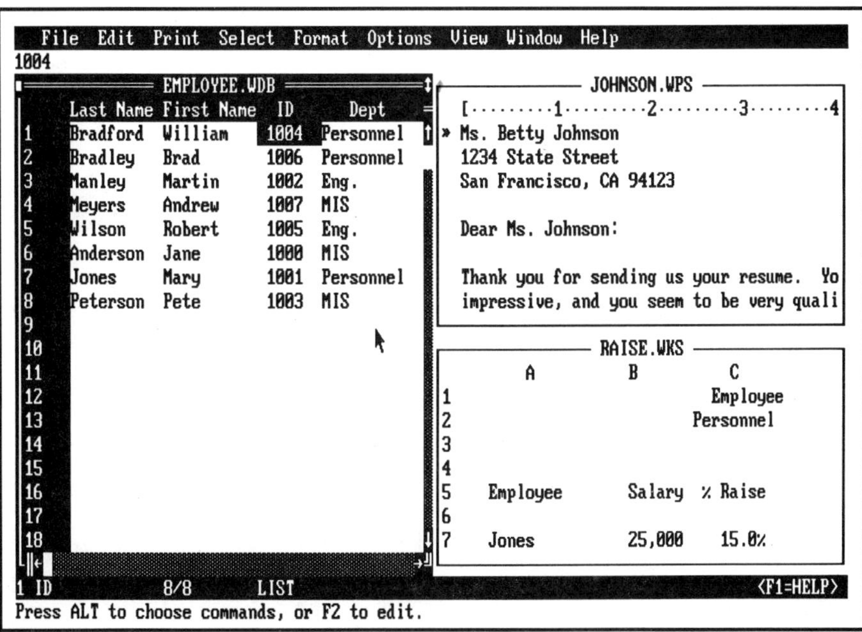

Figure 15.5: Three arranged windows

The Next Window command moves the cursor from window to window in a clockwise direction, and the Previous Window command moves the cursor counterclockwise.

The Arrange All command offers several nice features. First, you can see all open windows regardless of which window is active. (Normally, you can only see the windows that were opened *before* the active window.)

Second, because you can see all open windows, you can use your mouse to move to any window.

The disadvantage of arranging the windows is probably quite obvious: The windows are smaller than normal, so you can see only a minimal amount of text in each window. Consequently, you will probably arrange the windows for a specific task (for example, to copy data between files, to compare data in several files, etc.) and then return them to their normal sizes after you have finished your task.

Practice moving to different windows in your arranged window display, using any of the four techniques you learned earlier. Then, follow these steps to close one of the windows:

1. Move to the EMPLOYEE.WDB window.
2. Close this window. A "black hole" appears in place of the window—the windows need to be rearranged.
3. Choose Arrange All on the Window menu. Each window now consumes half of the screen, as shown in Figure 15.6.

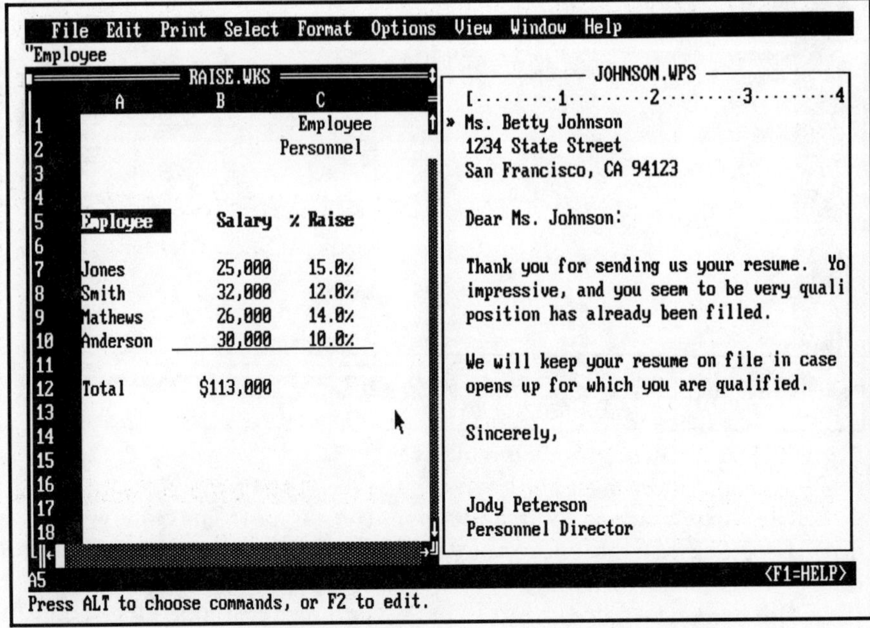

Figure 15.6: Two arranged windows

When you want to return the windows to full-screen size, you can choose the Maximize command on the Window menu or click on the Maximize icon. Keep the windows arranged for now.

ARRANGING THE WINDOWS MANUALLY

The Arrange All command moves and sizes the windows automatically, but it does not give you much control over where the windows are positioned. For example, in the previous exercise you used the Arrange All command when two windows were displayed, and the windows were placed side by side. If you want the windows stacked on top of each other, as shown in Figure 15.7, you have to manually move and size them. The Window menu offers Move and Size options; if you have a mouse, you can use the window icons.

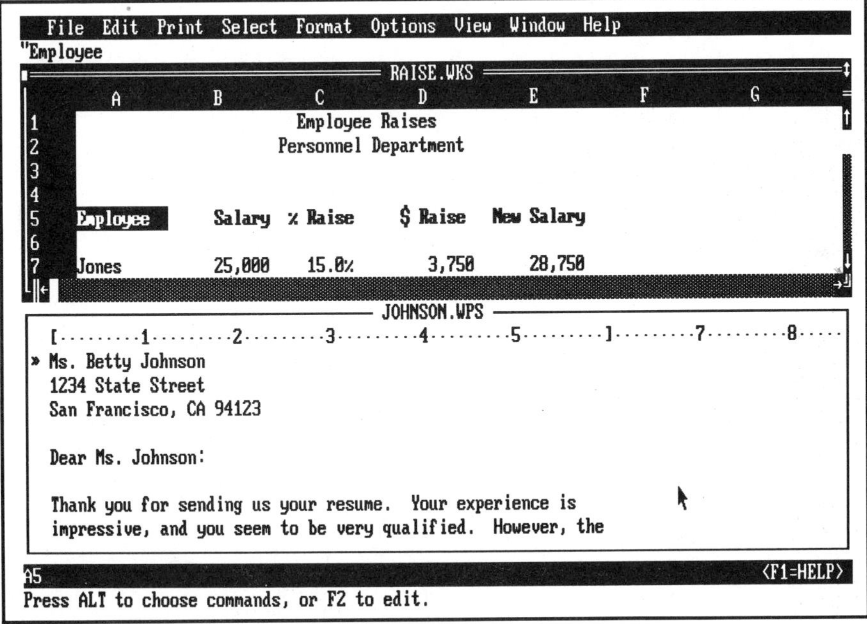

Figure 15.7: Two stacked windows

Sizing a Window

You change the size of a window by stretching or shrinking the window's lower-right corner. The upper-left window corner remains stationary. To make a window smaller, you move the lower-right corner up and/or to the left. To make a window larger, you move the corner down and/or to the right.

To change the size of a window with the Size option on the Window menu, follow these general steps:

- Go to the window you want to size.
- Choose the Size option on the Window menu. The bottom of the screen tells you to "Use DIRECTION keys to resize window, and press ENTER." Also notice that Works superimposes a thin frame over the normal window borders. It is this frame that you manipulate to change the window dimensions, not the actual window.
- Press the arrow key (↑, ↓, →, or ←) that corresponds to the direction in which you want to size the window. The lower-right corner of the window frame moves when you press an arrow key.
- When the window frame is the size you want it to be, press Enter.

If you have a mouse, follow these general steps to resize a window:

- Click inside the window you want to resize.
- Place the mouse pointer on the Size icon in the lower-right corner of the window. (The icon is circled in Figure 15.1.)
- Hold down the left mouse button. Works superimposes a thin frame over the normal window borders. It is this frame that you manipulate to change the window dimensions, not the actual window.
- Move the mouse pointer in the direction you want to size the window. The lower-right corner of the window frame moves as you move the mouse pointer.
- When the window frame is the size you want it to be, release the mouse button.

Moving a Window

You can position a window anywhere on the screen. The whole window doesn't even have to fit on the screen. To move a window with the Move option on the Window menu, follow these general steps:

- Go to the window you want to move.
- Choose the Move option on the Window menu. The bottom of the screen tells you to ''Use DIRECTION keys to move window, and press ENTER.'' As when you size a window, Works superimposes a thin frame over the normal window borders. It is this frame that you move, not the actual window.
- Press an arrow key (↑, ↓, →, or ←). The window frame trots in the direction of the arrow. Continue pressing until the window is positioned in its new location.
- Press Enter to complete the move.

If you have a mouse, follow these general steps to move a window:

- Click inside the window you want to move.
- Place the mouse pointer on the file name or anywhere along the double line at the top of the window.
- Hold down the left mouse button. As when you size a window, Works superimposes a thin frame over the normal window borders. It is this frame that you move, not the actual window.
- Move the mouse pointer in the direction you want to move the window.
- Release the mouse button to complete the move.

In the next section you will practice moving and sizing windows with the keyboard. If you have a mouse, skip to the section ''Hands-On Practice: Using the Mouse.''

Hands-On Practice: Using the Keyboard

Let's say you want to position the two windows so that they are stacked on top of each other (see Figure 15.7) instead of lying side by side. To do this, you have to size and move the windows.

First, resize the window on the right:

1. Move to the right-hand window.
2. Choose Size on the Window menu.
3. Press ↑ until the window frame is half of its current height.
4. Press Enter.

Now, move this window:

1. Choose Move on the Window menu.
2. Press ↓ and ← until the window frame is positioned in the lower-left corner of the screen. (The frame will partly cover the other window.)
3. Press Enter and the window moves to its new position.

Stretch this window across the width of the screen:

1. Choose Size on the Window menu.
2. Press → until the window frame spans the width of the screen.
3. Press Enter.

Change the size of the other window:

1. Press Ctrl-F6 to move to the next window.
2. Choose the Size command on the Window menu.
3. Press ↑ and → until the window frame fits in the top half of the screen.
4. Press Enter. Your screen should look similar to Figure 15.7.

Hands-On Practice: Using the Mouse

First, resize the window on the right:

1. Click inside the right-hand window.
2. Place the mouse pointer on the Size icon in the lower-right corner of the window.
3. Hold down the mouse button.
4. Move the mouse pointer up until the window frame is half of its current height.
5. Release the mouse button.

Now, move this window:

1. Place the mouse pointer on the file name or anywhere along the double line at the top of the window.
2. Hold down the mouse button.
3. Move the mouse pointer down and to the left until the window frame is positioned in the lower-left corner of the screen.
4. Release the mouse button.

Stretch this window across the width of the screen:

1. Place the mouse pointer on the Size icon in the lower-right corner of the window.
2. Hold down the mouse button.
3. Move the mouse pointer to the right until the window frame spans the width of the screen.
4. Release the mouse button.

Change the size of the other window:

1. Click inside the other window.

2. Place the mouse pointer on the Size icon in the lower-right corner of the window.
3. Hold down the mouse button.
4. Move the mouse pointer up and to the right until the window frame fits in the top half of the screen.
5. Release the mouse button. Your screen should look similar to Figure 15.7.

CREATING WINDOW PANES

In a large file, you may want to *split* the window so that you can simultaneously view two widely separated parts of the file. For example, in a spreadsheet you may want to see the yearly total column while you enter values in a monthly sales column. After you split a window, you can scroll the screen and move the cursor in each *pane* (section) to position the text you want to see. Since you can scroll panes independently, each pane has its own set of scroll bars.

In the word processor tool, you can create horizontal window panes, as shown in Figure 15.8. Notice that each pane has its own ruler and vertical scroll bars. In the spreadsheet tool and in the database tool's List view, you can split the screen horizontally, vertically, or both. Figure 15.9 displays a spreadsheet with a vertical window pane.

You can create window panes by using the Split option on the Window menu or by manipulating the Split icon with the mouse. (This icon is circled in Figure 15.1.) Follow these general steps to create horizontal and vertical panes using the Window menu's Split option:

- Choose Split on the Window menu. The message "Use DIRECTION keys to move split, and press ENTER" appears at the bottom of the screen.
- Press ↓ to move the ***horizontal split bar*** (double horizontal lines) to where you want to split the screen (usually near the middle).
- In the spreadsheet tool and in the database tool's List view, you can press → to move the ***vertical split bar*** (double vertical lines) to where you want to split the screen.
- Press Enter.

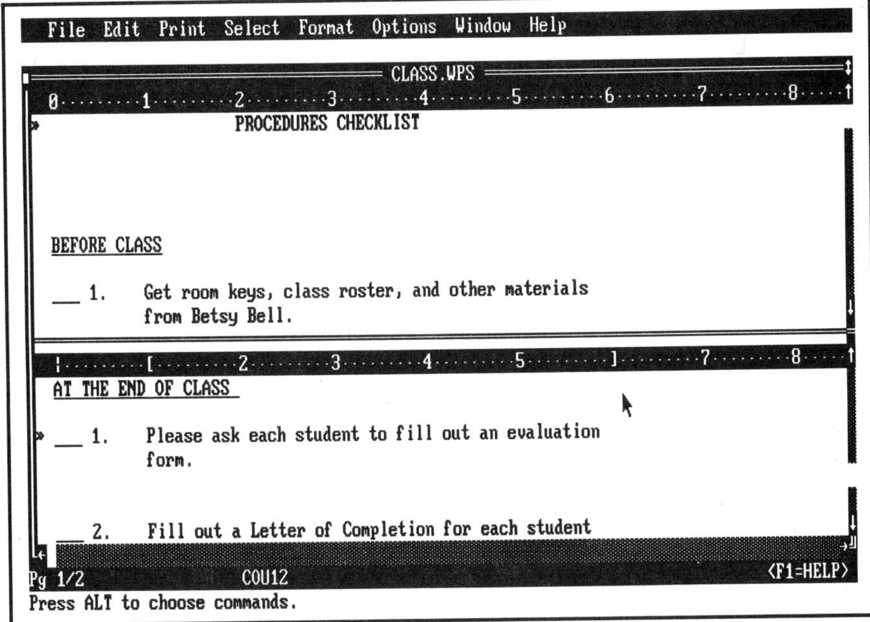

Figure 15.8: Horizontal window panes

If you have a mouse, you can follow these general steps to create horizontal panes:

- Place the mouse pointer on the Split icon in the upper-right corner of the window.
- Hold down the mouse button.
- Drag the horizontal split bar to where you want to split the screen.
- Release the mouse button.

To use the mouse to create a vertical pane in the spreadsheet tool or in the database tool's List view, follow the above steps, except drag the vertical split bar in the lower-left corner of the window.

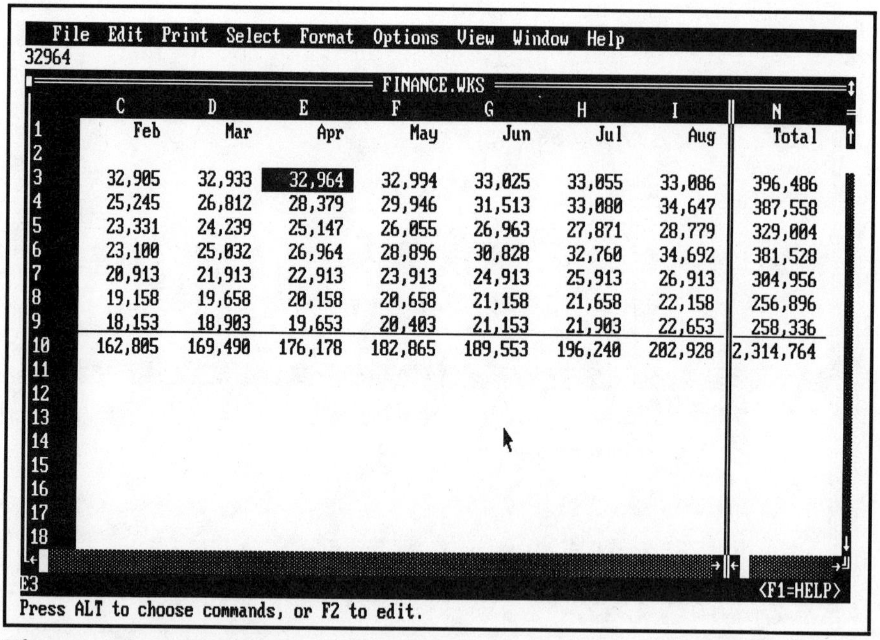

File Edit Print Select Format Options View Window Help
32964

FINANCE.WKS

	C	D	E	F	G	H	I	N
1	Feb	Mar	Apr	May	Jun	Jul	Aug	Total
2								
3	32,905	32,933	32,964	32,994	33,025	33,055	33,086	396,486
4	25,245	26,812	28,379	29,946	31,513	33,080	34,647	387,558
5	23,331	24,239	25,147	26,055	26,963	27,871	28,779	329,004
6	23,100	25,032	26,964	28,896	30,828	32,760	34,692	381,528
7	20,913	21,913	22,913	23,913	24,913	25,913	26,913	304,956
8	19,158	19,658	20,158	20,658	21,158	21,658	22,158	256,896
9	18,153	18,903	19,653	20,403	21,153	21,903	22,653	258,336
10	162,805	169,490	176,178	182,865	189,553	196,240	202,928	2,314,764
11								
12								
13								
14								
15								
16								
17								
18								

E3 <F1=HELP>
Press ALT to choose commands, or F2 to edit.

Figure 15.9: Vertical window panes

Let's create a horizontal window pane for the CLASS.WPS file that you used in Chapter 5. Follow these steps:

1. Close the open files on your screen.
2. Open CLASS.WPS.
3. Choose Split on the Window menu.
4. Press ↓ until the horizontal split bar is approximately in the middle of the screen.
5. Press Enter. Right now you see the same text in both window panes. In the next section, you will look at different text in each pane.

If you have a mouse, follow these steps to split the screen:

1. Place the mouse pointer on the Split icon in the upper-right corner of the window.

2. Hold down the mouse button.
3. Drag the horizontal split bar to the middle of the screen.
4. Release the mouse button. Right now you see the same text in both window panes. In the next section, you will look at different text in each pane.

The upper window pane shows the beginning of the file, and the lower pane shows the text that was displayed before you split the screen. The cursor is in the bottom pane.

USING WINDOW PANES

To move between window panes, you can use any of the following techniques:

- Press F6 to move to the next pane.
- Press Shift-F6 to move to the previous pane.
- Click the left mouse button inside the window pane.

You can scroll the text in each pane to see any part of the file. For example, if you are moving a paragraph, you may want to scroll the screen so that the text you want to move is in the top pane and the new location is in the bottom pane. Remember, each pane has its own cursor and scroll bars, so you can use any of your keyboard or mouse commands to move the cursor and scroll the screen.

In the bottom pane of your CLASS.WPS document, scroll to the last section of the document so that your screen looks similar to Figure 15.8. You should see the beginning of the document in the upper pane and the end of the document in the lower pane.

REMOVING WINDOW PANES

Window panes are not saved with the file, so one way to eliminate them is to close the file—the next time you open the file, the panes will be gone. But if you don't want to close the file yet, Works offers another way.

To remove window panes, you follow the same procedure you used to create them except that you drag the split bars into the window borders. For a horizontal window pane, you position the split bar as far up in the top window border as your ↑ or mouse pointer will go. For a vertical window pane, you drag the split bar into the left window border. Let's try it.

1. Choose Split on the Window menu.
2. Press ↑ until the split bar is in the upper window border. (The ruler temporarily disappears when the split bar is in the window border.)
3. Press Enter.

Or, if you have a mouse, follow these steps:

1. Place the mouse pointer anywhere along the split bar.
2. Hold down the mouse button.
3. Drag the split bar into the upper window border.
4. Release the mouse button.

You can now close the CLASS.WPS document.

SUMMARY

In this chapter you learned how to take advantage of one of Works's most powerful features: windows. Whether you have a mouse or just the keyboard, you can manipulate your windows in the following ways:

- Open up to eight files.
- Arrange the windows side by side so that all windows are clearly visible.
- Change a window's size.
- Move a window anywhere on the screen.
- Split a window into two or four sections.

EXERCISES

In the following exercises, you will practice arranging several windows on the screen. You can use the options on the Window menu or use the window icons, whichever method you prefer. Your goal is to make the window layout on your screen match the one shown in Figure 15.10. If you need help, refer to the sections indicated inside parentheses.

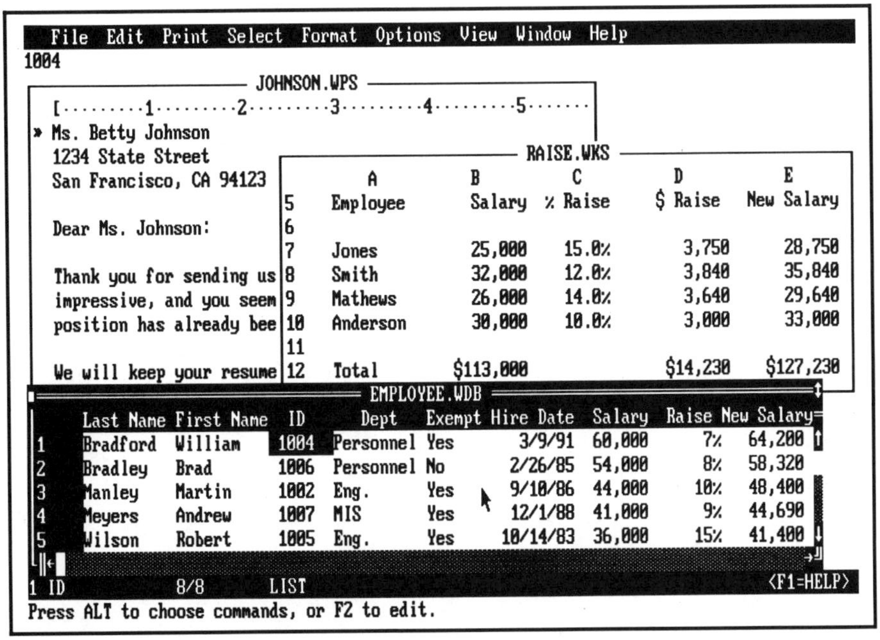

```
 File  Edit  Print  Select  Format  Options  View  Window  Help
1004
                          JOHNSON.WPS
  [.........1.........2.........3.........4.........5.......
» Ms. Betty Johnson
  1234 State Street                          RAISE.WKS
  San Francisco, CA 94123           A           B          C           D          E
                           5    Employee     Salary   % Raise     $ Raise   New Salary
  Dear Ms. Johnson:        6
                           7    Jones        25,000     15.0%       3,750       28,750
  Thank you for sending us 8    Smith        32,000     12.0%       3,840       35,840
  impressive, and you seem 9    Mathews      26,000     14.0%       3,640       29,640
  position has already bee 10   Anderson     30,000     10.0%       3,000       33,000
                           11
  We will keep your resume 12   Total      $113,000               $14,230     $127,230
                                EMPLOYEE.WDB
     Last Name First Name  ID     Dept    Exempt Hire Date  Salary  Raise New Salary
  1  Bradford  William    1004  Personnel Yes       3/9/91  60,000     7%   64,200
  2  Bradley   Brad       1006  Personnel No       2/26/85  54,000     8%   58,320
  3  Manley    Martin     1002  Eng.      Yes      9/10/86  44,000    10%   48,400
  4  Meyers    Andrew     1007  MIS       Yes      12/1/88  41,000     9%   44,690
  5  Wilson    Robert     1005  Eng.      Yes     10/14/83  36,000    15%   41,400
1 ID            8/8       LIST                                              <F1=HELP>
Press ALT to choose commands, or F2 to edit.
```

Figure 15.10: Three windows

1. Open three files. Figure 15.10 shows JOHNSON.WPS, RAISE.WKS, and EMPLOYEE.WDB, but you can open or create any three files.
2. Maximize the windows so that each window occupies the full screen. (See "Opening Multiple Files," page 417.)

3. Arrange the windows so that you can clearly see each window. (See "Arranging the Windows Automatically," page 423.)
4. Move and size the windows so they overlap as shown in Figure 15.10. (See "Arranging the Windows Manually," page 425.)
5. Close each of the files. (See "Closing Windows," page 422.)

AUTOMATING YOUR COMMANDS WITH MACROS

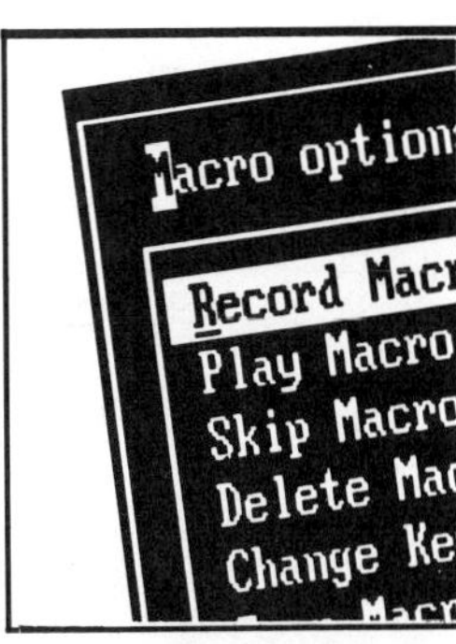

Imagine a hand coming out of your computer and typing on the keyboard for you. With Works's *macro* feature, you can automate lengthy command sequences so that all you have to do is press one or two keys (called your *playback keys*) and let Works take care of the rest.

Let's look at an example: printing. I normally save my file before I print, and this requires seven keystrokes: Press Alt (to bring up the menu bar), choose File, choose Save, press Alt, choose Print, choose Print again, and press Enter. Because of the number of keystrokes involved, I created a macro that does these commands for me when I press F4 (the playback key I assigned to the keystrokes). As you can clearly see from this example, macros are a big time-saver.

Sometimes you will want to create macros for commands that don't have a lot of keystrokes but are awkward to choose. For example, deleting a word requires that you press F8 twice and then press Del. These two keys are on opposite sides of the keyboard, so I created a macro that has the playback key Alt-W. This allows me to keep my hands on the keyboard when I delete a word.

Occasionally you will want to create temporary macros to help you with tedious editing jobs. Usually these tasks are one-time things, such as deleting five spaces from the beginning of 20 lines. It is unlikely you would want to keep this type of macro permanently, so after using the macro you can delete it.

Macros can do more than just automate your commands; they can automate your typing as well. For example, you can create a macro that types your signature block at the end of a letter or that types a standard paragraph that you commonly use in different letters.

The last section in this chapter, "Examples of Useful Macros," gives a bundle of suggestions for macros that you can use in each of the Works tools.

CREATING A MACRO

Macros are easy to create in Works because you can record your keystrokes just as you might record a voice or a song on a tape recorder. However, instead of recording on a cassette tape, you record into a special macro file named MACROS.INI. The equivalent of your tape recorder's record button is on a menu that you access with the Alt-/ key combination. The Macro

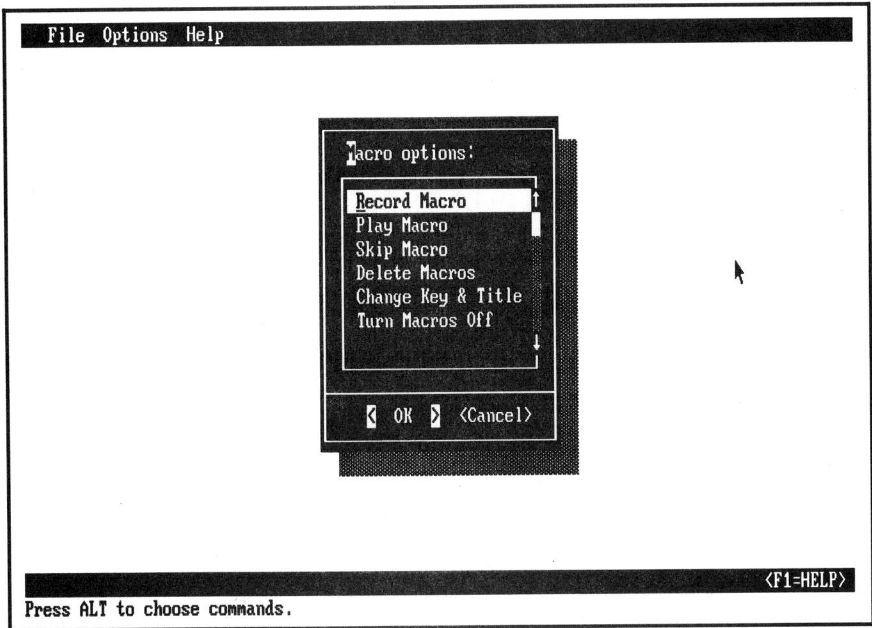

Figure 16.1: The Macro options dialog box

options dialog box is shown in Figure 16.1. To see this menu now, hold down Alt and press the slash (/) key.

Follow these general steps to record a macro:

- Set the scene for creating the macro. This could entail opening a file, positioning the cursor, or switching to a certain view. Do all the preliminary steps you would *not* want to record in the macro.
- Turn on the recorder by choosing Record Macro in the Macro options dialog box.
- Enter a playback key and a title. (See the section "Naming Your Macros" for a discussion of valid playback keys.)
- Enter the keystrokes you want to record. You *must* use your keyboard; mouse movement and clicks cannot be recorded.
- Turn off the recorder by choosing End Recording in the Macro options dialog box.

While the recorder is on, every key you press is recorded. If you make a mistake in the middle of the macro, you have two choices:

- Correct the mistake, and continue recording the macro. For example, if you chose the wrong menu option, press Esc to cancel the command and then choose the correct command.
- Turn off the recording, and restart the recording process.

One of the most common mistakes in recording a macro is to forget to turn off the recorder. If this happens, you will end up recording much more than you intended. Once you realize you have forgotten to turn off the recorder, you should turn it off and then record the macro again. When you assign the same playback key to a new macro, Works warns you that the key already has a macro and asks you whether you want to record anyway; choose OK.

Let's try the example I mentioned previously: a printing macro. Before you begin recording, open a short file, such as the JOHNSON.WPS document that you created in Chapter 3. Then, follow these steps to record a print macro:

1. If the Macro options dialog box is not already displayed, hold down Alt and press /.
2. Choose the Record Macro option.
3. Next to Playback key, press Ctrl-F4. *<ctrlf4>* is how Works shows the playback key.
4. Press ↓ or Tab to move next to Title, and type **Save and Print**.
5. Choose OK. The message *RECORD* appears in the bottom-right corner of the screen. Everything you type from here on is recorded—even mistakes!
6. Begin recording the keystrokes to save and print (don't use the mouse):
    - Choose Save on the File menu.
    - Choose Print on the Print menu.
    - Press Enter to choose Print, and your document will print.
7. Hold down Alt and press / to display the Macro options dialog box.
8. Choose End Recording. The RECORD message disappears.

PLAYING BACK A MACRO

To play back a macro you have recorded, you simply press the playback key you assigned to it. Now, use your print macro on a different file.

1. Close the current file.
2. Open another file (for example, RAISE.WKS).
3. Press Ctrl-F4. The following should happen:
    - The PLAYBACK message appears below the window.
    - The menus quickly flash on the screen as the macro executes the keystrokes you recorded.
    - Your current file prints.

Thus, anytime you want to save and print a file, you can press Ctrl-F4. Note that this macro assumes you have already assigned a name to the file you are saving and printing. If you run this macro without first giving the file a name, the macro will not work properly. (The file may not be saved in the proper format and will not print.)

What if you forget a macro's playback key? An option in the Macro options dialog box, Play Macro, lets you choose the macro from a list instead of pressing the playback key. Follow these general steps to play a macro when you can't remember the playback key:

- Press Alt-/ to display the Macro options dialog box.
- Choose Play Macro. A list of playback keys and titles is displayed. Figure 16.2 lists the macros you will be creating in this chapter.
- Highlight the macro name and press Enter (or double-click on the macro name). The macro will then be executed as if you had pressed the playback key.

Using the playback key is preferable to choosing the macro from a list because it requires fewer keystrokes (and that's the whole point—to save time and keystrokes). If you've created a lot of macros, it's a good idea to keep a list of your macro playback keys, and brief descriptions of them, next to your computer.

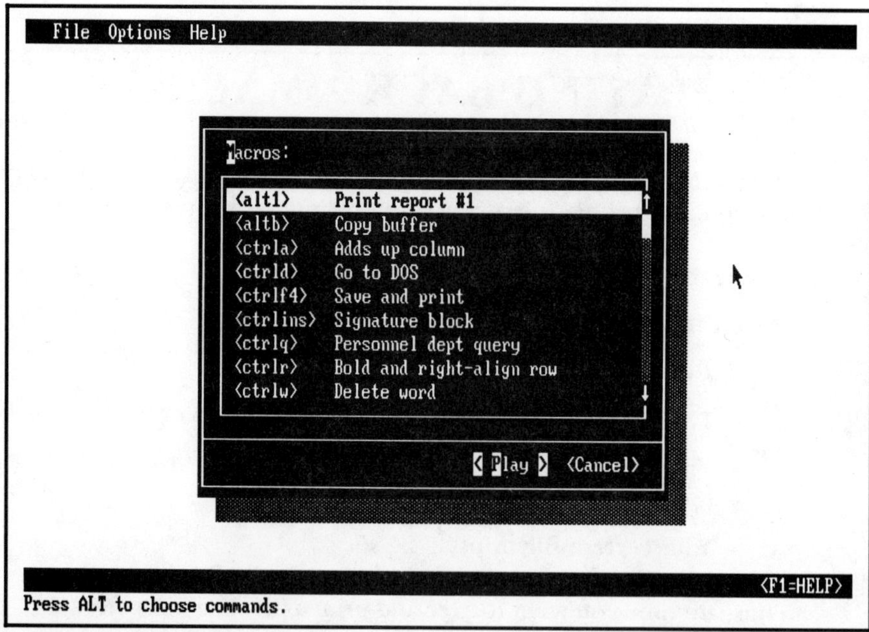

Figure 16.2: A list of macros

NAMING YOUR MACROS

There are many different keys you can use as playback keys. Here are a few examples:

- The function keys, by themselves or in conjunction with Ctrl, Shift, or Alt.
- Ctrl or Alt in tandem with the alphabet keys (A–Z), numeric keys (at the top of the keyboard only), or the special symbols (for example, [or]).

The only keys you cannot use as playback keys are Esc, Enter, →, ←, ↑, and ↓. These keys cannot name macros by themselves or in conjunction with Shift. However, these keys can name macros in conjunction with Ctrl or Alt. Using Alt with the arrow keys on the numeric keypad will *not* work; you can only use Alt with a separate cursor-movement keypad.

Even though Works lets you use your function keys and many different key combinations as playback keys, you should be careful that you don't use a key combination that is normally reserved for some other task. (Table 16.1 lists these combinations.) If you assign a playback key that is a Works key combination, the playback key takes precedence, and you won't be able to use the Works-defined command unless you disable all macros by choosing the Turn Macros Off command in the Macro options dialog box.

Table 16.1: Command Keys

KEY	COMMAND
Alt-C	Connect
Alt-D	Data
Alt-E	Edit menu
Alt-F	File menu
Alt-H	Help
Alt-O	Options
Alt-P	Print
Alt-S	Select
Alt-T	Format or Transfer
Alt-V	View
Alt-W	Window
Ctrl-B	Bold
Ctrl-C	Center
Ctrl-D	Print Date
Ctrl-E	No Lines Before Paragraph
Ctrl-F	Print File Name
Ctrl-G	Undo Hanging Indent
Ctrl-H	Hanging Indent
Ctrl-I	Italic
Ctrl-J	Justify
Ctrl-L	Left-align
Ctrl-M	Remove Indent on the Left
Ctrl-N	Indent on the Left
Ctrl-O	One Line Before Paragraph
Ctrl-P	Print Page Number

Table 16.1: Command Keys (continued)

KEY	COMMAND
Ctrl-R	Right-align
Ctrl-S	Strikethrough
Ctrl-T	Print Time
Ctrl-U	Underline
Ctrl-X	Normal Paragraph
F1	Help
F2	Edit
F3	Move
F4	Absolute Reference
F5	Goto
F6	Next Pane
F7	Repeat Search
F8	Select
F9	View Form/List, Calculate, Paginate Now
F10	Change Views
Shift-F3	Copy
Shift-F5	Next Name
Shift-F6	Previous Pane
Shift-F7	Repeat Copy/Format
Shift-F8	Select Column
Shift-F10	View Chart
Ctrl-F6	Next Window
Ctrl-F8	Select Row
Ctrl-semicolon	Insert Date
Ctrl-colon	Insert Time
Ctrl-equal sign	Subscript
Ctrl-plus sign	Superscript
Ctrl-spacebar	Plain Text

I suggest that you don't use Works key combinations for playback keys except for the commands you rarely use. For example, you probably frequently use the Ctrl-U keyboard shortcut for underlining, so you would not want to use it as a playback key. But if you never use Ctrl-S (Strikethrough), feel free to assign it to a macro. You definitely do not want to name a macro with a key combination that pulls down a menu (for example, Alt-F, which pulls down the File menu), because you will not be able to access that menu directly unless you use the mouse.

Because Works does not assign any function to F11, F12, and Ins, these keys make perfect macro playback keys. (Many keyboards do not have F11 or F12.)

EXAMPLES OF USEFUL MACROS

The following section lists macros that automate common Works tasks. It describes macros that can be used in any Works tool, in addition to tool-specific macros. You should consider these macros as a starting point for your own macro collection. Whenever you come across a command or a series of commands that requires too many keystrokes (only *you* can define how many is "too many"), you should record a macro.

Each macro discussion contains three parts:

- Preparation
- Record the Macro
- Play the Macro

The "Preparation" section describes the steps you must take before you record the macro. For example, it tells you which file to open or create, and where to place the cursor. Preparation is an important part of creating macros; if you don't "set the scene" correctly before you start recording, you may end up recording keystrokes that shouldn't be part of the macro.

The "Record the Macro" section lists the steps for turning on the macro recorder and naming your macro, in addition to the specific keystrokes to record. This section also suggests other variations of the macro, if applicable.

The "Play the Macro" section tells you what to do before playing the macro and how to invoke the macro.

GENERAL MACROS

There are many macros that can be used in any Works tool. You already recorded one of these general macros: printing. You will record two others: saving and going to DOS.

File Save

The File Save macro simply issues the Save command on the File menu. It doesn't take many keystrokes to save a file, but because you do it so often, you might want to assign a single key (for example, F11, F12, or Ins) as a playback key for saving.

Preparation

Open a file.

Record the Macro

1. Choose Record Macro in the Macro options dialog box.
2. Press F4 for the playback key.
3. Next to Title, type **Save file** and press Enter. You are now recording.
4. Choose Save on the File menu. (Remember, use your keyboard, not the mouse.)
5. Choose End Recording in the Macro options dialog box.

Play the Macro

Press F4.

Go to DOS

Works has a command that temporarily takes you to DOS so that you can give DOS commands (for example, DIR, CD, COPY) and then returns you to Works when you type *EXIT.* This command requires six keystrokes if you are not using a macro.

Preparation

If a menu is pulled down, you should press Esc to cancel it before recording or executing this macro. You can be in any Works tool or none at all. This macro's only requirement is that a pull-down menu cannot be displayed.

Record the Macro

1. Choose Record Macro in the Macro options dialog box.
2. Press Ctrl-d for the playback key. (If you frequently use Ctrl-d for the Print Date function, choose a different playback key.)
3. Next to Title, type **Go to DOS** and press Enter. You are now recording.
4. Choose Run Other Programs on the File menu.
5. Press ↓ to highlight *DOS prompt.*
6. Press Enter to choose the command.
7. Press Enter to choose OK. The DOS prompt (for example, C:\WORKS) appears.
8. Type **exit** and press Enter to return to Works.
9. Choose End Recording in the Macro options dialog box.

Even though you typed *exit* while the recorder was turned on, these keystrokes were not recorded because you were in DOS when you typed them.

Play the Macro

1. Press Esc if a pull-down menu is displayed.
2. Press Ctrl-d. The DOS prompt appears.
3. Type a DOS command, such as *DIR.*
4. To return to Works, type **exit** and press Enter.

WORD PROCESSOR MACROS

In this section, you will create three macros that you can use in the word processor tool. The first macro deletes a word, the second types a signature block at the end of a letter, and the third prints an address block from a letter on an envelope.

Delete Word

The Delete Word macro deletes the word that the cursor is on, regardless of where the cursor is in the word.

Preparation

1. Close any open files.
2. Open the JOHNSON.WPS file that you created in Chapter 3.
3. Place the cursor on any word.

Record the Macro

1. Choose Record Macro in the Macro options dialog box.
2. Press Ctrl-w for the playback key.
3. Next to Title, type **Delete word** and press Enter. You are now recording.
4. Press F8 twice to select the word.
5. Press Del to delete the selection.
6. Choose End Recording in the Macro options dialog box.

Play the Macro

1. Place the cursor on any word.
2. Press Ctrl-w.

If you have several consecutive words to delete, you can keep pressing Ctrl-w for each word.

Signature Block

The signature-block macro types the signature block (*Sincerely yours,* for example) at the end of a letter.

Preparation

1. Open the JOHNSON.WPS file, if necessary.
2. Delete the signature block at the end of the letter.
3. Place the cursor several rows below the last paragraph in the letter, where you want the signature block to appear.

Record the Macro

1. Choose Record Macro in the Macro options dialog box.
2. Press Ctrl-Ins for the playback key.
3. Next to Title, type **Signature block** and press Enter. You are now recording.
4. Type the appropriate closing (for example, *Sincerely yours* or *Yours truly*).
5. Press Enter five times.
6. Type your name (or the name of the person you are typing the letter for).
7. Press Enter.
8. Type your title (or the title of the person you are typing the letter for).
9. Press Enter.
10. If you are typing the letter for someone else, press Enter a few more times and type their initials, a colon, and your initials (for example, *JCS:rba*).
11. Choose End Recording in the Macro options dialog box.

If you type letters for several different people, you can create signature blocks for each person.

Play the Macro

1. Close the JOHNSON document without saving it.
2. Create a new word processor file.
3. Type the letter shown in Figure 16.3.

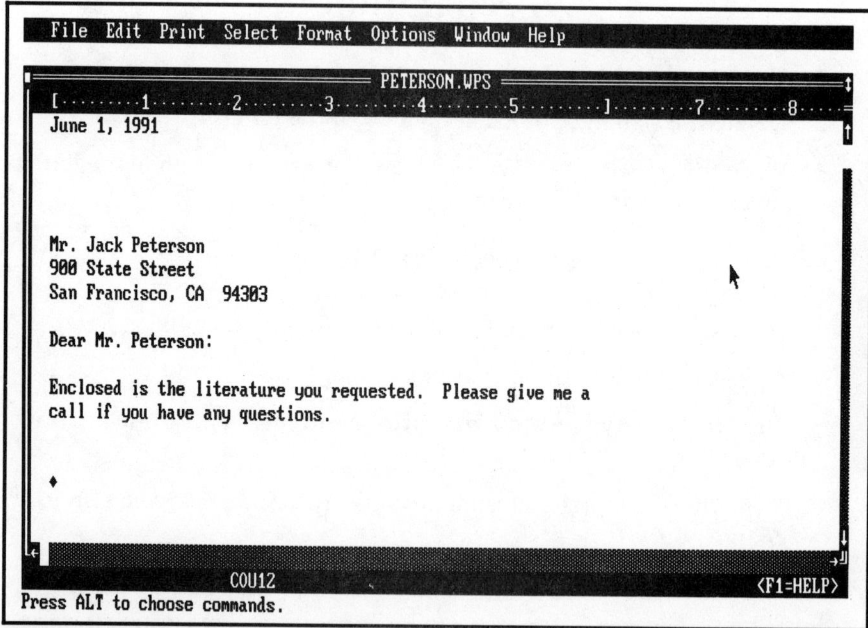

File Edit Print Select Format Options Window Help
PETERSON.WPS
June 1, 1991
Mr. Jack Peterson
900 State Street
San Francisco, CA 94303
Dear Mr. Peterson:
Enclosed is the literature you requested. Please give me a
call if you have any questions.
COU12
<F1=HELP>
Press ALT to choose commands.

Figure 16.3: A letter to type

4. Press Enter at the end of the letter to place the cursor where you want the address block to appear.
5. Press Ctrl-Ins. Your signature block is inserted.
6. Save the file with the name PETERSON.

Print an Envelope

The envelope macro prints the address block that appears at the top of a letter on an envelope. Printing an envelope is quite involved—but that makes it a perfect candidate for a macro. This macro copies the address block from the letter into a file that already has the correct page layout and margins for an envelope. It then prints the envelope and closes the file.

Preparation

1. Create a new word processor file that will hold the envelope settings.

2. Display the Page Setup & Margins dialog box and enter the settings shown in either Figure 16.4 or Figure 16.5. Figure 16.4 contains the appropriate settings for most printers; Figure 16.5 contains the settings for laser printers.
3. Save the file with the name ENVELOPE.
4. Close the file.
5. If necessary, open the document that you created in the last macro example, PETERSON.
6. Close any other open files. (Note: The macro will not work if you have additional files open.)
7. Turn on the printer, and insert an envelope.
8. Place the cursor at the beginning of the line containing the name (Mr. Jack Peterson).

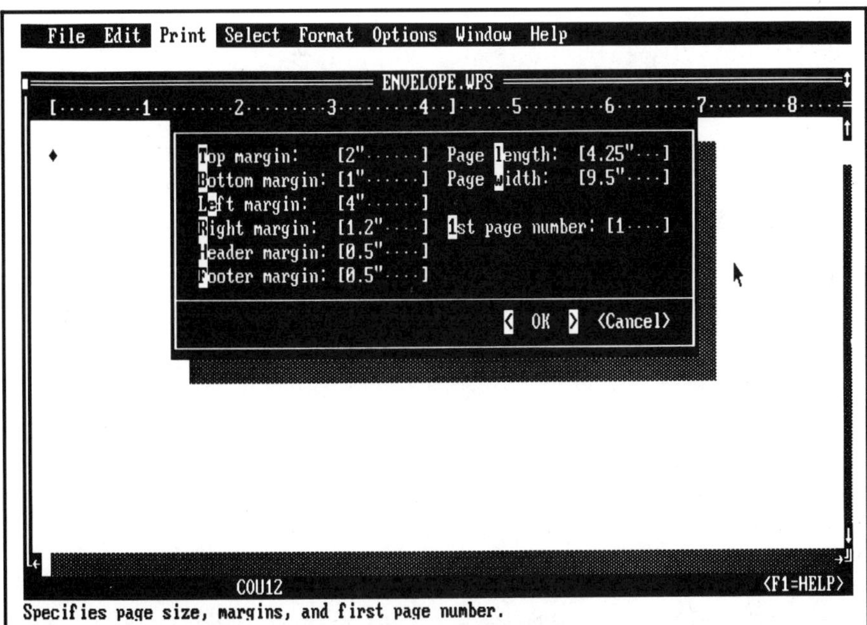

Figure 16.4: Envelope settings for most printers

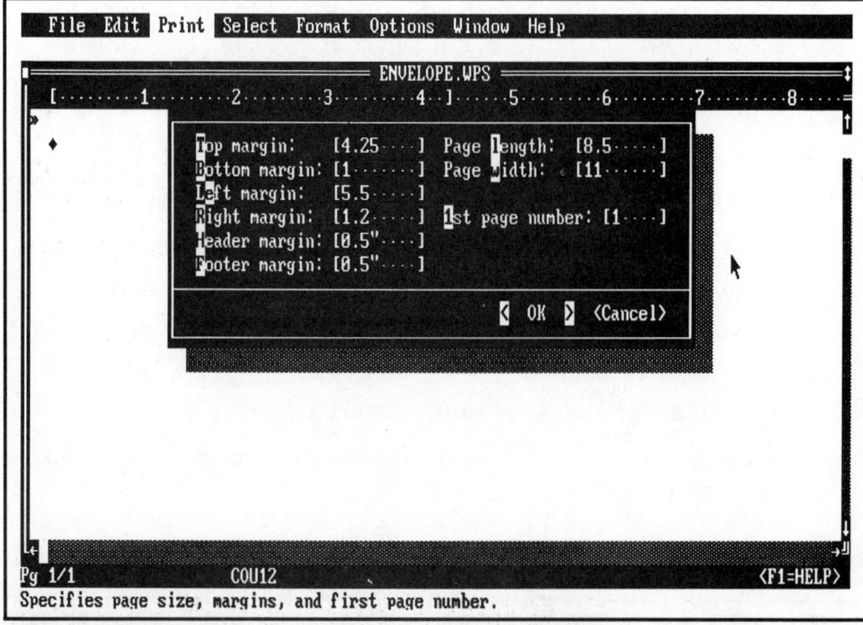

Figure 16.5: Envelope settings for laser printers

Record the Macro

1. Choose Record Macro in the Macro options dialog box.
2. Press Shift-F4 for the playback key.
3. Next to Title, type **Print envelope** and press Enter. You are now recording.
4. Choose Open Existing File on the File menu.
5. Type **envelope** and press Enter. (Don't use ↓ to highlight the name, because the position of the name on the list will change in the future, and then the macro will not work.)
6. Press Ctrl-F6 to switch back to the window containing your letter.
7. Press F8 to turn on Extend Selection.
8. Press ↓ four times to select the entire address block. Note that the fourth line is blank in this letter, but other letters may have an additional address line. You want the macro to select the entire address block, regardless of whether it has three or four lines.

9. Choose Copy on the Edit menu, or press Shift-F3.
10. Press Ctrl-F6 to go to the envelope window and press Enter. The address block is copied into the ENVELOPE file.
11. If you have a laser printer, you have to print the envelope in landscape orientation. Choose Printer Setup on the Print menu, highlight the landscape printer name (for example, HPLASLAN), and press Enter.
12. Choose Print on the Print menu.
13. Press Enter and the envelope prints.
14. Choose Close on the File menu, and press N to discard your changes. (You don't want to save the address block in the ENVELOPE file.)
15. If you have a laser printer, change back to your regular laser-printer name. Choose Printer Setup on the Print menu, highlight the regular laser-printer name (for example, HPLASER1), and press Enter.
16. Choose End Recording in the Macro options dialog box.

Play the Macro

For the envelope macro to work, you can have only one file open. If you have additional files open, the Next Window command (Ctrl-F6) in the macro will switch to the wrong window.

1. Close the PETERSON document.
2. Open the JOHNSON document.
3. Place the cursor at the beginning of the line containing the name.
4. Turn on the printer, and insert an envelope.
5. Press Shift-F4 to print the envelope.
6. Close the JOHNSON document.

SPREADSHEET MACROS

Because the spreadsheet tool doesn't offer keyboard shortcuts for formatting, you may want to create formatting macros. For example, you might want macros for adding style enhancements (bold, underline, italic) and numeric punctuation (dollar signs, decimal places, commas), as well as macros for changing cell alignment and column width. The first macro you will create changes both the style and alignment of a range of cells. The second spreadsheet macro you'll create automates the adding up of a column of numbers.

Format Column Headings

The Format Column Headings macro selects a row of headings, then goes into the Style dialog box and turns on right alignment and the bold style. To select the row of headings, the macro uses a keyboard shortcut mentioned in Chapter 7: Ctrl-→. This command moves the highlight to the last filled-in cell in the row. If you turn on the Extend Selection command (F8) before you press Ctrl-→, the entire row of column headings is selected.

Preparation

1. Create a new spreadsheet file.
2. Type the text and numbers shown in Figure 16.6. You will need to change the width of column A to 11. (Note: *Department* is in cell A1 and *Sales* is in B1.) The Profit column is a formula that subtracts Cost from Sales (for example, *=B3-C3.*)
3. Save the file with the name DPTSALES. It is very important that you save right now, because you will be closing the file without saving it after you record the macro.
4. Place the highlight on the first filled-in cell in the row of column headings (cell A1).

Record the Macro

1. Choose Record Macro in the Macro options dialog box.
2. Press Ctrl-r for the playback key.
3. Next to Title, type **Bold and right-align row** and press Enter. You are now recording.
4. Press F8 to turn on Extend Selection.
5. Press Ctrl-→ to move to the last heading.
6. Choose the Style command on the Format menu.

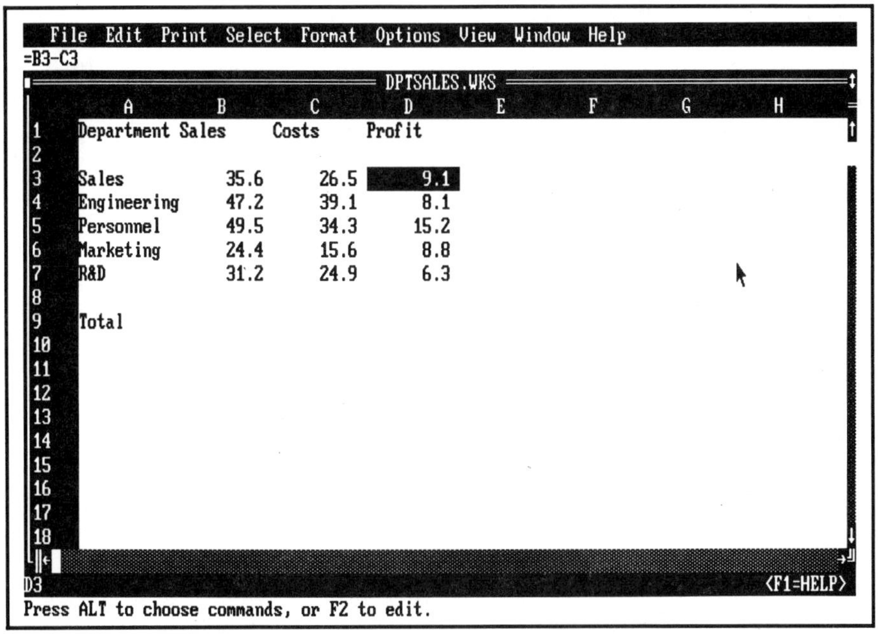

File Edit Print Select Format Options View Window Help
=B3-C3

DPTSALES.WKS

	A	B	C	D	E	F	G	H
1	Department Sales		Costs	Profit				
2								
3	Sales	35.6	26.5	9.1				
4	Engineering	47.2	39.1	8.1				
5	Personnel	49.5	34.3	15.2				
6	Marketing	24.4	15.6	8.8				
7	R&D	31.2	24.9	6.3				
8								
9	Total							
10								
11								
12								
13								
14								
15								
16								
17								
18								

D3 <F1=HELP>
Press ALT to choose commands, or F2 to edit.

Figure 16.6: A spreadsheet to create

7. Press R to turn on right alignment.
8. Press B to turn on bold.
9. Press Enter.
10. Choose End Recording in the Macro options dialog box.

If you have any blank cells in your row of column headings, the entire row will not be selected because the Ctrl-→ command uses blank cells as stop signs.

Play the Macro

1. Close the DPTSALES file without saving it.
2. Open the file again.
3. Place the highlight on the first filled-in cell in the row of column headings (cell A1).
4. Press Ctrl-r to format the headings.

Summing a Column

The macro that sums a column types the complete =SUM formula, including the range. It finds the beginning of the range by using the Ctrl-↑ command (it assumes there are no blank cells in the range). If the column has blank cells in the middle, you should not use this macro.

Preparation

1. The DPTSALES spreadsheet that you created in the previous macro should still be on your screen.
2. Place the highlight underneath the column of numbers you want to sum (on cell B9).

Record the Macro

1. Choose Record Macro in the Macro options dialog box.
2. Press Ctrl-a for the playback key.
3. Next to Title, type **Adds up column** and press Enter. You are now recording.
4. Type **=SUM(**
5. Press ↑ twice to move the highlight to the last number in the column.
6. Press F8 to turn on Extend Selection.
7. Press Ctrl-↑ to move the highlight to the first number in the column.
8. Type **)** and press Enter.
9. Choose End Recording in the Macro options dialog box.

This macro adds up any column of numbers, no matter how many numbers are in the column. As mentioned previously, the one exception is when the column has blank cells somewhere in the middle. If you want a macro that can accommodate blank cells, you have to create a macro that types only the beginning of the formula, *=SUM(,* and lets you finish the formula after you execute the macro.

Play the Macro

1. Place the highlight under the next column of numbers (on cell C9).
2. Press Ctrl-a to add up the column.
3. Go to the next column, and press Ctrl-a.
4. Save and close the file.

DATABASE MACROS

This section contains a couple of macros that are useful in the database tool. The first macro automates a database query, and the second macro retrieves and prints a database report.

Query

If you need to produce a list of certain records on a regular basis, you can create a macro to enter the criteria and perform the query for you.

Preparation

1. Open the EMPLOYEE.WDB database file that you created in Chapter 9.
2. If necessary, choose List on the View menu.

Record the Macro

1. Choose Record Macro in the Macro options dialog box.
2. Press Ctrl-q for the playback key.
3. Next to Title, type **Personnel dept query** and press Enter. You are now recording.
4. Press F5, the Goto key.
5. Type **Dept**, the name of the field you want to query, and press Enter. (This step places the highlight in the correct position before you go into Query view; it is important to do this now because it cannot be done in Query view.)
6. Choose Query on the View menu.

7. Choose Delete Query on the Edit menu to erase any existing criteria.
8. Enter your criterion: Type **Personnel** and press Enter.
9. Press F10 to display the list of records that matches the criterion. Your list should look similar to Figure 16.7.
10. Choose End Recording in the Macro options dialog box.

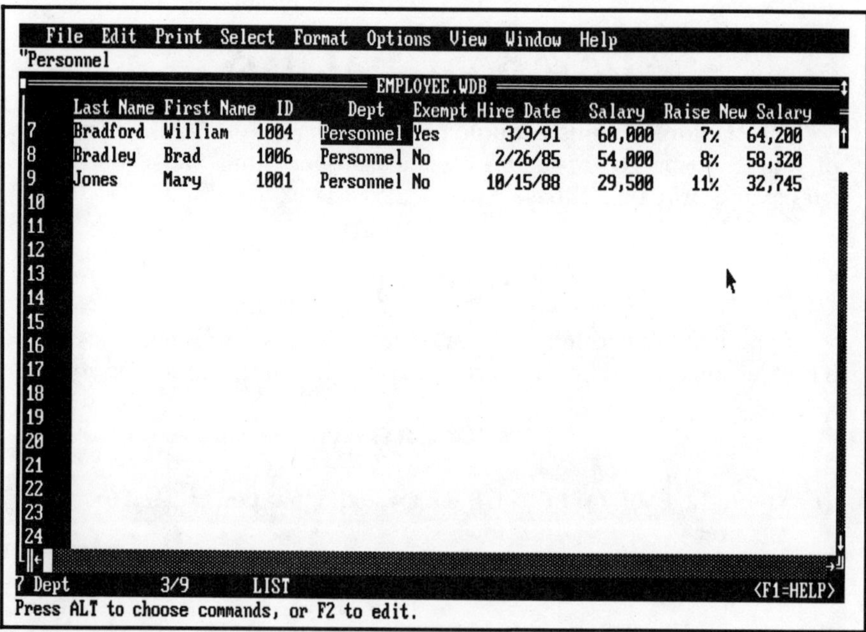

Figure 16.7: The list of records matching the query

If you like, you could carry this macro one step further and have it print the list.

Play the Macro

1. Choose Show All Records on the Select menu to cancel the query that you just performed and to display the entire database.
2. Press Ctrl-q to perform the query.
3. Before you record the next macro, choose Show All Records on the Select menu.

Report Printing

The Report Printing macro selects a report, goes into Report view, and then prints the report. This macro assumes you have already created a report for the database.

Preparation

1. If necessary, open the EMPLOYEE.WDB file.
2. Check the View menu to see that you have a report numbered *1*. You created this report in Chapter 11. Press Esc to clear the menu.
3. Turn on your printer.

Record the Macro

1. Choose Record Macro in the Macro options dialog box.
2. Press Alt-1 for the playback key. (Use the number on the top row of the keyboard, *not* on the numeric keypad.)
3. Next to Title, type **Print report #1** and press Enter. You are now recording.
4. Choose the report number, *1,* on the View menu.
5. Press Esc to clear the report from the screen.
6. Choose Print on the Print menu.
7. Press Enter to print.
8. Choose End Recording in the Macro options dialog box.

If you like, you can expand this macro so that it includes other steps before it prints the report. For example, you could have the macro sort the report by a specific field and/or perform a query to display certain records.

Play the Macro

1. Press F10 to return to List view.
2. Press Alt-1 to print the report.
3. Close the file.

COMMUNICATIONS MACROS

Both macros in this section help you save incoming data during a communications session. The first macro copies the buffer, and the second macro captures the data into a text file.

Copying the Buffer

This macro copies the communications buffer to a new word processor file so that you can save a record of your communications session.

Preparation

1. Close any open files.
2. Open a communications file.
3. Connect to a remote computer.
4. Disconnect from the computer.

Record the Macro

1. Choose Record Macro in the Macro options dialog box.
2. Press Alt-b for the playback key.
3. Next to Title, type **Copy buffer** and press Enter. You are now recording.
4. Choose All on the Select menu.
5. Choose Copy on the Edit menu (or press Shift-F3).
6. Choose Create New File on the File menu.
7. Choose New Word Processor.
8. Press Enter to copy the buffer into the new file.

At this point, you can turn off the recording so that you can edit and save the word processor file, or you can continue the macro so that it saves and closes the communications file.

9. Press Ctrl-Shift-F6 to move to the previous window.
10. Choose Save on the File menu.

11. Choose Close on the File menu.
12. Choose End Recording in the Macro options dialog box.

Play the Macro

1. Open a communications file, if necessary.
2. Close any other open files.
3. Connect to a remote computer.
4. Disconnect from the computer.
5. Press Alt-b to copy the buffer.
6. If desired, save the file with the name BUFFER.
7. Close the file.

Capturing Text

The Capturing Text macro turns on the Capture feature so that incoming text is saved into an existing text file. Since you must type a file name every time you capture text, it can be tedious to turn Capture on and off during a communications session. But with this macro, you can turn on Capture with your playback key and then turn it off by choosing the End Capture Text option on the Transfer menu.

Preparation

1. Create a word processor file.
2. Save the file with the name CAPTURE.TXT. (The file will be empty.) In the Save As dialogue box, press Alt-T to chose Text format. Choose OK to save without formatting.
3. Close this file.
4. Open a communications file.
5. Connect to the remote computer.

Record the Macro

1. Choose Record Macro in the Macro options dialog box.
2. Press Ctrl-8 for the playback key. (Use the number on the top row of the keyboard, not on the numeric keypad.)
3. Next to Title, type **Capture communications** and press Enter. You are now recording.
4. Choose Capture Text on the Transfer menu.
5. Type **CAPTURE.TXT** for the file name.
6. Press Enter to choose OK.
7. Press Enter to choose Append. (With this command, you tell Works to add captured text to the end of the existing file; every time you turn on the Capture feature, the new text will be appended to the old.)
8. Choose End Recording in the Macro options dialog box.
9. When you are ready to end the capture, choose End Capture Text on the Transfer menu.

I use this macro when I am logged on to HomeBanking. I play my macro to capture the text before HomeBanking displays a summary of my currenttransaction. (You will have to use the service awhile before you know exactly when this is.) After I have captured what I want, I choose the End Capture Text command on the Transfer menu. I repeat this process for every transaction.

Play the Macro

1. Make sure CAPTURE.TXT is *not* open.
2. Open a communications file and connect to a remote computer, if necessary.
3. When you want to capture text on your screen, press Ctrl-8.
4. To turn off Capture, choose End Capture Text on the Transfer menu.
5. Repeat steps 3 and 4 as many times as you want during the communications session.
6. Disconnect from the remote computer.
7. Open the CAPTURE.TXT file to see what you recorded.

SUMMARY

In this chapter you learned how to use Works's Macro feature to automate your commands and typing. In the process of learning how to create macros, you built yourself a useful collection of macros that you can use in the various Works tools. Several of the macros (the database macros in particular) are specific to the exercises, and you will probably want to delete them. To cancel a macro, use the Delete Macros command in the Macro options dialog box.

The exercises that follow will give you even more ideas for useful macros.

EXERCISES

In each of the following exercises, you will be given a brief description of a macro, and your goal is to record the macro and play it back successfully. If you need help, refer to the sections "Creating a Macro" and "Playing Back a Macro." Remember, before you create a macro, you need to "set the scene." This preparation usually means creating or opening a file and placing the cursor or highlight in the proper position.

1. Create a macro to change the right and left margins to 1″ each. This macro can be used in any Works tool, except the communications tool.
2. Record a macro to create a footer that prints the page number centered at the bottom of every page except page 1. The page number should have dashes around it (for example, *-2-*). This macro can be used in any Works tool, except the communications tool.
3. Create a word processor macro to delete the text from the cursor position to the end of the line. Hint: The macro should contain the following keystrokes:
   - *F8* to turn on Extend Selection.
   - *End* to highlight to the end of the line.
   - *Del* to delete the text.
4. Create a macro to insert a row in the spreadsheet tool.
5. Create a macro to format a row to Currency with no decimal places. The macro should select the row before formatting it. (See "Format Column Headings," page 454, for a hint on selecting a row in a macro.)
6. Create a macro to change the left and right margins to 0.5″ each and to select a small font size, such as Line Printer 8-point or Pica 8-point. This macro can be used in the spreadsheet and database tools.

INSTALLING AND STARTING WORKS

A

Before you can use Works, you must *install* the program on your computer. When you install Works, you copy the Works program disks and indicate what type of ***hardware*** (equipment) your computer has. The installation process takes about 15 minutes and is remarkably easy. Works provides a guided installation that essentially holds your hand through the entire process.

The first part of this appendix discusses what type of equipment you need to have in order to run Works. The next two sections help you install Works on a hard disk or a floppy disk—refer to whichever section applies to your computer. You will also learn how to modify your setup. The last section tells you how to start the Works program.

REQUIREMENTS

To run Works on your computer, you need the following hardware/software setup:

- 512K of memory (RAM).
- MS-DOS or PC-DOS, version 2.0 or higher.
- One of the following disk drive configurations:

  One hard disk (recommended for convenience and speed).
  Two 360K 5¼″ drives.
  One or two 1.2 Mb 5¼″ drives.
  One or two 720K 3½″ drives.
  One or two 1.44 Mb 3½″ drives.
- One of the following video cards: CGA, EGA, VGA, MCGA, Tandy 1000 Video Graphics, or Hercules. (A ***video card*** is the type of adapter your monitor is connected to; it is located inside your computer. If you don't know what type of video card you have, Works will suggest its "best guess" during installation.)
- A printer. (Works supports more than 200 different models.)

The following pieces of hardware are optional:

- A Microsoft or Microsoft-compatible mouse.
- A Hayes or Hayes-compatible modem.

You will also need the disks that came with Works. If you have 5 1/4" disks, your original disks should be labeled as follows:

Setup
Program
Accessories
Spell and Help
Thesaurus
Learning Works 1
Learning Works 2
Learning Works 3

If your copy of Works came with 3 1/2" disks, you should have the following original disks:

Setup and Learning Works 3
Program and Accessories
Spell, Help, and Thesaurus
Learning Works 1 and 2

The Setup disk that comes with Works includes an installation program that takes you through the complete process of copying Works to your hard disk or to a floppy disk. This process creates your *working copy.* The Setup program also asks you questions about what type of hardware you have. Before you begin the setup procedure, you need to know the following information about your hardware:

- Type of video card.
- Printer name and model (for example, Epson FX-80 or Hewlett-Packard LaserJet Series II).
- Whether you have printer cartridges. (*Cartridges* plug into the printer and determine what typefaces you can print. They are commonly used with laser printers.)
- Printer port (LPT1, LPT2, LPT3, COM1, or COM2). A *port* is the type of adapter that your printer is connected to. LPT1, LPT2, and LPT3 are *parallel* ports; COM1 and COM2 are *serial* ports. The

ports are sometimes labeled on the back of your computer. LPT1 is the most common.

- Whether you have a mouse.

If you can't find out any of the above information, don't despair—Works can usually correctly determine what type of video card you have and makes suggestions if you aren't sure of the answer to a question.

INSTALLING WORKS ON A HARD DISK

The Works program (including the thesaurus, speller, and accessories) requires approximately 1.4 million bytes (1.4 megabytes) of disk storage, and the tutorial consumes another 1 Mb. To see how much free space you have on your hard disk, do the following:

1. Turn on your computer.
2. Type **DIR** and press Enter. Look at the last line of the directory. Make sure the number of bytes free is greater than 1,400,000. If it's not, you will need to delete files to make room.

Assuming you have at least 1.4 Mb of free space on your hard disk, follow this procedure:

1. Put the Setup disk in drive A.
2. At the C:\> prompt, type **A:SETUP** and press Enter.

From here on, installing Works is simply a matter of reading the screens and answering the questions about your hardware. The screens are easy to read and self-explanatory.

When you come to the question about your printer, press PgDn to see additional printers. (They are listed in alphabetical order.) If your printer model is not on the displayed list, a couple of options are available to you. One option is to choose a generic printer name: "Standard Daisywheel" or "Standard or TTY printer." However, if you do this, you won't be able to take advantage of your printer's special features, such as underlining and bold.

Alternatively, you can choose the second option on the list, "Can't find my printer," and then read the accompanying message. (This screen is shown in Figure A.1.) To order the supplemental disk mentioned on this screen, or to see if Microsoft now supports your printer, contact Microsoft at the toll-free number listed on the screen. The supplemental disks also contain additional video-card files and a word processing conversion program. For information on using the Supplemental Setup disks, see "Modifying Your Hardware Setup" later in this chapter.

```
                M I C R O S O F T   W O R K S   S E T U P

  · If your printer is compatible with another printer in the list,
    you can go back and choose that other printer. To see if your
    printer is compatible, check your printer manual. If it is
    compatible, highlight "Go back and select another printer,"
    and press the ENTER key.
  · If your printer isn't compatible, or if you don't know, check
    the Conversion and Supplemental Setup coupon in your Works box.
    If you no longer have the coupon and are in the US, call the
    Microsoft Information Center at (800) 426-9400. If you no
    longer have the coupon and are not in the US, contact your
    local distributor or Microsoft subsidiary.

  Use the UP and DOWN keys to highlight your choice, and
  press the ENTER key.

               Go back and select another printer
               Continue without selecting a printer
               Cancel SETUP
```

Figure A.1: The "Can't find my printer" screen

After you answer questions pertaining to your monitor and printer, the Setup program asks you whether you want to copy the tutorial. The on-screen tutorial, called Learning Works, is designed to help you learn the Works program. If you like, you can use the tutorial as a supplemental learning tool to this book. Be aware, though, that Learning Works consumes an additional 1 Mb of hard disk space.

At this point, Works begins copying the floppy disks to the subdirectory you specified at the beginning of the setup procedure. The program will prompt you when you need to swap disks. After all the disks are copied, the Setup program asks a few more questions that deserve extra explanation.

Country: The country you choose affects the way Works displays numbers and dates. For example, if you choose France, currency is displayed in francs, commas and decimal points are reversed from the way they are used with numbers in the United States, and dates are displayed *en Francais.*

Mouse: If you answer *Yes* to the question about whether you have a mouse, the Setup program copies a file called MOUSE.COM into the root directory (C:\) and inserts a command in your AUTOEXEC.BAT file that runs the mouse program. (You will not see a question regarding a mouse if you already have a mouse installed.) What this all means is that every time you turn on your computer, the MOUSE.COM program is loaded. However, your mouse may use a program other than MOUSE.COM or require a different method for installation. If this is the case, you should follow the instructions that came with your mouse and answer *No* to Works's mouse question.

CONFIG.SYS: The CONFIG.SYS file contains your system configuration. For Works to run, this file needs to contain a line that says *FILES = XX,* where XX is a number greater than 15. If you know that your CONFIG.SYS file already contains this line, you can answer *No* to this question. Otherwise, choose *Yes.*

At the end of the installation, the Setup program displays several informational screens for you to read. You may then be instructed to reset your computer to activate the changes you made to the AUTOEXEC.BAT and CONFIG.SYS files. The quickest way to reset your computer is to press three keys simultaneously: Ctrl, Alt, and Del (Delete). Hold down Ctrl and Alt and keep these two keys depressed while you tap the Del key. This resetting process is similar to turning your computer off and on, but it's faster. It's sometimes called a ***warm boot*** because your computer is turned on (it's warm) when you do it. A ***cold boot*** is when you turn on the computer with the power switch.

INSTALLING WORKS ON A FLOPPY DISK SYSTEM

When you run the Setup program on a floppy disk system, Works creates a disk that you will use to run the Works program. This disk is called the Working Copy. The Works program is divided up into eight 360K 5¼″ disks or four 3½″ disks, because the entire program will not fit on a single disk. The capacity of your floppy disk drive determines how many of the Works disks can fit on your

Working Copy. If you have a 1.2 Mb or 1.44 Mb drive, everything except for the Thesaurus and Learning Works tutorial will fit on your Working Copy. But if you have a 360K drive, your Working Copy can only contain the main program; you will need to create separate disks for Accessories, Spell and Help, Thesaurus, and Learning Works. On a 720K drive, your Working Copy can hold the Program and Help files; you will need to create separate disks for Accessories, Spell, Thesaurus, and Learning Works.

Ideally, you should have two floppy drives so that you can keep the Working Copy in drive A and the disk you store your data on (called your ***data disk***) in drive B. If you have only one floppy drive, you will have to store the documents you create on your Working Copy, but it doesn't have much free space on it.

Before you run the Setup program, locate two blank floppy disks. One disk is your Working Copy, and the second disk is your data disk. You must prepare new disks before you can use them; this process is called *formatting*. Follow these steps to format your disks:

1. Insert your DOS disk in drive A.
2. Turn on the computer.
3. At the A> prompt, type **FORMAT A:** and press Enter.
4. Remove the DOS disk from drive A, and insert a blank disk.
5. Press Enter.
6. When the formatting procedure is finished, press Y and press Enter to format another disk.
7. Remove the formatted disk and label it *Working Copy.*
8. Insert a second blank disk, and press Enter to begin formatting.
9. When the second disk is formatted, press N and press Enter to end the formatting procedure.
10. Remove the formatted disk and label it *Data Disk.*

It's a good idea to *write-protect* your original Works disks before you continue. Write protection ensures that the originals will not be changed. To write-protect a 5¼" disk, put on a write-protect tab (a small piece of tape, usually silver or black, included in a new box of disks) so that it covers the notch on the disk. Figure A.2 illustrates where this notch is. On a 3½" disk, slide the small write-protect square so that the window is open. Figure A.3 points out the location of this square.

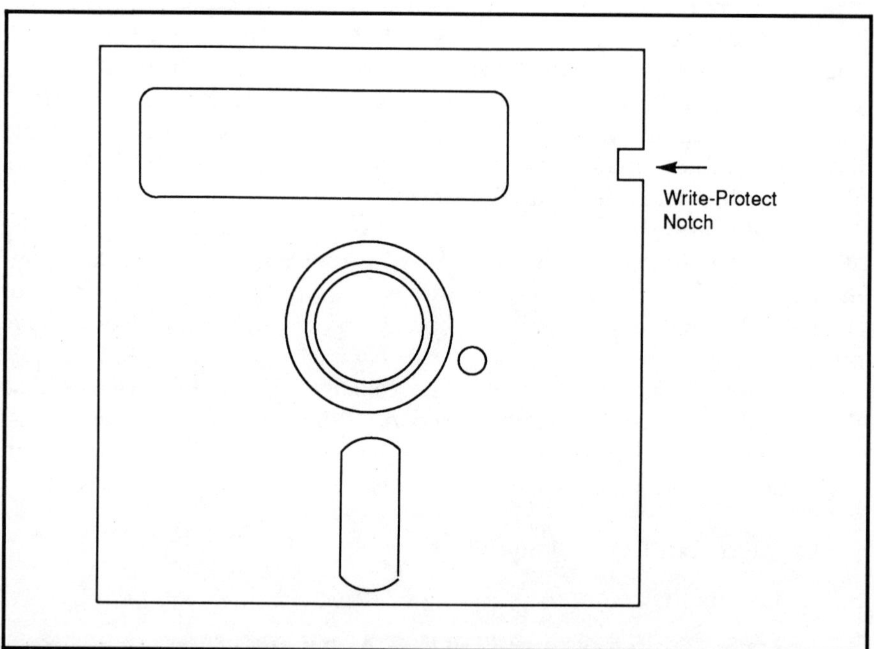

Figure A.2: The write-protect notch on a $5^{1}/_{4}''$ disk

CREATING THE WORKING COPY

You are now ready to use the Setup program to create your Working Copy.

1. Put the write-protected Setup disk in drive A.
2. Type **SETUP** and press Enter.

From here on, installation is simply a matter of reading the screens and answering the questions about your hardware. Intermittently, you will need to insert other disks, such as the Working Copy and Program disks, but the Setup program will let you know when you need to swap disks. The screens are easy to read and self-explanatory.

When you come to the question about your printer, press PgDn to see additional printers. (They are listed in alphabetical order.) If your printer model is not on the displayed list, a couple of options are available to you.

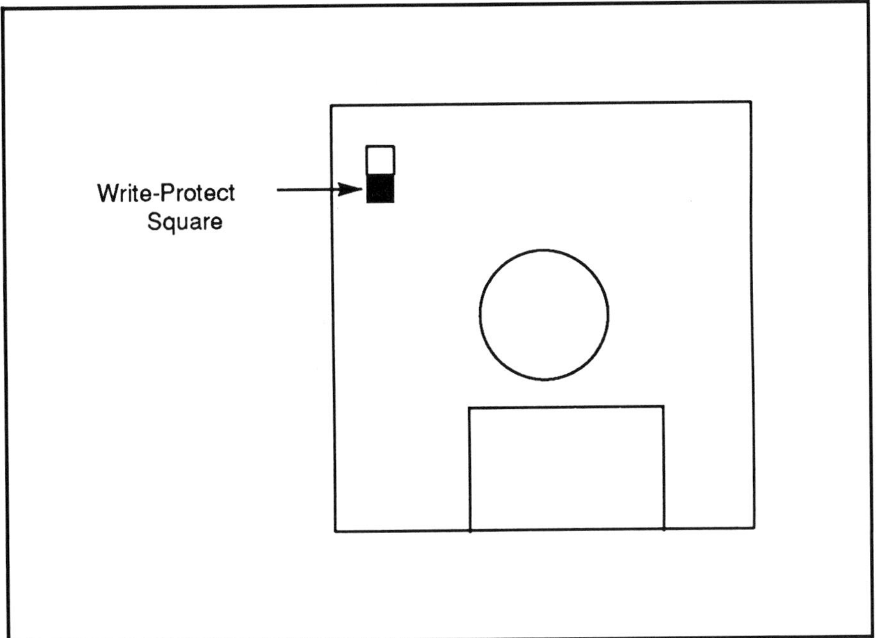

Figure A.3: The write-protect square on a 3½″ disk

One option is to choose a generic printer name: "Standard Daisywheel" or "Standard or TTY printer." However, if you do this, you won't be able to take advantage of your printer's special features, such as underlining and bold.

Alternatively, you can choose the second option on the list, "Can't find my printer," and then read the accompanying message. (This screen is shown in Figure A.1.) To order the supplemental disk mentioned on this screen, or to see if Microsoft now supports your printer, contact Microsoft at the toll-free number listed on the screen. The supplemental disks also contain additional video-card files and a word processing conversion program. For information on using the Supplemental Setup disks, see "Modifying Your Hardware Setup" later in this chapter.

Near the end of the installation, the program asks a few more questions that deserve extra explanation.

Country: The country you choose affects the way Works displays numbers and dates. For example, if you choose France, currency is displayed in francs, commas and decimal points are reversed from the way they are used with numbers in the United States, and dates are displayed *en Francais*.

Mouse: If you answer *Yes* to the question about whether you have a mouse, the Setup program inserts a command (MOUSE) in your AUTOEXEC-.BAT file that runs the mouse program. (You will not see a question regarding a mouse if you already have a mouse installed.) What this all means is that every time you turn on your computer, the MOUSE.COM program is loaded. However, your mouse may use a program other than MOUSE.COM or require a different method for installation. If this is the case, you should follow the instructions that came with your mouse and answer *No* to Works's mouse question.

CONFIG.SYS: The CONFIG.SYS file contains your system configuration. For Works to run, this file needs to contain a line that says *FILES = XX,* where XX is a number greater than 15. If you know that your CONFIG.SYS file already contains this line, you can answer *No* to this question. Otherwise, choose *Yes.*

At the end of the installation, the Setup program displays several informational screens for you to read. One of these screens lets you know which disks were not transferred to your Working Copy and instructs you to make backup copies of these disks. You should make a note of which disks you should back up. See "Backing Up Your Original Works Disks" for information on how to create backups.

You may then be instructed to reset your computer to activate the changes you made to the AUTOEXEC.BAT and CONFIG.SYS files. The quickest way to reset your computer is to press three keys simultaneously: Ctrl, Alt, and Del (Delete). Before you do this, insert your DOS disk in drive A. Then hold down Ctrl and Alt and keep these two keys depressed while you tap the Del key. This resetting process is similar to turning your computer off and on, but it's faster. It's sometimes called a *warm boot* because your computer is turned on (it's warm) when you do it. A *cold boot* is when you turn on the computer with the power switch.

BACKING UP YOUR ORIGINAL WORKS DISKS

The easiest way to create an exact duplicate of a floppy disk is to use the DISKCOPY command. Refer to the list of disks that you need to back up (the list you wrote at the end of Setup), and get out this number of disks. For example, on a 360K drive you need to make copies of the Accessories, Spell and Help, Setup, and Thesaurus disks, so you should get out four disks and label them appropriately. (They don't need to be formatted.) Optionally, you can make backups of the Learning Works disks. This on-screen tutorial is designed to help you learn the Works program, and if you like, you can use the tutorial as a supplemental learning tool to this book. If you want to use Learning Works, you will need to label additional disks.

To back up a disk when you have two disk drives of the same size (either two 3½" drives or two 5¼" drives), follow these steps:

1. Insert the DOS disk in drive A, if necessary. (Even though you are not copying the DOS disk, you need to insert it to use the DISKCOPY command.)
2. Type **DISKCOPY A: B:** and press Enter. The following message appears on the screen:

   Insert Source diskette in drive A:
   Insert Target diskette in drive B:
   Press any key when ready.

3. Insert the original disk in drive A and the blank disk in drive B.
4. Press any key.
5. When the copying process is complete, press Y to copy another disk.
6. Repeat steps 3–5 for each disk you have to copy.
7. Press N when you are finished.

To back up a disk when you have one drive, follow these steps:

1. Insert the DOS disk in drive A, if necessary. (Even though you are not copying the DOS disk, you need to insert it to use the DISKCOPY command.)
2. Type **DISKCOPY A: A:** and press Enter. The following message appears on the screen:

   Insert Source diskette in drive A:
   Press any key when ready.

3. Insert the original Works disk in drive A. Make sure this disk is write-protected.
4. Press any key.

5. When instructed, remove the original disk and insert the blank disk (called the *target* disk).
6. On some computers, you may need to swap the original and blank disks several times. Watch your screen carefully, and be sure to insert the proper disk.
7. When the copying process is complete, press Y to copy another disk.
8. Repeat steps 3–7 for each disk you have to copy.
9. Press N when you are finished.

MODIFYING YOUR HARDWARE SETUP

In the preceding sections you used the Setup program to create a working copy of Works on your hard disk or on a floppy disk and to specify your hardware configuration. As you will see in this section, the Setup program can also be used to modify settings in an existing copy of Works. If you get a printer or a mouse after installing Works, you can run the Setup program to tell Works about it. Also, if you choose not to copy the Learning Works tutorial when you initially install the program, you can use Setup to install it at a later date.

You *cannot* use Setup to change two of the settings you indicated in your initial installation: the country and the screen mode. (Note: You can change the screen mode if you tell Setup that you want to change your video card.) However, you can change these settings in Works by choosing Works Settings on the Options menu.

The procedure for modifying a working copy of Works is similar to creating a new one. The main difference is that Setup doesn't copy *all* the files—just the ones that have changed.

Turn on your computer and follow these steps, regardless of whether your Working Copy is on a hard disk or a floppy disk:

1. Insert the original Setup disk in drive A.
2. At the DOS prompt (A> or C:\>), type **A:SETUP** and press Enter.
3. When prompted, press Enter to continue.

4. Highlight *Modify an existing copy of Works 2.0* and press Enter.
5. Follow the on-screen instructions.

REMOVING A PRINTER

Although you can use the Setup program to add additional printers, you cannot delete a printer. The printers you add through Setup will appear in Works's Printer Setup dialog box forever—unless you delete the printer file from your Working Copy. Printer files have names that are similar to the name of the printer, and they always have the file extension .PRD. For example, the printer file for the Epson FX-80 printer is EPSONFX.PRD.

Follow these steps to delete a printer file:

1. Insert your Working Copy in drive A. On a hard disk, change to the Works subdirectory (for example, type **CD\WORKS**).
2. Type **DIR *.PRD** to list all the printer files. Locate the printer name that you want to delete.
3. Type **DEL name.PRD**, where *name* is the name of the printer file that you want to delete. Press Enter.

The first time you load Works after you delete the .PRD file, you will get an error message telling you that Works cannot find the file. Choose Cancel or press Esc to clear the message, and you will not be bothered with this error message again.

USING THE SUPPLEMENTAL SETUP DISKS

The Setup disk contains the most commonly used video cards and printers. If your hardware is not listed when you run the Setup program, it could be located on one of the Supplemental Setup disks, available from Microsoft. You can get these disks by sending in the Conversion and Supplemental Setup coupon in your Works box; if you have lost the coupon, call Microsoft at 800-426-9400. Once you have received these disks, run the Setup program with the Supplemental Setup 1 disk instead of the original Setup disk.

Follow these steps to use the Supplementary Setup disks:

1. Insert the Supplemental Setup 1 disk in drive A.
2. Type **A:SETUP** and press Enter.
3. When prompted, press Enter to continue.
4. Highlight *Modify an existing copy of Works 2.0* and press Enter.
5. Follow the on-screen instructions. You will see several additional selections for video cards and about three times as many printer choices.
6. Once you have answered all the questions, you may be prompted to insert the Supplemental Setup 2 disk or the original Setup disk, depending on which disk the video card or printer file is located.

STARTING WORKS

After you have run the Setup program, you are ready to start Works. The procedure varies depending on whether you are running Works from a hard disk or a floppy disk.

If you have a hard disk, follow these steps:

1. Turn on your computer, if necessary.
2. Using the CD command in DOS, change to the directory containing Works. For example, if you named the directory *WORKS* during the setup procedure, you should type **CD\WORKS** and press Enter.
3. Type **WORKS** and press Enter. After a moment you will see the Works opening menu.

To start Works on a floppy-based system, you use the Working Copy disk you created during the setup procedure. Follow these steps:

1. Insert your DOS disk in drive A and turn on your computer, if necessary.
2. Once you see the A> prompt, remove the DOS disk and insert the Working Copy in drive A.

3. Type **WORKS** and press Enter. After a moment you will see the Works opening menu.

Because the entire set of Works disks cannot fit on a single floppy, at certain points while using Works, you will be prompted to insert a different disk. For example, if you are in the word processor tool and give the command to check your document for spelling mistakes, Works may tell you to insert the Spell disk. You remove the Working Copy and insert the Spell disk. After spell-checking is finished, Works tells you when to reinsert the Working Copy.

DOCUMENTS FOR CHAPTER 5

B

APPENDIX B

This appendix contains the documents referred to in Chapter 5. The name of the document appears at the top of each page. You can create all the documents before you begin Chapter 5, or you can type the documents when they are referred to in the text.

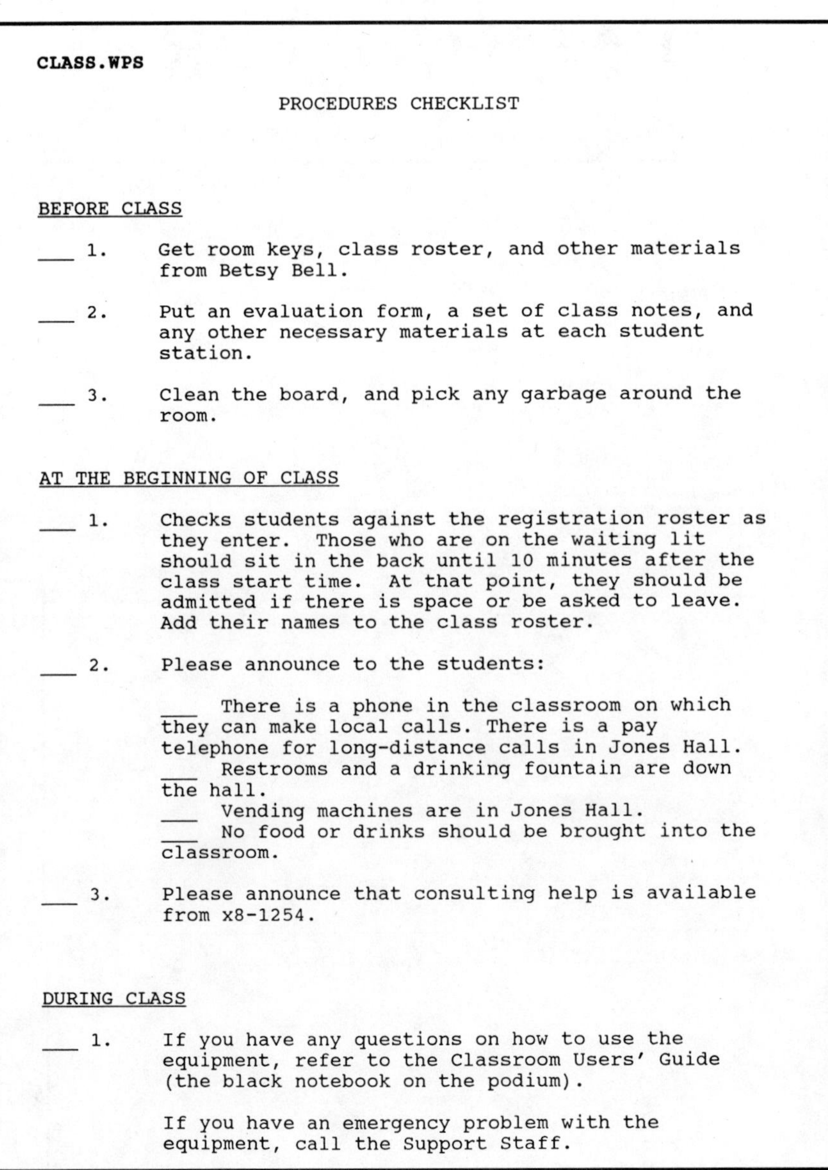

CLASS.WPS

PROCEDURES CHECKLIST

BEFORE CLASS

___ 1. Get room keys, class roster, and other materials from Betsy Bell.

___ 2. Put an evaluation form, a set of class notes, and any other necessary materials at each student station.

___ 3. Clean the board, and pick any garbage around the room.

AT THE BEGINNING OF CLASS

___ 1. Checks students against the registration roster as they enter. Those who are on the waiting lit should sit in the back until 10 minutes after the class start time. At that point, they should be admitted if there is space or be asked to leave. Add their names to the class roster.

___ 2. Please announce to the students:

___ There is a phone in the classroom on which they can make local calls. There is a pay telephone for long-distance calls in Jones Hall.
___ Restrooms and a drinking fountain are down the hall.
___ Vending machines are in Jones Hall.
___ No food or drinks should be brought into the classroom.

___ 3. Please announce that consulting help is available from x8-1254.

DURING CLASS

___ 1. If you have any questions on how to use the equipment, refer to the Classroom Users' Guide (the black notebook on the podium).

If you have an emergency problem with the equipment, call the Support Staff.

AT THE END OF CLASS

___ 1. Please ask each student to fill out an evaluation form.

___ 2. Fill out a Letter of Completion for each student who needs one.

PGBREAK.WPS

Ms. Mary Smith
ABC Company
789 Second Street
San Francisco, CA 94033

Dear Ms. Smith:

Enclosed are the prices you requested in your recent phone call.

Please give me a call if you have any questions. Thank you for your interest.

Sincerely,

Robert Johnson

PRICE LIST

PART NUMBER	DESCRIPTION	PRICE
AK5K-907	Liquid Paper	12.59/box
PI49-065	Post-Its	5.74/box
BP33-012	Ball Point Pens	17.99/box

CONTRACT.WPS

CONTRACT

A. NAME represents that he (she) is free to enter into this agreement.

B. NAME agrees that all rights to all projects developed under this agreement will belong to the company.

C. Any changes herein shall be made by mutual agreement in writing between the company and NAME.

PRICES.WPS

PRICE LIST

PART NUMBER	DESCRIPTION	PRICE
AK5K-907	Liquid Paper	12.59/box
PI49-065	Post-Its	5.74/box
BP33-012	Ball Point Pens	17.99/box

REQUEST.WPS

Mr. John Roberts
XYZ Company
4322 State Street
San Jose, CA 94122

Dear Mr. Roberts:

Enclosed are the prices you requested in your recent phone call.

Please give me a call if you have any questions. Thank you for your interest.

Sincerely,

Robert Johnson

SPREADSHEET AND DATABASE FUNCTIONS

C

Chapter 6 introduced you to two of the built-in functions that Works offers: SUM and AVG. As you saw, these functions provide you with a shortcut to entering what would otherwise be a long, complicated formula. For example, instead of having to type =(B5+B6+B7+B8+B9+B10)/6, you can type =AVG(B5:B10).

This appendix explains all 57 of the functions that can be used in the spreadsheet and database tools. These functions are categorized as follows:

FUNCTION TYPE	EXAMPLE
Statistical	Calculating the standard deviation or variance.
Mathematical	Rounding a number.
Logical	Determining whether something is true or false and displaying different results depending on the answer.
Lookup	Looking up a result in a table.
Date and Time	Entering the date automatically.
Depreciation	Computing an asset's depreciation expense using the straight-line method.
Cash-Flow Analysis	Calculating the amount of a mortgage payment.
Engineering	Computing a logarithm.

The following general rules apply to functions:

- They begin with an equal sign.
- They usually contain one or more *arguments.* An argument can be a number, formula, cell reference, or range. For example, the argument in the SUM function is the cell range to be totaled.
- If the function has more than one argument, a comma separates each one.
- Arguments are enclosed with parentheses. If the function doesn't have any arguments, you must still include parentheses.

STATISTICAL FUNCTIONS

You have already learned the two most common statistical functions: SUM and AVG. The other statistical functions are COUNT, MAX (maximum), MIN (minimum), STD (standard deviation), and VAR (variance). In the following examples, refer to Figure C.1.

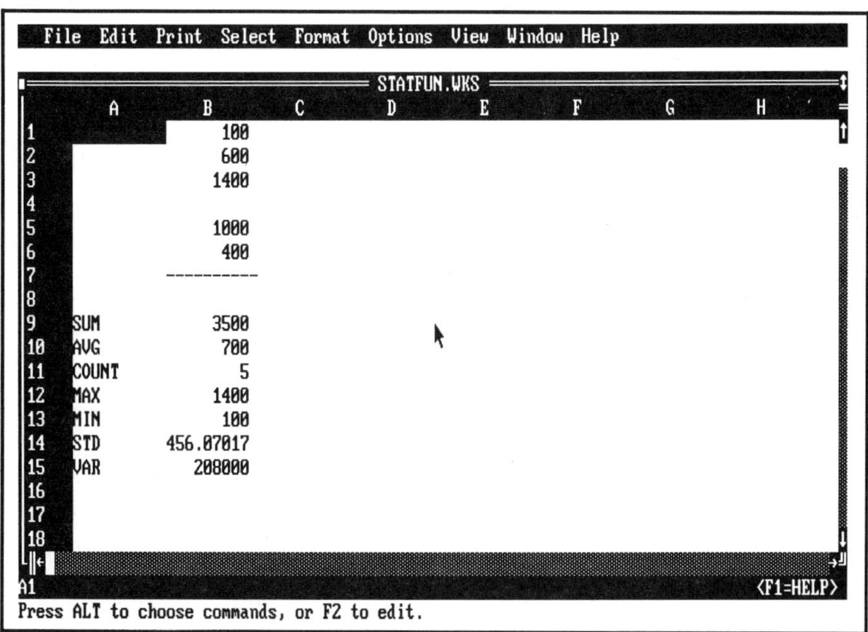

Figure C.1: Statistical functions

SUM: Totaling a Range

The SUM function totals the values in a range. You can use this function to add up a column or a row.

Syntax

= SUM(*range*)

Example

= SUM(B1:B6)

AVG: Averaging a Range

The AVG function totals the values in a range, counts how many values are in the range, and then divides the total by the number of values. Blank cells are not counted as values, but text cells are treated as zero values. Therefore, do not include a text cell in the average range.

Syntax

= AVG(*range*)

Example

= AVG(B1:B6)

COUNT: Counting the Number of Entries in a Range

The COUNT function counts the number of nonblank cells in the range. Each cell in the range that contains a number, a formula, or text counts as 1. Thus, if the range contains 25 cells, but 3 of them are blank, the count would be 22. This function can be used to count the number of records in a database.

Syntax

= COUNT(*range*)

Example

= COUNT(B1:B6)

MAX: Finding the Highest Value in a Range

The MAX function displays the largest value in a range. You can use this function to determine which person, product, or division in your company made the most money, or who had the highest score on a test.

Syntax

= MAX(*range*)

Example

= MAX(B1:B6)

MIN: Finding the Lowest Value in a Range

The MIN function displays the lowest value in a range. You can use this function to quickly pinpoint the product with the worst sales record.

Syntax

= MIN(*range*)

Example

= MIN(B1:B6)

STD and VAR: Measuring the Dispersion of a Range

Variance tells you how much the values in a range vary from the range's average. The standard deviation is simply the square root of the variance. The higher the standard deviation is, the more widely dispersed the values are.

Syntax

= STD(*range*)
= VAR(*range*)

Examples

= STD(B1:B6)
= VAR(B1:B6)

MATHEMATICAL FUNCTIONS

The mathematical functions manipulate your numbers in different ways. You can take a number and round it (ROUND), or find its square root (SQRT), absolute value (ABS), and integer value (INT). You can also generate a random number (RAND), and find the remainder after dividing two numbers (MOD).

ABS: Finding the Absolute Value of a Number

The absolute value is a number's positive value. The *value* argument can be a number, a formula, or a cell reference.

Syntax

= ABS(*value*)

Examples

FORMULA	RESULT
= ABS(– 20)	20
= ABS(– 20*5)	100

=ABS(20)	20
=ABS(C3)	30

[C3 = -30]

INT: Displaying a Number's Integer

An integer is a whole number without any decimal places—the numbers to the right of the decimal point are truncated without rounding the remaining number.

Syntax

=INT(*value*)

Examples

FORMULA	RESULT
=INT(125.67)	125
=INT(C3)	– 100

[C3 = – 100.456]

MOD: Finding the Remainder

MOD is an abbreviation for *modulus,* a mathematical term that refers to the remainder of the division of two numbers. For example, if you divide 7 (the numerator) by 3 (the denominator), the remainder (modulus) is 1.

Syntax

=MOD(*numerator,denominator*)

Examples

FORMULA	RESULT
= MOD(18,4)	2
= MOD(20,4)	0
= MOD(C3,D3)	3

[C3 = 23 and D3 = 5]

RAND: Generating a Random Number

The RAND function generates a random number between 0 and 1 (but not including 1). A new random number is generated each time the spreadsheet is recalculated. (The spreadsheet is recalculated every time you make an entry or press F9.) To get larger random numbers, you can multiply the function by a number like 100 or 1000, as shown in the second example below. To get whole random numbers, you can use the INT function, as shown in the third example below. The RAND function does not have any arguments, but you must still use the parentheses.

Syntax

= RAND()

Examples

FORMULA	RESULT
= RAND()	A random number between 0 and 1 (not including 1).
= RAND()*1000	A random number between 0 and 1000 (not including 1000).
= INT(RAND()*1000)	A random whole number between 0 and 1000.

ROUND: Rounding Off a Number's Decimal Places

The numeric formatting commands change the number of decimal places that are displayed, but they do not alter the cell's actual contents; thus, when you refer to a formatted cell in a formula, Works uses the actual number with all its decimal places. If you want a formula to use a rounded number in a calculation, you can use the ROUND function. In the function's arguments, you indicate which number or cell to round and the number of decimal places to round to.

Syntax

=ROUND(*value,number of decimal places*)

Examples

FORMULA	RESULT
=ROUND(200.54,0)	201
=ROUND(A4,0)+ROUND(B4,0)	2

[A4 = 1.4 and B4 = 1.4 (formatted to zero decimal places). Note that without rounding, the screen would show 1 plus 1 equals 3.]

SQRT: Calculating the Square Root of a Number

The SQRT function calculates the square root of a number, formula, or cell reference. The value must be positive.

Syntax

=SQRT(*value*)

Examples

FORMULA	RESULT
= SQRT(25)	5
= SQRT(A3 * 20)	10

[A3 = 5]

LOGICAL FUNCTIONS

With the logical functions, you can look at the contents of a cell and display different results depending on what the cell contains. The main logical function is *IF;* the other functions are usually arguments in IF formulas.

IF: Handling Multiple Responses in One Formula

The IF function places different responses in a cell depending on whether a condition is true or false. A condition uses the following logical operators:

OPERATOR	DESCRIPTION
=	Equal to
>	Greater than
> =	Greater than or equal to
<	Less than
< =	Less than or equal to
<>	Not equal to

The IF function's condition argument uses one of the above operators to compare two values; the values can be numbers typed into the formula, cell references, or field names in a database. Examples of valid conditions are *B7>C7, B7 = 100,* and *sales>50000.*

The IF function has three arguments. The ***condition*** tests to see whether something is true or false. If the condition is true, the ***true value*** is displayed in the cell. But if the condition is false, the ***false value*** is displayed. Use the IF function whenever you have more than one possible answer in a cell.

Syntax

= IF(*condition,true value,false value*)

Example

= IF(actual>quota,10%,0)

This formula might be entered into a salesperson's bonus field in a database. What this formula says is, "If the salesperson's actual sales are greater than the quota (meaning the condition is true), then display 10% in the bonus field. Otherwise, if actual sales are *not* greater than the quota (meaning the condition is false), then display 0 in the field."

NA: When Data Are Not Available

Sometimes while you are entering data in a spreadsheet, you discover that an important number is missing. Rather than leaving the cell blank, you can enter the Not Available function, = NA(). If you leave the cell blank, your results may be misleading. But if you enter the NA function, any formula that uses the unavailable data also displays *N/A,* until the = NA() is replaced with the actual number.

Syntax

= NA()

Example

= NA()

ISNA: Determining If Data Are Unavailable

The ISNA function checks to see whether a cell contains N/A. If the tested cell contains N/A, *1* is displayed in the cell; otherwise, *0* is displayed. In other words, 1 signifies true and 0 signifies false. A true result occurs if the cell contains =NA() or a formula that references a cell containing =NA(). ISNA is most frequently used as a condition argument in an IF function. (See the example below.)

Syntax

=ISNA(*cell*)

Example

=IF(ISNA(A5),10,5)

This formula reads as follows: "If A5 displays N/A, then display 10. If A5 displays anything other than N/A, display 5."

ERR: Flagging an Error

The ERR function displays *ERR* in a cell; it doesn't use any arguments. Any formula that references the cell containing the error message also displays ERR until the =ERR() is removed. ERR is frequently used as a *true value* or *false value* in an IF formula. You can use it to flag an error situation—for example, when a cell contains a number outside of an acceptable range. (See the example below.)

Syntax

=ERR()

Example

=IF(B20>30000,ERR(),B20*1.07)

Assume that cell B20 contains a total invoice amount and that 30,000 is the credit limit. This formula reads as follows: "If cell B20 is greater than

30,000, then display ERR. Otherwise, if B20 is not greater than 30,000, then multiply B20 by 1.07." This formula calls attention to any situation where a customer's order exceeds the credit limit.

ISERR: Determining If an Error Exists

The ISERR function checks to see whether a cell contains ERR. If the tested cell contains ERR, *1* is displayed in the cell; otherwise, *0* is displayed. In other words, 1 signifies true and 0 signifies false. A true result occurs if the cell contains =ERR() or a formula that references a cell displaying ERR(). ISERR is most frequently used as a condition argument in an IF function. (See the example below.)

Syntax

=ISERR(*cell*)

Example

=IF(ISERR(A5/A6),0,A5/A6)

The purpose of this formula is to prevent an error message from appearing if a cell is divided by zero. If A6 contains a zero, the division of A5 by A6 will produce an ERR. This formula checks to see if A5/A6 results in an error. If it does, a zero is displayed. Otherwise, the result of A5/A6 is displayed.

TRUE and FALSE: Finding the Truth

The TRUE function displays a 1, and the FALSE function displays a 0. Neither function uses any arguments. Both functions can be used in IF formulas to see whether you entered a complex condition correctly.

Syntax

=TRUE()
=FALSE()

Example

= IF(A5/50 >A6 * 100,TRUE(),FALSE())

This formula displays a 1 if the condition is true or a 0 if the condition is false.

LOOKUP FUNCTIONS

Works offers a variety of ways to look up information: VLOOKUP (vertical lookup), HLOOKUP (horizontal lookup), INDEX (horizontal and vertical lookup), and CHOOSE (lookup in a list). Think of these functions as ways to automatically enter data. Instead of referring to a table in a book or on a piece of paper, you can refer to a table in the spreadsheet and have Works look up the value for you.

VLOOKUP: Looking Up Values Indexed by Columns

An income-tax table is the perfect example of a vertical lookup table. You locate your income in the first column of the table. Then, you go across to the column associated with your filing status (single, married filing jointly, etc.) and find your tax liability.

The VLOOKUP function has three arguments: lookup value, table range, and column number. The *lookup value* is the number you are looking up in the table (for example, your income). The *table range* is where the lookup table is entered in the spreadsheet. The *column number* refers to which column the answer is located in; counting begins with 0 (the first column's number is 0, the second column's number is 1, etc.). For example, if your filing status is single, the column number is 1; if you are married filing jointly, the column number is 2.

The first column of the vertical lookup table must be in ascending order. If the lookup value does not exactly match an entry in the first column, the largest number that is less than the lookup value is chosen.

Syntax

= VLOOKUP(*lookup value,table range,column number*)

Example

Figure C.2 displays the spreadsheet and lookup table for this example. The vertical lookup table is shown on the right side of the screen in the figure.

=VLOOKUP(B3,$F$3:$G$9,1)

This formula tells Works to look up the contents of cell B3 (15,000) in the lookup table (F3:G9) and find and display the discount in the first column. Notice the dollar signs in the table range—these absolute reference symbols let you copy the formula without changing the table range references. (See Chapter 7 for more information on absolute references.)

HLOOKUP: Looking Up Values Indexed by Rows

The only difference between horizontal and vertical lookups is in how the table is organized. In a vertical lookup, Works looks *down the first*

```
  File  Edit  Print  Select  Format  Options  View  Window  Help
=VLOOKUP(B3,$F$3:$G$9,1)
                                   LOOKUP.WKS
              A            B       C      D      E        F       G        H        I
1   Customer          Sales  Discount   :   Vertical   Sales  Discount
2                                       :   Lookup:
3   Anderson & Sons  15,000        2%   :              10,000       0%
4   Pete & Pete      30,000        8%   :              15,000       2%
5   Johnson Bros.    12,000        0%   :              20,000       4%
6   Bascom Inc.      40,000       12%   :              25,000       6%
7                                       :              30,000       8%
8                                       :              35,000      10%
9                                       :              40,000      12%
10                                      :--------------------------
11
12  ----------------------------------------------------------------------
13  Horizontal Lookup:
14
15          10,000  15,000  20,000  25,000  30,000  35,000  40,000
16              0%      2%      4%      6%      8%     10%     12%
17
18
C3                                                                 <F1=HELP>
Press ALT to choose commands, or F2 to edit.
```

Figure C.2: Lookup tables

column to locate the lookup value. In a horizontal lookup, Works looks *across the first row* to locate the lookup value.

The HLOOKUP function has three arguments: lookup value, table range, and row number. The *lookup value* is the number you are looking up in the table. The *table range* is where the lookup table is entered in the spreadsheet. The *row number* refers to which row the answer is located in; counting begins with 0.

The first row of the horizontal lookup table must be in ascending order. If the lookup value does not exactly match an entry in the first row, the largest number that is less than the lookup value is chosen.

Syntax

=HLOOKUP(*lookup value,table range,row number*)

Example

Figure C.2 displays the spreadsheet and lookup table for this example. The horizontal lookup table is shown at the bottom of the screen in the figure.

=HLOOKUP(B3,$A$15:$G$16,1)

This formula tells Works to look up the contents of cell B3 (15,000) in the lookup table (A15:G16) and find and display the discount in the first row. Notice the dollar signs in the table range—these absolute reference symbols let you copy the formula without changing the table range references. (See Chapter 7 for more information on absolute references.)

INDEX: Looking Up Values Indexed by Rows and Columns

The INDEX function allows you to look up values horizontally and vertically. The INDEX function has three arguments: table range, column number, and row number. The *table range* is where the lookup table is entered in the spreadsheet. The *column number* refers to which column the answer is located in; counting begins with 0 (the first column's number is 0, the second column's number is 1, etc.). The *row number* refers to which row the answer is located in; counting begins with 0. The result of this function is the value in the cell at the intersection of the column and row numbers.

The first row and first column of the lookup table must be numbered beginning with 1.

Syntax

= INDEX(*table range,column number,row number*)

Example

Figure C.3 displays the spreadsheet and index table for this example. The index is shown at the right side of the screen in the figure.

File Edit Print Select Format Options View Window Help

=INDEX($F$1:$H$11,B3,C3)

INDEX.WKS

	A	B	C	D	E	F	G	H
1	Employee	Code	Yrs.	Rate		Index:	1	2
2						1	20	15
3	Johnson	2	5	56		2	30	23
4	Jones	2	4	38		3	40	30
5	Smith	1	2	30		4	50	38
6	Anderson	1	7	110		5	75	56
7						6	100	75
8						7	110	83
9						8	115	86
10						9	120	90
11						10	125	94
12								
13								
14								
15								
16								
17								
18								

D3 <F1=HELP>

Press ALT to choose commands, or F2 to edit.

Figure C.3: Index table

= INDEX($F$1:$H$11,B3,C3)

This formula tells Works to look up the contents of cells B3 and C3 in the lookup table (F1:H11) and find and display the value at their intersection. Because B3 contains 2, Works looks in the column numbered 2 at the top; because C3 contains 5, Works looks in the row numbered 5 at the left. The value at the intersection of the table's column 2 and row 5 is 56. Notice the dollar signs in the table range—these absolute reference symbols let you copy the formula without changing the table range references. (See Chapter 7 for more information on absolute references.)

CHOOSE: Looking Up Values in a List

The HLOOKUP, VLOOKUP, and INDEX functions all perform their lookups in a table. The CHOOSE function looks up a value from a list of values entered as arguments in the formula (each value in the list is separated by a comma). Though the list can contain as many values as you want, you will probably use this function if you have only a few values to look up. If you have more than a few values to look up, use one of the table functions.

The first argument in the CHOOSE function is *choice*. The choice indicates which of the values in the list you want to choose. The choice of the first value is 0, the second value is 1, the third value is 2, and so on.

Syntax

=CHOOSE(*choice,value 0,value 1,value 2,value n*)

Example

=CHOOSE(A3,15%,20%,25%)

If A3 contains 1, the result of this formula is 20%. If A3 contains 0, the result is 15%.

COLS and ROWS: Counting the Number of Columns and Rows

The COLS function counts the number of columns in a range; the ROWS function counts the number of rows. The *range* argument can be expressed as cell references or as a name. You can use these functions to determine the size of a print range.

Syntax

= COLS(*range*)
= ROWS(*range*)

Examples

FORMULA	RESULT
= COLS(A4:L98)	12
= ROWS(A4:L98)	95

DATE AND TIME FUNCTIONS

Works offers a variety of functions specific to dates and times. You can use the NOW and DATE functions to enter dates and the TIME function to enter time. The DAY, MONTH, YEAR, MINUTE, and SECOND functions allow you to manipulate specific parts of the date or time.

Dates and times are actually stored as numbers so that you can do calculations with them. For example, you can subtract two dates to see how many days have passed. The number associated with a date is the number of days that have passed since December 31, 1899. The number associated with a time is the fractional portion of the day. For example, at 6 a.m., a quarter of the day has passed, so its time number is 0.25.

DATE: Entering a Date

The easiest way to enter a date is to type it in. For example, to enter the date May 15, 1991, type *5/15/91*. Do not type the date with dashes (for example, 5-15-91), because it will be entered as text, not as a number. Another way to enter a date is to use the DATE function. This function displays the date number until you format the cell to Time/Date (see the example below). Because it requires more work than typing the date directly, there really is little need for this function.

Syntax

= DATE(*year,month,day*)

Example

FORMULA	RESULT	AFTER FORMATTING
=DATE(91,5,15)	33373	5/15/91

NOW: Entering the Current Date and Time

You use the NOW function to display the current date or time. This function displays a number until you format the cell to either a date or time format. The NOW function is dynamic and is updated every time you open a file. This function is only as accurate as your computer's system clock; so, if your clock is off, NOW will be off also.

Syntax

=NOW()

Example

It is noon on May 15, 1991.

FUNCTION	RESULT	DATE FORMAT	TIME FORMAT
=NOW()	33373.5	5/15/91	12:00 PM

Note: The integer portion (33373) represents the date; the decimal place (.5) represents the time.

DAY: Displaying the Day of the Month

The DAY function extracts the day of the month from a date and displays the day as a number between 1 and 31. The *date* argument can be a cell containing a date or a date enclosed in single quote marks.

Syntax

=DAY(*date*)

Examples

FORMULA	RESULT
=DAY('5/15/91')	15
=DAY(A5)	7

[A5 = 10/7/92]

MONTH: Displaying the Month

The MONTH function extracts the month from a date and displays the month as a number between 1 and 12. The *date* argument can be a cell containing a date or a date enclosed in single quote marks. This function can also be used to query a date field in a database. For example, to find all dates in the month of June, the condition would be =MONTH()=6.

Syntax

=MONTH(*date*)

Examples

FORMULA	RESULT
=MONTH('5/15/91')	5
=MONTH(A5)	10

[A5 = 10/7/92]

YEAR: Displaying the Year

The YEAR function extracts the year from a date and displays the year as a double-digit number (for example, *92* represents 1992). The *date* argument can be a cell containing a date or a date enclosed in single quote marks. This function can also be used to query a date field in a database. For example, to find all dates in the year 1990, the condition would be =YEAR()=90.

Syntax

= YEAR(*date*)

Examples

FORMULA	RESULT
= YEAR('5/15/91')	91
= YEAR(A5)	92

[A5 = 10/7/92]

TIME: Entering a Time

The easiest way to enter a time is to type it in. For example, to enter the time nine o'clock in the morning, type *9:00* or *9 AM.* Another way to enter a time is to use the TIME function. This function displays the time number until you format the cell to Time/Date (see the example below). Because it requires more work than typing the time directly, there really is little need for this function.

The time should be entered according to a 24-hour clock. Thus, the hour of 2 PM is 14, not 2. Even though you may not be concerned with seconds, you still must enter something (for example, a zero) for the *second* argument.

Syntax

= TIME(*hour,minute,second*)

Examples

FORMULA	RESULT	AFTER FORMATTING
= TIME(9,30,0)	.39588333	9:30 AM
= TIME(15,45,30)	.6565972	3:45 PM

HOUR: Displaying the Hour

The HOUR function extracts the hour from a given time and displays the hour as a number between 0 (midnight) and 23 (11 PM). The *time* argument can be a cell containing a time or a time enclosed in single quote marks.

Syntax

= HOUR(*time*)

Examples

FUNCTION	RESULT
= HOUR('9:30:0')	9
= HOUR(A5)	15

[A5 = 3:45 PM]

MINUTE: Displaying the Minute

The MINUTE function extracts the minute from a given time and displays the minute as a number between 0 and 59. The *time* argument can be a cell containing a time or a time enclosed in single quote marks.

Syntax

= MINUTE(*time*)

Examples

FUNCTION	RESULT
= MINUTE('9:30:0')	30
= MINUTE(A5)	45

[A5 = 3:45 PM]

SECOND: Displaying the Second

The SECOND function extracts the second from a given time and displays the second as a number between 0 and 59. The *time* argument can be a cell containing a time or a time enclosed in single quote marks.

Syntax

= SECOND(*time*)

Examples

FUNCTION	RESULT
= SECOND('9:30:0')	0
= SECOND(A5)	30

[A5 = 3:34:30 PM]

DEPRECIATION FUNCTIONS

Works offers three functions to calculate depreciation: straight-line, double declining balance, and sum-of-the-years-digits. To use these functions, you need to know the asset's *cost* (the amount you purchased it for), *life* (the number of years you will use the asset), and *salvage value* (the amount the asset is worth at the end of its life).

SLN: Computing Depreciation with the Straight-Line Method

With the straight-line depreciation method, the same amount is depreciated each year. To use the SLN function, you need to know the asset's *cost, salvage value,* and *life.*

Syntax

= SLN(*cost,salvage value,life*)

Example

= SLN(15000,3000,5)

In this example, you purchase a car for $15,000. You expect to use the car for 5 years, at which time it will be worth $3000. Using the straight-line method, this formula shows that the depreciation expense for each year is $2400.

DDB: Computing Depreciation with the Double Declining Balance Method

With the double declining balance method, the depreciation expense is higher in the earlier years of the asset's life than in the latter years. To use the DDB function, you need to know the asset's *cost, salvage value, life,* and *period.* The *period* argument indicates the year for which you want to calculate depreciation. (The depreciation expense for each year is different, unlike with straight-line depreciation.)

Syntax

= DDB(*cost,salvage value,life,period*)

Example

= DDB(15000,3000,5,1)

In this example, you purchase a car for $15,000. You expect to use the car for 5 years, at which time it will be worth $3000. Using the double declining balance method, this formula shows that the depreciation expense for the first year is $6000.

SYD: Computing Depreciation with the Sum-of-the-Years-Digits Method

With the sum-of-the-years-digits method, the depreciation expense is somewhat higher in the earlier years of the asset's life than in the latter years, but the expense is more evenly distributed than in the double declining balance method. To use the SYD function, you need to know the asset's *cost, salvage value, life,* and *period.* The *period* argument indicates the year for which you want to calculate depreciation.

Syntax

= SYD(*cost,salvage value,life,period*)

Example

= SYD(15000,3000,5,1)

In this example, you purchase a car for $15,000. You expect to use the car for 5 years, at which time it will be worth $3000. Using the sum-of-the-years-digits method, this formula shows that the depreciation expense for the first year is $4000.

FUNCTIONS FOR CASH-FLOW ANALYSIS

If you are contemplating making an investment, you can use Works's financial functions to analyze the investment's suitability and profitability. You can calculate an investment's future value, present value, net present value, and internal rate of return. You can also calculate how long you need to hold onto an investment to reach a specified value in the future. Probably the most commonly used financial function is PMT, which you can use to calculate monthly mortgage payments.

PMT: Computing Payment Amounts

The PMT function calculates loan payments based on a fixed interest rate. Besides the *rate,* the PMT function requires two other arguments: *principal* (amount that you are borrowing) and *term* (how long you are borrowing the money for). Make sure the term, rate, and payment use the same unit. For example, to calculate a monthly payment, the term and interest rate have to be expressed in months.

Syntax

=PMT(*principal,rate,term*)

Example

=PMT(300000,0.1/12,30*12)

In this example, the principal amount is $300,000, the monthly interest rate is 10% divided by 12, and the term is 30 years times 12. The monthly mortgage payment would be $2633.

FV: Computing the Future Value of a Stream of Payments

The future value function, FV, totals the amount of money you will have in the future if you invest a set amount each period, given a certain interest rate. The arguments in the FV function are *payment* (amount invested each period), *rate* (the interest rate you expect to earn), and *term* (the number of periods during which you will invest).

Syntax

=FV(*payment,rate,term*)

Example

=FV(2000,9%,35)

In this example, you are investing $2000 each year for 35 years, with an expected interest rate of 9% a year. The formula shows that at the end of 35 years, you would have $431,422.

PV: Computing the Present Value of an Annuity

The present value is what a future stream of payments would be worth today. The arguments in the PV function are *payment* (amount paid to you each period), *rate* (the estimated discount rate), and *term* (the number of periods during which payments will be made to you).

Syntax

= PV(*payment,rate,term*)

Example

= PV(50000,9%,20)

In this example, you just won a million dollars in the state lottery. You will get $50,000 each year for 20 years, and the discount rate is assumed to be 9% a year. The formula shows that the present value of the million dollars is $456,427. (This is how much the state would have to set aside for your winnings.)

NPV: Computing the Net Present Value

Net present value is similar to present value except that the payments are not equal, nor are they at fixed intervals. The payments are contained in a spreadsheet range and are referenced as an argument in the NPV function.

Syntax

= NPV(*rate,range*)

Example

= NPV(12%,A2:A5)

In this example, the discount rate is 12% and the payments are in the spreadsheet range A2:A5. This range contains the following payment amounts: 1000, 1500, 2000, and 3000. If you were considering investing in this annuity, you should pay no more than the net present value: $5419.

IRR: Computing the Internal Rate of Return on a Cash-Flow Series

The IRR function calculates the internal rate of return on a cash-flow series (outgoing and incoming cash). This function requires two arguments. The first is a guess as to what you think the rate of return might be; it must be between 0 and 1 (or in terms of percentages, between 0% and 100%). The guess does not affect the results unless your guess is off by more than 0.5 (50%). If the cell displays *ERR,* your guess was too far off—guess again. The second argument is the range that contains the cash payments and receipts. Outgoing payments should be entered as negative numbers; cash receipts should be entered as positive numbers.

Syntax

= IRR(*rate,range*)

Example

= IRR(15%,A2:A5)

In this example, you are guessing that the IRR is around 15%. The cash-flow series is in the spreadsheet range A2:A5. This range contains the following values: – 5000 (your initial investment), 1500, 2000, and 3000. The formula shows that the internal rate of return is 0.127 (12.7%).

RATE: Calculating the Return on a Lump-Sum Payment

The RATE function is similar to IRR except that the investment's income comes in the form of a single payment at the end of a period. You have to specify the investment's *present value* (what you paid for it), *future value* (what you expect to sell it for), and the *term* (how long you will be holding the investment).

Syntax

= RATE(*future value,present value,term*)

Example

= RATE(240000,168000,2)

In this example, you are buying a house for $168,000, and you expect to sell it for $240,000 after owning it for two years. The formula shows that the rate of return on your investment is 19.5%.

TERM: Computing the Term of a Cash Flow

The TERM function calculates the number of years it takes to reach a certain future value, given a fixed interest rate. It assumes that a series of equal payments are made during each period.

Syntax

= TERM(*payment,rate,future value*)

Example

= TERM(10000,11%,100000)

The results of this formula indicate that if you invested $10,000 per year at 11%, it would take 7.1 years to accumulate $100,000.

CTERM: Computing the Term on a Lump-Sum Payment

Like the TERM function, CTERM calculates the number of years it takes to reach a certain future value, given a fixed interest rate. This function assumes, though, that you make a single payment at the beginning of the period.

Syntax

= CTERM(*rate,future value,present value*)

Example

= CTERM(11%,20000,10000)

If you make a single investment of $10,000 and it earns interest at a rate of 11% each year, this formula shows that it would take 6.6 years to double your money.

ENGINEERING FUNCTIONS

Works contains a set of functions that are intended for scientific and engineering applications. Most of these functions are trigonometric: sine, cosine, tangent, arcsine, arccosine, and arctangent. You can also compute pi and logarithms.

The trigonometric functions measure angles in *radians,* rather than in degrees. A radian is a unit of measurement based on pi.

PI: Using Pi

The PI function, which doesn't have any arguments, displays the value of the pi constant (3.1415926536). *Pi* is the ratio of a circle's circumference to its diameter. Because the trigonometric functions use the radian as their unit of measurement, which is based on pi, you can use the PI function to convert degrees to radians. The following is the basic formula for converting degrees to radians: degrees * pi/180. The second example below converts a 90-degree angle to radians.

Syntax

=PI()

Examples

FORMULA	RESULT
=PI()	3.14... (radians)
=90*PI()/180	1.57 (radians)

COS: Computing a Cosine

The COS function calculates the cosine of an angle measured in radians.

Syntax

= COS(*radians*)

Examples

FORMULA	RESULT
= COS(1.047)	0.5
= COS(A5)	0.866

[A5: = 30*PI()/180]

SIN: Computing a Sine

The SIN function calculates the sine of an angle measured in radians.

Syntax

= SIN(*radians*)

Examples

FORMULA	RESULT
= SIN(1.047)	0.866
= SIN(A5)	0.5

[A5: = 30*PI()/180]

TAN: Computing a Tangent

The TAN function calculates the tangent of an angle measured in radians.

Syntax

= TAN(*radians*)

Examples

FORMULA	RESULT
= TAN(1.047)	1.73
= TAN(A5)	0.577

[A5: = 30*PI()/180]

ACOS: Computing an Arccosine

The ACOS function converts a cosine to radians. *Cosine* is the function's argument. The cosine value must be between − 1 and 1 (inclusive).

Syntax

= ACOS(*cosine value*)

Examples

FORMULA	RESULT
= ACOS(0)	1.57 radians
= ACOS(A5)	1.047 radians

[A5 = 0.5]

ASIN: Computing an Arcsine

The ASIN function converts a sine to radians. *Sine* is the function's argument. The sine value must be between − 1 and 1 (inclusive).

Syntax

= ASIN(*sine value*)

Examples

FORMULA	RESULT
= ASIN(1)	1.57 radians
= ASIN(A5)	– 0.927 radians

[A5 = – 0.8]

ATAN: Computing an Arctangent

The ATAN function converts a tangent to radians. *Tangent* is the function's argument.

Syntax

= ATAN(*tangent value*)

Examples

FORMULA	RESULT
= ATAN(3)	1.25 radians
= ATAN(A5)	– 1.37 radians

[A5 = – 5]

ATAN2: Computing a Four-Quadrant Arctangent

The ATAN2 function converts a tangent defined by x and y coordinates to radians. The coordinates are the function's two arguments.

Syntax

= ATAN2(*x-coordinate,y-coordinate*)

Examples

FORMULA	RESULT
=ATAN2(0,1)	1.57 radians
=ATAN2(A5,B5)	3.14 radians

[A5 = −1, B5 = 0]

LOG: Calculating Logarithms

The LOG function calculates the base-10 logarithm of a number. The number cannot be zero or negative.

Syntax

=LOG(*value*)

Examples

FORMULA	RESULT
=LOG(10)	1
=LOG(A5)	2

[A5 = 100]

LN: Calculating Natural Logarithms

Like LOG, the LN function calculates a logarithm of a number, but LN computes the log in base *e* (LOG uses base 10). Base *e* is the constant 2.71828.... The value must be positive.

Syntax

=LN(*value*)

Examples

FORMULA	RESULT
= LN(2.7)	0.993
= LN(A5)	2

[A5 = 7.389]

EXP: Using Exponents

The EXP function raises the *e* constant (2.71828...) to the specified power. It performs the inverse operation of the LN function.

Syntax

= EXP(*power*)

Examples

FORMULA	RESULT
= EXP(1)	2.718
= EXP(2)	7.389

index

A

B

C

D

G

H

I

J

K

L

M

N

O

P

Q

T

X

Y

Z

Selections from The SYBEX Library

SPREADSHEETS AND INTEGRATED SOFTWARE

1-2-3 for Scientists and Engineers

William J. Orvis

371pp. Ref. 733-9

This up-to-date edition offers fast, elegant solutions to common problems in science and engineering. Complete, carefully explained techniques for plotting, curve fitting, statistics, derivatives, integrals and differentials, solving systems of equations, and more; plus useful Lotus add-ins.

The ABC's of 1-2-3 (Second Edition)

Chris Gilbert
Laurie Williams

245pp. Ref. 355-4

Online Today recommends it as "an easy and comfortable way to get started with the program." An essential tutorial for novices, it will remain on your desk as a valuable source of ongoing reference and support. For Release 2.

The ABC's of 1-2-3 Release 2.2

Chris Gilbert
Laurie Williams

340pp. Ref. 623-5

New Lotus 1-2-3 users delight in this book's step-by-step approach to building trouble-free spreadsheets, displaying graphs, and efficiently building databases. The authors cover the ins and outs of the latest version including easier calculations, file linking, and better graphic presentation.

The ABC's of 1-2-3 Release 2.3

Chris Gilbert
Laurie Williams

350pp. Ref. 837-8

Computer Currents called it "one of the best tutorials available." This new edition provides easy-to-follow, hands-on lessons tailored specifically for computer and spreadsheet newcomers—or for anyone seeking a quick and easy guide to the basics. Covers everything from switching on the computer to charts, functions, macros, and important new features.

The ABC's of 1-2-3 Release 3

Judd Robbins

290pp. Ref. 519-0

The ideal book for beginners who are new to Lotus or new to Release 3. This step-by-step approach to the 1-2-3 spreadsheet software gets the reader up and running with spreadsheet, database, graphics, and macro functions.

The ABC's of 1-2-3 for Windows

Robert Cowart

300pp; Ref. 682-0

This friendly introduction covers the new Windows-compatible 1-2-3 speadsheet, with tutorials suitable for Windows newcomers—even those using a computer for the first time. Easy-to-follow lessons show how to build business spreadsheets, create graphs to illustrate the numbers, print worksheets and graphs, use the database manager, and more.

The ABC's of Excel on the IBM PC

Douglas Hergert

326pp. Ref. 567-0

This book is a brisk and friendly introduction to the most important features of Microsoft Excel for PC's. This beginner's book discusses worksheets, charts, database operations, and macros, all with hands-on examples. Written for all versions through Version 2.

The ABC's of Quattro Pro 3

Alan Simpson
Douglas Wolf

338pp. Ref. 836-6

This popular beginner's tutorial on Quattro Pro 2 shows first-time computer and spreadsheet users the essentials of electronic number-crunching. Topics range from business spreadsheet design to error-free formulas, presentation slide shows, the database, macros, more.

The Complete Lotus 1-2-3 Release 3 Handbook

Greg Harvey

700pp. Ref. 600-6

Everything you ever wanted to know about 1-2-3 is in this definitive handbook. As a Release 3 guide, it features the design and use of 3D worksheets, and improved graphics, along with using Lotus under DOS or OS/2. Problems, exercises, and helpful insights are included.

Lotus 1-2-3 2.2 On-Line Advisor Version 1.1

SYBAR, Software Division of SYBEX, Inc.

Ref. 935-8

Need Help fast? With a touch of a key, the Advisor pops up right on top of your Lotus 1-2-3 program to answer your spreadsheet questions. With over 4000 index citations and 1600 pre-linked cross-references, help has never been so easy to find. Just start typing your topic and the Lotus 1-2-3 Advisor does all the look-up for you. Covers versions 2.01 and 2.2. Software package comes with 3½" and 5¼" disks. **System Requirements:** IBM compatible with DOS 2.0 or higher, runs with Windows 3.0, uses 90K of RAM.

Lotus 1-2-3 Instant Reference Release 2.2 SYBEX Prompter Series

Greg Harvey
Kay Yarborough Nelson

254pp. Ref. 635-9

The reader gets quick and easy access to any operation in 1-2-3 Version 2.2 in this handy pocket-sized encyclopedia. Organized by menu function, each command and function has a summary description, the exact key sequence, and a discussion of the options.

Lotus 1-2-3 Release 2.3 Instant Reference

Judd Robbins

175pp; Ref. 658-8

The concise guide to 1-2-3 commands, functions, and options covers all versions of release 2—offering on-the-job help and quick reminders in a compact, easy-to-use format. Entries are organized alphabetically and provide a summary description, exact syntax, complete options, a brief discussion with examples, and valuable tips.

Lotus 1-2-3 for Windows Instant Reference

Gerald E. Jones

175pp; Ref. 864-5

This complete quick-reference guide to 1-2-3 for Windows includes an overview of new features, and a special section on Windows. Concise, alphabetized entries present and briefly explain every feature and function of the software—for a quick reminder, or fast help with new options. Each entry provides a summary, exact syntax, complete options, and examples.

Mastering Enable/OA

Christopher Van Buren
Robert Bixby

540pp. Ref 637-5

This is a structured, hands-on guide to integrated business computing, for users who want to achieve productivity in the shortest possible time. Separate in-depth sections cover word processing, spreadsheets, databases, telecommunications, task integration and macros.

Mastering Excel 3 on the Macintosh

Marvin Bryan

586pp; Ref. 800-9

Turn here for in-depth coverage of today's Excel, and how to make the most of its enhanced capabilities—including those applicable to System 7. For all user levels: clear, jargon-free explanations and exercises for the beginner are complemented by advanced information and tips for the power user.

Mastering Excel 3 for Windows

Carl Townsend

625pp. Ref. 643-X

A new edition of SYBEX's highly praised guide to the Excel super spreadsheet, under Windows 3.0. Includes full coverage of new features; dozens of tips and examples; in-depth treatment of specialized topics, including presentation graphics and macros; and sample applications for inventory control, financial management, trend analysis, and more.

Mastering Framework III

Douglas Hergert
Jonathan Kamin

613pp. Ref. 513-1

Thorough, hands-on treatment of the latest Framework release. An outstanding introduction to integrated software applications, with examples for outlining, spreadsheets, word processing, databases, and more; plus an introduction to FRED programming.

Mastering Freelance Plus

Donald Richard Read

411pp. Ref. 701-0

A detailed guide to high-powered graphing and charting with Freelance Plus. Part I is a practical overview of the software. Part II offers concise tutorials on creating specific chart types. Part III covers drawing functions in depth. Part IV shows how to organize and generate output, including printing and on-screen shows.

Mastering Quattro Pro 3

Gene Weisskopf

618pp. Ref. 841-6

A complete hands-on guide and on-the-job reference, offering practical tutorials on the basics; up-to-date treatment of advanced capabilities; highlighted coverage of new software features, and expert advice from author Gene Weisskopf, a seasoned spreadsheet specialist.

Mastering SuperCalc5

Greg Harvey
Mary Beth Andrasak

500pp. Ref. 624-3

This book offers a complete and unintimidating guided tour through each feature. With step-by-step lessons, readers learn about the full capabilities of spreadsheet, graphics, and data management functions. Multiple spreadsheets, linked spreadsheets, 3D graphics, and macros are also discussed.

Quattro Pro 3 Instant Reference

Gene Weisskopf

225pp; Ref. 822-X

A superb quick reference for anyone using Quattro Pro 3. This pocket guide offers quick access to instructions on all menu commands, @ functions, and macro keywords. Beginners will use this book to pick up the basics, while more experienced users will find it a handy place to check unusual or specialized commands.

Teach Yourself Lotus 1-2-3 Release 2.2

Jeff Woodward

250pp. Ref. 641-3

Readers match what they see on the screen with the book's screen-by-screen action sequences. For new Lotus users, topics include computer fundamentals, opening and editing a worksheet, using graphs, macros, and printing typeset-quality reports. For Release 2.2.

Understanding 1-2-3 Release 2.3

Rebecca Bridge Altman

700pp. Ref. 856-4

This comprehensive guide to 1-2-3 spreadsheet power covers everything from basic concepts to sophisticated business applications. New users will build a solid foundation; intermediate and experienced users will learn how to refine their spreadsheets, manage large projects, create effective graphics, analyze databases, master graphics, more.

Understanding 1-2-3 for Windows

Douglas Hergert

700pp; Ref. 845-9

This all-new guide to 1-2-3 is written especially for the new Windows version. There are self-contained chapters for beginning, intermediate and advanced users, with business-oriented coverage of such topics as the Windows environment, worksheet development, charting, functions, database management, macro programming, and data sharing.

Understanding PFS: First Choice

Gerry Litton

489pp. Ref. 568-9

From basic commands to complex features, this complete guide to the popular integrated package is loaded with step-by-step instructions. Lessons cover creating attractive documents, setting up easy-to-use databases, working with spreadsheets and graphics, and smoothly integrating tasks from different First Choice modules. For Version 3.0.

Up & Running with Excel for Windows

D.F. Scott

140pp; Ref. 880-7

In just 20 easy steps, you can learn the fundamentals of Excel for Windows. This concise, no-nonsense approach is ideal for computer-literate users who are upgrading from an earlier version of Excel, or migrating from another spreadsheet program.

Up & Running with Lotus 1-2-3 Release 2.2

Rainer Bartel

139pp. Ref 748-7

Start using 1-2-3 in the shortest time possible with this concise 20-step guide to the major features of the software. Each "step" is a self-contained, time-coded lesson (taking 15, 30, 45 or 60 minutes to complete) focused on a single aspect of 1-2-3 operations.

Up & Running with 1-2-3 Release 2.3

Robert M. Thomas

140pp. Ref. 872-6

Get a fast start with this 20-step guide to 1-2-3 release 2.3. Each step takes just 15 minutes to an hour, and is preceded by a clock icon, so you know how much time to budget for each lesson. This book is great for people who want to start using the program right away, as well as for potential 1-2-3 users who want to evaluate the program before purchase.

Up & Running with Lotus 1-2-3 Release 3.1

Kris Jamsa

141pp. Ref. 813-0

A 20-step overview of the new 3.1 version of 1-2-3. The first twelve steps take you through the fundamentals of creating, using and graphing worksheets. Steps 13 through 15 explain the database, and the balance of the book is dedicated to 3.1's powerful WYSIWYG capabilities.

Up & Running with Lotus 1-2-3 for Windows

Robert M. Thomas

140pp; Ref. 73-4

The ideal book for computer-literate users who are new to spreadsheets, upgrading from a previous version of 1-2-3, or migrating from another spreadsheet program. In just 20 concise lessons, you learn the essentials of the new 1-2-3 for Windows, with no time wasted on necessary detail.

Up & Running with Quattro Pro 3

Peter Aitken

140pp. Ref.857-2

Get a fast start with this 20-step guide to Quattro Pro 3. Each step takes just 15 minutes to an hour, and is preceded by a clock icon, so you know how much time to budget for each lesson. This book is great for people who want to start using the program right away, as well as for potential Quattro Pro 3 users who want to evaluate the program before purchase.

OPERATING SYSTEMS

The ABC's of DOS 4

Alan R. Miller

275pp. Ref. 583-2

This step-by-step introduction to using DOS 4 is written especially for beginners. Filled with simple examples, *The ABC's of DOS 4* covers the basics of hardware, software, disks, the system editor EDLIN, DOS commands, and more.

The ABC's of DOS 5

Alan Miller

267pp. Ref. 770-3

This straightforward guide will haven even first-time computer users working comfortably with DOS 5 in no time. Step-by-step lessons lead users from switching on the PC, through exploring the DOS Shell, working with directories and files, using essential commands, customizing the system, and trouble shooting. Includes a tear-out quick reference card and function key template.

ABC's of MS-DOS (Second Edition)

Alan R. Miller

233pp. Ref. 493-3

This handy guide to MS-DOS is all many PC users need to manage their computer files, organize floppy and hard disks, use EDLIN, and keep their computers organized. Additional information is given about utilities like Sidekick, and there is a DOS command and program summary. The second edition is fully updated for Version 3.3.

The ABC's of SCO UNIX

Tom Cuthbertson

263pp. Re. 715-0

A guide especially for beginners who want to get to work fast. Includes hands-on tutorials on logging in and out; creating and editing files; using electronic mail; organizing files into directories; printing; text formatting; and more.

The ABC's of Windows 3.0

Kris Jamsa

327pp. Ref. 760-6

A user-friendly introduction to the essentials of Windows 3.0. Presented in 64 short lessons. Beginners start with lesson one, while more advanced readers can skip ahead. Learn to use File Manager, the accessory programs, customization features, Program Manager, and more.

DESQview Instant Reference

Paul J. Perry

175pp. Ref. 809-2

This complete quick-reference command guide covers version 2.3 and DESQview 386, as well as QEMM (for managing expanded memory) and Manifest Memory Analyzer. Concise, alphabetized entries provide exact syntax, options, usage, and brief examples for every command. A handy source for on-the-job reminders and tips.

DOS 3.3 On-Line Advisor Version 1.1

SYBAR, Software Division of SYBEX, Inc.

Ref. 933-1

The answer to all your DOS problems. The DOS On-Line Advisor is an on-screen reference that explains over 200 DOS error messages. 2300 other citations cover all you ever needed to know about DOS. The DOS On-Line Advisor pops up on top of your working program to give you quick, easy help when you need it, and disappears when you don't. Covers thru version 3.3. Software package comes with 3½" and 5¼" disks. **System Requirements:** IBM compatible with DOS 2.0 or higher, runs with Windows 3.0, uses 90K of RAM.

DOS Instant Reference SYBEX Prompter Series

Greg Harvey
Kay Yarborough Nelson

220pp. Ref. 477-1

A complete fingertip reference for fast, easy on-line help:command summaries, syntax, usage and error messages. Organized by function—system commands, file commands, disk management, directories, batch files, I/O, networking, programming, and more. Through Version 3.3.

DOS 5: A to Z

Gary Masters

900pp; Ref. 805-X

A personal guru for every DOS 5 user! This comprehensive, "all you need to know" guide to DOS 5 provides detailed, A-to-Z coverage of DOS 5 commands, options, error messages, and dialog boxes—with syntax, usage, and plenty of examples and tips. It also includes hundreds of informative, in-depth articles on DOS 5 terminology and concepts.

DOS 5 Instant Reference

Robert M. Thomas

200pp. Ref. 804-1

The comprehensive quick guide to DOS—all its features, commands, options, and versions—now including DOS 5, with the new graphical interface. Concise, alphabetized command entries provide exact syntax, options, usage, brief examples, and applicable version numbers. Fully cross-referenced; ideal for quick review or on-the-job reference.

The DOS 5 User's Handbook

Gary Masters
Richard Allen King

400pp. Ref. 777-0

This is the DOS 5 book for users who are already familiar with an earlier version of DOS. Part I is a quick, friendly guide to new features; topics include the graphical interface, new and enhanced commands, and much more. Part II is a complete DOS 5 quick reference, with command summaries, in-depth explanations, and examples.

Essential OS/2 (Second Edition)

Judd Robbins

445pp. Ref. 609-X

Written by an OS/2 expert, this is the guide to the powerful new resources of the OS/2 operating system standard edition 1.1 with presentation manager. Robbins introduces the standard edition, and details multitasking under OS/2, and the range of commands for installing, starting up, configuring, and running applications. For Version 1.1 Standard Edition.

Essential PC-DOS (Second Edition)

Myril Clement Shaw
Susan Soltis Shaw

332pp. Ref. 413-5

An authoritative guide to PC-DOS, including version 3.2. Designed to make experts out of beginners, it explores everything from disk management to batch file programming. Includes an 85-page command summary. Through Version 3.2.

Graphics Programming Under Windows

Brian Myers
Chris Doner

646pp. Ref. 448-8

Straightforward discussion, abundant examples, and a concise reference guide to graphics commands make this book a must for Windows programmers. Topics range from how Windows works to programming for business, animation, CAD, and desktop publishing. For Version 2.

Inside DOS: A Programmer's Guide

Michael J. Young

490pp. Ref. 710-X

A collection of practical techniques (with source code listings) designed to help you take advantage of the rich resources intrinsic to MS-DOS machines. Designed for the experienced programmer with a basic understanding of C and 8086 assembly language, and DOS fundamentals.

Mastering DOS (Second Edition)

Judd Robbins

722pp. Ref. 555-7

"The most useful DOS book." This seven-part, in-depth tutorial addresses the needs of users at all levels. Topics range from running applications, to managing files and directories, configuring the system, batch file programming, and techniques for system developers. Through Version 4.

Mastering DOS 5

Judd Robbins

800pp. Ref.767-3

"The DOS reference to keep next to your computer," according to PC Week, this highly acclaimed text is now revised and expanded for DOS 5. Comprehensive tutorials cover everything from first steps for beginners, to advanced tools for systems developers—with emphasis on the new graphics interface. Includes tips, tricks, and a tear-out quick reference card and function key template.

Mastering SunOS

Brent D. Heslop
David Angell

588pp. Ref. 683-9

Learn to configure and manage your system; use essential commands; manage files; perform editing, formatting, and printing tasks; master E-mail and external communication; and use the SunView and new Open Window graphic interfaces.

Mastering Windows 3.0

Robert Cowart

592pp. Ref.458-5

Every Windows user will find valuable how-to and reference information here. With full details on the desktop utilities; manipulating files; running applications (including non-Windows programs); sharing data between DOS, OS/2, and Windows; hardware and software efficiency tips; and more.

Understanding DESQview

Rick Altman

300pp; Ref. 665-0

An in-depth, practical introduction to multitasking and memory management with DESQview, including DESQview 386 and QEMM. Learn to swap programs in and out of memory, transfer data between windows, use scripts to automate essential tasks, run programs in the background, and more.

Understanding DOS 3.3

Judd Robbins

678pp. Ref. 648-0

This best selling, in-depth tutorial addresses the needs of users at all levels with many examples and hands-on exercises. Robbins discusses the fundamentals of DOS, then covers manipulating files and directories, using the DOS editor, printing, communicating, and finishes with a full section on batch files.

Understanding Hard Disk Management on the PC

Jonathan Kamin

500pp. Ref. 561-1

This title is a key productivity tool for all hard disk users who want efficient, error-free file management and organization. Includes details on the best ways to conserve hard disk space when using several memory-guzzling programs. Through DOS 4.

Up & Running with DR DOS 5.0

Joerg Schieb

130pp. Ref. 815-7

Enjoy a fast-paced, but thorough introduction to DR DOS 5.0. In only 20 steps, you can begin to obtain practical results: copy and delete files, password protect your data, use batch files to save time, and more.

Up & Running with DOS 3.3

Michael-Alexander Beisecker

126pp. Ref. 750-9

Learn the fundamentals of DOS 3.3 in just 20 basic steps. Each "step" is a self-contained, time-coded lesson, taking 15 minutes to an hour to complete. You learn the essentials in record time.

Up & Running with DOS 5

Alan Simpson

150pp. Ref. 774-6

A 20-step guide to the essentials of DOS 5—for busy users seeking a fast-paced overview. Steps take only minutes to complete, and each is marked with a timer clock, so you know how long each one will take. Topics include installation, the DOS Shell, Program Manager, disks, directories, utilities, customization, batch files, ports and devices, DOSKEY, memory, Windows, and BASIC.

Up & Running with Windows 3.0

Gabriele Wentges

117pp. Ref. 711-8

All the essentials of Windows 3.0 in just twenty "steps"—self-contained lessons that take minutes to complete. Perfect for evaluating the software or getting a quick start with the new environment. Topics include installation, managing windows, using keyboard and mouse, using desktop utilities, and built-in programs.

Windows 3.0 Instant Reference

Marshall Moseley

195pp. Ref. 757-6

This concise, comprehensive pocket reference provides quick access to instructions on all Windows 3.0 mouse and keyboard commands. It features step-by-step instructions on using Windows, the applications that come bundled with it, and Windows' unique help facilities. Great for all levels of expertise.

DATABASES

The ABC's of dBASE III PLUS

Robert Cowart

264pp. Ref. 379-1

The most efficient way to get beginners up and running with dBASE. Every 'how' and 'why' of database management is demonstrated through tutorials and practical dBASE III PLUS applications.

The ABC's of dBASE IV 1.1

Robert Cowart

350pp, Ref. 632-4

The latest version of dBASE IV is featured in this hands-on introduction. It assumes no previous experience with computers or database management, and uses easy-to-follow lessons to introduce the concepts, build basic skills, and set up some practical applications. Includes report writing and Query by Example.

The ABC's of FoxPro 2 (Second Edition)

Scott D. Palmer

308pp; Ref. 877-7

This fast, friendly introduction to database management is now in a new edition for version 2. Concise tutorials show you how to use essential FoxPro features and commands, while hot tips give you special pointers for avoiding pitfalls. Covers everything from simple customer files to multi-file databases.

The ABC's of Paradox 3.5 (Second Edition)

Charles Siegel

334pp, Ref. 785-1

This easy-to-follow, hands-on tutorial is a must for beginning users of Paradox 3.0 and 3.5. Even if you've never used a computer before, you'll be doing useful work in just a few short lessons. A clear introduction to database management and valuable business examples make this a "right-to-work" guide for the practical-minded.

The ABC's of Q & A 4

Trudi Reisner

232pp; Ref. 824-6

A popular introduction to Q & A 4, packed with step-by-step tutorials for beginners. Learn to create databases, use the word processor, print out reports, and more. Easy instructions incorporate practical business applications. With special coverage of the Intelligent Assistant.

Advanced Techniques in dBASE III PLUS

Alan Simpson

454pp. Ref. 369-4

A full course in database design and structured programming, with routines for inventory control, accounts receivable, system management, and integrated databases.

TO JOIN THE SYBEX MAILING LIST OR ORDER BOOKS
PLEASE COMPLETE THIS FORM

NAME ______________________ COMPANY ______________________

STREET ______________________ CITY ______________________

STATE ______________________ ZIP ______________________

☐ PLEASE MAIL ME MORE INFORMATION ABOUT **SYBEX** TITLES

ORDER FORM (There is no obligation to order)

PLEASE SEND ME THE FOLLOWING:

TITLE	QTY	PRICE
______________	_____	_____
______________	_____	_____
______________	_____	_____
______________	_____	_____
TOTAL BOOK ORDER	_____	$_____

CUSTOMER SIGNATURE ______________________

SHIPPING AND HANDLING PLEASE ADD $2.00 PER BOOK VIA UPS _____

FOR OVERSEAS SURFACE ADD $5.25 PER BOOK PLUS $4.40 REGISTRATION FEE _____

FOR OVERSEAS AIRMAIL ADD $18.25 PER BOOK PLUS $4.40 REGISTRATION FEE _____

CALIFORNIA RESIDENTS PLEASE ADD APPLICABLE SALES TAX _____

TOTAL AMOUNT PAYABLE _____

☐ CHECK ENCLOSED ☐ VISA
☐ MASTERCARD ☐ AMERICAN EXPRESS

ACCOUNT NUMBER ______________________

EXPIR. DATE _____ DAYTIME PHONE ______________

CHECK AREA OF COMPUTER INTEREST:

☐ BUSINESS SOFTWARE

☐ TECHNICAL PROGRAMMING

☐ OTHER: ______________________

THE FACTOR THAT WAS MOST IMPORTANT IN YOUR SELECTION:

☐ THE SYBEX NAME

☐ QUALITY

☐ PRICE

☐ EXTRA FEATURES

☐ COMPREHENSIVENESS

☐ CLEAR WRITING

☐ OTHER ______________________

OTHER COMPUTER TITLES YOU WOULD LIKE TO SEE IN PRINT:

____

____

OCCUPATION

☐ PROGRAMMER

☐ SENIOR EXECUTIVE

☐ COMPUTER CONSULTANT

☐ SUPERVISOR

☐ MIDDLE MANAGEMENT

☐ ENGINEER/TECHNICAL

☐ CLERICAL/SERVICE

☐ BUSINESS OWNER/SELF EMPLOYED

☐ TEACHER

☐ HOMEMAKER

☐ RETIRED

☐ STUDENT

☐ OTHER: ______________

CHECK YOUR LEVEL OF COMPUTER USE

☐ NEW TO COMPUTERS

☐ INFREQUENT COMPUTER USER

☐ FREQUENT USER OF ONE SOFTWARE PACKAGE:

NAME ________________________

☐ FREQUENT USER OF MANY SOFTWARE PACKAGES

☐ PROFESSIONAL PROGRAMMER

OTHER COMMENTS:

____

____

____

____

____

____

____

PLEASE FOLD, SEAL, AND MAIL TO SYBEX

SYBEX, INC.
2021 CHALLENGER DR. #100
ALAMEDA, CALIFORNIA USA
94501

SEAL

Database Tool

Editing Keys

Copy Previous Record's Data in Current Field	Ctrl-'	Copy Selection	Shift-F3
Display Report	Shift-F10	Edit Field Data	F2
Help	F1	Move Selection	F3
Quit Report and Query Views	F10	Repeat Copy or Format	Shift-F7
Repeat Search	F7	Switch between Form/List Views	F9

Keys for Moving between Records and Fields in Form View

Next record	Ctrl-PgDn or Ctrl-↓
Previous record	Ctrl-PgUp or Ctrl-↑
First record	Ctrl-Home
End of database	Ctrl-End
Specific record number	F5
Next screen of form	PgDn
Previous screen of form	PgUp
Next field	Tab
Previous field	Shift-Tab
Specific field	F5

Moving between Records and Fields with the Mouse in Form View

Next record	Click on down arrow in scroll bar
Previous record	Click on up arrow in scroll bar
First record	Click on scroll box at top of scroll bar
Specific field	Click on dotted line next to field name

Keys for Moving the Highlight in List View

(See Spreadsheet Tool, "Keys for Moving the Highlight")

Selection Keys in List View

Extend selection	F8	Record	Ctrl-F8
Field	Shift-F8	Database	Ctrl-Shift-F8

SYBEX Computer Books are different.

Here is why . . .

At SYBEX, each book is designed with you in mind. Every manuscript is carefully selected and supervised by our editors, who are themselves computer experts. We publish the best authors, whose technical expertise is matched by an ability to write clearly and to communicate effectively. Programs are thoroughly tested for accuracy by our technical staff. Our computerized production department goes to great lengths to make sure that each book is well-designed.

In the pursuit of timeliness, SYBEX has achieved many publishing firsts. SYBEX was among the first to integrate personal computers used by authors and staff into the publishing process. SYBEX was the first to publish books on the CP/M operating system, microprocessor interfacing techniques, word processing, and many more topics.

Expertise in computers and dedication to the highest quality product have made SYBEX a world leader in computer book publishing. Translated into fourteen languages, SYBEX books have helped millions of people around the world to get the most from their computers. We hope we have helped you, too.

For a complete catalog of our publications: